ANNUAL EDITIONS

Criminal Justice 11/12

Thirty-Fifth Edition

EDITOR

Joanne Naughton
Mercy College, Dobbs Ferry

Joanne Naughton is an assistant professor of Criminal Justice at Mercy College. Professor Naughton is a former member of the New York City Police Department, where she encountered most aspects of police work as a police officer, detective, sergeant, and lieutenant. She is also a former staff attorney with The Legal Aid Society where she represented indigent criminal defendants, and has taught at John Jay College of Criminal Justice. She received her BA and JD at Fordham University.

McGraw Hill

Connect
Learn
Succeed™

The McGraw·Hill Companies

ANNUAL EDITIONS: CRIMINAL JUSTICE, THIRTY-FIFTH EDITION

Published by McGraw-Hill, a business unit of The McGraw-Hill Companies, Inc., 1221 Avenue of the Americas, New York, NY 10020. Copyright © 2012 by The McGraw-Hill Companies, Inc. All rights reserved. Previous editions © 2011, 2010, and 2009. No part of this publication may be reproduced or distributed in any form or by any means, or stored in a database or retrieval system, without the prior written consent of The McGraw-Hill Companies, Inc., including, but not limited to, in any network or other electronic storage or transmission, or broadcast for distance learning.

Some ancillaries, including electronic and print components, may not be available to customers outside the United States.

Annual Editions® is a registered trademark of The McGraw-Hill Companies, Inc.

Annual Editions is published by the **Contemporary Learning Series** group within the McGraw-Hill Higher Education division.

1 2 3 4 5 6 7 8 9 0 QDB/QDB 1 0 9 8 7 6 5 4 3 2 1

ISBN 978-0-07-805088-6
MHID 0-07-805088-X
ISSN 0272-3816 (print)
ISSN 2159-1032 (online)

Managing Editor: *Larry Loeppke*
Developmental Editor: *Dave Welsh*
Permissions Coordinator: *Shirley Lanners*
Marketing Specialist: *Alice Link*
Project Manager: *Robin A. Reed*
Design Coordinator: *Margarite Reynolds*
Buyer: *Susan K. Culbertson*
Cover Graphics: *Kristine Jubeck*
Media Project Manager: *Sridevi Palani*

Compositor: Laserwords Private Limited
Cover Images: Royalty-Free/CORBIS (inset); National Geographic/SuperStock (background)

Editors/Academic Advisory Board

Members of the Academic Advisory Board are instrumental in the final selection of articles for each edition of ANNUAL EDITIONS. Their review of articles for content, level, and appropriateness provides critical direction to the editors and staff. We think that you will find their careful consideration well reflected in this volume.

ANNUAL EDITIONS: Criminal Justice 11/12
35th Edition

EDITOR

Joanne Naughton
Mercy College, Dobbs Ferry

Preface

During the 1970s, Criminal Justice emerged as an appealing, vital, and unique academic discipline. It emphasizes the professional development of students who plan careers in the field, and attracts those who want to know more about a complex social problem and how this country deals with it. Criminal Justice incorporates a vast range of knowledge from a number of specialties, including law, history, and the behavioral and social sciences. Each specialty contributes to our fuller understanding of criminal behavior and of society's attitudes toward deviance.

In view of the fact that the criminal justice system is in a constant state of flux, and because the study of criminal justice covers such a broad spectrum, today's students must be aware of a variety of subjects and topics. Standard textbooks and traditional anthologies cannot keep pace with the changes as quickly as they occur. In fact, many such sources are already out-of-date the day they are published. *Annual Editions: Criminal Justice 11/12* strives to maintain currency in matters of concern by providing up-to-date commentaries, articles, reports, and statistics from the most recent literature in the criminal justice field.

This volume contains units concerning crime and justice in America, victimology, the police, the judicial system, juvenile justice, and punishment and corrections. The articles in these units were selected because they are informative as well as provocative. The selections are timely and useful in their treatment of ethics, punishment, juveniles, courts, and other related topics.

Included in this volume are a number of features designed to be useful to students, researchers, and professionals in the criminal justice field. These include the table of contents, which summarizes each article, and features key concepts in bold italics; *a topic guide* for locating articles on specific subjects; a list of relevant *Internet References*; a comprehensive section on crime statistics; and a glossary. In addition, each unit is preceded by an overview that provides a background for informed reading of the articles, emphasizes critical issues, and presents key points to consider.

We would like to know what you think of the selections contained in this edition of *Annual Editions: Criminal Justice.* Please fill out the postage-paid article rating form on the last page and let us know your opinions. We change or retain many of the articles based on the comments we receive from you, the reader. Help us to improve this anthology—annually.

Joanne Naughton

Joanne Naughton
Editor

Contents

UNIT 1
Crime and Justice in America

The concepts in bold italics are developed in the article. For further expansion, please refer to the Topic Guide.

UNIT 2
Victimology

UNIT 3
The Police

The concepts in bold italics are developed in the article. For further expansion, please refer to the Topic Guide.

UNIT 4
The Judicial System

The concepts in bold italics are developed in the article. For further expansion, please refer to the Topic Guide.

UNIT 5
Juvenile Justice

The concepts in bold italics are developed in the article. For further expansion, please refer to the Topic Guide.

UNIT 6
Punishment and Corrections

The concepts in bold italics are developed in the article. For further expansion, please refer to the Topic Guide.

The concepts in bold italics are developed in the article. For further expansion, please refer to the Topic Guide.

Correlation Guide

The *Annual Editions* series provides students with convenient, inexpensive access to current, carefully selected articles from the public press. **Annual Editions: Criminal Justice 11/12** is an easy-to-use reader that presents articles on important topics such as the *justice system, victims, punishment, policing,* and many more. For more information on *Annual Editions* and other *McGraw-Hill Contemporary Learning Series* titles, visit www.mhhe.com/cls.

This convenient guide matches the units in **Annual Editions: Criminal Justice 11/12** with the corresponding chapters in two of our best-selling McGraw-Hill Introductory Criminal Justice textbooks by Inciardi, Bohm/Haley, and Masters et al.

Annual Editions: Criminal Justice 11/12	Criminal Justice, 9/e by Inciardi	Introduction to Criminal Justice, 6/e by Bohm/Haley	Criminal Justice: Realities and Challenges, by Masters et al.
Unit 1: Crime and Justice in America	**Chapter 1:** "Criminal Justice" in America	**Chapter 1:** Crime and Justice in the United States	**Chapter 1:** What Is the Criminal Justice System? **Chapter 2:** Types of Crime **Chapter 3:** Causes of Crime
Unit 2: Victimology	**Chapter 9:** Police Misconduct and Police Integrity	**Chapter 2:** Crime and Its Consequences	**Chapter 14:** Understanding and Helping Victims
Unit 3: The Police	**Chapter 6:** Police Systems in the United Stated: History and Structure **Chapter 7:** Enforcing the Law and Keeping the Peace: The Nature and Scope of Police Work **Chapter 8:** The Law of Arrest, Search, and Seizure: Police and the Constitution **Chapter 9:** Police Misconduct and Police Integrity	**Chapter 5:** History and Structure of American Law Enforcement **Chapter 6:** Policing: Roles, Styles, and Functions **Chapter 7:** Policing America: Issues and Ethics	**Chapter 5:** Overview of Policing **Chapter 6:** Policing Operations **Chapter 7:** Legal and Special Issues in Policing
Unit 4: The Judicial System	**Chapter 10:** The Structure of American Courts **Chapter 11:** The Courtroom Work Group and the Right to Counsel **Chapter 12:** The Business of the Court: From First Appearance through Trial **Chapter 13:** Sentencing, Appeal, and the Judgment of Death	**Chapter 8:** The Administration of Justice **Chapter 9:** Sentencing, Appeals, and the Death Penalty	**Chapter 8:** The Courts **Chapter 9:** Pretrial and Trial **Chapter 10:** Sentencing
Unit 5: Juvenile Justice	**Chapter 18:** Juvenile Justice: An Overview	**Chapter 13:** Juvenile Justice	**Chapter 15:** Juvenile Justice
Unit 6: Punishment and Corrections	**Chapter 14:** From Walnut Street to Alcatraz: The American Prison Experience **Chapter 15:** Penitentiaries, Prisons, and Other Correctional Institutions: A Look Inside the Inmate World **Chapter 16:** Prison Conditions and Inmate Rights **Chapter 17:** Probation, Parole, and Community-Based Correction	**Chapter 10:** Institutional Corrections **Chapter 11:** Prison Life, Inmate Rights, Release, and Recidivism **Chapter 12:** Community Corrections	**Chapter 10:** Sentencing **Chapter 11:** Overview of Corrections **Chapter 12:** Jails and Prisons **Chapter 13:** Community Corrections

Topic Guide

This topic guide suggests how the selections in this book relate to the subjects covered in your course. You may want to use the topics listed on these pages to search the web more easily.

On the following pages a number of websites have been gathered specifically for this book. They are arranged to reflect the units of this Annual Editions reader. You can link to these sites by going to www.mhhe.com/cls.

All the articles that relate to each topic are listed below the bold-faced term.

Internet References

The following Internet sites have been selected to support the articles found in this reader. These sites were available at the time of publication. However, because websites often change their structure and content, the information listed may no longer be available. We invite you to visit www.mhhe.com/cls for easy access to these sites.

Annual Editions: Criminal Justice 11/12

General Sources

American Society of Criminology
www.bsos.umd.edu/asc/four.html

This is an excellent starting place for study of all aspects of criminology and criminal justice, with links to international criminal justice, juvenile justice, court information, police, governments, and so on.

Federal Bureau of Investigation
www.fbi.gov

The main page of the FBI website leads to lists of the most wanted criminals, uniform crime reports, FBI case reports, major investigations, and more.

National Archive of Criminal Justice Data
www.icpsr.umich.edu/NACJD/index.html

NACJD holds more than 500 data collections relating to criminal justice; this site provides browsing and downloading access to most of the data and documentation. NACJD's central mission is to facilitate and encourage research in the field of criminal justice.

Social Science Information Gateway
http://sosig.esrc.bris.ac.uk

This is an online catalog of thousands of Internet resources relevant to social science education and research. Every resource is selected and described by a librarian or subject specialist. Enter "criminal justice" under Search for an excellent annotated list of sources.

UNIT 1: Crime and Justice in America

Sourcebook of Criminal Justice Statistics Online
www.albany.edu/sourcebook

Data about all aspects of criminal justice in the United States are available at this site, which includes more than 600 tables from dozens of sources. A search mechanism is available.

UNIT 2: Victimology

National Crime Victim's Research and Treatment Center (NCVC)
www.musc.edu/cvc

At this site, find out about the work of the NCVC at the Medical University of South Carolina, and click on Related Resources for an excellent listing of additional web sources.

Office for Victims of Crime (OVC)
www.ojp.usdoj.gov/ovc

Established by the 1984 Victims of Crime Act, the OVC oversees diverse programs that benefit the victims of crime. From this site you can download a great deal of pertinent information.

UNIT 3: The Police

ACLU Criminal Justice Home Page
www.aclu.org/CriminalJustice/CriminalJusticeMain.cfm

This "Criminal Justice" page of the American Civil Liberties Union website highlights recent events in criminal justice, addresses police issues, lists important resources, and contains a search mechanism.

Law Enforcement Guide to the World Wide Web
http://leolinks.com

This page is dedicated to excellence in law enforcement. It contains links to every possible related category: community policing, computer crime, forensics, gangs, and wanted persons are just a few.

Violent Criminal Apprehension Program (VICAP)
www.state.ma.us/msp/unitpage/vicap.htm

VICAP's mission is to facilitate cooperation, communication, and coordination among law enforcement agencies and provide support in their efforts to investigate, identify, track, apprehend, and prosecute violent serial offenders. Access VICAP's data information center resources here.

UNIT 4: The Judicial System

Center for Rational Correctional Policy
www.correctionalpolicy.com

This is an excellent site on courts and sentencing, with many additional links to a variety of criminal justice sources.

Justice Information Center (JIC)
www.ncjrs.org

Provided by the National Criminal Justice Reference Service, this JIC site connects to information about corrections, courts, crime prevention, criminal justice, statistics, drugs and crime, law enforcement, and victims.

National Center for Policy Analysis (NCPA)
www.public-policy.org/~ncpa/pd/law/index3.html

Through the NCPA's "Idea House," you can click onto links to an array of topics that are of major interest in the study of the American judicial system.

U.S. Department of Justice (DOJ)
www.usdoj.gov

The DOJ represents the American people in enforcing the law in the public interest. Open its main page to find information about the U.S. judicial system. This site provides links to federal government web servers, topics of interest related to the justice system, documents and resources, and a topical index.

UNIT 5: Juvenile Justice

Gang Land: The Jerry Capeci Page
www.ganglandnews.com

Although this site particularly addresses organized-crime gangs, its insights into gang lifestyle—including gang families and their influence—are useful for those interested in exploring issues related to juvenile justice.

Internet References

Institute for Intergovernmental Research (IIR)
www.iir.com

The IIR is a research organization that specializes in law enforcement, juvenile justice, and criminal justice issues. Explore the projects, links, and search engines from this home page. Topics addressed include youth gangs and white collar crime.

National Criminal Justice Reference Service (NCJRS)
http://virlib.ncjrs.org/JuvenileJustice.asp

NCJRS, a federally sponsored information clearinghouse for people involved with research, policy, and practice related to criminal and juvenile justice and drug control, provides this site of links to full-text juvenile justice publications.

Partnership Against Violence Network
www.pavnet.org

The Partnership Against Violence Network is a virtual library of information about violence and youths at risk, representing data from seven different federal agencies—a one-stop searchable information resource.

UNIT 6: Punishment and Corrections

American Probation and Parole Association (APPA)
www.appa-net.org

Open this APPA site to find information and resources related to probation and parole issues, position papers, the APPA code of ethics, and research and training programs and opportunities.

The Corrections Connection
www.corrections.com

This site is an online network for corrections professionals.

Critical Criminology Division of the ASC
www.critcrim.org

Here you will find basic criminology resources and related government resources, provided by the American Society of Criminology, as well as other useful links. The death penalty is also discussed.

David Willshire's Forensic Psychology & Psychiatry Links
http://members.optushome.com.au/dwillsh/index.html

This site offers an enormous number of links to professional journals and associations. It is a valuable resource for study into possible connections between violence and mental disorders. Topics include serial killers, sex offenders, and trauma.

Oregon Department of Corrections
http://egov.oregon.gov/DOC/TRANS/CC/cc_welcome.shtml

Open this site for resources in such areas as crime and law enforcement and for links to U.S. state corrections departments.

UNIT 1

Crime and Justice in America

Unit Selections

1. **What Is the Sequence of Events in the Criminal Justice System?** *Report to the Nation on Crime and Justice,* Bureau of Justice Statistics
2. **Plugging Holes in the Science of Forensics,** Henry Fountain
3. **Picked from a Lineup, on a Whiff of Evidence,** John Schwartz
4. **Organizational Learning and Islamic Militancy,** Michael Kenney
5. **The Death of the War on Drugs,** Lawrence T. Jablecki
6. **The Wrong Man,** David Freed
7. **Universal Policing: Counterterrorism Lessons from Northern Ireland,** Justin Schoeman

Learning Outcomes

After reading this unit, you will be able to:

• Critically assess the arguments for the "war on drugs."

• Explain from the perspective of the "wrong man" what damage can be done when law enforcement focuses on a suspect about whom they have little more than mere suspicion.

• List the steps that follow a successful investigation.

• Discuss the use of dogs in law enforcement investigations.

• Consider the problems of terrorism in light of the lessons of Northern Ireland.

• Explain the concept of metis, and its importance in fighting terrorism.

Student Website
www.mhhe.com/cls

Internet Reference
Sourcebook of Criminal Justice Statistics Online
www.albany.edu/sourcebook

Crime continues to be a major problem in the United States. Court dockets are full, our prisons are overcrowded, probation and parole caseloads are overwhelming, and our police are being urged to do more. The bulging prison population places a heavy strain on the economy of the country. Clearly, crime is a complex problem that defies simple explanations or solutions. While the more familiar crimes of murder, rape, assault, and drug law violations are still with us, international terrorism has become a pressing worry. The debate also continues about how best to handle juvenile offenders, sex offenders, and those who commit acts of domestic violence. Crime committed using computers and the Internet also demands attention from the criminal justice system.

Annual Editions: Criminal Justice 11/12 focuses directly upon crime in America and the three traditional components of the criminal justice system: police, the courts, and corrections. It also gives special attention to crime victims in the victimology unit and to juveniles in the juvenile justice unit. The articles presented in this section are intended to serve as a foundation for the materials presented in subsequent sections.

The unit begins with "What Is the Sequence of Events in the Criminal Justice System?", an article that reveals that the response to crime is a complex process, involving citizens as well as many agencies, levels, and branches of government. Then, Henry Fountain reports on a study by a panel of experts that said it was time to put more science in forensic science in "Plugging Holes in the Science of Forensics." In "Picked from a Lineup on a Whiff of Evidence," John Schwartz writes about the use of dogs to sniff out drugs and other contraband, and reports on the methods of a dog handler in Texas that have come under fierce attack. In "Organizational Learning and Islamic Militancy," Michael Kenney discusses the essential qualities terrorists need in order to be successful in carrying out acts of political violence.

Next, Lawrence Jablecki is critical of this country's drug policies in "The Death of the War on Drugs." In "The Wrong Man," David Freed chronicles the investigation of the deadly anthrax attacks following 9/11, which led to the naming of an innocent man as the culprit.

This unit ends with "Universal Policing: Counterterrorism Lessons from Northern Ireland", an article by Justin Schoeman,

© Mikael Karlsson/Arresting Images

in which he argues that the lessons learned fighting the counterinsurgency in Northern Ireland can be applied to similar battles against terror in Iraq and Afghanistan.

What Is the Sequence of Events in the Criminal Justice System?

The Private Sector Initiates the Response to Crime

This first response may come from individuals, families, neighborhood associations, business, industry, agriculture, educational institutions, the news media, or any other private service to the public.

It involves crime prevention as well as participation in the criminal justice process once a crime has been committed. Private crime prevention is more than providing private security or burglar alarms or participating in neighborhood watch. It also includes a commitment to stop criminal behavior by not engaging in it or condoning it when it is committed by others.

Citizens take part directly in the criminal justice process by reporting crime to the police, by being a reliable participant (for example, a witness or a juror) in a criminal proceeding and by accepting the disposition of the system as just or reasonable. As voters and taxpayers, citizens also participate in criminal justice through the policymaking process that affects how the criminal justice process operates, the resources available to it, and its goals and objectives. At every stage of the process from the original formulation of objectives to the decision about where to locate jails and prisons to the reintegration of inmates into society, the private sector has a role to play. Without such involvement, the criminal justice process cannot serve the citizens it is intended to protect.

The Response to Crime and Public Safety Involves Many Agencies and Services

Many of the services needed to prevent crime and make neighborhoods safe are supplied by noncriminal justice agencies, including agencies with primary concern for public health, education, welfare, public works, and housing. Individual citizens as well as public and private sector organizations have joined with criminal justice agencies to prevent crime and make neighborhoods safe.

Criminal Cases Are Brought by the Government Through the Criminal Justice System

We apprehend, try, and punish offenders by means of a loose confederation of agencies at all levels of government. Our American system of justice has evolved from the English common law into a complex series of procedures and decisions. Founded on the concept that crimes against an individual are crimes against the State, our justice system prosecutes individuals as though they victimized all of society. However, crime victims are involved throughout the process and many justice agencies have programs which focus on helping victims.

There is no single criminal justice system in this country. We have many similar systems that are individually unique. Criminal cases may be handled differently in different jurisdictions, but court decisions based on the due process guarantees of the U.S. Constitution require that specific steps be taken in the administration of criminal justice so that the individual will be protected from undue intervention from the State.

The description of the criminal and juvenile justice systems that follows portrays the most common sequence of events in response to serious criminal behavior.

Entry into the System

The justice system does not respond to most crime because so much crime is not discovered or reported to the police. Law enforcement agencies learn about crime from the reports of victims or other citizens, from discovery by a police officer in the field, from informants, or from investigative and intelligence work.

Once a law enforcement agency has established that a crime has been committed, a suspect must be identified and apprehended for the case to proceed through the system. Sometimes, a suspect is apprehended at the scene; however, identification of a suspect sometimes requires an extensive investigation. Often, no one is identified or apprehended. In some instances, a suspect is arrested and later the police determine that no crime was committed and the suspect is released.

Prosecution and Pretrial Services

After an arrest, law enforcement agencies present information about the case and about the accused to the prosecutor, who will decide if formal charges will be filed with the court. If no charges are filed, the accused must be released. The prosecutor can also drop charges after making efforts to prosecute (*nolle prosequi*).

A suspect charged with a crime must be taken before a judge or magistrate without unnecessary delay. At the initial appearance, the judge or magistrate informs the accused of the charges and decides whether there is probable cause to detain the accused person. If the offense is not very serious, the determination of guilt and assessment of a penalty may also occur at this stage.

Often, the defense counsel is also assigned at the initial appearance. All suspects prosecuted for serious crimes have a right to be represented by an attorney. If the court determines the suspect is indigent and cannot afford such representation, the court will assign counsel at the public's expense.

A pretrial-release decision may be made at the initial appearance, but may occur at other hearings or may be changed at another time during the process. Pretrial release and bail were traditionally intended to ensure appearance at trial. However, many jurisdictions permit pretrial detention of defendants accused of serious offenses and deemed to be dangerous to prevent them from committing crimes prior to trial.

The court often bases its pretrial decision on information about the defendant's drug use, as well as residence, employment, and family ties. The court may decide to release the accused on his/her own recognizance or into the custody of a third party after the posting of a financial bond or on the promise of satisfying certain conditions such as taking periodic drug tests to ensure drug abstinence.

In many jurisdictions, the initial appearance may be followed by a preliminary hearing. The main function of this hearing is to discover if there is probable cause to believe that the accused committed a known crime within the jurisdiction of the court. If the judge does not find probable cause, the case is dismissed; however, if the judge or magistrate finds probable cause for such a belief, or the accused waives his or her right to a preliminary hearing, the case may be bound over to a grand jury.

A grand jury hears evidence against the accused presented by the prosecutor and decides if there is sufficient evidence to cause the accused to be brought to trial. If the grand jury finds sufficient evidence, it submits to the court an indictment, a written statement of the essential facts of the offense charged against the accused.

Where the grand jury system is used, the grand jury may also investigate criminal activity generally and issue indictments called grand jury originals that initiate criminal cases. These investigations and indictments are often used in drug and conspiracy cases that involve complex organizations. After such an indictment, law enforcement tries to apprehend and arrest the suspects named in the indictment.

Misdemeanor cases and some felony cases proceed by the issuance of an information, a formal, written accusation submitted to the court by a prosecutor. In some jurisdictions, indictments may be required in felony cases. However, the accused may choose to waive a grand jury indictment and, instead, accept service of an information for the crime.

In some jurisdictions, defendants, often those without prior criminal records, may be eligible for diversion from prosecution subject to the completion of specific conditions such as drug treatment. Successful completion of the conditions may result in the dropping of charges or the expunging of the criminal record where the defendant is required to plead guilty prior to the diversion.

Adjudication

Once an indictment or information has been filed with the trial court, the accused is scheduled for arraignment. At the arraignment, the accused is informed of the charges, advised of the rights of criminal defendants, and asked to enter a plea to the charges. Sometimes, a plea of guilty is the result of negotiations between the prosecutor and the defendant.

If the accused pleads guilty or pleads *nolo contendere* (accepts penalty without admitting guilt), the judge may accept or reject the plea. If the plea is accepted, no trial is held and the offender is sentenced at this proceeding or at a later date. The plea may be rejected and proceed to trial if, for example, the judge believes that the accused may have been coerced.

If the accused pleads not guilty or not guilty by reason of insanity, a date is set for the trial. A person accused of a serious crime is guaranteed a trial by jury. However, the accused may ask for a bench trial where the judge, rather than a jury, serves as the finder of fact. In both instances the prosecution and defense present evidence by questioning witnesses while the judge decides on issues of law. The trial results in acquittal or conviction on the original charges or on lesser included offenses.

After the trial a defendant may request appellate review of the conviction or sentence. In some cases, appeals of convictions are a matter of right; all States with the death penalty provide for automatic appeal of cases involving a death sentence. Appeals may be subject to the discretion of the appellate court and may be granted only on acceptance of a defendant's petition for a *writ of certiorari*. Prisoners may also appeal their sentences through civil rights petitions and *writs of habeas corpus* where they claim unlawful detention.

Sentencing and Sanctions

After a conviction, sentence is imposed. In most cases the judge decides on the sentence, but in some jurisdictions the sentence is decided by the jury, particularly for capital offenses.

In arriving at an appropriate sentence, a sentencing hearing may be held at which evidence of aggravating or mitigating circumstances is considered. In assessing the circumstances surrounding a convicted person's criminal behavior, courts often rely on presentence investigations by probation agencies or other designated authorities. Courts may also consider victim impact statements.

The sentencing choices that may be available to judges and juries include one or more of the following:

- the death penalty
- incarceration in a prison, jail, or other confinement facility
- probation—allowing the convicted person to remain at liberty but subject to certain conditions and restrictions such as drug testing or drug restrictions such as drug testing or drug treatment

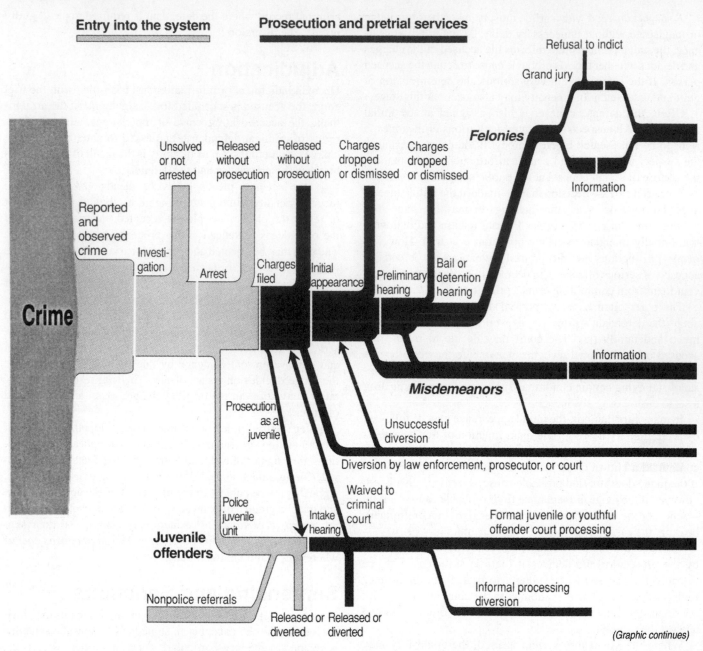

Entry into the system

Prosecution and pretrial services

Figure 1

Note: This chart gives a simplified view of caseflow through the criminal justice system. Procedures vary among jurisdictions. The weights of the lines are not intended to show the actual size of caseloads.

- fines—primarily applied as penalties in minor offenses
- restitution—requiring the offender to pay compensation to the victim. In some jurisdictions, offenders may be sentenced to alternatives to incarceration that are considered more severe than straight probation but less severe than a prison term. Examples of such sanctions include boot camps, intense supervision often with drug treatment and testing, house arrest and electronic monitoring, denial of Federal benefits, and community service.

In many jurisdictions, the law mandates that persons convicted of certain types of offenses serve a prison term. Most jurisdictions permit the judge to set the sentence length within certain limits, but some have determinate sentencing laws that stipulate a specific sentence length that must be served and cannot be altered by a parole board.

Corrections

Offenders sentenced to incarceration usually serve time in a local jail or a State prison. Offenders sentenced to less than 1 year generally go to jail; those sentenced to more than 1 year go to prison. Persons admitted to the Federal system or a State prison system may be held in prison with varying levels of custody or in a community correctional facility.

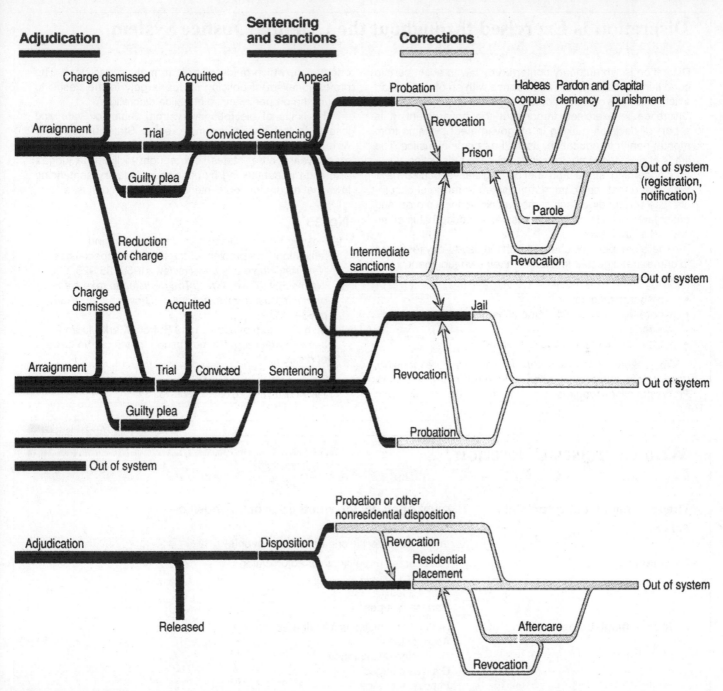

Adjudication **Sentencing and sanctions** **Corrections**

Figure 1 *(continued)*

Source: Adapted from *The challenge of crime in a free society*. President's Commission on Law Enforcement and Administration of Justice, 1967. This revision, a result of the Symposium on the 30th Anniversary of the President's Commission, was prepared by the Bureau of Justice Statistics in 1997.

A prisoner may become eligible for parole after serving a specific part of his or her sentence. Parole is the conditional release of a prisoner before the prisoner's full sentence has been served. The decision to grant parole is made by an authority such as a parole board, which has power to grant or revoke parole or to discharge a parolee altogether. The way parole decisions are made varies widely among jurisdictions.

Offenders may also be required to serve out their full sentences prior to release (expiration of term). Those sentenced under determinate sentencing laws can be released only after

they have served their full sentence (mandatory release) less any "goodtime" received while in prison. Inmates get goodtime credits against their sentences automatically or by earning them through participation in programs.

If released by a parole board decision or by mandatory release, the releasee will be under the supervision of a parole officer in the community for the balance of his or her unexpired sentence. This supervision is governed by specific conditions of release, and the releasee may be returned to prison for violations of such conditions.

Discretion Is Exercised throughout the Criminal Justice System

Discretion is "an authority conferred by law to act in certain conditions or situations in accordance with an official's or an official agency's own considered judgment and conscience."[1] Discretion is exercised throughout the government. It is a part of decision making in all government systems from mental health to education, as well as criminal justice. The limits of discretion vary from jurisdiction to jurisdiction.

Concerning crime and justice, legislative bodies have recognized that they cannot anticipate the range of circumstances surrounding each crime, anticipate local mores, and enact laws that clearly encompass all conduct that is criminal and all that is not.[2]

Therefore, persons charged with the day-to-day response to crime are expected to exercise their own judgment within limits set by law. Basically, they must decide—

- whether to take action
- where the situation fits in the scheme of law, rules, and precedent
- which official response is appropriate.[3]

To ensure that discretion is exercised responsibly, government authority is often delegated to professionals. Professionalism requires a minimum level of training and orientation, which guide officials in making decisions. The professionalism of policing is due largely to the desire to ensure the proper exercise of police discretion.

The limits of discretion vary from State to State and locality to locality. For example, some State judges have wide discretion in the type of sentence they may impose. In recent years, other states have sought to limit the judge's discretion in sentencing by passing mandatory sentencing laws that require prison sentences for certain offenses.

Notes

1. Roscoe Pound, "Discretion, dispensation and mitigation: The problem of the individual special case," *New York University Law Review* (1960) 35:925, 926.
2. Wayne R. LaFave, *Arrest: The decision to take a suspect into custody* (Boston: Little, Brown & Co., 1964), p. 63–184.
3. Memorandum of June 21, 1977, from Mark Moore to James Vorenberg, "Some abstract notes on the issue of discretion."

Bureau of Justice Statistics (www.ojp.usdoj.gov/bjs/). January 1998. NCJ 167894. To order: 1-800-732-3277.

Who Exercises Discretion?

These criminal justice officials . . .	must often decide whether or not or how to—
Police	Enforce specific laws Investigate specific crimes; Search people
Prosecutors	File charges or petitions for adjudication Seek indictments Drop cases Reduce charges
Judges or magistrates	Set bail or conditions for release Accept pleas Determine delinquency Dismiss charges Impose sentence Revoke probation
Correctional officials	Assign to type of correctional facility Award privileges Punish for disciplinary infractions
Paroling authorities	Determine date and conditions of parole Revoke parole

Recidivism

Once the suspects, defendants, or offenders are released from the jurisdiction of a criminal justice agency, they may be processed through the criminal justice system again for a new crime. Long term studies show that many suspects who are arrested have prior criminal histories and those with a greater number of prior arrests were more likely to be arrested again. As the courts take prior criminal history into account at sentencing, most prison inmates have a prior criminal history and many have been incarcerated before. Nationally, about half the inmates released from State prison will return to prison.

The Juvenile Justice System

Juvenile courts usually have jurisdiction over matters concerning children, including delinquency, neglect, and adoption. They also handle "status offenses" such as truancy and running away, which are not applicable to adults. State statutes define which persons are under the original jurisdiction of the juvenile court. The upper age of juvenile court jurisdiction in delinquency matters is 17 in most States.

The processing of juvenile offenders is not entirely dissimilar to adult criminal processing, but there are crucial differences. Many juveniles are referred to juvenile courts by law enforcement officers, but many others are referred by school officials, social services agencies, neighbors, and even parents, for behavior or conditions that are determined to require intervention by the formal system for social control.

At arrest, a decision is made either to send the matter further into the justice system or to divert the case out of the system, often to alternative programs. Examples of alternative programs include drug treatment, individual or group counseling, or referral to educational and recreational programs.

When juveniles are referred to the juvenile courts, the court's intake department or the prosecuting attorney determines whether sufficient grounds exist to warrant filing a petition that requests an adjudicatory hearing or a request to transfer jurisdiction to criminal court. At this point, many juveniles are released or diverted to alternative programs.

All States allow juveniles to be tried as adults in criminal court under certain circumstances. In many States, the legislature *statutorily excludes* certain (usually serious) offenses from the jurisdiction of the juvenile court regardless of the age of the accused. In some States and at the Federal level under certain circumstances, prosecutors have the *discretion* to either file criminal charges against juveniles directly in criminal courts or proceed through the juvenile justice process. The juvenile court's intake department or the prosecutor may petition the juvenile court to *waive* jurisdiction to criminal court. The juvenile court also may order *referral* to criminal court for trial as adults. In some jurisdictions, juveniles processed as adults may upon conviction be sentenced to either an adult or a juvenile facility.

In those cases where the juvenile court retains jurisdiction, the case may be handled formally by filing a delinquency petition or informally by diverting the juvenile to other agencies or programs in lieu of further court processing.

If a petition for an adjudicatory hearing is accepted, the juvenile may be brought before a court quite unlike the court with jurisdiction over adult offenders. Despite the considerable discretion associated with juvenile court proceedings, juveniles are afforded many of the due-process safeguards associated with adult criminal trials. Several States permit the use of juries in juvenile courts; however, in light of the U.S. Supreme Court holding that juries are not essential to juvenile hearings, most States do not make provisions for juries in juvenile courts.

In disposing of cases, juvenile courts usually have far more discretion than adult courts. In addition to such options as probation, commitment to a residential facility, restitution, or fines, State laws grant juvenile courts the power to order removal of children from their homes to foster homes or treatment facilities. Juvenile courts also may order participation in special programs aimed at shoplifting prevention, drug counseling, or driver education.

Once a juvenile is under juvenile court disposition, the court may retain jurisdiction until the juvenile legally becomes an adult (at age 21 in most States). In some jurisdictions, juvenile offenders may be classified as youthful offenders which can lead to extended sentences.

Following release from an institution, juveniles are often ordered to a period of aftercare which is similar to parole supervision for adult offenders. Juvenile offenders who violate the conditions of aftercare may have their aftercare revoked, resulting in being recommitted to a facility. Juveniles who are classified as youthful offenders and violate the conditions of aftercare may be subject to adult sanctions.

The Governmental Response to Crime Is Founded in the Intergovernmental Structure of the United States

Under our form of government, each State and the Federal Government has its own criminal justice system. All systems must respect the rights of individuals set forth in court interpretation of the U.S. Constitution and defined in case law.

State constitutions and laws define the criminal justice system within each State and delegate the authority and responsibility for criminal justice to various jurisdictions, officials, and institutions. State laws also define criminal behavior and groups of children or acts under jurisdiction of the juvenile courts.

Municipalities and counties further define their criminal justice systems through local ordinances that proscribe the local agencies responsible for criminal justice processing that were not established by the State.

Congress has also established a criminal justice system at the Federal level to respond to Federal crimes such as bank robbery, kidnaping, and transporting stolen goods across State lines.

The Response to Crime Is Mainly a State and Local Function

Very few crimes are under exclusive Federal jurisdiction. The responsibility to respond to most crime rests with State and local governments. Police protection is primarily a function of cities and towns. Corrections is primarily a function of State governments. Most justice personnel are employed at the local level.

Critical Thinking

1. Explain discretion and how it is exercised in the criminal justice system.
2. What are the steps that follow once a suspect is arrested by police and charged with a crime?

From *Report to the Nation on Crime and Justice,* January 1998. Published by Office of Justice/U.S. Department of Justice.

Plugging Holes in the Science of Forensics

HENRY FOUNTAIN

It was time, the panel of experts said, to put more science in forensic science.

A report in February by a committee of the National Academy of Sciences found "serious problems" with much of the work performed by crime laboratories in the United States. Recent incidents of faulty evidence analysis—including the case of an Oregon lawyer who was arrested by the F.B.I. after the 2004 Madrid terrorist bombings based on fingerprint identification that turned out to be wrong—were just high-profile examples of wider deficiencies, the committee said. Crime labs were overworked, there were few certification programs for investigators and technicians, and the entire field suffered from a lack of oversight.

But perhaps the most damning conclusion was that many forensic disciplines—including analysis of fingerprints, bite marks and the striations and indentations left by a pry bar or a gun's firing mechanism—were not grounded in the kind of rigorous, peer-reviewed research that is the hallmark of classic science. DNA analysis was an exception, the report noted, in that it had been studied extensively. But many other investigative tests, the report said, "have never been exposed to stringent scientific scrutiny."

While some forensic experts took issue with that conclusion, many welcomed it. And some scientists are working on just the kind of research necessary to improve the field. They are refining software and studying human decision-making to improve an important aspect of much forensic science—the ability to recognize and compare patterns.

The report was "basically saying what many of us have been saying for a long time," said Lawrence Kobilinsky, chairman of the department of sciences at John Jay College of Criminal Justice in New York. "There are a lot of areas in forensics that need improvement."

Barry Fisher, a past president of the American Academy of Forensic Sciences and a former director of the crime laboratory at the Los Angeles County Sheriff's Department, said he and others had been pushing for this kind of independent assessment for years. "There needs to be a demonstration that this stuff is reliable," he said.

It's not that there hasn't been any research in forensic science. But over the years much of it has been done in crime labs themselves. "It hasn't gotten to the level where they can state findings in a rigorous scientific way," said Constantine Gatsonis, director of the Center for Statistical Sciences at Brown University and co-chairman of the National Academy of Sciences committee. And rather than being teased out in academic papers and debated at scientific conferences, "a lot of this forensic stuff is being argued in the courtroom," Mr. Fisher said. "That's not the place to validate any kind of scientific information."

Much forensic research has been geared to improving technologies and techniques. These studies can result in the kinds of gee-whiz advances that may show up in the next episode of the "C.S.I." series—a technique to obtain fingerprints from a grocery bag or other unlikely source, for example, or equipment that enables analyses of the tiniest bits of evidence.

This kind of work is useful, Dr. Kobilinsky said, "but it doesn't solve the basic problem."

DNA analysis came out of the biological sciences, and much money and time has been spent developing the field, resulting in a large body of peer-reviewed research. So when a DNA expert testifies in court that there is a certain probability that a sample comes from a suspect, that claim is grounded in science.

As evidence to be analyzed, DNA has certain advantages. "DNA has a particular structure, and can be digitized," Dr. Gatsonis said. So scientists can agree, for example, on how many loci on a DNA strand to use in their analyses, and computers can do the necessary computations of probability.

"Fingerprints are a lot more complicated," Dr. Gatsonis said. "There are a lot of different ways you can select features and make comparisons." A smudged print may have only a few ridge endings or other points for comparison, while a clear print may have many more. And other factors can affect prints, including the material they were found on and the pressure of the fingers in making them.

Sargur N. Srihari, an expert in pattern recognition at the University at Buffalo, part of the New York state university system, is trying to quantify the uncertainty. His group did much of the research that led to postal systems that can recognize handwritten addresses on envelopes, and he works with databases of fingerprints to derive probabilities of random correspondence between two prints.

Most features on a print are usually represented by X and Y coordinates and by an angle that represents the orientation of the particular ridge where the feature is located. A single print can have 40 or more comparable features.

Dr. Srihari uses relatively small databases, including an extreme one that contains fingerprints from dozens of identical twins (so the probability of matches is high), and employs the results to further refine mathematical tools for comparison that would work with larger populations.

"These numbers are not easy to come by at this point," he said. The goal is not individualization—matching two prints with absolute certainty—but coming up with firm probabilities that would be very useful in legal proceedings.

Other researchers are compiling databases of their own. Nicholas D. K. Petraco, an assistant professor at John Jay College, is studying microscopic tool marks of the kind made by a screwdriver when a burglar jimmies a window. It has been hypothesized that no two screwdrivers leave exactly the same pattern of marks, although that has never been proved. So Dr. Petraco is systematically making marks in jeweler's wax and other materials, creating images of them under a stereo microscope and quantifying the details, assembling a database that can eventually be mined to determine probabilities that a mark matches a certain tool.

Dr. Petraco, a chemist with a strong background in computer science, looks to industry for ideas about pattern recognition—the tools that a company like Netflix uses, for example, to classify people by the kinds of movies they like. "A lot of computational machinery goes into making those kinds of decisions," he said.

He figures that if something works for industry, it will work for forensic science. "You don't want to invent anything new," he said, because that raises legal issues of admissibility of evidence.

The work takes time, but the good news is that the data stays around forever. So as software improves, the probabilities should get more accurate. "Algorithms and data comparison evolve over time," Dr. Petraco said.

But it may not be possible to develop useful databases in some disciplines—bite mark analysis, for example. "Using a screwdriver, that's very straightforward and simple," said Ira Titunik, a forensic odontologist and adjunct professor at John Jay College. But bites involve numerous teeth, and there are other factors, including condition of the skin, that may make it difficult to quantify them for purposes of determining probabilities.

A few researchers are looking at how errors creep into forensic analysis. The National Institute of Standards and Technology recently established a working group on fingerprints, with statisticians, psychologists and others, "to try to understand the circumstances that lead to human error," said Mark Stolorow, director of the Office of Law Enforcement Standards at the institute.

In Britain, Itiel Dror, a psychologist who studies decision-making processes, is already looking at human factors. "I like to say the mind is not a camera, objectively and passively recording information," said Dr. Dror, who has a consulting firm and is affiliated with University College London. "The brain is an active and dynamic device."

He has conducted studies that show that when working on an identification, fingerprint examiners can be influenced by what else they know about a case. In one experiment, he found that the same examiner can come to different conclusions about the same fingerprint, if the context is changed over time.

The same kinds of contextual biases arise with other decision-makers, said Dr. Dror, who works with the military and with financial and medical professionals. He thinks one reason forensic examiners often do not acknowledge that they make errors is that in these other fields, the mistakes are obvious. "In forensics, they don't really see it," he said. "People go to jail."

Forensics experts say the need for research like Dr. Dror's and Dr. Srihari's does not mean that disciplines like fingerprint analysis will turn out to be invalid. "I have no doubt that fingerprint evidence and firearms evidence, once looked into by the appropriate research entities, are going to be shown to be very reliable and good," said Mr. Fisher, the former American Academy of Forensic Sciences president.

Dr. Kobilinsky said people should not jump to the conclusion that forensic science is bad science. "There's a lot of experience and knowledge that goes into somebody's expertise," he said.

"It's not junk science. But that doesn't mean it shouldn't be improved."

Critical Thinking

1. How do errors creep into forensic analysis?
2. What is meant by contextual bias?

Picked from a Lineup, on a Whiff of Evidence

JOHN SCHWARTZ

Houston—A dog's sniff helped put Curvis Bickham in jail for eight months. Now that the case against him has been dropped, he wants to tell the world that the investigative technique that justified his arrest smells to high heaven.

The police told Mr. Bickham they had tied him to a triple homicide through a dog-scent lineup, in which dogs choose a suspect's smell out of a group. The dogs are exposed to the scent from items found at a crime scene, and are then walked by a series of containers with samples swabbed from a suspect and from others not involved in the crime. If the dog finds a can with a matching scent, it signals—stiffening, barking or giving some other alert its handler recognizes.

Dogs' noses have long proved useful to track people, and the police rely on them to detect drugs and explosives, and to find the bodies of victims of crime and disaster. A 2004 report by the F.B.I. states that use of scent dogs, properly conducted, "has become a proven tool that can establish a connection to the crime."

Scent lineups, however, are different. Critics say that the possibilities of cross-contamination of scent are great, and that the procedures are rarely well controlled. Nonetheless, although some courts have rejected evidence from them, the technique has been used in many states, including Alaska, Florida, New York and Texas, said Lawrence J. Myers, an associate professor of animal behavior at the Auburn University College of Veterinary Medicine.

In particular, the methods of the dog handler in Mr. Bickham's case, and in a half-dozen others that are the basis of lawsuits, have come under fierce attack.

The handler, Deputy Keith A. Pikett of the Fort Bend County, Tex., Sheriff's Department, is "a charlatan," said Rex Easley, a lawyer in Victoria, Tex., who represents a man falsely accused by the police of murdering a neighbor. Deputy Pikett, the lawyer said, "devised an unreliable dog trick to justify local police agencies' suspicions" for producing search warrants and arrests.

Deputy Pikett, who declined to be interviewed, works in the town of Richmond, southwest of Houston, but he has served as a busy consultant to law enforcement agencies around the state, using his home-trained bloodhounds—he has given them names that include Columbo, Quincy and Clue—to sniff out crime. A native of Buffalo, N.Y., he has by his own estimate in court testimony performed thousands of scent lineups since the 1990s. His lawyer said the techniques were effective.

Thomas Lintner, the chief of the F.B.I. laboratory's evidence response team unit, said the agency used scents only to follow a trail to a suspect or to a place associated with him, and not to identify one person out of several. The 2004 F.B.I. report warned that dog scent work "should not be used as primary evidence," but only to corroborate other evidence.

In several of the cases that were based on Deputy Pikett's dogs, however, the scent lineups appear to have provided the primary evidence, even when contradictory evidence was readily available. Mr. Bickham spent eight months in jail after being identified in a scent lineup by Deputy Pikett's dogs, until another man confessed to the killings. In an interview, Mr. Bickham scoffed at the accusation that he had taken part in three murders, noting that he has been hobbled by bone spurs and diabetes and is partially blind.

Ronald Curtis, another Houston man jailed on the basis of Deputy Pikett's dogs, was released from jail nine months after being accused of a string of burglaries. Store videos showed that the burglar did not resemble him. "Nobody was listening," Mr. Curtis said.

Both he and Mr. Bickham are filing civil lawsuits over their treatment in federal court on Wednesday.

The first person to file such a suit, in January, was Michael Buchanek, a retired captain with the Victoria County, Tex., Sheriff's Department and a client of Mr. Easley. After Deputy Pikett's dogs identified him, Mr. Buchanek said the police "just kept telling me, 'the dogs don't lie—we know you did it.'" After months of uncertainty, DNA evidence implicated another man who later confessed to the crime.

As Mr. Easley examined the case, he sought the opinion of animal investigation experts who reviewed Deputy Pikett's work and responded with incredulity. Robert Coote, the head of a British canine police unit, reviewed videos of Deputy Pikett's scent lineup in the Buchanek case and stated, "If it was not for the fact that this is a serious matter, I could have been watching a comedy."

Mr. Easley shared his findings with colleagues at the Innocence Project of Texas, a legal defense organization, which released a report last month that excoriated dog scent lineups as a "junk science injustice." Jeff Blackburn, the chief counsel for the group, said Deputy Pickett merely gave the police the match they had hoped for.

Mr. Myers, the animal behavior expert, suggested that handlers like Deputy Pikett might believe in the dogs and the methods, but might allow samples to become contaminated or inadvertently allow the dogs to pick up on subtle, even unconscious signals from handlers or detectives.

"They just don't realize they're doing it wrong," he said.

Randall Morse, an assistant Fort Bend county attorney who is representing Deputy Pikett, said the dogs provided information, not conclusions of guilt or innocence.

"Pikett doesn't arrest anybody," Mr. Morse said. "Our dogs don't say, You murdered somebody. They don't even say, You committed a crime. They just say, We picked up your scent."

Mr. Morse said scent lineups had proved their worth, as in the case of Bart Whitaker, a Texan who hired friends to kill his family in 2003. Deputy Pikett's dogs helped identify the trigger man from eight suspects. Mr. Whitaker is now on death row, and his accomplices are in prison.

"We believe in this stuff," Mr. Morse said.

Mr. Blackburn of the Innocence Project noted that the Whitaker case involved a great deal of corroborating evidence beyond the dogs.

"Our estimate right now is we've got 15 to 20 people who are in prison right now based on virtually nothing but Pikett's testimony," he said. "That's a big problem."

Donna Hawkins, a spokeswoman for the Harris County district attorney's office in Houston, said she could not comment on the dispute over dog scent lineups or on the re-examination of cases that involved them. "Cases will be evaluated on an individual basis, considering all relevant evidence," Ms. Hawkins said.

As for Mr. Bickham, he said he had lost his home while in jail and had struggled to restart his barbecue stand; he sold his cars to hire his lawyer. These days, he said, he is easily agitated, cries readily and is taking antidepressants.

"I lost everything," Mr. Bickham said, because of "a nothing case."

Critical Thinking

1. How does a scent lineup work?
2. How does the FBI use dogs' ability to detect scents?
3. What are the criticisms of scent lineups?

Organizational Learning and Islamic Militancy

Law enforcement may be able to exploit terrorists' inexperience to deter attacks.

MICHAEL KENNEY

Like other forms of criminal deviance, terrorism requires expertise that combines knowledge with practice.

Terrorists with knowledge and practical experience are more likely to carry out "successful" attacks than those lacking both of these essential qualities. However, some extremists are more informed—and experienced—than others.

Well-educated people do not necessarily make good terrorists. The medical doctors behind the failed 2007 car bombings in London and Glasgow, Scotland, lacked the bomb-making skills of the petty criminals who killed 56 people in the London Tube and bus bombings two years before. Terrorism is a craft involving its own particular set of skills and knowledge that practitioners must develop to be good at it. This begs an important yet little understood question: How do terrorists get the experience—and expertise—they need to carry out acts of political violence?

To answer this question, I carried out five months of fieldwork on Islamic militancy in Britain and Spain, home to two of the most devastating terrorist attacks since Sept. 11.[1] I interviewed many militants, including former Guantánamo Bay detainees and members of al-Muhajiroun. I also interviewed dozens of law enforcement officials and intelligence analysts from the Federal Bureau of Investigation, the London Metropolitan Police Service, the Spanish Civil Guard and other agencies. I complemented these interviews with news reports, studies and court documents from criminal proceedings in Britain and Spain.

While terrorists gain knowledge of their craft through formal study and practice, the method of diffusion depends on the knowledge being gained. Abstract technical knowledge, what the ancient Greeks called "techne," can be codified in documents and communicated in "small, explicit, logical steps."[2] Islamic terrorists gain the techne involved in bomb making and weapons handling by reading manuals and other documents that provide detailed, systematic instructions. Alternatively, they attend training camps where experienced practitioners teach these clear, logical and deadly steps as part of their curriculum. This technical knowledge is universal; it does not vary across local settings. Would-be terrorists may gain abstract knowledge for carrying out attacks at a training camp in Waziristan, Pakistan; a farmhouse outside Madrid, Spain; or from an online training manual.

While terrorists gain knowledge of their craft through formal study and practice, the method of diffusion depends on the knowledge being gained.

Not all knowledge can be gained in this manner. Practitioners of a specific tradecraft, such as medicine, law enforcement or terrorism, often rely on intuitive, practical knowledge, what the Greeks called "métis." Practitioners develop métis gradually, by engaging in the activity itself, rather than by formal study. Terrorists may learn the techne involved in building bombs, shooting weapons and other activities by studying manuals or receiving formal instruction. However, to develop hands-on competence they must put the book down and practice. Practice may not make perfect, but it does build skills. To become a competent terrorist, one must build bombs, fire guns or survey targets, gaining the practical "know-how" that is essential for carrying out successful attacks. Unlike techne, métis is not "settled knowledge;" it varies across local contexts.[3] What works in one location may not work in another. Street smarts in London are different from "cave smarts" in Afghanistan. The tradecraft needed to succeed in urban terrorism in the

West is not easily gained from training in guerrilla warfare, even as taught at the best al-Qaida camps.

In fact, Islamic terrorists are often short on métis; the experiential knowledge needed to carry out attacks in local settings is far removed from their training sites. Even battle-hardened militants typically develop their violent métis by taking part in one or more jihads in Afghanistan, Bosnia, Chechnya, Iraq or Kashmir. Militants' combat knowledge, however useful in those locales, is essentially limited to guerrilla warfare. Such métis does not necessarily translate into effective urban terrorism in Western countries, where success requires local knowledge, street smarts and a talent for clandestine operations.

The Sept. 11 attacks provide a striking and diagnostic case. The hijackers Nawaf al-Hazmi and Khalid al-Mihdhar were veteran jihadists who trained in Afghanistan and fought in Bosnia. For all their training and combat experience, both militants were unprepared for their original roles as pilots in the operation. Renting an apartment in southern California, let alone learning English and completing pilot training, proved a daunting task, requiring the help of English-speaking residents who knew the area. Not coincidentally, those recruited to replace the duo, Mohammed Atta, Marwan al Shehh and Ziad Jarrah, lived in Germany for years before joining al-Qaida. These "educated, technical men . . . did not need to be told how to live in the West;" they already knew how.[4] Atta and his colleagues drew on their English-speaking skills and experience from living in Germany to perform satisfactory, if imperfect, tradecraft in the operation.

Unlike the Sept. 11 hijackers, Mohammed Siddique Khan and his co-conspirators in the 2005 London bombings grew up in the country they attacked. Their knowledge of British culture and society and their natural command of English were instrumental in carrying out their suicide bombings. Two of the bombers, Khan and Shehzad Tanweer, received training in Pakistan. Yet any techne they gained there merely complemented the métis they already had from living in Britain for so long. The London bombers drew on their local knowledge and experience to move around the country and get the explosive materials they needed without being disrupted by law enforcement.

Similarly, the Madrid train bombers drew on their own métis, gained from living in Spain for many years, to carry out their attacks in 2004. Many conspirators, such as Jamal Ahmidan and Serhane ben Abdelmajid Fakhet, were originally from North Africa. Yet they settled permanently in Madrid and were fluent in Spanish, which helped them prepare for the operation. Other key participants, including José Emilio Suárez Trashorras, the former miner who provided access to the explosives, were natural born citizens who had lived in Spain their entire lives.

Ahmidan, Trashorras and others had another critical source of métis: criminal experience in drug trafficking. Ahmidan was a veteran hashish and Ecstasy smuggler who had previously killed a man. Rafa Zouhier was an

Related Research

A number of NIJ-funded studies have contributed to our understanding of how terrorists learn:

Brian Jackson led a team of RAND Corp. researchers who examined how several terrorist groups gather information and develop tactical innovations in their attacks.[5] The study suggests that counterterrorism efforts become more effective as law enforcement officers assess and anticipate terrorists' efforts to change how they operate.

Mark Hamm drew on court documents from the American Terrorism Study and criminological literature on social learning to explore how terrorists carry out violent attacks.[6]

The study examined how certain opportunities and skills contributed to terrorists' ability to commit crimes. In other cases, events or lack of skill prevented planned crimes.

Other scholars have explored how terrorists train their supporters in the tactics and techniques of guerrilla warfare and terrorism.[7] Combined with earlier literature on terrorism contagion[8] and recent scholarship on suicide bombings,[9] these studies are helping us develop more effective counterterrorism policies and practices, providing clues to short-circuit terrorists' learning process.

experienced drug dealer who provided Ahmidan the connection to Trashorras, who had a history of hashish trafficking. All of these criminals drew on their contacts and practical knowledge of drug trafficking and explosives to play essential roles in the bombings.

As in the United States after Sept. 11, today in Britain and Spain it has become increasingly difficult for would-be terrorists to acquire the métis they need to carry out attacks. Counterterrorism agencies have cracked down on militants following the London and Madrid bombings and other incidents. In recent years, law enforcement and intelligence officers in all three countries have created a hostile environment for Islamic terrorists, intercepting their communications, arresting them and disrupting their plots. Unlike techne, which can be gained from knowledge-based artifacts, métis is learned by doing. This presents militants with a dilemma. To develop hands-on knowledge for carrying out attacks, they must practice building bombs, using firearms and performing related activities. Yet in doing so, they expose themselves to potential surveillance and disruption by security officials.

The most important lesson is that terrorists' chance of exposure grows as the counterterrorism environment around them becomes increasingly vigilant. The reason is simple: lack of practice leads to a lack of métis that in turn leads to mistakes that alert law enforcement officers can detect. To remain below the radar of police officers and suspicious neighbors, militants have adopted security-enhancing measures. They may wait until the last day of training before allowing students to fire their weapons or detonate their bombs. These precautions help preserve security, but they do not allow participants to practice what they have learned. Yet gaining a feel or knack for terrorism comes from repeated practice and direct experience, not from abstract knowledge codified in documents, no matter how detailed their instructions and accurate their recipes.

Terrorists' chance of exposure grows as the counterterrrorism environment around them becomes increasingly vigilant. Lack of practice leads to mistakes that alert law enforcement officers can detect.

Terrorists are not the only ones who rely on their practical knowledge of local areas. Law enforcement officers draw on their own métis, developed from patrolling community beats, to identify and disrupt illicit activity. Law enforcement officers have detailed knowledge of local resources of interest to potential terrorists, including fertilizer suppliers, explosives manufacturers and gun dealers. Their routine policing activities and their contacts in the communities they serve also provide opportunities to note suspicious behavior among potential militants.[10]

Because they know when something is amiss in the neighborhood, local law enforcement officers play a critical role in counterterrorism. To improve their skills, officers must be able to recognize the warning signs of terrorism-related surveillance and other preparatory acts, such as building explosives. Dead flowers outside the covered window of an inner-city apartment, the gradual lightening of a young man's hair color or apartment trash littered with empty containers of hydrogen peroxide are subtle signals. To the untrained eye these signs may not mean much, but to the knowing observer they can provide clues for identifying bomb-making laboratories. Law enforcement officers who can recognize and act on these warning signs will make a valuable contribution to counterterrorism in the months and years ahead.

For More Information

Learn more at NIJ's terrorism Web page: www.ojp.usdoj.gov/nij/topics/crime/terrorism/welcome.htm.

Read an *NIJ Journal* article about how domestic terrorists prepare for their attacks. See www.ojp.usdoj.gov/nij/journals/260/terroristbehavior.htm.

Notes

1. Kenney, M., *Organizational Learning and Islamic Militancy,* final report submitted to the National Institute of Justice, U.S. Department of Justice, Washington, DC: May 2009 (NCJ 226808), www.ncjrs.gov/pdffiles1/nij/grants/226808.pdf.

2. Scott, J.C., *Seeing Like a State: How Certain Schemes to Improve the Human Condition Have Failed,* New Haven: Yale University Press, 1998: 320. See also Detienne, M., and J.P. Vernant, *Cunning Intelligence in Greek Culture and Society,* Sussex: The Harvester Press, 1978; and Nussbaum, M.C., *The Fragility* of *Goodness: Luck and Ethics in Greek Tragedy and Philosophy,* Cambridge: Cambridge University Press, 1986.

3. Scott, *Seeing Like a State,* 312–315, 320.

4. Wright, L., *The Looming Tower: Al-Qaeda and the Road to 9/11,* New York: Alfred A. Knopf, 2006: 309.

5. Jackson, B.A., J.C. Baker, K. Cragin, J. Parachini, H.R. Trujillo, and P. Chalk, *Aptitude for Destruction, Volume 1: Organizational Learning in Terrorist Groups and Its Implications for Combating Terrorism,* report prepared for the National Institute of Justice, U.S. Department of Justice, Washington, DC: 2005 (NCJ 211208), www.rand.org/pubs/monographs/2005/RAND_MG331.pdf; and Jackson, B.A., J.C. Baker, P. Chalk, K. Cragin, J.V. Parachini, and H.R. Trujillo, *Aptitude for Destruction, Volume 2: Case Studies of Organizational Learning in Five Terrorist Groups,* Santa Monica, CA: RAND Corp., 2005.

6. Hamm, M.S., *Crimes Committed by Terrorist Groups: Theory, Research, and Prevention,* final report submitted to the National Institute of Justice, U.S. Department of Justice, Washington, DC: September 2005 (NCJ 211203), www.ncjrs.gov/pdffiles1/nij/grants/211203.pdf. Also see Hamm, M.S., *Terrorism as Crime: From Oklahoma City to Al-Qaeda and Beyond,* New York: New York University Press, 2007.

7. Forest, J., ed., *Teaching Terror: Knowledge Transfer in the Terrorist World,* Lanham: Rowman & Littlefield, 2006; Forest, J., ed., *The Making of a Terrorist: Recruitment, Training, and Root Causes, Volume Two: Training,* Westport: Praeger Security International, 2006; Kenney, M., *From Pablo to Osama: Trafficking and Terrorist Networks, Government Bureaucracies, and Competitive Adaptation,* University Park: Pennsylvania State University Press, 2007; Nesser, P., "How Did Europe's Global Jihadis Obtain Training for Their Militant Causes?" *Terrorism and Political Violence* 20 (2) (2008): 234–256; and A. Stenerson, "The Internet: A Virtual Training Camp?" *Terrorism and Political Violence* 20 (2) (2008): 215–233.

8. Heyman, E., and E. Mickolus, "Observations on Why Violence Spreads," *International Studies Quarterly* 24 (2) (1980): 299–305; Russell, C.A., L.J. Banker, Jr., and B.H. Miller, "Out-Inventing the Terrorist," in *Terrorism: Theory and Practice,* ed. Y. Alexander, D. Carlton, and P. Wilkinson, Boulder: Westview, 1979: 3–42; R.T. Holden, "The Contagion of Aircraft Hijacking," *American Journal of Sociology* 91 (4) (1986): 874–904; and Midlarsky, M.I., M. Crenshaw, and F. Yoshida, "Why Violence Spreads: The Contagion of International Terrorism," *International Studies Quarterly* 24 (2) (1980): 262–298.

9. Bloom, M., *Dying to Kill: The Allure of Suicide Terror,* New York: Columbia University Press, 2005; Pape, R.A., *Dying to Win: The Strategic Logic of Suicide Terrorism,* New York: Random House, 2005; Gambetta, D., ed., *Making Sense of Suicide Missions,* expanded and updated edition, Oxford: Oxford University Press, 2006.

10. Bayley, D.H., and D. Weisburd, "Cops and Spooks: The Role of the Police in Counterterrorism," in *To Protect and to Serve: Policing in an Age of Terrorism,* ed. D. Weisburd, T.E. Feucht, I Hakimi, L.F. Mock, and S. Perry, New York: Springer, 2009: 92.

Critical Thinking

1. What is métis and why are Islamic terrorists often lacking it?
2. Why do terrorists' chances of exposure grow as the counter-terrorism environment becomes vigilant?

MICHAEL KENNEY is assistant professor of political science and public policy in the School of Public Affairs, Pennsylvania State University.

From *National Institute of Justice Journal,* issue 265, April 2010, pp. 18–21. Published by U.S. Department of Justice.

The Death of the War on Drugs

LAWRENCE T. JABLECKI

In his first interview as the nation's new drug czar, Gil Kerlikowske told the *Wall Street Journal* that the phrase "war on drugs" should be retired because it implies that citizens who use illegal substances are enemies of the state to be conquered and destroyed. Instead of viewing the vast majority of these citizens as criminals deserving of punishment, a new paradigm should embrace them as members of our communities deserving of opportunities to establish or renew healthy and productive lives.

There are certainly no new arguments available to employ in support of or in opposition to current U.S. drug policies. Instead, we are locked in an ideological contest between two conflicting and not mutually exclusive philosophical perspectives, both of which have existed for many centuries. More specifically, the contest is between the perspective that a genuinely free society maximizes the rights and freedoms of its citizens, in turn allowing them to think, say, and act as they please as long as they don't harm or injure their fellow citizens. The other perspective emphasizes the claim that a stable social order can't be maintained in the absence of the legal enforcement of a rather long list of the shared moral values of its citizens. In short, this contest is what the eighteenth century Scottish philosopher David Hume called the perpetual struggle between the liberty of the individual and the authority of the state. And what can't be emphasized enough is that this isn't a struggle between the armies of good and evil. Much too often, defenders on both sides are persuaded that truth and justice are on theirs, and they have allowed their zeal to sink to the level of inflammatory attacks on the motivation and personal characteristics of their opponents. Regardless of our moral stance on a cluster of very divisive issues, all of us should heed the sage comments of the philosopher Isaiah Berlin in his 1958 "Two Concepts of Liberty" lecture: "If, as I believe, the ends of men are many, and not all of them are in principle compatible with each other, then the possibility of conflict—and of tragedy—can never be wholly eliminated from human life, either personal or social. The necessity of choosing between absolute claims is then an inescapable characteristic of the human condition."

I am enormously proud to be an American citizen and wouldn't choose to live in another country. I am, however, unequivocally ashamed that during the last thirty years, our criminal justice policies (federal and state) have sealed our identity as the nation that incarcerates a higher percentage of its population than any other country in the world. The dominant crime control policies are driven by a harsh retributive view of punishment committed to the belief that the only criteria are the seriousness of the offense and the criminal history of the defendant. Making no claim to originality, we have been beguiled by an addiction more powerful than all the drugs combined, namely, vengeance. This is a bitter pill that honesty obliges us to swallow.

There is a wealth of scholarly bickering about the feasibility of determining the actual number of non-violent drug offenders in U.S. federal, state, and private prisons. In his 2004 book, *Thinking about Crime: Sense and Sensibility in American Penal Culture* (Oxford University Press), Michael Tonry makes the worthy claim that

Many thousands of people are serving decades long sentences in federal prisons for non-violent drug crimes. Their misfortune is to have been sentenced in federal courts before avoidance of sentencing guidelines by federal judges and prosecutors became common practice. Hundreds of thousands of people, mostly but not only of minority and disadvantaged backgrounds, have spent much of their young adulthood in prison for drug crimes. Their misfortune is that unwisely, but for young people not uncommonly, and typically as a result of peer influences and teenagers' sense of invincibility, they experimented with drug use, got hooked, and got caught—in a time when antidrug policies were unprecedentedly harsh.

It would be a major error in judgment to claim that the tough law-and-order campaigns of those seeking to retain or attain public office and well-financed lobbyists urging the construction of more prisons, particularly private prisons, were solely responsible for the realities presented by Tonry. Members of Congress and state legislators would not have been able to craft and pass harsh penalties without the strong support of their constituents. Fortunately, the opinions and sensibilities of a fast growing number of our citizens are moving in the direction of believing that the war of prohibition, cradication, and harsh penalties are costing far too much in terms of human fatalities and consuming far too much of our federal and state resources. Many groups of vocal dissenters using electronic mass communication are focusing on these items for an agenda for change: the medical use of marijuana; the de-criminalization of the possession of small amounts of marijuana; the still unresolved issue of the wide disparity in the disposition of cases involving crack and powder cocaine; access to clean syringes to reduce the spread of HIV and hepatitis C; and new medical research involving prescription heroin or heroin replacements with the goals of improving health and reducing crime.

The Uniform Crime Report of 2007 compiled by the FBI contains the following data: of the over fourteen million reported arrests, 1.8 million or 13 percent were for drug abuse violations. Of those, 47.5 percent were for marijuana and of that number 89 percent were for possession, the others involving the sale and manufacture or growing. Three of every four persons in the group of drug violators were under the age of thirty. It is a given that many thousands in this group had a significant criminal history and it is equally true that many thousands did not. This means that many thousands of young offenders with no criminal history are caught in the very wide net of criminal justice and the majority of them must endure a grueling process of adjudication which brands them with a conviction and the status of being a criminal.

A radical proposal, which I believe is realistically feasible, would retrain the same professionals who administer our criminal justice systems to create so-called pre-prosecution agreements which still send a message of societal disapproval, but leave no permanent scars. The specific guts of the proposal are as follows: all persons arrested for possessing small amounts of any illegal substance, excluding it's sale or manufacture, who have no criminal history shall be granted a one-time only pre-prosecution agreement not to exceed one year. Within thirty days of accepting this agreement, they shall complete a substance abuse evaluation by a state-certified substance abuse counselor approved by the local jurisdiction and follow any recommendations of said counselor. Within thirty days of successful completion of this agreement the local jurisdiction and the state's criminal records division shall destroy and expunge all records of the case, excepting a list of the participants. Any participant who is arrested and convicted of any new criminal offense before completion of the program is subject to prosecution of the original offense.

The prosecutors in every local jurisdiction of this country have the explicit or inherent authority to create these programs and they certainly have the discretionary authority to dispose of numerous felony arrests by using this option. I am not embracing the claim that people who violate the criminal laws have any kind of a right that obliges the state to provide a comprehensive menu of services to fix the causes of their illegal conduct. I am claiming that there is a compelling public interest to do so.

The demise of the war on drugs can be accomplished if President Obama musters the political courage to use the presidential bully pulpit to win public and congressional support for the National Criminal Justice Commission Act of 2009 coauthored by Senators Jim Webb (D-VA) and Arlen Specter (D-PA). The purpose of this commission is to, in the words of the legislation, "undertake a comprehensive review of the criminal justice system, make findings related to current federal and state criminal justice policies and practices, and make reform recommendations for the president, Congress, and state governments to improve public safety, cost-effectiveness, overall prison administration, and fairness in the implementation of the nation's criminal justice system."

The commission will have eleven members, the chair to be appointed by President Obama and the other ten members to be appointed by various elected officials. Hopefully, the majority of these ten members will be private citizens who are nationally recognized experts and whose collective experience embraces the specified areas of law enforcement, criminal justice, national security, prison administration, prisoner reentry, public health (including drug addiction and mental health), victims' rights and social services.

If this commission is enacted and its final product receives strong public support and congressional approval, it can deal a death blow to the present international perception that the United States is a rogue nation whose criminal justice system is at war with its own citizens.

Critical Thinking

1. What are the arguments in favor of ending the war on drugs?
2. How can it be accomplished?

LAWRENCE T. JABLECKI, PhD, is a lecturer in the Master of Liberal Studies Program at Rice University and an adjunct professor of philosophy in the prison program of the University of Houston at Clear Lake. For eighteen years he was the director of the adult probation department in Brazoria County, Texas.

From *The Humanist*, September/October 2009, pp. 6–8. Copyright © 2009 by Lawrence T. Jablecki, PhD. Reprinted by permission of the author.

The Wrong Man

In the fall of 2001, a nation reeling from the horror of 9/11 was rocked by a series of deadly anthrax attacks. As the pressure to find a culprit mounted, the FBI, abetted by the media, found one. The wrong one. This is the story of how federal authorities blew the biggest anti-terror investigation of the past decade—and nearly destroyed an innocent man. Here, for the first time, the falsely accused, Dr. Steven J. Hatfill, speaks out about his ordeal.

DAVID FREED

The first anthrax attacks came days after the jetliner assaults of September 11, 2001. Postmarked Trenton, New Jersey, and believed to have been sent from a mailbox near Princeton University, the initial mailings went to NBC News, the *New York Post,* and the Florida-based publisher of several supermarket tabloids, including *The Sun* and *The National Enquirer.* Three weeks later, two more envelopes containing anthrax arrived at the Senate offices of Democrats Tom Daschle and Patrick Leahy, each bearing the handwritten return address of a nonexistent "Greendale School" in Franklin Park, New Jersey. Government mail service quickly shut down.

The letters accompanying the anthrax read like the work of a jihadist, suggesting that their author was an Arab extremist—or someone masquerading as one—yet also advised recipients to take antibiotics, implying that whoever had mailed them never really intended to harm anyone. But at least 17 people would fall ill and five would die—a photo editor at *The Sun*; two postal employees at a Washington, D.C., mail-processing center; a hospital stockroom clerk in Manhattan whose exposure to anthrax could never be fully explained; and a 94-year-old Connecticut widow whose mail apparently crossed paths with an anthrax letter somewhere in the labyrinth of the postal system. The attacks spawned a spate of hoax letters nationwide. Police were swamped with calls from citizens suddenly suspicious of their own mail.

Americans had good reason to fear. Inhaled anthrax bacteria devour the body from within. Anthrax infections typically begin with flu-like symptoms. Massive lesions soon form in the lungs and brain, as a few thousand bacilli propagate within days into literally trillions of voracious parasitic microbes. The final stages before death are excruciatingly painful. As their minds disintegrate, victims literally drown in their own fluids. If you were to peer through a microscope at a cross-section of an anthrax victim's blood vessel at the moment of death, it would look, says Leonard A. Cole, an expert on bioterrorism at Rutgers University, "as though it were teeming with worms."

The pressure on American law enforcement to find the perpetrator or perpetrators was enormous. Agents were compelled to consider any and all means of investigation. One such avenue involved Don Foster, a professor of English at Vassar College and a self-styled literary detective, who had achieved modest celebrity status by examining punctuation and other linguistic fingerprints to identify Joe Klein, who was then a *Newsweek* columnist, as the author of the anonymously written 1996 political novel, *Primary Colors.* Foster had since consulted with the FBI on investigations of the Unabomber and Atlanta's Centennial Olympic Park bombing, among other cases. Now he was asked to analyze the anthrax letters for insights as to who may have mailed them. Foster would detail his efforts two years later in a 9,500-word article for *Vanity Fair.*

Surveying the publicly available evidence, as well as documents sent to him by the FBI, Foster surmised that the killer was an American posing as an Islamic jihadist. Only a limited number of American scientists would have had a working knowledge of anthrax. One of those scientists, Foster concluded, was a man named Steven Hatfill, a medical doctor who had once worked at the Army's elite Medical Research Institute of Infectious Diseases (USAMRIID), which had stocks of anthrax.

On the day al-Qaeda struck the World Trade Center and the Pentagon with hijacked jetliners, Hatfill was recovering from nasal surgery in his apartment outside the gates of Fort Detrick, Maryland, where USAMRIID is housed. *We're at war,* he remembers thinking as he watched the news that day—but he had no idea that it was a war in which he himself would soon become collateral damage, as the FBI came to regard him as a homegrown bioterrorist, likely responsible for some of the most unsettling multiple murders in recent American history. His story provides a cautionary tale about how federal authorities, fueled by the general panic over terrorism, embraced conjecture and coincidence as evidence, and blindly pursued one suspect while the real anthrax killer roamed free for more than six years. Hatfill's experience is also the wrenching saga of how an American citizen who saw himself as a patriot came to be vilified and presumed guilty, as his country turned against him.

"It's like death by a thousand cuts," Hatfill, who is now 56, says today. "There's a sheer feeling of hopelessness. You can't fight back. You have to just sit there and take it, day after day, the constant drip-drip-drip of innuendo, a punching bag for the government and the press. And the thing was, I couldn't understand why it was happening to me. I mean, I was one of the *good* guys."

> **You have to just sit there and take it, day after day, the constant drip-drip-drip of innuendo, a punching bag for the government and the press. I couldn't understand why it was happening to me. I was one of the *good* guys.**

Don Foster, the Vassar professor, was among those who set the wheels of injustice in motion. Scouring the Internet, Foster found an interview that Hatfill had given while working at the National Institutes of Health, in which he described how bubonic plague could be made with simple equipment and used in a bioterror attack. Foster later tracked down an unpublished novel Hatfill had written, depicting a fictional bioterror attack on Washington. He discovered that Hatfill had been in Rhodesia (present-day Zimbabwe) during an anthrax outbreak there in the late 1970s, and that he'd attended medical school near a Rhodesian suburb called Greendale—the name of the invented school in the return address of the anthrax letters mailed to the Senate. The deeper Foster dug, the more Hatfill looked to him like a viable suspect.

"When I lined up Hatfill's known movements with the postmark locations of reported biothreats," Foster later wrote, "those hoax anthrax attacks appeared to trail him like a vapor cloud."

In February 2002, Foster tried to interest the FBI in Hatfill, but says he was told that Hatfill had a good alibi. "A month later, when I pressed the issue," Foster wrote, "I was told, 'Look, Don, maybe you're spending too much time on this.'"

Meanwhile, Barbara Hatch Rosenberg, a passionate crusader against the use of bioweapons, was also convinced that an American scientist was to blame for the anthrax attacks. In an interview with the BBC in early 2002, she theorized that the murders were the result of a top-secret CIA project gone awry, and that the FBI was hesitant to arrest the killer because it would embarrass Washington. A molecular biologist and professor of environmental science who had once served as a low-level bioweapons adviser to President Clinton, Rosenberg had taken it upon herself to look into the anthrax murders, and her investigations had independently led her to Hatfill. (Hatfill says he believes Rosenberg was made aware of him by a former acquaintance, a defense contractor with whom Hatfill had clashed over a proposed counter-anthrax training program intended for the U.S. Marshals Service.) Rosenberg wrote a paper she called "Possible Portrait of the Anthrax Perpetrator,"

which was disseminated on the Internet. Although Rosenberg would later deny ever having identified him publicly or privately, the specific details of her "Portrait" made it clear she had a particular suspect in mind: Steven Hatfill.

Foster says he met Rosenberg over lunch in April 2002, "compared notes," and "found that our evidence had led us in the same direction." Weeks dragged on while he and Rosenberg tried to interest the FBI in their theories, but the bureau remained "stubbornly unwilling to listen." Two months later, her "patience exhausted," Rosenberg, according to Foster, met on Capitol Hill with Senate staff members "and laid out the evidence, such as it was, hers and mine." Special Agent Van Harp, the senior FBI agent on what by then had been dubbed the "Amerithrax" investigation, was summoned to the meeting, along with other FBI officials.

Rosenberg criticized the FBI for not being aggressive enough. "She thought we were wasting efforts and resources in a particular—or in several areas, and should focus more on who she concluded was responsible for it," Harp would later testify.

"Did she mention Dr. Hatfill's name in her presentation?" Hatfill's attorney, former federal prosecutor Thomas G. Connolly, asked Harp during a sworn deposition.

"That's who she was talking about," Harp testified.

Exactly a week after the Rosenberg meeting, the FBI carried out its first search of Hatfill's apartment, with television news cameras broadcasting it live.

In his deposition, Harp would dismiss the timing of the search as coincidental.

Beryl Howell, who at the time of the investigation was serving as Senator Patrick Leahy's point person on all matters anthrax, recently told me that asking Harp and other lead agents to sit down with the "quite persistent" Rosenberg was never meant to pressure the FBI to go after Hatfill. The meeting, Howell says, was intended simply to ensure that investigators cooperated with other experts outside the bureau and objectively considered all theories in the case in order to solve it more quickly.

"Whether or not Rosenberg's suspicions about Hatfill were correct was really not my business," Howell says. "It was really law enforcement's prerogative to figure that one out."

There was enough circumstantial evidence surrounding Hatfill that zealous investigators could easily elaborate a plausible theory of him as the culprit. As fear about the anthrax attacks spread, government and other workers who might have been exposed to the deadly spores via the mail system were prescribed prophylactic doses of Cipro, a powerful antibiotic that protects against infection caused by inhaled anthrax. Unfamiliar to the general population before September 2001, Cipro quickly became known as the anti-anthrax drug, and prescriptions for it skyrocketed.

As it happened, at the time of the anthrax attacks, Hatfill was taking Cipro.

Hatfill's eccentricity also generated suspicion among colleagues and FBI agents. Bench scientists tend toward the sedate and gymnasium-challenged. Steve Hatfill was a flag-waving, tobacco-chewing weight lifter partial to blood-rare steaks and black safari suits that showed off his linebacker's physique, a physician with a bawdy sense of humor and a soldier's ethos, who told stories over cocktails of parachuting from military aircraft and battling Communists in Africa. While few people who knew him could deny his intellect or his passion as a researcher, some found him arrogant and blustery. Others feared him. Even his allies acknowledge that Hatfill could sometimes come across as different. "If you try to link Steve and the word *normal,* they're not going to match up," says Jim Cline, a retired Special Forces sergeant major and anti-terror expert who worked with Hatfill from 1999 to 2002 at Science Applications International Corporation (SAIC), a large defense contractor.

It also happened that Hatfill was familiar with anthrax. He had done his medical training in Africa, where outbreaks of anthrax infections have been known to occur among livestock herds. In 1999, after going to work for SAIC, Hatfill had a hand in developing a brochure for emergency personnel on ways to handle anthrax hoax letters. In the long run-up to Operation Iraqi Freedom, he also oversaw the construction of a full-scale model designed to show invading U.S. troops what a mobile Iraqi germ-warfare lab might look like and how best to destroy it. But while he possessed a working knowledge of *Bacillus anthracis,* Hatfill had never worked in any capacity with the spore-forming, rod-shaped bacterium.

"I was a virus guy," he told me, "not a bacteria guy."

Still, when FBI agents asked to interview him 10 months after the anthrax murders, Hatfill says he wasn't surprised. In their hunt for what he believed were the foreign terrorists who had sent the letters, Hatfill assumed that agents were routinely interviewing every scientist who'd ever worked at USAMRIID, including those, like himself, who had never set foot in the high-security laboratory where anthrax cultures were kept. Hatfill answered the agents' questions and willingly took a polygraph test, which he says he was told he passed.

"I thought that was the end of it," Hatfill says. "But it was only the beginning."

In June, agents asked to "swab" his apartment. Hatfill complied, feeling he had nothing to hide. On June 25, 2002, after signing a consent form at the FBI's field office in nearby Frederick, Maryland, he came home to find reporters and camera crews swarming. TV helicopters orbited overhead. "There's obviously been a leak," Hatfill says one of the agents told him. He was driven to a Holiday Inn to escape the crush of news media and sat in a motel room, watching incredulously as a full-blown search of his home played out on national television. The experience was surreal.

Agents conducted a second search five weeks later amid a repeated media circus. This time they came equipped with a warrant and bloodhounds. The dogs, Hatfill would later learn, had been responsible for false arrests in other cases. Hatfill says he innocently petted one of the hounds, named Tinkerbell. The dog seemed to like him. "He's identified you from the anthrax letters!" Tinkerbell's handler exclaimed.

"It took every ounce of restraint to stop from laughing," Hatfill recalls. "They said, 'We know you did it. We know you

didn't mean to kill anyone.' I said, 'Am I under arrest?' They said no. I walked out, rented a car, and went to see an attorney about suing the hell out of these people."

The FBI raided Hatfill's rented storage locker in Ocala, Florida, where his father owned a thoroughbred horse farm; the agency also searched a townhouse in Washington, D.C., owned by his longtime girlfriend, a slim, elegant accountant whom Hatfill calls "Boo." (To guard her privacy, he asked that her real name not be used.) Agents rifled through Boo's closets and drawers, breaking cherished keepsakes. "They told me, 'Your boyfriend murdered five people,'" she said to me recently, unable to talk about it without tears.

Hatfill was fired from SAIC. The official explanation given was that he had failed to maintain a necessary security clearance; the real reason, he believes, was that the government wanted him fired. He immediately landed the associate directorship of a fledgling Louisiana State University program designed to train firefighters and other emergency personnel to respond to terrorist acts and natural disasters, a job that would have matched the $150,000 annual salary he'd been getting at SAIC. But after Justice Department officials learned of Hatfill's employment, they told LSU to "immediately cease and desist" from using Hatfill on any federally funded program. He was let go before his first day. Other prospective employment fell through. No one would return his calls. One job vanished after Hatfill emerged from a meeting with prospective employers to find FBI agents videotaping them. His savings dwindling, he moved in with Boo.

By this time, the FBI and the Justice Department were so confident Hatfill was guilty that on August 6, 2002, Attorney General John Ashcroft publicly declared him a "person of interest"—the only time the nation's top-law-enforcement official has ever so identified the subject of an active criminal investigation. Agents grilled Hatfill's friends, tapped his phone, installed surveillance cameras outside Boo's condo, and for more than two years, shadowed him day and night, looking for any grounds on which to arrest him.

Many of Hatfill's friends, worried for their own reputations, abandoned him as the FBI gave chase. Certain of Hatfill's innocence, his former colleague Jim Cline was among the few who stood by him, afraid that his increasingly socially isolated friend would kill himself to escape his torment. "When you have the world against you," Cline says, "and only a few people are willing to look you in the eye and tell you, 'I believe you'— I mean, to this day, I really don't know how the guy survived."

Virtually everywhere Hatfill went, the FBI went too, often right behind him—a deliberately harassing tactic called "bumper locking." Hatfill believes that local authorities joined in tormenting him at the behest of the Justice Department. Coming home from dinner one Friday night, he was pulled over by a Washington, D.C., police officer who issued him a warning for failing to signal a lane change. Three blocks later, another cop stopped him, again for not using his turn signal. The officer asked if he'd been drinking. Hatfill said he'd had one Bloody Mary. He was ordered out of his car. "Not unless you're going to arrest me," Hatfill says he responded indignantly. The officer obliged. Hatfill spent the weekend in jail and would later be ordered to attend a four-day alcohol counseling program. The police, he says, refused to administer a blood-alcohol test that would have proved he wasn't drunk.

Connolly, Hatfill's attorney, offered to have Hatfill surrender his passport and be outfitted with a tracking device, to have FBI agents ride with him everywhere, to show them that they were wasting their time. The offer was rejected. "They were purposely sweating him," Connolly says, "trying to get him to go over the edge."

Much of what authorities discovered, they leaked anonymously to journalists. The result was an unrelenting stream of inflammatory innuendo that dominated front pages and television news. Hatfill found himself trapped, the powerless central player in what Connolly describes as "a story about the two most powerful institutions in the United States, the government and the press, ganging up on an innocent man. It's Kafka."

With Hatfill's face splashed all over the news, strangers on the street stared. Some asked for his autograph. Hatfill was humiliated. Embarrassed to be recognized, he stopped going to the gym. He stopped visiting friends, concerned that the FBI would harass them, too. Soon, he stopped going out in public altogether. Once an energetic and ambitious professional who reveled in 14-hour workdays, Hatfill now found himself staring at the walls all day. Television became his steady companion.

"I'd never really watched the news before," Hatfill says, "and now I'm seeing my name all over the place and all these idiots like Geraldo Rivera asking, 'Is this the anthrax animal? Is this the guy who murdered innocent people?' You might as well have hooked me up to a battery. It was sanctioned torture."

I'm seeing my name all over the place and all these idiots like Geraldo Rivera asking, 'Is this the guy who murdered innocent people?' You might as well have hooked me up to a battery. It was sanctioned torture.

Hatfill decided to redecorate Boo's condo as a distraction from the news. He repainted, hung wallpaper, learned to install crown molding. He also began drinking.

An afternoon glass of red wine became three or more. At night, Hatfill would stay up late, dipping Copenhagen tobacco and getting drunk while waiting in a smoldering rage for his name to appear on television, until finally he would pass out and wake up gagging on the tobacco that had caught in his throat, or stumble around and "crash into something." Boo would help him to bed. After a few anguished hours of sleep, Hatfill would see her off to work, doze past noon, then rise to repeat the cycle, closing the blinds to block the sun and the video camera the FBI had installed on a pole across the street. For a while, Boo bought newspapers, so the two of them could fume over the latest lies that had been published about him. But soon he asked her to stop bringing them home, because he couldn't take it anymore.

Steven Hatfill was born on October 24, 1953, and raised with a younger sister in Mattoon, Illinois. His father designed and sold electrical substations. His mother dabbled in interior decorating. He studied piano, soloed a glider at 14, and wrestled for the varsity team in high school. By his own admission, he was a poor student. "I never took a book home," Hatfill says. But he read plenty on his own, especially about science and the military. In 1971, he enrolled at Southwestern College, a small liberal-arts school in Kansas affiliated with the Methodist Church, where he majored in biology and signed up for a Marine Corps summer leadership course with dreams of piloting jet fighters. But when his vision was measured at less than 20/20, he opted out of the program rather than accept a navigator slot. Midway through his sophomore year, he left college and went to Africa.

Hatfill says he always wanted to help people in the developing world. He got his chance at a remote Methodist mission hospital in what is now the Democratic Republic of the Congo, where he learned blood chemistry, parasitology, and basic hematology in a rudimentary lab. A year later, he returned to the United States; he graduated from Southwestern in 1975, and signed up for the Army.

He took a direct-enlistment option to join the Green Berets, attended parachute school, trained as a radio operator, and was assigned to the Army's 7th Special Forces Group at Fort Bragg, North Carolina. When a back injury eventually disqualified him from serving with an operational A-Team, Hatfill reentered civilian life. He joined the National Guard, married the daughter of a Methodist surgeon he had worked with in Africa, and returned to Mattoon to work the night shift as a security guard at a radiator factory. His marriage soon faltered. After they separated, his wife delivered their only child, a girl. Hatfill would not see his daughter for 27 years.

From 1978 to 1994, Hatfill lived in Africa. He earned a medical degree from the Godfrey Huggins School of Medicine in Salisbury, Rhodesia, and saw combat as a volunteer medic with the territorial forces of the Rhodesian army, eventually being attached to a unit called the Selous Scouts, which was renowned for its ruthlessness in battle. While he was in Rhodesia, Hatfill says, a truck he was riding in was ambushed by Marxist insurgents. Leaping from the truck, he landed on his face, badly breaking his nose. For decades afterward he would have trouble breathing—which is why, in September 2001, he finally elected to have surgery on his sinuses, an operation that would lead doctors to prescribe him Cipro, to guard against infection.

Following his medical internship in Africa, he spent 14 months as the resident physician at an Antarctic research base. He went on to obtain three master's degrees in the hard sciences from two South African universities and finish a doctoral thesis in molecular cell biology that described a new marker for radiation-induced leukemia.

Hatfill returned once more to the United States in 1994. He painted barns for six months on his father's horse farm before taking a one-year fellowship to study a cancer protein at Oxford University. He parlayed the Oxford fellowship into a job researching cancer, HIV, and Lyme disease at the National

Institutes of Health in Bethesda, Maryland. In September 1997, Hatfill accepted a two-year fellowship as a medical doctor and hematologist to study Ebola and other hemorrhagic fevers at USAMRIID. He was earning $45,000 a year.

Part of his research involved fatal viral experiments on macaque monkeys. Sometimes, with permission from staff veterinarians, Hatfill would slip the animals Reese's Peanut Butter Cups to assuage his own guilt over helping cause them harm. He found his USAMRIID assignment both anguishing and rewarding. Some months, he never took a day off. "It's altruism, in a way," Hatfill says. "You're trying to find cures for diseases to help people who have no other means of help. It was a privilege just to be there."

The FBI would later speculate that Hatfill had somehow gained access to anthrax cultures while working at USAMRIID, perhaps through an inadvertently unlocked door. Drawing in part on the work of the Vassar professor Foster and the anti-bioweapons activist Rosenberg, federal investigators began trying to connect bits of circumstantial evidence, assembling them into a picture of Hatfill as the anthrax killer.

He'd been in Britain and Florida, respectively, when two letters with fake anthrax were mailed from those locations. His girlfriend was Malaysian-born—and a hoax package had been sent from Malaysia to a Microsoft office in Nevada. He'd been in Africa during a major anthrax outbreak in the late 1970s. Rhodesia's capital city has that suburb called Greendale—and, as noted, "Greendale School" was the return address on the anthrax letters sent to Daschle and Leahy. He'd written that unpublished novel, which Don Foster had unearthed, about a bioterror attack on Washington. He was close to Bill Patrick, widely recognized as the father of America's bioweapons program, whom he'd met at a conference on bioterror some years earlier. And, of course, he'd taken Cipro just before the anthrax attacks.

The government became convinced all of it had to amount to something.

It didn't.

The FBI's sleuthing had produced zero witnesses, no firm evidence, nothing to show that Hatfill had ever touched anthrax, let alone killed anyone with it. So thin was the bureau's case that Hatfill was never even indicted. But that didn't stop the FBI from focusing on him to the virtual exclusion of other suspects.

In law enforcement, there is a syndrome known as "detective myopia." Former Los Angeles Police Chief Daryl F. Gates told me he suspected that FBI agents had succumbed to this condition, becoming so focused on Hatfill that they lost their objectivity. "This mostly happens when the case is important and there is pressure to solve it," Gates says. "In the case of the FBI, the pressure most certainly can be, and is, political. When a congressman may be a victim of anthrax—well, the case needs to be solved or the suspect made impotent."

Special Agent Harp, who initially headed the anthrax investigation, conceded after Hatfill sued the government in August 2003 that the FBI had been sensitive to accusations

that it had stumbled in other high-profile investigations, and that it had consciously sought to assure the public that it was working hard to crack the anthrax murders. Part of providing such assurance involved actively communicating with news reporters. Questioned under oath, Harp admitted to serving as a confidential source for more than a dozen journalists during the case, but he insisted that he had never leaked privileged information about Hatfill, or anyone else for that matter.

Hatfill's attorney has his doubts. After taking Harp's deposition, Connolly says, he went home and half-jokingly told his wife, "We're building a bomb shelter. If these are the guys in charge of our national security, we're all in serious trouble."

In their own depositions, both John Ashcroft and Robert Mueller, the FBI director, said they had expressed concern to underlings about news leaks that appeared to single out and smear Hatfill. Both, however, denied any knowledge of who specifically was doing the leaking.

In August of 2002, following the searches of his apartment, Hatfill held two press conferences to proclaim his innocence. He offered to undergo, and eventually took, blood and handwriting tests in an attempt to help clear his name. "I want to look my fellow Americans directly in the eye and declare to them, 'I am not the anthrax killer,'" Hatfill told reporters. "I know nothing about the anthrax attacks. I had absolutely nothing to do with this terrible crime. My life is being destroyed by arrogant government bureaucrats who are peddling groundless innuendo and half-information about me to gullible reporters, who in turn repeat this to the public in the guise of news."

One newspaper reporter even called Boo's former in-laws in Canada, inquiring whether Hatfill had had anything to do with the death of her late husband—who had succumbed to a stroke a year before Boo met Hatfill. The call, Boo says, prompted her former brother-in-law to fly to Washington and demand, "What are you doing, living with this murderer?"

Months passed with Hatfill cloistered in Boo's condominium, watching television and drinking alone. He binged on chocolate and fried chicken, putting on weight, growing too lethargic and depressed to even get on the bathroom scale. He developed heart palpitations. He wondered whether he was losing his mind.

Remembering what her boyfriend was like back then, Boo grows emotional. "I got tired of cleaning up your vomit," she tells him over dinner at an Indian restaurant down the street from her condo. Tears stream down her cheeks. Hatfill chokes up too, the trauma still raw nearly eight years later.

"Every human being has to feel a part of a tribe," he explains. "It's programmed into us. And you have to feel that you're contributing to something. They tried to take all that away from me. No tribe wanted me. I just didn't feel of value to anything or anyone. I had Boo. Boo was my only tribe."

The next morning, driving through Georgetown on the way to visit one of his friends in suburban Maryland, I ask Hatfill how close he came to suicide. The muscles in his jaw tighten.

"That was never an option," Hatfill says, staring straight ahead. "If I would've killed myself, I would've been automatically judged by the press and the FBI to be guilty."

Some journalists became convinced there was plenty pointing to Hatfill's guilt. Among those beating the drum early and loud, in the summer of 2002, was Nicholas Kristof, a columnist for *The New York Times*. At least initially, Kristof stopped short of naming Hatfill publicly, instead branding him with the sinister-sounding pseudonym "Mr. Z." Without identifying his sources, in a July column Kristof wrote:

> If Mr. Z were an Arab national, he would have been imprisoned long ago. But he is a true-blue American with close ties to the U.S. Defense Department, the C.I.A. and the American biodefense program. On the other hand, he was once caught with a girlfriend in a biohazard "hot suite" at Fort Detrick, surrounded only by blushing germs.

> With many experts buzzing about Mr. Z behind his back, it's time for the F.B.I. to make a move: either it should go after him more aggressively, sifting thoroughly through his past and picking up loose threads, or it should seek to exculpate him and remove this cloud of suspicion.

One of those threads, Kristof reported, pointed to the possibility that Mr. Z was a genocidal racist who had carried out germ warfare to slaughter innocent black Africans. Kristof addressed his column directly to the FBI:

> Have you examined whether Mr. Z has connections to the biggest anthrax outbreak among humans ever recorded, the one that sickened more than 10,000 black farmers in Zimbabwe in 1978–80? There is evidence that the anthrax was released by the white Rhodesian Army fighting against black guerrillas, and Mr. Z has claimed that he participated in the white army's much-feared Selous Scouts. Could rogue elements of the American military have backed the Rhodesian Army in anthrax and cholera attacks against blacks?

Kristof didn't mention that the majority of soldiers in the Rhodesian army, and in Hatfill's unit, were black; or that many well-respected scientists who examined the evidence concluded that the Rhodesian anthrax outbreak emerged naturally when cattle herds went unvaccinated during a turbulent civil war. Kristof also failed to mention that Mr. Z had served in that war as a lowly private. To have been involved in some sort of top-secret Rhodesian germ-weapons program "would've been like a Pakistani army private being brought in to work on a project at Los Alamos," Hatfill says today.

Kristof wrote that Mr. Z had shown "evasion" in repeated FBI polygraph examinations. He also claimed that following the anthrax attacks, Mr. Z had accessed an "isolated residence" that Kristof described as a possible safe house for American intelligence operatives where, the columnist reported, "Mr. Z gave Cipro to people who visited it." Other journalists would later describe this mysterious residence as a "remote cabin," a kind of Ted Kaczynski-style hideout where a deranged scientist could easily have prepared anthrax for mailing.

In fact, the "cabin" was a three-bedroom weekend home with a Jacuzzi on 40 acres of land in rural Virginia owned by a longtime friend of Hatfill's, George R. Borsari Jr., an avuncular Washington communications lawyer and retired Army lieutenant colonel. Borsari says he found speculation that his place had been a haven for spies or bioterrorists laughable.

When an FBI agent asked Borsari if he would allow a search of the property, Borsari said no. "I told him, 'I'm not going to be a part of your publicity game,'" Borsari says. No search was ever conducted, but by then the damage to Hatfill had been done.

In late 2001, before being publicly implicated in the anthrax attacks, Hatfill had attended a weekend dinner party at Borsari's Virginia retreat along with more than a dozen other guests, including some of Hatfill's co-workers at the defense contractor where he was then employed. Borsari, who'd read a recent article about anthrax-fighting drugs, said he jokingly asked Hatfill, "Hey, by the way, we're your friends. How come we don't have any Cipro?" Hatfill advised him to go to a hospital if he felt he'd been exposed to anthrax. In subsequent news reports, Hatfill was alleged to have warned everyone to begin taking Cipro, as if to suggest that another attack was imminent. "You can't make this stuff up," Borsari later told me. "But, apparently, they did."

Though he cannot prove it, Hatfill says he believes that a friend-turned-political-enemy heard about the Cipro conversation from a co-worker who was at Borsari's house that night, misconstrued it, and passed it on to federal agents. The same former friend, Hatfill asserts, also was responsible for undermining his efforts to secure a higher security clearance that would have enabled him to work on top-secret CIA projects when he was employed at SAIC.

The former friend, who works today at a high level within the intelligence community and requested anonymity after I contacted him, denies Hatfill's version of events. He says he never approached the FBI regarding Hatfill, but would not discuss whether he ever talked with agents about him, suggesting instead that simmering workplace conflicts between Hatfill and former colleagues at USAMRIID could have prompted someone there to "drop a dime to the bureau." "Steve always saw himself as having the purest of motivations. I don't think that was always apparent to everyone around him," the former friend says. "There's a line from *Tom Jones,* 'It's not enough to be good. You have to be seen as being good.' I don't think Steve ever learned that lesson."

Though the two have not spoken in more than a decade, he says he still regards Hatfill warmly.

The feelings are hardly mutual. Hatfill believes that his former friend helped perpetuate false and damaging rumors about him. As evidence for this assertion, Hatfill says he once confided to him about having taken a shower with a female colleague inside the decontamination area of a USAMRIID lab. The story, according to Hatfill, was a fiction meant to amuse and titillate. He says he told the story to no one other than this one friend. As the FBI began focusing on Hatfill in July 2002, *The Times*'s Nicholas Kristof would report Hatfill's fictitious laboratory dalliance as fact.

Hatfill would later sue *The New York Times* for that and a host of other alleged libels. The case would eventually be dismissed, after a judge ruled that Hatfill was a public figure. To successfully sue for defamation, public figures must prove that a publication acted with "actual malice."

In late 2002, news bulletins reported that either an unnamed tipster or bloodhounds, depending on which report was to be believed, had led FBI agents to a pond in the Maryland countryside about eight miles from Hatfill's former apartment. There, divers discovered what was described as a makeshift laboratory "glove box." Reports speculated that Hatfill, a certified SCUBA diver, had used the airtight device to stuff anthrax microbes into envelopes underwater to avoid contaminating himself. *The Washington Post* reported that "vials and gloves wrapped in plastic" also were recovered from the water. Tests to determine the presence of anthrax produced "conflicting results," *The Post* reported, yet so "compelling" were these finds that the FBI would later pay $250,000 to have the pond drained in search of more evidence. Nothing retrieved from the pond ever linked Hatfill, or anyone else, to the murders. According to some news reports, the laboratory "glove box" turned out to be a homemade turtle trap. But the pond story helped keep alive the public perception that FBI agents were hot on the trail, with Hatfill in their sights.

At Connolly's urging, Hatfill reluctantly agreed to a few informal, one-on-one get-togethers with journalists to show them he was no monster. The effort did little to stanch the flow of negative reporting. Two weeks after Hatfill met with CBS correspondent Jim Stewart, in May 2003, Stewart aired a story on the *CBS Evening News*. The anchor, Dan Rather, read the lead-in:

Rather: It has been more than a year and half now since the string of deadly anthrax attacks in this country, and still no arrests, even though investigators believe they know who the culprit is and where he is. CBS News correspondent Jim Stewart is on the case and has the latest.

Stewart: Bioweapons researcher Dr. Steven Hatfill, sources confirm, remains the FBI's number-one suspect in the attacks, even though round-the-clock surveillance and extensive searches have failed to develop more than what sources describe as a "highly circumstantial" case.

And now one possible outcome, sources suggest, is that the government could bring charges against Hatfill unrelated to the anthrax attacks at all, if they become convinced that's the only way to stop future incidents. Not unlike, for example, the income-tax evasion charges finally brought against Al Capone, when evidence of racketeering proved elusive.

After watching Stewart's report that night, Hatfill recalls, "I just lost it." He left an angry message on Stewart's voice mail, vowing to sue. It was, as Hatfill looks back, the last straw. "I just decided I wasn't going to let it get to me anymore. Screw 'em," Hatfill says. "I mean, what more could the press and the FBI do to me than they already had?"

Plenty, as it turned out.

Boo was driving Hatfill to a paint store a week later when FBI agents in a Dodge Durango, trying to keep up with them, blew through a red light in a school zone with children present. Hatfill says he got out of his car to snap a photo of the offending agents and give them a piece of his mind. The Durango sped away—running over his right foot. Hatfill declined an ambulance ride to the hospital; unemployed, he had no medical insurance. When Washington police arrived, they issued him a ticket for "walking to create a hazard." The infraction carried a $5 fine. Hatfill would contest the ticket in court and lose. The agent who ran over his foot was never charged.

"People think they're free in this country," Hatfill says. "Don't kid yourself. This is a police state. The government can pretty much do whatever it wants."

Sitting alone day after day, Boo's condo by now completely redecorated, Hatfill realized that he needed something else to keep his mind occupied while waiting for his day in court. He decided to act as though he were starting medical school all over. He dug out his old textbooks and began studying. The hours flew by.

"I was back on familiar ground, something I knew and understood. It was therapy," Hatfill says. "There wasn't any doubt in my mind that there would be a payday eventually," from lawsuits against those who had destroyed his reputation. "At that point, it became a waiting game for me. Everything else became tolerable."

One afternoon, Hatfill was reading a scientific publication about problems researchers were having in developing promising new antibiotics, when he had a life-changing thought. Many antibiotics and anti-cancer agents, he knew, are synthesized from plants or derived from fungi found in jungles and rainforests. Instead of transporting samples to the lab, why not take the lab to the samples? The concept so excited him that Hatfill ran out and bought modeling clay to begin crafting his vision of a floating laboratory. FBI agents tailed him to a local hobby shop and back.

In the aftermath of the Indian Ocean tsunami that killed more than 200,000 people, Hatfill joined a relief effort and flew to Sri Lanka in early 2005. Tending to the sick and injured reminded him that he still had something to contribute to the world. Finally, he says, he stopped worrying about the press and the FBI. He stopped constantly looking over his shoulder.

By early 2007, after fresh investigators were brought in to reexamine evidence collected in the anthrax case, the FBI came to believe what Hatfill had been saying all along: he'd never had access to the anthrax at USAMRIID; he was a virus guy. The FBI, meanwhile, began to focus on someone who had enjoyed complete access: senior microbiologist Bruce Edward Ivins.

Ivins had spent most of his career at USAMRIID, working with anthrax. Agents had even sought his advice and scientific expertise early in their investigation of Hatfill. Now they subjected Ivins to the same harsh treatment they'd given Hatfill, placing Ivins under 24-hour surveillance, digging into his past, and telling him he was a murder suspect. Soon Ivins was banned from the labs where he had labored for 28 years. In July 2008, following a voluntary two-week stay in a psychiatric clinic for treatment of depression and anxiety, Ivins went home and downed a fatal dose of Tylenol. He was 62.

Less than two weeks later, the Justice Department officially exonerated Steven Hatfill. Six years had passed since he was first named a person of interest.

As it had done with Hatfill, the press dissected the pathology of Ivins's life, linking him, however speculatively, to the murders. Ivins was a devout Catholic, which could've explained why anthrax was sent to two pro-choice senators, Daschle and Leahy. Reports said that Ivins harbored homicidal urges, especially toward women. He had purportedly been obsessed with a particular sorority, Kappa Kappa Gamma, ever since being rebuffed by one of its members while attending the University of Cincinnati, which could've explained why the anthrax letters were mailed from a box near a storage facility used by the sorority's Princeton chapter. Ivins, of course, was no longer alive to defend himself. But in him, the FBI had found a suspect against whom tangible evidence existed.

Ivins had been the sole custodian of a large flask of highly purified anthrax spores genetically linked to those found in the letters. He had allegedly submitted purposely misleading lab data to the FBI in an attempt to hide the fact that the strain of anthrax used in the attacks was a genetic match with the anthrax in his possession. He had been unable to provide a good explanation for the many late nights he'd put in at the lab, working alone, just before the attacks. Agents found that he had been under intense pressure at USAMRIID to produce an anthrax vaccine for U.S. troops. A few days after the anthrax letters were postmarked, Ivins, according to the FBI, had sent an e-mail to a former colleague, who has never been publicly identified, warning: "Bin Laden terrorists for sure have anthrax and sarin gas," and have "just decreed death to all Jews and all Americans." The language was similar to the anthrax letters that warned, "We have this anthrax . . . Death to America . . . Death to Israel."

Following his suicide, some of Ivins's friends insisted that the FBI had pressured him into doing what Hatfill would not. Ivins's own attorney, Paul F. Kemp, disagrees. "Dr. Ivins had a host of psychological problems that he was grappling with, that existed long before the anthrax letters were mailed, and long after," Kemp told me.

Though Hatfill's apartment in Frederick was less than a quarter mile from Ivins's modest home on Military Road, and both men worked at Fort Detrick at the same time, Hatfill says the two never met. Hatfill was surprised when the FBI ultimately pinned the anthrax murders on a fellow American scientist.

"I thought it would eventually be proven that al-Qaeda was behind the attacks," he says.

In the years since the attacks, postal officials have equipped more than 270 processing and distribution centers with sensors that "sniff" the air around virtually every piece of incoming mail to detect deadly biohazards. The sensors have never picked up so much as a whiff of anthrax, according to a Postal Inspection Service spokesman, Peter Rendina. "Your mail," Rendina says, "is safer today than at any other time in our history."

The same, Hatfill believes, cannot be said about American civil liberties. "I was a guy who trusted the government," he says. "Now, I don't trust a damn thing they do." He trusts reporters even less, dismissing them as little more than lapdogs for law enforcement.

The media's general willingness to report what was spoonfed to them, in an effort to reassure a frightened public that an arrest was not far off, is somewhat understandable considering the level of fear that gripped the nation following 9/11. But that doesn't "justify the sliming of Steven Hatfill," says Edward Wasserman, who is the Knight Professor of Journalism Ethics at Washington and Lee University, in Virginia. "If anything, it's a reminder that an unquestioning media serves as a potential lever of power to be activated by the government, almost at will."

In February 2008, Reggie B. Walton, the U.S. District Court judge presiding over Hatfill's case against the government, announced that he had reviewed secret internal memos on the status of the FBI's investigation and could find "not a scintilla of evidence that would indicate that Dr. Hatfill had anything to do with" the anthrax attacks.

Four months later, the Justice Department quietly settled with Hatfill for $5.82 million. "It allowed Doc to start over," Connolly, his lawyer, says.

For Hatfill, rebuilding remains painful and slow. He enters post offices only if he absolutely must, careful to show his face to surveillance cameras so that he can't be accused of mailing letters surreptitiously. He tries to document his whereabouts at all times, in case he should ever need an alibi. He is permanently damaged, Hatfill says. Yet he still professes to love America. "My country didn't do this to me," he is quick to point out. "A bloated, incompetent bureaucracy and a broken press did. I wouldn't be doing what I'm doing today if I didn't still love my country."

Much of Hatfill's time these days is devoted to teaching life-saving medical techniques to military personnel bound for combat. They are his "band of brothers," and the hours he spends with them, Hatfill says, are among his happiest. He also serves as an adjunct associate professor of emergency medicine at George Washington University.

Then there is his boat.

Hatfill has committed $1.5 million to building his floating genetic laboratory, a futuristic-looking vessel replete with a helicopter, an operating room to treat rural indigenous peoples, and a Cordon Bleu-trained chef. Hatfill intends to assemble a scientific team and cruise the Amazon for undiscovered or little-known plants and animals. From these organisms, he hopes to develop new medications for leukemia, and for tuberculosis and other diseases that have been growing increasingly resistant to existing antibiotics. Any useful treatments, he says, will be licensed to pharmaceutical companies on the condition that developing nations receive them at cost. Hatfill hopes to christen the boat within two years. Scientists at USAMRIID, where the FBI once suspected him of stealing anthrax, have expressed tentative interest in helping him mount his expedition.

In addition to suing the Justice Department for violating his privacy and *The New York Times* for defaming him, Hatfill also brought a libel lawsuit against Don Foster, *Vanity Fair*, and *Reader's Digest,* which had reprinted Foster's article. The lawsuit led to a settlement whose dollar amount all parties have agreed to keep confidential. The news media, which had for so long savaged Hatfill, dutifully reported his legal victories, but from where he stands, that hardly balanced things on the ledger sheet of journalistic fairness.

Three weeks after the FBI exonerated Hatfill, in the summer of 2008, Nicholas Kristof apologized to him in *The New York Times* for any distress his columns may have caused. The role of the news media, Kristof wrote on August 28, is "to afflict the comfortable and comfort the afflicted. Instead, I managed to afflict the afflicted."

Many others who raised critical questions about Hatfill have remained silent in the wake of his exoneration. Barbara Hatch Rosenberg, the molecular biologist who spurred the FBI to pursue Hatfill, retired two years ago. Through a former colleague, she declined to be interviewed for this article. Jim Stewart, the television correspondent whose report compared Hatfill to Al Capone, left CBS in 2006. Stewart admitted in a deposition to having relied, for his report, on four confidential FBI sources. When I reached the former newsman at his home in Florida, Stewart said he couldn't talk about Hatfill because he was entertaining houseguests. When I asked when might be a good time to call back, he said, "There isn't a good time," and hung up.

"The entire unhappy episode" is how Don Foster, the Vassar professor who wrote the *Vanity Fair* article, sums up Hatfill's story and his own role in it. Foster says he no longer consults for the FBI. "The anthrax case was it for me," he told me recently. "I'm happier teaching. Like Steven Hatfill, I would prefer to be a private person."

The government was convinced that all the circumstantial evidence pointing to Hatfill had to amount to something. It didn't.

Foster says he never intended to imply that Hatfill was a murderer, yet continues to stand by his reporting as "inaccurate in only minor details." I asked if he had any regrets about what he'd written.

"On what grounds?" he asked.

"The heartache it caused Hatfill. The heartache it caused you and *Vanity Fair.*"

Foster pondered the question, then said, "I don't know Steven Hatfill. I don't know his heartache. But anytime an American citizen, a journalist, a scientist, a scholar, is made the object of unfair or inaccurate public scrutiny, it's unfortunate. It's part of a free press to set that right."

This past February, the Justice Department formally closed its investigation of the 2001 anthrax attacks, releasing more than 2,500 pages of documents, many of them heavily redacted, buttressing the government's assertion that Bruce Ivins was solely responsible for the anthrax letters.

When I asked FBI spokesperson Debra Weierman how much money had been spent chasing Hatfill, she said the bureau was unable to provide such an accounting. She would neither confirm nor deny that the FBI ever opened any administrative inquiries into the news leaks that had defamed him. The FBI, she said, was unwilling to publicly discuss Hatfill in any capacity, "out of privacy considerations for Dr. Hatfill." Weierman referred me instead to what she described as an "abundance of information" on the FBI's Web site.

Information about the anthrax case is indeed abundant on the bureau's Web site, with dozens of documents touting the FBI's efforts to solve the murders. Included is a transcript of a press conference held in August 2008, a month after Ivins's suicide, in which federal authorities initially laid out the evidence they had amassed against him. But beyond a handful of questions asked by reporters that day, in which his last name is repeatedly misspelled, and a few scant paragraphs in the 96-page executive summary of the case, there is no mention anywhere on the FBI's Web site of Steven Hatfill.

Critical Thinking

1. What do you think the FBI hoped to accomplish by "bumper locking" Hatfill, having him harassed by local law enforcement, causing him to be fired from his jobs?

2. Were the media reports about the anthrax investigation reliable?

3. Is there any more evidence that Ivins did it than there was against Hatfill?

DAVID FREED is a screenwriter and former investigative reporter for the *Los Angeles Times,* where he shared in a Pulitzer Prize for coverage of the 1992 Rodney King riots.

From *The Atlantic,* May 2010, pp. 46, 48–56. Copyright © 2010 by The Atlantic Media Co. www.theatlantic.com. Distributed by Tribune Media Services.

Universal Policing
Counterterrorism Lessons from Northern Ireland

JUSTIN SCHOEMAN

Over the past several hundred years, ongoing conflicts have occurred in Northern Ireland between members of the Catholic and Protestant communities. This feud, most recently known as The Troubles, has evolved from a local religious clash to an insurgency movement against Northern Ireland and British authorities. The Police Service of Northern Ireland worked closely with the British military to end escalating violence in the region. The relationship between these two bodies developed from the police supporting the military and vice versa. With the use of counterinsurgency tactics, the government of Northern Ireland worked with the Catholic community and members of the insurgency to compromise on dividing issues.[1]

Lessons learned from counterinsurgency efforts in Northern Ireland incorporate fundamental principles both universal to people across the globe and capable of cutting through cultural lines. Therefore, they could be applied to similar battles in Iraq and Afghanistan. The Northern Ireland authorities successfully phased out British conventional military to allow for police supremacy, creating a police force that the people of Northern Ireland perceived not only as legitimate but one that addressed grievances within the disgruntled community as well.

History

The struggle in Ireland dates back as far as 1691 when the British military defeated Irish General Patrick Sarsfield and continued to occupy Ireland. This loss was the last organized resistance to English rule in Ireland; the new opposition involved conflict waged without rules and by irregular methods.[2] As Ireland remained under British rule for hundreds of years, the feud between the Protestants and the Catholics became extremely bitter. The Irish Catholics felt marginalized due to the closeness between the Protestants and the British government. Random acts of violence between Catholics and Protestants continued as the years passed. In May 1921, the Government of Ireland Act divided Ireland into the six predominantly Protestant counties of Ulster in the north and the remaining 26 primarily Catholic counties in the south. Northern Ireland was created as an "Irish Free State" with British dominion status, falling short of complete sovereignty.[3]

Increase in Hostility

In the late 1960s, the tipping point of Catholic hostility emerged. Police harassment, exclusion from public service appointments, and the refusal of Catholic political representatives in parliament increased the community's sense of alienation. From this impression of isolation originating from the government, including the Royal Ulster Constabulary (RUC), the Provisional Irish Republican Army (PIRA)—an offshoot of the Irish Republican Army (IRA)—organized itself into a paramilitary organization to defend the Catholic minority's civil rights and to unite Ireland. Protestant and Catholic paramilitary groups clashed in the streets of Northern Ireland using terrorist tactics, killing hundreds of innocent victims. In response, the British military attempted to crack down on the militant groups by conducting house-to-house searches and establishing internment-holding facilities for potential PIRA members. These approaches caused the perceived pro-Protestant British military to lose more legitimacy, resulting in additional PIRA recruits. The cycle of violence continued throughout Ireland with shootings and then bombings in Belfast, Derry, Birmingham, and Dublin. The violence came to a dramatic pause after Protestants and members from the political arm of the IRA and the British government signed the 1998 Good Friday Agreement. This political ceasefire ended a majority of the paramilitary violence in Northern Ireland by adopting political concessions agreeable to all parties.[4]

From 1969 to 1998, approximately 3,251 deaths resulted from terrorist activity during The Troubles. An overwhelming number of those killed were civilians, including more than 50 children under 14 years of age. Over 30,000 people were injured or maimed.[5] The British Army sustained a total 719 deaths from The Troubles in Northern Ireland during the same period. An analysis of the soldiers' deaths illustrated the type of terrorist activity undertaken by the IRA/PIRA. While operating within a sympathetic locality, the IRA/PIRA could choose their targets and operate at an advantage over the British Army. This advantage could only be overcome with training and the cooperation of the RUC. Due to terrorist activity, 176 members of the British Army were considered murdered by the IRA/PIRA (24.4 percent of all fatalities). Many of these soldiers, part-time members of the Ulster Defence Regiment, were killed on their way to and from work. Casualties that resulted from direct operational contact with the enemy only accounted for 26.2 percent of the total. A majority of the British Army's casualties were caused by bombs, land mines, and booby-trap devices.[6]

Identification of Roles

Police agencies and militaries have very different roles when dealing with insurgencies. Therefore, the two units must work together to better fulfill their joint mission. Based on experiences in Northern Ireland, British Royal Marine Colonel Mike Page stated that the military mission during the infancy of counterinsurgency events should involve stabilizing the area and preparing for the police, a civilian corps, to take a primary role in securing the community. As the violence within the community subsides and the police become ready to cope with the environment, a political process should be set in place to address the problems that originally stimulated the insurgency. While police strength evolves, the military should begin to play a supporting role. Toward the end of the counterinsurgency campaign, the military's presence within the community must terminate or become almost nonexistent. Ensuring cooperation between the police and the military throughout the course of the counterinsurgency campaign and phasing out military operations as irregular warfare progresses into police-type incidents proves essential to developing a reasonable end state for the mission.

Police agencies and militaries . . . must work together to better fulfill their joint mission.

Resolutions

One of the main reasons The Troubles occurred in Northern Ireland involved the Catholic community's perception of the police as illegitimate. The Good Friday Agreement in 1998 resulted in the organization of the Independent Commission on Policing, which sought to review the Police Service of Northern Ireland and make recommendations on how to improve the police force. After the analysis, the commission made 175 recommendations that would make police services more transparent, accountable, and representative of the Northern Ireland community. The Historical Enquiries Team, a policing group organized to reexamine all of the deaths that occurred as a result of the security situation in Northern Ireland between 1969 and 1998, attempted to bring closure to the families of those killed during The Troubles. A Human Rights Body was formed to review police training and policies, ensuring the preservation of human rights principles. To distance itself from the British (a major point of friction) and mirror the Northern Ireland populous, the RUC changed its name and reformed into the Police Service of Northern Ireland (PSNI) in 2001 and mandated that approximately 50 percent of the police force [be] Catholics. These and other PSNI programs brought the battle-fatigued community and police services closer together, resulting in fewer acts of violence.

To address grievances and public complaints, the PSNI initiated internal police service programs, along with external groups, to guarantee unbiased and fair law enforcement. Programs started by the police entailed the adoption of a Policing Board of Northern Ireland and a District Policing Partnership. Although these programs review different policing issues, they oversee police actions. Further, the PSNI created the Ombudsman's Office to review

use-of-force issues and shooting incidents.[7] One concern evaluated by the Ombudsman's Office involved the use of an incapacitating spray during riot events to control crowds as a less lethal option in the use-of-force criterion.

Conclusion

Religious groups in Iraq or Afghanistan model those of Northern Ireland. Each community has internal friction in which one or two parties feel marginalized. Citizens in every community in the world want not only a stable and secure place to live but to be treated fairly as well. Counterinsurgency efforts should follow the successful Northern Ireland example by phasing out the military's presence as stability increases and establishing a legitimate civilian police service—one that is transparent, fair, and unbiased and addresses the community's needs.

Notes

1. Colonel Mike Page, speech to the U.S. Marine Corps University Command and Staff College (Quantico, VA, February 22, 2008).

2. Tom Geraghty, *The Irish War* (Baltimore, MD: Johns Hopkins University Press, 2000), xxii.

3. BBC History, *Northern Ireland: The Troubles*, "The Road to Northern Ireland, 1167 to 1921," www.bbc.co.uk/history/recent/troubles/overview_ni_article_01.shtml (accessed June 24, 2009).

4. BBC History, *Northern Ireland: The Troubles*, "The Road to Northern Ireland, 1963 to 1985," www.bbc.co.uk/history/recent/troubles/the_troubles_article_08.shtml (accessed June 24, 2009).

5. Geraghty, v.

6. Ron Austin, "British Army Fatal Casualties—Ulster Troubles, 1969–1998," http://goliath.ecnext.com/coms2/gi_0199-3300357/British-Army-fatal-casualties-Ulster.html (accessed June 24, 2009).

7. Superintendent Gary Gracey (PSNI), speech to the U.S. Marine Corps University Command and Staff College (Quantico, VA, February 21, 2008).

Critical Thinking

1. What lessons can be learned from the Northern Ireland experience?

2. What changes came about as a result of the Good Friday Agreement of 1998?

3. What grievances did the Catholic minority have?

Special Agent **JUSTIN SCHOEMAN** serves in the Leadership Development Unit at the DEA Academy.

From *FBI Law Enforcement Bulletin* by Justin Shocman, April 2010, pp. 8–11. Published by Federal Bureau of Investigation, www.fbi.gov.

UNIT 2
Victimology

Unit Selections

Learning Outcomes

After reading this unit, you will be able to:

- Evaluate statistics more critically.

- Recognize some of the problems inherent in cases of elder abuse.

- Understand that immigrants have unique problems in their relations with law enforcement.

- Be able to understand the concept of honor killings.

- Discuss the different options about reporting sexual violence.

Student Website
www.mhhe.com/cls

Internet References

National Crime Victim's Research and Treatment Center (NCVC)
www.musc.edu/cvc
Office for Victims of Crime (OVC)
www.ojp.usdoj.gov/ovc

For many years, crime victims were not considered an important topic for criminological study. Now, however, criminologists consider that focusing on victims and victimization is essential to understanding the phenomenon of crime. The popularity of this area of study can be attributed to the early work of Hans Von Hentig and the later work of Stephen Schafer. These writers were the first to assert that crime victims play an integral role in the criminal event, that their actions may actually precipitate crime, and that unless the victim's role is considered, the study of crime is not complete.

In recent years, a growing number of criminologists have devoted increasing attention to the victim's role in the criminal justice process. Generally, areas of particular interest include establishing probabilities of victimization risks, studying victim precipitation of crime and culpability, and designing services expressly for victims of crime. As more criminologists focus their attention on the victim's role in the criminal process, victimology will take on even greater importance.

This unit provides a sharp focus on several key issues. The lead article "Telling the Truth about Damned Lies and Statistics," by Joel Best, discusses the need for good statistics in order to talk sensibly about social problems.

Amanda White's first-person account of her harrowing experience follows next in "The Face of Domestic Violence." The phenomenon of honor killings is explained by Cynthia Fuchs Epstein in her report "Death by Gender." Philip Bulman describes two recent studies about a previously hidden problem in "Elder Abuse Emerges from the Shadows of Public Consciousness."

© Purestock/Getty Images

Next, Sabrina Garcia reports in "Options for Reporting Sexual Violence: Developments over the Past Decade," about how "blind reporting" can help victims file reports safely. "The U Visa: An Effective Resource for Law Enforcement" by Stacey Ivie and Natalie Nanasi is an article that tells about the problems faced by immigrant victims of serious crimes.

The final article in this section, "Victim Satisfaction with the Criminal Justice System," presents the results of research on whether the victims of domestic violence who call the police are satisfied with the outcome.

Telling the Truth about Damned Lies and Statistics

JOEL BEST

The dissertation prospectus began by quoting a statistic—a "grabber" meant to capture the reader's attention. The graduate student who wrote this prospectus undoubtedly wanted to seem scholarly to the professors who would read it; they would be supervising the proposed research. And what could be more scholarly than a nice, authoritative statistic, quoted from a professional journal in the student's field?

So the prospectus began with this (carefully footnoted) quotation: "Every year since 1950, the number of American children gunned down has doubled." I had been invited to serve on the student's dissertation committee. When I read the quotation, I assumed the student had made an error in copying it. I went to the library and looked up the article the student had cited. There, in the journal's 1995 volume, was exactly the same sentence: "Every year since 1950, the number of American children gunned down has doubled."

This quotation is my nomination for a dubious distinction: I think it may be the worst—that is, the most inaccurate—social statistic ever.

What makes this statistic so bad? Just for the sake of argument, let's assume that "the number of American children gunned down" in 1950 was one. If the number doubled each year, there must have been two children gunned down in 1951, four in 1952, eight in 1953, and so on. By 1960, the number would have been 1,024. By 1965, it would have been 32,768 (in 1965, the F.B.I. identified only 9,960 criminal homicides in the entire country, including adult as well as child victims). By 1970, the number would have passed one million; by 1980, one billion (more than four times the total U.S. population in that year). Only three years later, in 1983, the number of American children gunned down would have been 8.6 billion (nearly twice the earth's population at the time). Another milestone would have been passed in 1987, when the number of gunned-down American children (137 billion) would have surpassed the best estimates for the total human population throughout history (110 billion). By 1995, when the article was published, the annual number of victims would have been over 35 trillion—a really big number, of a magnitude you rarely encounter outside economics or astronomy.

Thus my nomination: estimating the number of American child gunshot victims in 1995 at 35 trillion must be as far off—as hilariously, wildly wrong—as a social statistic can be. (If anyone spots a more inaccurate social statistic, I'd love to hear about it.)

Where did the article's author get this statistic? I wrote the author, who responded that the statistic came from the Children's Defense Fund, a well-known advocacy group for children. The C.D.F.'s *The State of America's Children Yearbook 1994* does state: "The number of American children killed each year by guns has doubled since 1950." Note the difference in the wording—the C.D.F. claimed there were twice as many deaths in 1994 as in 1950; the article's author reworded that claim and created a very different meaning.

It is worth examining the history of this statistic. It began with the C.D.F. noting that child gunshot deaths had doubled from 1950 to 1994. This is not quite as dramatic an increase as it might seem. Remember that the U.S. population also rose throughout this period; in fact, it grew about 73 percent—or nearly double. Therefore, we might expect all sorts of things—including the number of child gunshot deaths—to increase, to nearly double, just because the population grew. Before we can decide whether twice as many deaths indicate that things are getting worse, we'd have to know more. The C.D.F. statistic raises other issues as well: Where did the statistic come from? Who counts child gunshot deaths, and how? What is meant by a "child" (some C.D.F. statistics about violence include everyone under age 25)? What is meant by "killed by guns" (gunshot-death statistics often include suicides and accidents, as well as homicides)? But people rarely ask questions of this sort when they encounter statistics. Most of the time, most people simply accept statistics without question.

Certainly, the article's author didn't ask many probing, critical questions about the C.D.F.'s claim. Impressed by the statistic, the author repeated it—well, meant to repeat it. Instead, by rewording the C.D.F.'s claim, the author created a mutant statistic, one garbled almost beyond recognition.

But people treat mutant statistics just as they do other statistics—that is, they usually accept even the most implausible claims without question. For example, the journal editor who accepted the author's article for publication did not bother to consider the implications of child victims doubling each year. And people repeat bad statistics: The graduate student copied the garbled statistic and inserted it into the dissertation prospectus. Who knows whether still other readers were impressed by the author's statistic and remembered it or repeated it? The article remains on the shelf in hundreds of libraries, available to anyone who needs a dramatic quote. The lesson should be clear: Bad statistics live on; they take on lives of their own.

Some statistics are born bad—they aren't much good from the start, because they are based on nothing more than guesses or dubious data. Other statistics mutate; they become bad after being mangled (as in the case of the author's creative rewording). Either way, bad statistics are potentially important: They can be used to stir up public outrage or fear; they can distort our understanding of our world; and they can lead us to make poor policy choices.

The notion that we need to watch out for bad statistics isn't new. We've all heard people say, "You can prove anything with statistics." The title of my book, *Damned Lies and Statistics*, comes from a famous aphorism (usually attributed to Mark Twain or Benjamin Disraeli): "There are three kinds of lies: lies, damned lies, and statistics." There is even a useful little book, still in print after more than 40 years, called *How to Lie With Statistics*.

We shouldn't ignore all statistics, or assume that every number is false. Some statistics are bad, but others are pretty good. And we need good statistics to talk sensibly about social problems.

Statistics, then, have a bad reputation. We suspect that statistics may be wrong, that people who use statistics may be "lying"—trying to manipulate us by using numbers to somehow distort the truth. Yet, at the same time, we need statistics; we depend upon them to summarize and clarify the nature of our complex society. This is particularly true when we talk about social problems. Debates about social problems routinely raise questions that demand statistical answers: Is the problem widespread? How many people—and which people—does it affect? Is it getting worse? What does it cost society? What will it cost to deal with it? Convincing answers to such questions demand evidence, and that usually means numbers, measurements, statistics.

But can't you prove anything with statistics? It depends on what "prove" means. If we want to know, say, how many children are "gunned down" each year, we can't simply guess—pluck a number from thin air: 100, 1,000, 10,000, 35 trillion, whatever. Obviously, there's no reason to consider an arbitrary guess "proof" of anything. However, it might be possible for someone—using records kept by police departments or hospital emergency rooms or coroners—to keep track of children who have been shot; compiling careful, complete records might give us a fairly accurate idea of the number of gunned-down children. If that number seems accurate enough, we might consider it very strong evidence—or proof.

The solution to the problem of bad statistics is not to ignore all statistics, or to assume that every number is false. Some statistics are bad, but others are pretty good, and we need statistics—good statistics—to talk sensibly about social problems. The solution, then, is not to give up on statistics, but to become better judges of the numbers we encounter. We need to think critically about statistics—at least critically enough to suspect that the number of children gunned down hasn't been doubling each year since 1950.

A few years ago, the mathematician John Allen Paulos wrote *Innumeracy*, a short, readable book about "mathematical illiteracy." Too few people, he argued, are comfortable with basic mathematical principles, and this makes them poor judges of the numbers they encounter. No doubt this is one reason we have so many bad statistics. But there are other reasons, as well.

Social statistics describe society, but they are also products of our social arrangements. The people who bring social statistics to our attention have reasons for doing so; they inevitably want something, just as reporters and the other media figures who repeat and publicize statistics have their own goals. Statistics are tools, used for particular purposes. Thinking critically about statistics requires understanding their place in society.

While we may be more suspicious of statistics presented by people with whom we disagree—people who favor different political parties or have different beliefs—bad statistics are used to promote all sorts of causes. Bad statistics come from conservatives on the political right and liberals on the left, from wealthy corporations and powerful government agencies, and from advocates of the poor and the powerless.

In order to interpret statistics, we need more than a checklist of common errors. We need a general approach, an orientation, a mind-set that we can use to think about new statistics that we encounter. We ought to approach statistics thoughtfully. This can be hard to do, precisely because so many people in our society treat statistics as fetishes. We might call this the mind-set of the awestruck—the people who don't think critically, who act as though statistics have magical powers. The awestruck know they don't always understand the statistics they hear, but this doesn't bother them. After all, who can expect to understand magical numbers? The reverential fatalism of the awestruck is not thoughtful—it is a way of avoiding thought. We need a different approach.

One choice is to approach statistics critically. Being critical does not mean being negative or hostile—it is not cynicism. The critical approach statistics thoughtfully; they avoid the extremes of both naive acceptance and cynical rejection of the numbers they encounter. Instead, the critical attempt to evaluate numbers, to distinguish between good statistics and bad statistics.

The critical understand that, while some social statistics may be pretty good, they are never perfect. Every statistic is a way of summarizing complex information into relatively simple numbers. Inevitably, some information, some of the complexity, is lost whenever we use statistics. The critical recognize that this is an inevitable limitation of statistics. Moreover, they realize that every statistic is the product of choices—the choice between defining a category broadly or narrowly, the choice of one measurement over another, the choice of a sample. People choose definitions, measurements, and samples for all sorts of reasons: Perhaps they want to emphasize some aspect of a problem; perhaps it is easier or cheaper to gather data in a particular way—many considerations can come into play. Every statistic is a compromise among choices. This means that every definition—and every measurement and every sample—probably has limitations and can be criticized.

Being critical means more than simply pointing to the flaws in a statistic. Again, every statistic has flaws. The issue is whether a particular statistic's flaws are severe enough to damage its usefulness. Is the definition so broad that it encompasses too many false positives (or so narrow that it excludes too many false negatives)? How would changing the definition alter the statistic? Similarly, how do the choices of measurements and samples affect the statistic? What would happen if different measures or samples were chosen? And how is the statistic used? Is it being interpreted appropriately, or has its meaning been mangled to create a mutant statistic? Are the comparisons that are being made appropriate, or are apples being confused with oranges? How do different choices produce the conflicting numbers found in stat wars? These are the sorts of questions the critical ask.

As a practical matter, it is virtually impossible for citizens in contemporary society to avoid statistics about social problems. Statistics arise in all sorts of ways, and in almost every case the people promoting statistics want to persuade us. Activists use statistics to convince us that social problems are serious and deserve our attention and concern. Charities use statistics to encourage donations. Politicians use statistics to persuade us that they understand society's problems and that they deserve our support. The media use statistics to make their reporting more dramatic, more convincing, more compelling. Corporations use statistics to promote and improve their products. Researchers use statistics to document their findings and support their conclusions. Those with whom we agree use statistics to reassure us that we're on the right side, while our opponents use statistics to try and convince us that we are wrong. Statistics are one of the standard types of evidence used by people in our society.

It is not possible simply to ignore statistics, to pretend they don't exist. That sort of head-in-the-sand approach would be too costly. Without statistics, we limit our ability to think thoughtfully about our society; without statistics, we have no accurate ways of judging how big a problem may be, whether it is getting worse, or how well the policies designed to address that problem actually work. And awestruck or naive attitudes toward statistics are no better than ignoring statistics; statistics have no magical properties, and it is foolish to assume that all statistics are equally valid. Nor is a cynical approach the answer; statistics are too widespread and too useful to be automatically discounted.

It would be nice to have a checklist, a set of items we could consider in evaluating any statistic. The list might detail potential problems with definitions, measurements, sampling, mutation, and so on. These are, in fact, common sorts of flaws found in many statistics, but they should not be considered a formal, complete checklist. It is probably impossible to produce a complete list of statistical flaws—no matter how long the list, there will be other possible problems that could affect statistics.

The goal is not to memorize a list, but to develop a thoughtful approach. Becoming critical about statistics requires being prepared to ask questions about numbers. When encountering a new statistic in, say, a news report, the critical try to assess it. What might be the sources for this number? How could one go about producing the figure? Who produced the number, and what interests might they have? What are the different ways key terms might have been defined, and which definitions have been chosen? How might the phenomena be measured, and which measurement choices have been made? What sort of sample was gathered, and how might that sample affect the result? Is the statistic being properly interpreted? Are comparisons being made, and if so, are the comparisons appropriate? Are there competing statistics? If so, what stakes do the opponents have in the issue, and how are those stakes likely to affect their use of statistics? And is it possible to figure out why the statistics seem to disagree, what the differences are in the ways the competing sides are using figures?

At first, this list of questions may seem overwhelming. How can an ordinary person—someone who reads a statistic in a magazine article or hears it on a news broadcast—determine the answers to such questions? Certainly news reports rarely give detailed information on the processes by which statistics are created. And few of us have time to drop everything and investigate the background of some new number we encounter. Being critical, it seems, involves an impossible amount of work.

In practice, however, the critical need not investigate the origin of every statistic. Rather, being critical means appreciating the inevitable limitations that affect all statistics, rather than being awestruck in the presence of numbers. It means not being too credulous, not accepting every statistic at face value. But it also means appreciating that statistics, while always imperfect, can be useful. Instead of automatically discounting every statistic, the critical reserve judgment. When confronted with an interesting number, they may try to learn more, to evaluate, to weigh the figure's strengths and weaknesses.

Of course, this critical approach need not—and should not—be limited to statistics. It ought to apply to all the evidence we encounter when we scan a news report, or listen to a speech—whenever we learn about social problems. Claims about social problems often feature dramatic, compelling examples; the critical might ask whether an example is likely to be a typical case or an extreme, exceptional instance. Claims about social problems often include quotations from different sources, and the critical might wonder why those sources have spoken and why they have been quoted: Do they have particular expertise? Do they stand to benefit if they influence others? Claims about social problems usually involve arguments about the problem's causes and potential solutions. The critical might ask whether these arguments are convincing. Are they logical? Does the proposed solution seem feasible and appropriate? And so on. Being critical— adopting a skeptical, analytical stance when confronted with claims—is an approach that goes far beyond simply dealing with statistics.

Statistics are not magical. Nor are they always true—or always false. Nor need they be incomprehensible. Adopting a critical approach offers an effective way of responding to the numbers we are sure to encounter. Being critical requires more thought, but failing to adopt a critical mind-set makes us powerless to evaluate what others tell us. When we fail to think critically, the statistics we hear might just as well be magical.

Critical Thinking

1. Why are there bad statistics?
2. How can one approach statistics critically?
3. What was wrong with the following statement made in 1995: "Every year since 1950 the number of American children gunned down has doubled"?

JOEL BEST is a professor of sociology and criminal justice at the University of Delaware. This essay is excerpted from *Damned Lies and Statistics: Untangling Numbers from the Media, Politicians, and Activists,* published by the University of California Press and reprinted by permission. Copyright © 2001 by the Regents of the University of California.

As seen in *Chronicle of Higher Education,* May 4, 2001, pp. B7–B9; originally appeared in *Damned Lies and Statistics: Untangling Numbers from the Media, Politicians, and Activists* by Joel Best (University of California Press, 2001). Copyright © 2001 by University of California Press. Reprinted by permission via Rightslink.

The Face of Domestic Violence

How could Amanda White have stayed with a husband who beat her over and over again? A young mom opens up about what she went through and why she believed it would all get better.

SARAH ELIZABETH RICHARDS, AS TOLD TO HER BY AMANDA WHITE

First Signs of Trouble

I sat in my mom's house not knowing what to do.

My body still ached from being beaten by my husband a day earlier. But he kept pleading through the door: "I was drunk. I'm sorry. I'll never do that to you again. I know I need help." I had a 2-week-old baby. I wanted to believe him. I opened the door.

I had a crush on Dietrich White back in junior high. When I ran into him almost a decade later in 1997, I was 21 and even more attracted to his sexy smile and blue eyes. I was thrilled when he asked me out. I was living with my mom in Hot Springs, Arkansas, while I took time off from college to heal from complications of endometriosis surgery. I tried to fill my time by running a booth-rental business in a crafts mall, but many of my friends were away at school and I was lonely.

Dietrich and I became a couple and spent nearly every day together. He said we were soul mates, brought me flowers, and took me on a trip to Florida. Two months later we were engaged. We moved in together in Little Rock (about an hour away from my mom), where Dietrich owned a carpet-cleaning business. I intended to return to school, but Dietrich said he earned enough to support us, so I could spend my time decorating our home and planning my dream wedding.

Dietrich and I rarely argued, but sometimes he got jealous and claimed I looked at other men. I was flattered that he was so in love with me that he couldn't stand the idea of me being with someone else. I wish I had known then that jealousy is often a warning sign of an abusive personality.

Our idyllic life didn't last long. Within a few months Dietrich had lost many of his customers and became distant. We had our first fight when I couldn't find him at his jobsite one afternoon; I smelled beer on his breath when he came home. "Where the hell have you been?" I demanded. He lied that he had been working and headed for the shower. I got so mad I threw a glass-covered candle at the bathtub. Dietrich stormed over and slapped me hard across the face. No one had ever hit me before, and I was stunned. "Did you just hit me?" I screamed.

"You made me do it!" I remember him shouting back. "You have no right to attack me when I've been working."

Later I apologized, and he said, "We never need to do that again." I tried to forget about the incident, but the next day my mother saw my black eye. "He was drinking, and I started it," I tried to explain. She exploded. "I don't care about the circumstances," she said. "No man can do that!"

Dietrich's irrational jealousy erupted again a month later when he accused me of sleeping with a friend of his. He canceled our wedding, which was just two weeks away, and asked me to move out. My parents lost thousands of dollars, but my mother was relieved. I was devastated.

On what would have been our wedding day I found out I was pregnant. After my endometriosis surgery, my doctor had told me I was infertile, so we hadn't been using birth control. The timing was terrible, but I was thrilled to learn I could have kids. My mom urged me to have the baby on my own, but I didn't want to be a single mother. Besides, I believed that a child would complete our little family and make things better.

Pain and Denial

When I was eight months pregnant we finally got married—in a judge's office. Then, after our son was born, Dietrich's business tanked and we had to move in with my mom. After she left for work one morning he said he had overheard us talking about my high school boyfriend and accused me of planning to see him. When I denied it he called me a liar and punched me several times in the face. I fell and the baby started screaming. I had never seen Dietrich this enraged. "Please stop!" I begged hysterically as I tried to reach the baby. He'd calm down and let me nurse the baby, but then he'd explode and come at me again.

At first I had white flashes in front of my eyes and a pounding pressure in my head, but my adrenaline kicked in and I felt dazed and couldn't tell where I'd been hit. Seven long hours later he told me to wash the blood off my face. I thought the nightmare was over, but as soon as I climbed into the tub he came into the bathroom and started choking me under the water until I passed out. I was sure I was going to die. He must have pulled my head out of the water in time because I came to, stumbled out of the bathroom and discovered that he'd taken the baby. By the time I called my sister-in-law to come get me, Dietrich had returned. He had calmed down, told me the baby was at his mother's house and took me to the hospital.

My mom found me in the ER, where they examined my black eyes and bruises. When the doctor asked what happened, I said I fell down a flight of stairs. He didn't ask any more questions and I was released. When we got home, Dietrich had brought back the baby, but my mom made him leave. She called the police the next day, but they said you have to call within four hours of a domestic-violence incident in order for them to make an arrest (the state law has since been changed to 12 hours). That evening Dietrich came over to apologize. He said he'd been drunk the night before. He swore he'd go to Alcoholics Anonymous. He promised we'd go to couples counseling. Three days later I let him back in.

My mom was furious. It's hard to explain how anyone could stay with someone after being hurt like that, but I had convinced myself it was because of the alcohol and that this one incident had gotten out of control. I knew that Dietrich loved me. I wanted to believe he was truly sorry and would never harm me again.

A Fresh Start?

I felt reassured when Dietrich made good on his pledge to attend a couple of AA meetings. He thought we needed a clean slate, so in the fall of 1998 we moved almost 1,000 miles away to Tampa, Florida. Those days were the best of our marriage. He found work laying down tile; I helped out while the baby slept. We took our son swimming in the ocean, and Dietrich toted him around in a baby carrier. He also fussed over me and bought me a beautiful silk bathrobe and diamond bracelet. I really thought he had changed.

But six months later Dietrich couldn't get any more work. That's when he started to abuse me again. During an argument he pushed me and broke my arm. Again I lied to doctors at the hospital and said I had fallen down the stairs. And to my surprise I found out I was pregnant. We eventually ran out of money and moved back to Arkansas. After our second son was born, in November 1999, Dietrich attacked my mom when she tried to stop him from driving drunk with the baby in the car.

In 2001, three years into our marriage, I finally got up the courage to leave. My parents were so relieved and rented me a house. Dietrich begged me to come back, but even though I learned I was pregnant for the third time, I stayed strong and filed for divorce. He said there was no way I could care for three kids on my own, and that scared me. So by the time I delivered a third son, Dietrich and I were back together.

Hitting Rock Bottom

I know it sounds crazy now, but I really didn't think I was a battered woman—at least not yet. Then one May night in 2002 Dietrich beat me so badly with a child's chair that he broke my nose, shattered my knuckles, and fractured several bones in my face. My mom called the police. My hair was full of blood and my body was covered in gashes and bruises. I needed 65 stitches; Dietrich was arrested and charged with domestic battery in the first degree. The court added child endangerment charges since he had attacked me with the kids around. While he spent some time in jail, he was released on bond.

You'd think the severity of that beating would have been the last straw. This time, though, I thought jail had really scared him. During Thanksgiving at his parents' house that year he acted as if he had really missed me and the boys. I was moved by his sincerity and, during a weak moment, yes, we had sex. As luck would have it, since Dietrich would never let me use birth control, I got pregnant for the fourth time.

As the Arkansas trial drew closer, Dietrich started to unravel under the pressure and, afraid of jail time, fled to Ohio. He threatened that if I didn't join him, he would kill my family. Now that I knew what he was capable of, I was terrified he would do it. So I told my parents I was taking the kids to see friends but instead left for Ohio. They frantically called Dietrich's relatives and hired a private investigator but couldn't find me for more than a year. I wasn't surprised that the beatings continued in Ohio, but I was shocked when one night in 2004 someone called the police, and they arrested Dietrich *and* me. We had a fourth son by then, and I was charged with child endangerment for allowing the kids to witness the violence.

A New Life

The threat of losing my kids was the turning point. I had no idea how much they had suffered. I was devastated when I looked through their coloring books and saw they had scratched out all the faces. I thought I had protected them by making sure they were in another room or sleeping. But who was I kidding? Of course they heard the fighting and saw the bruises. Of course they lived in constant fear, too.

I knew I had to make it up to them and prove myself as a mom. So I completed all the court's required parenting classes and attended a domestic-violence support group. Dietrich begged me to drop the charges from the beating in Arkansas, which would increase his sentence. But I wouldn't do it. My mom was so proud. In the end he was sentenced to serve 18 years in prison. After seven years of marriage, our divorce became final in 2005.

At age 30 I returned to Arkansas to start over. Now I work for the Saline County Safe Haven, a local domestic-violence shelter. I've testified before the state legislature to raise money, and I speak to women to help them recognize the signs of abuse. I was proudest, though, when I completed my training to be a police officer. I was recruited to handle domestic-violence calls, and it feels great to help women find a shelter or get legal help. More than anything, I try to make them understand that they're choosing to continue the cycle of abuse every time they go back. I wish I had learned that lesson sooner.

The boys know their father is in jail and isn't allowed to contact them. They don't talk about him much, but occasionally one might say, "I wish our dad wasn't so mean so he could be with us." I put them each in counseling for about a year, and except for some minor anger issues they all seem to have recovered. I'm proud of them. They're all so loving, get good grades, and play school sports. I spend as much time as possible with them and organize my schedule so I can be home when they get out of school.

Dietrich will be eligible for parole in June, and I know he'll get out eventually. He may try to find me and get me to come back as he did before, but I'm a different person now. I won't let anyone hurt us ever again.

Critical Thinking

1. Is it sometimes OK for a woman to hit a man, especially if he has provoked her?
2. Should the wife in Ohio in 2004 have been arrested?
3. Is there anything more doctors should have done?

Death by Gender

CYNTHIA FUCHS EPSTEIN

Finally, the atrocity of gendercide—the murder and mutilation of victims selected by sex—is getting prominent attention in the press. Through feminist online activism, but more prominently through the efforts of *New York Times* columnist Nicholas Kristof (in his new book *Half the Sky,* written with his wife, Sheryl WuDunn, and in his *New York Times* column), a socially embedded and systematic assault on women and girls in much of the world has been brought to public consciousness. The crimes at issue range from the killing of girls and women—often by their fathers, brothers, or male cousins, acting for the "honor" of the family—to the trafficking of women as sex slaves and to their forced recruitment as suicide bombers.

I will focus in this article on honor killing because the act is so vile. Further, the concept is difficult to dislodge. The notion of "honor" is at the core of many conflicts within and between societies all over the world, although it has been substantially reduced in the West. But, notions of honor underpin the marriage system in the tribal societies that are common in the Middle East and many parts of Africa. The most important connections between tribes are based on kinship and marriage, and value in the marriage market depends on female "virtue"—so girls and women must be tightly controlled to assure the "purity" of these social connections. Girls' families won't invest emotionally in them because they typically leave their birth families while very young and are brought into their husband's families as outsiders whose purpose is to bear children and take care of elderly family members. Without personal or social resources, they often are forced to be the servants or slaves of men in their birth families and then again in the families they enter by marriage. In "honor societies," which are characteristic of much of the developing world, girls and women are denied the protections that outside affiliations and affection might provide. Deviation from the rules imposed by male authorities may label a female as "contaminated" and elicit harsh sanctions. At its most serious, contamination is decreed when a women or girl is believed to have sought or had a sexual connection outside marriage—whether she acts from a desire to choose her own mate or is a victim of rape. Whether it has occurred within or outside the family, sexual contamination may be punished by murder. Thus, in some societies, the murder of girls and woman is justified by perceived social and moral infractions, and women are held in strict segregation to guard against these possibilities.

The belief that women are symbolic bearers of the honor of the clan or tribe is widely held, most often in Muslim countries but in others as well. And although Islamic law, or sharia, does not mandate honor killing as a punishment, it is practiced in many Islamic communities, openly so in some of them. It can be found also in some other groups, such as the Sikhs. There are lesser violations of honor for which girls and women are sometimes killed, like failing to comply with restrictive dress codes—wearing makeup or taking off the head scarf or hijab, for example—or for dating or merely appearing with unrelated boys or men in public. (According to the Al Arabia Web site, a Saudi father killed his daughter for chatting with a man on Facebook.) Trying to escape an arranged marriage is another important violation of traditional family norms that may merit death—as in the case of a young British woman who was stabbed to death by her father in London in 2002 when her family heard a love song dedicated to her on the radio and suspected that she had a boyfriend she had chosen for herself. A similar report comes from Turkey.

Women who protest forced marriage and abusive husbands can become targets of honor killings. And women and girls who have been raped can be doomed to death at the hands of a kinsman—or be forced to kill themselves to shield the rapist, if he himself is a kinsman, from punishment by the civil authorities. The dishonor of rape is so great that it can be used for political purposes. In January 2009, an Iraqi woman, Samira Ahmed Jassim, confessed to organizing the rapes of more than eighty women so that their shame would make them susceptible to recruitment as suicide bombers by al Qaeda. Twenty-eight of the women were said to have carried out suicide attacks.

The Turkish Human Rights Directorate reported in 2008 that in Istanbul alone there is one honor killing every week; more than one thousand occurred there in the preceding five years. UNICEF reported that in the Gaza Strip and the West Bank, according to 1999 figures, two-thirds of all murders were probably honor killings. In 2003, anthropologist/journalist James Emery of the Metropolitan State College of Denver stated that in the Palestinian communities of the West Bank, Gaza Strip, Israel, and Jordan, dishonored women were executed in their homes, in open fields, and occasionally in public before cheering crowds. Honor killings, Emery reported, account for virtually all recorded murders of Palestinian women. Although there are attempts by organizations such as the Women's Affairs

Technical Committee (WATC) and other NGOs to provide education and practical services to protect and assist women, they have had little success so far.

Death because of gender is arguably a leading cause of female homicide in many societies, but gendercide occurs in other ways: in 1990 the Nobel laureate Amartya Sen wrote in the *New York Review of Books* that more than one hundred million women were missing from the world as a result of sex-selective abortion and ill treatment. No doubt, the number has increased as girls continue to be selectively pruned in such places as India and Pakistan—not only by the poor who under-nourish their girl babies but also by members of the middle class who use sonograms to determine the sex of a fetus and then abort the females. The truth is that gender is regarded as a birth defect in much of the world, and this fact is neither analyzed nor addressed.

The officially reported estimates of the numbers of women who die in honor killings range from five thousand to ten thousand a year. (The UN Population Fund has estimated the total at five thousand a year, and that figure was reported by the secretary-general to the UN General Assembly in 2006.) But these numbers underestimate the actual toll because most honor murders are recorded as suicides or accidental deaths—or are not recorded at all. And the reports cannot begin to describe the terror girls and women must feel when they know that any aberrant behavior might provoke their fathers or close kin to kill them. Commentators in the West who suggest that women freely choose to conform to restrictions on their behavior and dress are not sensitive to the lurking threat of deadly punishment for violations of the codes. It is ludicrous to suggest that Islamic women decide for themselves to wear restrictive clothing and head coverings, given the possible consequences of not doing so.

Surprisingly, the support for honor killings is not limited to tribal societies but exists also among individuals living in traditional communities in modern societies. Even there, women who "go astray" and violate the bonds of marriage or assume individual identities often face physical assault. A poll by the BBC's Asia network, for example, found that one in ten young British Asians believe that honor killings can be justified. And in a poll of five hundred Hindus, Sikhs, Christians, and Muslims reported in 2009 by the online Women's E-news, one-tenth said they would condone the murder of someone who "disrespected" their family's honor.

Honor killings are not identified as a critically important instance of women's degraded status in many societies, and the practice is rarely condemned by the educated and sophisticated members of the societies in which the killings occur—nor by the social activists or leaders of the "free world." Nicholas Cohen, a writer for *Standpoint* magazine, asks why the outrage against apartheid does not extend to the women who are segregated and locked in their own homes, forced into arranged marriages, or raped and stoned. Why, he asks, do the societies that tolerate such practices not face irate Western boycotts or demonstrations in front of their embassy buildings?

It is clear, however, that the practice and the reasoning behind it will be difficult to erase. The protection of women's honor is an important part of the symbolic glue of kin groups that are, in many societies, the essential political bodies that maintain social order. Sociologists like Roger Friedland and Mounira Charrad have argued that control over women and marriage ensures that tribal groups can fully regulate the relationships between clans. (This is not so different from the marriages negotiated between the royal houses and aristocratic families of many countries in the West up to the early twentieth century.) Young women have to have unsullied reputations, and of course, they have to be virgins. Offering the bloodied sheets of the marital bed to relatives of the bride and groom is still necessary in many countries of the world.

Friedland has criticized the lack of awareness by political scientists (to say nothing of the media experts) who attempt to understand societies such as Afghanistan and Pakistan without attending to the tribal alliances created by marriages engineered by tribal elders. The obedience of women (actually girls, because these marriages are typically of underage children) is essential, and so the discipline over them is intense. Charrad, a sociologist studying the tribal foundations of the former French colonies of Algeria, Morocco, and Tunisia, similarly points to the political importance of tribal alliances created through the exchange of women.

Of course, men also are affected by these exchanges, but the men stay in their families of origin and it is the exchanged women who are forced to leave their places of birth and childhood. Because girls are married off early and torn from their families, they are powerless in the new environments to which they come as strangers. They are virtual slaves in the women's quarters of their new families.

Why do some women and girls internalize these views of honor and defend the very practices that enslave them? Why do we hear accounts of mothers who hold down their daughters as their husbands plunge knives into them or who observe the stoning that kills them? Or who insist that their daughters be circumcised when they know the pain and future discomfort this practice will bring?

Taken as child brides into the homes of their husbands, the only power these women have comes later in life as the mothers of sons who may, or may not, support them—and as the mothers of daughters, whom they can help to control but can't protect. They have learned the costs of deviance, and they teach those costs to, and even impose them on, their daughters. The resistance to the education of girls in Afghanistan, by the Taliban and also, sometimes, by their own parents, is now well known, but girls' education is poor in many other regions where their "honor" is the most important thing about them—as in Pakistan, for example, and parts of India.

Are things getting better? Attempts by international human rights associations and women's rights organizations to impose penalties for honor killings have recently been undercut at the UN. According to ESCR-FEM, the online listserv for Women's Economic, Social and Cultural Rights, the UN Human Rights Council adopted a resolution in 2009 "promoting human rights and fundamental freedoms through a better understanding of *traditional* values of humankind. . ." [emphasis added]. The vote was twenty-six in favor, fifteen against, with six abstentions.

The resolution was proposed by Russia and supported by the Arab League and the Organization of the Islamic Conference, a grouping of fifty-seven UN member states. Human Rights organizations across the globe strongly opposed it, declaring that its passage would set a destructive precedent by affirming a concept ("traditional values") often used to legitimize human rights abuses. The nongovernmental Cairo Institution for Human Rights Studies issued a statement expressing deep concern over the text. It declared that "such a concept has been used in the Arab region to justify treating women as second class citizens, female genital mutilation, honor crimes, child marriage, and other practices that clearly contradict international human rights standards."

There are a number of organizations devoted to improving the conditions of girls' and women's lives in the countries where those lives are most at risk. They include the International Initiative on Maternal Mortality and Human Rights and the Association for Women's Rights in Development, the Center for Women's Global Leadership, and the International Women's Rights Action Watch–Asia Pacific. Some organizations devoted to improving the situation of women are connected to agencies of the United Nations. It is more than thirty years since 90 percent of the member countries of the United Nations signed on to the Convention on the Elimination of all forms of Discrimination Against Women, which proclaimed that women's rights are human rights. But many of the signatories are countries in which the worst practices are carried out against women. Ironically, the United States has not signed.

What is to be done? We know that individuals' hearts and minds are difficult to change, but we also know that with proper incentives and political will they can sometimes change swiftly. Perhaps it is time for world leaders to insist on basic standards of human rights as a precondition for full commercial and diplomatic relations regardless of a country's religion or traditional culture. And perhaps it is also time for the resurgence of a woman's movement in the United States that will connect with the fledgling women's movements in countries of the Global South to form an alliance that will act politically to insist that women's and girls' rights be on the agenda of every international meeting.

Critical Thinking

1. What is the purpose of honor killings?
2. Why would some women defend honor killings?
3. Other than murder, how else does death by gender occur?

CYNTHIA FUCHS EPSTEIN is Distinguished Professor of Sociology at The Graduate Center of the City University of New York. Among her books are *Woman's Place, Women in Law*, and *Deceptive Distinctions*.

Elder Abuse Emerges from the Shadows of Public Consciousness

Two recent studies shed light on the prevalence and detection of an often overlooked crime.

PHILIP BULMAN

Detective Cherie Hill was skeptical, to say the least.

An elderly woman was trying to convince her that her grandson, who lived with her, had not hurt her. Standing in the police station in Anaheim, Calif., surrounded by half a dozen family members, the woman told Hill that a cereal box had fallen on her wrist and caused a bruise. Hill, an experienced elder abuse investigator, looked closely at the bruising, which went all the way around her wrist. She surmised that a cereal box—even a large, airborne cereal box—would not likely wrap itself around someone's wrist when it landed and cause that degree of bruising. Then there was the additional bruise on her face that police officers had noticed when they first responded to the call. The 23-year old grandson had been arrested and was in jail. Hill suspected that family members were now pressuring the woman to recant to get the grandson released. She had initially told neighbors that her grandson had grabbed her and hit her.

Hill asked Dr. Laura Mosqueda to examine the bruises. Mosqueda is director of geriatrics at the University of California, Irvine Medical Center. She has also studied bruising in the elderly to determine a scientific basis for distinguishing accidental bruises from abusive bruises. Mosqueda believed the bruising was abusive. In addition, during the conversation the elderly woman, who had dementia, repeated that her grandson had grabbed her.

Prosecutors later charged the grandson with elder abuse. He was found guilty. The judge in the case placed the young man on probation and issued a protective order. Two pioneering studies of bruising in the elderly sponsored by the National Institute of Justice helped investigators in this and many other cases, Hill said.

"These studies are really important for law enforcement," she said. "It has completely changed the way prosecutors handle these cases. It's just really phenomenal."

> These studies are really important for law enforcement. It has completely changed the way prosecutors handle these cases.

Many people believe that bruising in elderly people is normal because they are more likely to experience accidental falls. Indeed, a combination of factors such as thinner skin and less subcutaneous fat does make bruising more common among older people than their younger peers. So researchers decided to study "normal" bruising in elderly people and then follow up with a separate study of bruising that resulted from physical abuse.

A Scientific Look at Bruising

To learn what normal bruising looked like, researchers recruited 101 people, 65 or older, with an average age of 83. Trained interviewers went to their homes every day for six weeks. Participants undressed and were examined from head to toe for bruises. Each bruise was photographed, and the interviewers documented their location, size and color and noted how long it took for the bruises to fade. The researchers found that 90 percent of the bruises were on the extremities. Not a single accidental bruise was found on the neck, ears, genitals, buttocks or soles of the feet. Of the 20 large bruises (larger than 5 centimeters—about 2 inches—in diameter) only one occurred on the trunk of the body. Red and purple were the most common colors on the first day that a bruise appeared. However, some fresh bruises were yellow, a significant finding because many people believe that yellow bruises are more likely to be older. Indeed, yellow was the most common color in bruises that stayed visible for more than three weeks.

Once researchers knew what accidental bruising looked like, they turned their attention to deliberately inflicted bruising. Stark differences emerged. The team of researchers examined 67 people, 65 and older, who had been reported to adult protective services as possible abuse victims. An expert panel confirmed the abuse before including the people in the study. Seventy-two percent of those who had been physically abused within 30 days before examination had bruises. When compared with the previous group (who had not been abused), they had significantly larger bruises. Another important finding is that 91 percent knew what caused their bruises. Only 28.6 percent of the comparison group—those who had normal, non-abusive bruising—remembered the incident that caused their accidental bruises.

Abusive bruises are often larger. More than half are 2 inches or larger in diameter. The physically abused elders were much more likely to have bruises on the head and neck, especially the face, and on the posterior torso. Researchers also noted significant bruising on the right arm, perhaps because people raised their arms in an attempt to block an attacker.

Aileen Wigglesworth, a gerontologist and assistant professor at the University of California, Irvine, worked on both studies. Wigglesworth said that although the studies give police and prosecutors forensic markers that are vital tools in elder abuse cases, more work remains on other fronts, even on basic issues like the credibility of people who ask for help.

"People tend not to believe elders," she said.

Some people assume that memory loss and dementia afflict all elders, making them unreliable witnesses. The reality is that even some people with dementia can talk about abuse; they may forget small details, but they are likely to remember emotionally charged events.

"With dementia, they don't remember things with no emotional content," Wigglesworth said.

People who work in the field face a host of other challenges as well. Elders typically want to protect family members and are reluctant to report abuse. Sometimes family members are striving to take care of an elderly person but fall short. This may not involve outright abuse, but neglect or the simple inability to care properly for an elderly person. In those cases social service agencies can often help, Wigglesworth said.

Critical Thinking

1. What did researchers learn about the differences between "normal bruising" and "abusive bruising"?

2. What are some problems police might have when dealing with elderly victims?

Cherie Hill and Aileen Wigglesworth spoke at the 2009 NIJ Conference. To see a brief interview go to: www.ojp.usdoj.gov/nij/journals/media.htm.

From *National Institute of Justice Journal,* issue 265, April 2010, pp. 4–5. Published by U.S. Department of Justice.

Options for Reporting Sexual Violence: Developments over the Past Decade

SABRINA GARCIA, MA AND MARGARET HENDERSON, MPA

"Blind reporting can give victims of sexual violence, and other sensitive crimes, a safe haven to file a report at the same time that it removes that refuge from their assailants."[1] For the victim, the benefit of such a system lies in having time to build trust with the law enforcement officer and to consider all of the implications of participating in reporting, investigating, or prosecuting the case *before* making a decision whether to proceed. For the law enforcement agency, this type of reporting can help gain intelligence about the local incidence and perpetration of all sexual violence in the community, as well as build trust and credibility with populations vulnerable to assault.

Developments in the field and changing social expectations have made law enforcement agencies reconsider and refine their processes for working with victims of sexual violence. Careful thought, clear direction, and institutional commitment are required to set up graduated reporting systems that respect the circumstances and challenges of victims, provide consistent response by investigators over time, and gather intelligence and evidence that will ultimately achieve law enforcement's primary goal: to protect and serve.

Major Changes

Since 1999, these developments have affected the terms used to describe this practice and applied the concept to parallel processes. The two major changes involved the U.S. Department of Defense establishing a graduated reporting system (confidential, restricted, and unrestricted) in all branches of the military in 2004. Then, in 2005, Violence Against Women legislation (VAWA 2005) mandated that states afford forensic medical examinations to victims of sexual assault *without* 1) requiring cooperation with law enforcement or participation in the criminal justice system and 2) incurring any out-of-pocket expenses.[2]

U.S. Military Process

By 2004, the Department of Defense implemented landmark policies to address the incidence of sexual violence taking place within the military. They originally distinguished three levels of reporting.[3]

1. Confidential reporting: The service member reports the victimization to specified officials and gains access to supportive services. The service providers are not required to automatically report the incident to law enforcement or initiate an official investigation.
2. Restricted reporting: The service member reports the victimization to specified officials and gains access to supportive services. The service providers will not inform law enforcement unless the victim consents or an established exception is exercised under DoD Directive 6495.01.
3. Unrestricted reporting: The service member reports the victimization and gains access to supportive services. Both the report and any details from the service providers are reportable to law enforcement and may be used to initiate the official investigative process.

VAWA 2005 Mandate

States that do not comply with the VAWA 2005 requirement regarding forensic examinations will not be eligible to receive STOP Violence Against Women Formula Grant Program funds. According to the Office on Violence Against Women (OVW), "In fiscal year 2009, the STOP Program awarded almost $116 million in grant funds. Since 1995, OVW has made approximately 353 awards to states and territories, totaling more than $750 million, to address domestic violence, dating violence, sexual assault, and stalking."[4] This funding enables states to introduce innovations and improvements to their client services, law enforcement, and judicial systems.

Of importance, VAWA 2005 emphasizes health care and evidence collection, *not* reporting to law enforcement. It requires states to meet these forensic requirements but does not mandate a particular strategy for compliance. States, therefore, vary in their approaches.[5] Moreover, states also are not required to implement restricted reporting processes, but many are doing so voluntarily.[6]

...VAWA 2005 emphasizes health care and evidence collection, *not* reporting to law enforcement.

OVW's Web site offers some frequently asked questions, including one concerning the effect of the VAWA 2005 forensic examination requirement on law enforcement. "Many victims refuse to undergo examinations because they are not ready to report the sexual assault to the police. Advocates for sexual assault victims maintain that the VAWA 2005 forensic examination requirement will encourage more victims to undergo examinations directly following the crime, thereby preserving forensic evidence for future prosecutions when victims are ready to cooperate with law enforcement. Jurisdictions that have implemented anonymous reporting, including the U.S. Military, have found this to be true."[7]

Term Usage

Law enforcement officials and other professionals who work with victims of sexual violence might be unclear about the distinguishing characteristics among the terms *blind, restricted, confidential, Jane Doe,* or *anonymous* reporting processes and might use them differently. To aid the law enforcement community, the authors offer a clarification of these terms and provide general guidance on setting up these systems of reporting. They use the term *restricted reporting* to refer to processes in which victims contact law enforcement for assistance and the term *anonymous reporting* for those in which victims seek medical intervention and evidence collection but not necessarily investigation as set forth in VAWA 2005.[8]

In anonymous reporting processes, the victims are given a code number at the hospital that they can use to identify themselves if they choose to report at a later time. They are not required to cooperate with law enforcement or criminal justice authorities. Generally speaking, no direct connection is made between the victim and law enforcement officials unless the victim is willing to request their involvement. An advantage to anonymous reporting is that the integrity of the evidence is maintained while the victims have time to heal, consider their options, and make decisions. A disadvantage concerns hospitals and law enforcement investing resources in collecting and storing evidence that might not be used.

Twofold Benefits

For Victims

In addition to dealing with the ordeal of the violence itself, victims also might be traumatized by the reactions of family, friends, or the professionals from whom they seek help. Historically, too many survivors experienced revictimization through the law enforcement and criminal justice processes. Reporting systems that force—or are *perceived* to force—immediate all-or-nothing decisions whether to pursue investigation understandably scare off some victims. In contrast, allowing time to create dialogue between the victim and the law enforcement

officer has the added benefit of building trust between them as well. A victim who trusts the integrity of the investigator is more likely to withstand the potential challenges, intrusions, or disappointments of the investigative process.

For Law Enforcement

Law enforcement officers might initially experience frustration in spending time with a victim who is uncertain about following through or in their being held back from a compelling investigation. However, victim-friendly reporting processes constitute an investment in both building positive community relationships and in gathering intelligence related to the commission of sexually violent crimes.

Agencies that implement some form of graduated reporting options likely will experience an increase in the initial reports that develop into formal investigations. For example, in 2005, the first year of the Department of Defense's graduated reporting system, 108 (24.8 percent) of the 435 victims who initially used the confidential reporting mechanism later chose to file formal reports.[9] And, for the Chapel Hill, North Carolina, Police Department, 22 percent of these types of reports developed into formal investigations over a period of 10 years.[10]

An advantage to anonymous reporting is that the integrity of the evidence is maintained while the victims have time to heal, consider their options, and make decisions.

Untapped Potential

These graduated reporting options represent an innovation from over a decade ago that some in law enforcement have yet to fully embrace. Room for expansion in terms of both philosophy and implementation could prove beneficial for both victims and the law enforcement community. Where such systems exist, one learning opportunity now relates to how best to use the information while maintaining any promised expectations of confidentiality.

Using the Data

The initial report acts as a foundation document, offering the first account presented by the victim that can link to a suspect's method of operation, description, crime location, or identity. The information also might inform other existing investigations of the same or related types of crime or patterns of perpetration. The information presented to law enforcement by the victim of sexual violence is potentially unavailable by any other means or through any other person. Similarly, narcotics and vice operations commonly practice receiving, but not acting upon, such information to make the best strategic use of the data.

Specific information for any crime is primarily gained from two distinct sources, the victim and the offender. As law enforcement is aware, gaining access to a crime through the "eyes of a victim" lends unique insight to an offender's behavior and motivation. It also can provide links to other crimes that

Basic Steps in Establishing a Restricted Reporting System

1. Clarify the goal of setting up a flexible system of reporting. Is the law enforcement agency interested in strengthening its service to victims, reacting to negative publicity, or responding to emerging trends in the field? If the ultimate goal is to investigate and enable the successful prosecution of more cases of sexual violence, the agency must understand that it might take a long time to gain the trust of the community.

2. Identify the resources available to support the system. Which staff will be trained and involved in receiving reports from victims? What kind of private office space is available for the interviews?

3. Designate who will receive, document, store, or have access to the information. Create a secure location for storing this information, preferably away from other records.

4. Determine the circumstances or processes in which information might be shared across types of investigations within the agency. For example, consider a situation in which a rape victim discloses significant information about a drug dealer. When does the victim of sexual violence hold all authority over the information shared? When might information related to the drug supply, storage, or sales be shared, anonymously or not, with another investigator?

5. Set forth the circumstances or processes in which information might be shared with other helping professionals outside the agency, such as the rape crisis center, sexual assault nurse examiner, or sexual assault response team. The victim should be informed of and preferably have the opportunity to clarify how much information must or could be shared with which other people.

6. Consider creating an information sheet that describes the reporting system for others so that they will understand the intention, the process, the involved staff, and any limitations victims should consider. Decide how best to share this information within the agency, directly with victims, or throughout the community.

7. Create a standardized intake form that, along with the details of the sexual offense, clarifies the victim's preferences for sharing or receiving information, conditions for future contact, and expected next steps. Similarly, standardized categorization of the information will aid in analyzing the report, retrieving data, and matching specific characteristics across investigations.

8. Institute training for and reinforcement of the following basic principles for working with victims of sexual violence:

   - Establish and uphold a policy of confidentiality. It is the basis of trust.
   - Accept as little or as much information as the victim is willing to provide. Putting pressure on the victim for immediate and full disclosure can threaten the sense of trust placed in the officer and sense of safety with the process.
   - Take information whenever the victim might offer it. A delay in disclosure might reflect more on the victim's sense of support than on the validity of the statement.
   - Allow information from third parties. Some victims might feel so threatened that they will only share information through other parties, such as the rape crisis center.
   - Clarify options for future contact. Specify the means (phone, e-mail, in person), the content (first name or professional title, code phrase, full disclosure), and the circumstances (if another victim comes forth, if more evidence is discovered).
   - Maintain these reports in separate files unless the victim decides to file a formal report.
   - Consistently categorize the information within each report.
   - Compare the information with that in other formal investigative reports to provide an ongoing analysis of sexual assault reports.

might not seem connected due to their nonsexualized presentation. Related crimes that can easily be overlooked are property crimes, such as breaking and entering, burglary, carjacking, or robbery. Perpetrators might employ these strategies to gain access to potential victims for the purpose of sexual assault.

However, data collection and analysis must be grounded in the specific dynamics of sexual violence perpetration and victimization. The relationship between law enforcement and a confidential informant who provides drug or vice intelligence, for example, will not parallel the one between law enforcement and a victim of sexual violence.

Relating to Victims

For victims to risk talking at all, law enforcement officers should demonstrate a basic knowledge about the potential emotional and behavioral reactions to the violence and convey an understanding

of the negative personal impact of working through the justice system. Affirming the challenges of both experiences (the violence and the reporting) does not mean the officers accept the victims' accounts with unquestioning belief but simply that they convey a basic understanding of some part of the experience.[11] It is appropriate to share legal definitions or potential interpretations of behavior, recognizing that sex offenders are effective in using these myths and misunderstandings to convince victims that their actions contributed to the sexually violent outcome of the encounter. Too often and too accurately, victims delay or avoid reporting the crime because the perpetrator has convinced them that no one else will believe or care.

Linking Cases

Once a victim talks with an officer, another challenge lies in taking the initiative to consistently code and study the report.

Comparison of Anonymous and Restricted Reporting Systems

	Anonymous Reporting to Hospitals	Restricted or Blind Reporting
Authority behind the system	VAWA 2005 requires states to provide victims medical intervention and evidence collection at no charge and with no obligation to report to law enforcement.	established at the discretion of individual law enforcement agencies.
The evidence or information is collected by	the hospital.	an investigator or specialist designated by the agency.
The evidence or information is stored by	a central repository for the state.	the designated investigator or specialist.
The victim has the option to	report to law enforcement or take no action.	file a blind report (share information) or file a full report (request an investigation).
The evidence or information	is stored until the victim files a report with law enforcement, who retrieves and processes the medical evidence.	the victim specifies how the agency might use the information contained within a blind report. If a full report is filed, the evidence or information is processed for the investigation.

The end goal is to achieve case linkage through comparative analysis.

To structure reported information into a usable format, developing a restricted reporting form and using it consistently prove critical. The structure of the form should enable easy review with other formally submitted police reports. Assigning responsibility to one person, such as the department's crime analyst, investigation commander, or sex crime specialist, is a preferred way to consistently maintain and analyze the reports. In addition to asking traditional questions about the perpetrator, weapons, vehicle, and crime, this form also can be used to track custody of evidence kits or other collected evidence, as well as the strategies employed to identify, groom, isolate, intimidate, or control the victim. As a beginning, expectations of the information contained within the reports should be considered from four perspectives.

1. Collection: Designate space on the report form to document how the information and evidence were obtained, as well as from whom, where, and when.
2. Collation: Sort the information into specific categories, such as the time frame when crimes were committed, locations, and victimology.
3. Analysis: Note the specific behaviors, features, controls, or dialogue/monologue by offender and victim. These characteristics can demonstrate ritualized behaviors or scripted language required by the perpetrator to complete the offense.
4. Dissemination: Clarify how, when, what, and with whom the information is shared, with the victim's permission. This includes internal and external sharing with professional peers or multidisciplinary teams.

If the victim decides to proceed with a full investigation, the original restricted report and the official incident report should be cross-coded by number. This will allow for easy retrieval of the information.

> **Agencies that implement some form of graduated reporting options likely will experience an increase in the initial reports that develop into formal investigations.**

Conclusion

Setting up restricted reporting systems helps ensure that law enforcement agencies receive a more accurate account of the crimes committed within their jurisdictions. These endeavors provide a venue for victims to satisfy their need to notify others of the potential for harm, gain faith in a complex process unknown to them, and receive the response that they deserve.

As with most innovative techniques that address specialized crimes, law enforcement organizations should take time up front to clarify their goals for implementing the system and the resources they are willing to direct toward sustaining it. Planning and providing training for both the process of reporting and the dynamics of sexual violence also is critical for successful implementation. In the end, agencies should remember that the lack of confidential reporting can create a picture-perfect community but not always a safe one.

Notes

1. Sabrina Garcia and Margaret Henderson, "Blind Reporting of Sexual Violence," *FBI Law Enforcement Bulletin,* June 1999, 12–16.
2. Access http://frwebgate.access.gpo.gov/cgi-bin/getdoc.cgi?dbname=109_cong_bills&docid=f:h3402enr.txt.pdf for the complete text of VAWA 2005.
3. The Web site for the U.S. Department of Defense Sexual Assault Prevention and Response, www.sapr.mil, now lists only two options for reporting—restricted and unrestricted—and refers to the policy on confidentiality for specific personnel.

4. See, the Office on Violence Against Women website at www.ovw.usdoj.gov/stop_grant_desc.htm.

5. States needing technical assistance in reaching compliance should contact the Maryland Coalition Against Sexual Assault (MCASA), which was designated by the Office on Violence Against Women as the national technical assistance provider on this issue. Information regarding this project can be found at www.mcasa.org.

6. See the Office on Violence Against Women website at www.ovw.usdoj.gov.

7. For further information on forensic examination requirements and other STOP Program requirements, please visit www.ovw.usdoj.gov/docs/FAQ_FINAL_nov_21_07.pdf or contact the Office on Violence Against Women at 800 K Street, NW, Washington, DC 20530, Phone: (202) 307-6026 and Fax: (202) 305-2589.

8. One disadvantage of using the term *Jane Doe* in relation to sexual assault forensic exams is that law enforcement often uses this phrase to refer to unidentified victims for whom investigations are initiated. In the circumstances addressed by VAWA 2005, investigation will not begin until or unless the victim decides to do so.

9. See Department of Defense Report of Sexual Assaults in CY 2005 at www.sapr.mil/contents/references/2005%20RTC%20Sexual%20Assaults.pdf.

10. Statistics provided by Sabrina Garcia, Chapel Hill, North Carolina, Police Department.

11. Local rape crisis centers and state sexual assault coalitions are sources for training about the victim's perspective.

Critical Thinking

1. What are the benefits of the various options for reporting victimization, to the victims and to law enforcement?

2. Are there any disadvantages to any of these options?

Ms. Garcia is the domestic violence/sexual assault specialist for the Chapel Hill, North Carolina, Police Department. **Ms. Henderson** is the associate director of the Public Intersection Project at the School of Government, University of North Carolina at Chapel Hill.

From *FBI Law Enforcement Bulletin* by Sabrina Garcia and Margaret Henderson, May 2010, pp. 1–8. Published by Federal Bureau of Investigation, www.fbi.gov.

The U Visa
An Effective Resource for Law Enforcement

Stacey Ivie, MEd and Natalie Nanasi, JD

Law enforcement personnel strive for strong connections with all citizens. In pursuit of this goal, striking an appropriate balance—one that punishes wrongdoers while protecting victims—can present a challenge. One way that officers not only can foster better relationships with immigrant communities but also increase offender accountability, promote public safety, and help ensure that crimes translate into convictions is to promote awareness of the U visa, which provides important immigration benefits to cooperating crime victims.

The authors believe that the fear of deportation has created a class of silent victims and undermined officers' attempts at community-oriented policing among immigrant populations. They opine that the U visa helps improve relations with these communities, increase the reporting of criminal activity, enable provision of services to victims, and enhance the prosecution of violent perpetrators. Also, the authors feel that officers may have misconceptions about the U visa and not recognize its effectiveness as a tool. They hope that this article will help clarify the intent, purpose, and benefits of the U visa to the law enforcement community.

Description of the U Visa

Congress created the U visa—available to immigrant victims of a wide range of serious crimes—as part of the Victims of Trafficking and Violence Protection Act of 2000, recognizing that many of these individuals, with temporary or no legal status, fear that assisting law enforcement could lead to deportation.[1] By providing noncitizen victims a means of stabilizing their legal status, the U visa encourages them to report the crimes. It helps to curtail criminal activity, protect the innocent, and encourage victims to "fully participate in proceedings that will aid in bringing perpetrators to justice."[2] The U visa also can promote contact with law enforcement officers within isolated communities, which provides valuable assistance to individuals at heightened risk of victimization.

The U visa provides an avenue to legal status for immigrant crime victims who 1) have suffered substantial physical or mental abuse as a result of victimization; 2) possess information regarding the activity; and 3) offer a source of help in the investigation or prosecution.[3] The incident in question must have violated U.S. law or occurred within the nation's borders (including Indian country and military installations) or one of its territories or possessions.

The qualifying criminal activities covered by the U visa include a long list of serious offenses or the attempt, conspiracy, or solicitation to commit any of them. Unlike other protections available to battered immigrants (such as those provided under the Violence Against Women Act), eligibility for a U visa does not depend on a marriage between the victim and abuser or the legal status of the perpetrator.[4]

To obtain a U visa, victims must demonstrate to the U.S. Citizenship and Immigration Services (USCIS) their willingness to cooperate in a qualifying investigation or prosecution by law enforcement entities, such as federal, state, or local police agencies; prosecutors; judges; or any other appropriate authority. This definition includes organizations with criminal investigative jurisdiction in their respective areas of expertise (e.g., Child Protective Services, the Equal Employment Opportunity Commission, and the Department of Labor).[5]

Benefits for Victims

Approved U-visa petitioners receive temporary legal status and work authorization, which allows these victims to support themselves and rebuild their lives in safety while assisting law enforcement.[6] After 3 years, they may gain eligibility for lawful permanent resident status (i.e., a Green Card). Such benefits make the U visa an effective tool for bringing victims, particularly those of domestic violence who may depend on the perpetrator for legal status or economic support, out of the shadows. Research shows that "immigrant battered women want . . . the violence to stop, but culture, lack of support and immigration status limit their ability to deal with the violence and make them particularly vulnerable to failure in their attempts to escape a battering relationship."[7] Often, these victims find it difficult to break free as social "isolation, exacerbated by lack of social contacts, geographic isolation, and limited mastery of English or cultural alienation . . . interferes with detection and accountability, makes it easier for the batterer to ignore social sanctions, promotes increased marital dependence, and increases intrafamilial exclusivity and intensity."[8] The prospect of a U visa may eliminate the person's fear of calling the police for help, and, once connected to legal and social service systems (e.g., victim-witness advocates, battered-women's shelters, health- and child-care programs), some of the pressures that discourage victims of domestic violence to leave a relationship may be alleviated, allowing them to ultimately break the cycle of abuse.

Moreover, financial concerns pose significant barriers that prevent victims of crimes, such as domestic violence, from leaving and attaining economic self-sufficiency. Because battered immigrant women are not eligible for many work opportunities and public benefits, they and their children must choose between remaining in a violent situation or facing starvation and poverty. The U visa, therefore, can afford noncitizen victims of domestic violence the same opportunities as survivors with U.S. citizenship and allow them to obtain the resources crucial in helping them escape from abusive situations.[9]

With immigrant victims no longer afraid to cooperate . . . the subsequent increase in reporting will ensure the identification and apprehension of more violent criminals.

Advantages for Law Enforcement

Cooperative Victims

With immigrant victims no longer afraid to cooperate with the police, the subsequent increase in reporting will ensure the identification and apprehension of more violent criminals. Additionally, victim participation in the investigation or prosecution of cases increases the likelihood of convictions. The resulting accountability of offenders can lead to defendant rehabilitation, which, in turn, ultimately may increase the number of productive members of society, reduce crime rates, and promote public safety for all members of a community.

Use of the U visa also may cause a decline in recidivism, or the repetition of certain crimes, thus decreasing the frustration of officers and the loss of financial assistance and other services needed by victims. These issues prove particularly prominent in domestic violence cases. Statistics show that "on average, women . . . leave and return to an abusive relationship five times before permanently leaving. . . ."[10] Those five incidents may have involved law enforcement responding to the scene and spending numerous hours on a case, thereby decreasing officers' availability to other crime victims. Perhaps, the prosecutor spent time and financial resources to create an evidence-based prosecution with a limited chance of conviction. In such instances, the U visa can increase the likelihood of victim cooperation, thereby eliminating these wasted hours.

Offenses Covered by the U Visa

To obtain a U visa, the immigrant must be the victim of one or more qualifying crimes; the attempt, conspiracy, or solicitation to commit any of the acts; or any similar activity in violation of federal, state, or local criminal law.

Rape	Torture
Trafficking	Incest
Domestic violence	Sexual assault
Abusive sexual contact	Prostitution
Sexual exploitation	Female genital mutilation
Being held hostage	Peonage
Involuntary servitude	Slave trade
Kidnapping	Abduction
Unlawful criminal restraint	False imprisonment
Blackmail	Extortion
Manslaughter	Murder
Felonious assault	Witness tampering
Obstruction of justice	Perjury

8 U.S.C. 1101(a)(15)(U)(iii)

Moreover, recidivism rates logically will decrease when public service resources are provided to undocumented victims of certain pattern crimes. The ability to earn an income and receive financial assistance may drastically change the outlook of victims who had no prospect for life modification prior to the availability of the U visa, allowing them to leave a violent relationship.

Last, use of the U visa also can eliminate the current conflict faced by officers who respond to domestic violence scenes. Like many other states, the commonwealth of Virginia mandates public assistance for victims of domestic abuse. The Virginia Code requires that the officer "provide the allegedly abused person, both orally and in writing, information regarding the legal and community resources available. . . ."[11] However, this directive conflicts with the prohibition against immigrant victims receiving public benefits, creating a confusing situation for first responders. Putting noncitizen victims of domestic violence on the path to legal status can resolve this inconsistency.

Community-Oriented Policing

Community-oriented policing "promotes and supports organizational strategies to address the causes and reduce the fear of crime and social disorder through problem-solving tactics and police-community partnerships."[12] In short, this law enforcement model is based on the principle that only the partnership of police and citizens can successfully address the problem of crime in communities. The U.S. Department of Justice promotes community-oriented policing as a highly effective problem-solving model.

Fear of deportation breaks down the ties that bind the police and the community, and, without a joint venture involving both participants and the trust that must exist between the two parties, community-oriented policing will not work. Use of the

U visa can address this fear, giving victims more confidence about calling the police and increasing trust between community members and those sworn to protect and serve.

Fear of deportation breaks down the ties that bind the police and the community . . .

Frequently Asked Questions

Although the U visa can provide substantial benefits to both victims and officers, the authors recognize that valid questions and concerns exist that may limit its acceptance and effectiveness in the law enforcement community. The answers to some frequently asked questions can help address these issues.

- *What role do law enforcement agencies have in the application process?* Agencies only complete the 3-page Form I-918 Supplement B, U Nonimmigrant Status Certification (i.e., the "law enforcement certification form"), which simply requires the department's information; the details of the crime; and the victim's personal data, knowledge of the incident, and helpfulness to the investigation or prosecution. Signing the form does not indicate sponsorship of the immigrant. Although the form bears significant weight because it demonstrates that the individual has met several of the eligibility criteria, the USCIS decides whether to grant the U visa only after evaluating the totality of the circumstances. However, a U visa will not be issued without a signed law enforcement certification.

- *Who can sign the law enforcement certification form?* Heads of certifying agencies or any supervisory employee they appoint (i.e., a designated certifier) can sign the form. A designated certifier should know the certification requirements thoroughly and be readily identifiable and accessible to immigrant crime victims; this simplifies the process for applicants, serves as a quality control measure, and prevents abuse of the U visa.

- *What if the victim stops cooperating?* Certifying departments may notify USCIS if victims do not meet their ongoing responsibility to cooperate with law enforcement officers. However, agencies should recognize when a victim may have suffered abuse-related trauma (e.g., post-traumatic stress disorder or other debilitating emotional or physical condition) or legitimately fear retaliation from perpetrators; in such situations, agencies should be mindful of withdrawing or refusing certification. Departments also should remember that issuance of a U visa does not require any case outcomes or milestones; a victim must only be helpful.[13] Last, USCIS assumes "an ongoing need for the applicant's assistance"; if authorities no longer need help, the victims have fulfilled their obligation to law enforcement.[14]

- *Is there a quid pro quo?* No. The U visa is not given in exchange for filing a police report or for testimony at trial.

For Additional Information

www.uscis.gov
www.tahirih.org
www.legalmomentum.org/our-work/
immigrant-women-program

- *Are some eligible victims criminals due to their illegal presence in the United States?* The Immigration and Nationality Act (INA) determines an individual's legal status. In enacting the Victims of Trafficking and Violence Prevention Act and creating the U visa, Congress modified the INA. The federal government weighed all of the interests involved and ultimately created a legal status for cooperating crime victims, regardless of their means of entry into the country, based on the determination that "the purpose of the U nonimmigrant classification is to strengthen the ability of law enforcement agencies to investigate and prosecute such crimes as domestic violence, sexual assault, and trafficking in persons, while offering protection to alien crime victims in keeping with the humanitarian interests of the United States."[15]

- *Will U visas increase the filing of false police reports?* To combat false reporting, law enforcement officials should conduct a thorough investigation of any alleged crime to determine its authenticity. Concerning a false allegation, not only should officers not sign the U-visa certification form but they should initiate a criminal charge for the filing of a false police report. However, no evidence indicates that an agency's use of the U visa will lead to the filing of false claims. The U visa covers crimes that are serious, predominantly violent, difficult to fabricate, and that carry dire legal consequences for the perpetrator. Additionally, immigrants hesitant to contact authorities regarding a real crime because of their fear of deportation probably would not do so to report a false one. Moreover, U-visa regulations protect against its abuse in this way. First, they specifically exclude "a person . . . culpable for the qualifying criminal activity" from U-visa eligibility.[16] Further, if applicants cannot demonstrate a true crime's occurrence, their suffering from the incident, or their cooperation with law enforcement, they cannot obtain a U visa.

- *Do law enforcement agencies have to sign U-visa certification forms?* The federal government does not mandate that law enforcement agencies implement a U-visa certification process. It only serves as a resource designed to augment the effectiveness of a criminal investigation or prosecution. However, departments that decline participation may prevent the identification and punishment of violent perpetrators. Moreover, refusing to certify a qualifying victim not only undermines the purpose of the federal law but decreases an agency's ability to combat crime, apprehend perpetrators, foster relationships within immigrant communities, and provide crucial assistance to victims of violent crime.

Conclusion

The fear of deportation can cause immigrant communities to cut themselves off from police and not offer information about criminal activity, even when victimized. Consequently, predators remain on the street, emboldened because they know they can strike with a degree of impunity. As a result, societies face increased crime, including serious offenses, and the perpetrators victimize and endanger everyone, not just illegal immigrants.[17]

The U visa can alleviate the concerns of immigrant communities, open lines of communication, and enhance public safety for all. It then helps law enforcement officers fulfill their ultimate goal of ensuring the well-being of those they serve.

Notes

1. New Classification for Victims of Criminal Activity; Eligibility for "U" Nonimmigrant Status, Background and Legislative Authority, retrieved from http://bibdaily.com/pdfs/E7-17807.pdf. See also www.ilrc.org/resources/U%20Visa/Frequently%20Asked%20Questions.html.

2. www.uscis.gov/files/pressrelease/U-visa_05Sept07.pdf

3. The U visa is available to individuals with temporary immigration status (e.g., student, employment-based, and tourist visas or Temporary Protected Status), as well as undocumented persons with no legal status.

4. Because of their experience and expertise, the authors use examples of domestic violence and other crimes against women throughout the article. However, the U visa is available to both men and women and serves as a useful tool against a wide range of violent crimes.

5. 8 C.F.R. §214.14(a)(2) (defining a "certifying agency" for U-visa purposes).

6. Pursuant to 8 U.S.C. 1184(p)(2), the maximum number of issued U visas may not exceed 10,000 per fiscal year.

7. M.A. Dutton and G.A. Hass, "The Use of Expert Testimony Concerning Battering and Its Effects on Immigrant Women;" retrieved from www.legalmomentum.org/site/DocServer/wwwappendixcesperttestimonyconcerningbattering.pdf?docID=631.

8. Joyce Nielson, Russell Endo, and Barbara Ellington, "Social Isolation and Wife Abuse: A Research Report," in *Intimate Violence: Interdisciplinary Perspectives,* ed. Emilio C. Viano (Bristol, PA: Taylor and Francis, 1992); and Bruce Rounsaville, "Theories in Marital Violence: Evidence from a Study of Battered Women," *Victimology: An International Journal* 11 (1978): 21.

9. National Immigration Law Center Fact Sheet on the Women Immigrants Safe Harbor Act; retrieved from www.nilc.org/immspbs/cdev/wish/WISH_2pgr_3-26-04.pdf.

10. www.ncptsd.va.gov/ncmain/ncdocs/fact_shts/fs_domestic_violence.html

11. VA Criminal Procedure Code §19.2-81.3.

12. U.S. Department of Justice, Office of Community Oriented Policing Services, "What Is Community Policing?" retrieved from www.cops.usdoj.gov/Default.asp?Item=36. See also David Allender, "Community Policing: Exploring the Philosophy," *FBI Law Enforcement Bulletin,* March 2004, 18–22; Clyde Cronkhite, "Fostering Community Partnerships That Prevent Crime and Promote Quality of Life," *FBI Law Enforcement Bulletin,* May 2005, 7–10; John Ellison, "Community Policing: Implementation Issues," *FBI Law Enforcement Bulletin,* April 2006, 12–16; and Carl Peed, "The Community Policing Umbrella," *FBI Law Enforcement Bulletin,* November 2008, 22–24.

13. U visa regulations broadly define the concept of helpfulness, to include victims who have been helpful in the past, are currently being helpful, or are likely to be helpful in the future. 8 CFR 214.14(b)(3).

14. 8 C.F.R. §214.14(a)(2).

15. U Visa Regulations, Document Summary, 8 C.F.R. § 214.14.

16. 8 C.F.R. §214.01(a)(14)(iii).

17. David Harris, "Avoidable Disaster: Police Enforcing U.S. Immigration Law"; retrieved from http://jurist.law.pitt.edu/forumy/2006/10/avoidable-disaster-police-enforcing-us.php.

Critical Thinking

1. How would you describe the U Visa?

2. Do you see any problems that might arise from using it?

3. Might the U Visa encourage false reporting?

Detective **STACEY IVIE** serves with the Alexandria, Virginia, Police Department. **Ms. NATALIE NANASI** is an attorney with the Tahirih Justice Center in Falls Church, Virginia.

From *FBI Law Enforcement Bulletin* by Stacey Ivie and Natalie Nanasi, October 2009, pp. 10–16. Published by Federal Bureau of Investigation, www.fbi.gov.

Victim Satisfaction with the Criminal Justice System

New research suggests that victims of domestic violence who initially turn to the criminal justice system for intervention may be so dissatisfied with the outcome that they do not call the police the next time they need help.

Researchers Eve Buzawa and the late Gerald Hotaling asked women in 353 domestic violence cases in the Quincy District Court (QDC) in Quincy, Massachusetts, to assess the role of the police, prosecutors, victim advocates, and judges and to rate their level of satisfaction.[1] They found that in 55 percent of the cases, women were generally satisfied with the outcome. In 17 percent, victims were dissatisfied.

The researchers found several common variables in the satisfied cases: the incidents were less serious, the offender was less dangerous, the victim said she felt some control and wanted the case to go forward, and the victim reported experiencing less violence in her past.

Dissatisfied victims appeared to have been involved in more serious incidents with highly dangerous offenders and were more likely to have disagreed with the police about the offender's arrest. These victims were also 16 times more likely than satisfied victims to report that they had experienced both sexual and severe physical abuse before the age of 18. As a group, dissatisfied victims appeared to be more willing to leave offenders or unwilling (or afraid) to directly confront the abuser, even if they were separated.

For the researchers, the bottom line was that victim satisfaction in domestic violence cases appeared to hinge on the extent to which the victim felt control over ending the violence in the incident, control over her offender's future conduct—and even over the criminal justice system. When the victim had a low sense of control, satisfaction with the system decreased significantly.

Consequences of Victim Dissatisfaction

Having identified the common variables in cases of satisfied and dissatisfied victims, Buzawa and Hotaling then examined what, if any, consequences flowed from dissatisfaction. The second stage of the study focused on the connection between victim dissatisfaction and willingness to report future victimizations. The researchers tracked 118 women for a year after the original study to see if they reported any new incidents or sought civil restraining orders.

Of the 118 women, 49 percent admitted that they had been revictimized. Of these, 22 percent reported the incidents to the police. Contrary to the presumption that "more serious" offenses get reported to the police, victims who reported the new incident were more likely to report less serious offenses, like violations of restraining orders, than they were to reach out for assistance due to a physical assault. Women who reported new abuse to the police also generally reported that the abuse was becoming more serious.

Women who chose not to report new incidents of abuse were:

- The least likely to have resisted the arrest of the offender during the first incident.
- The least likely to have been dissatisfied with how the police initially handled the incident.
- The most likely, by the conclusion of the case, to feel that the actions of the police negatively affected their safety and to complain that they wanted the prosecutor to make charges against the offender more severe.

Women who chose not to report new incidents of abuse also were likely to have experienced sexual abuse as a child. This finding coincides with other research that suggests a link between a woman's history of abuse and her likelihood of reporting revictimization to police. The researchers theorize that "for an individual who has experienced abuse through the 'life course,' reporting this latest incident to the police may be viewed as a useless ritualism."[2]

Balancing Different Perspectives

In the past, victims of domestic violence often expressed dissatisfaction with the lack of aggressive response to domestic assault by police, prosecutors, and the courts. Now, researchers have discovered, the pendulum may have swung the other way.

Mandatory arrest policies in many jurisdictions and implementation of "full enforcement" protocols have resulted in more cases being prosecuted whether the victim wants to proceed or not.

Women who are the victims of domestic abuse usually want to enhance their own safety, maintain economic viability, protect their children, and have an opportunity to force an abuser to participate in batterers' counseling programs. They are less concerned about upholding the law or deterring future abuse—the main objectives of the police, prosecutor, and judge.

Victim Services Increase Positive Experiences

Women who take advantage of victim service programs tend to have more positive outcomes and are more likely to report satisfaction, according to one study.[3] Researchers found that women benefit the most when the criminal justice system and nonprofit and community-based agencies collaborate and coordinate their efforts. Such cooperation results in more positive outcomes and greater victim satisfaction. Treating victims with respect, offering them positive encouragement, refraining from engaging in negative interactions, and most importantly, creating a sense of control increased the odds of positive outcomes in the victim's view.

Researchers concluded that the most positive outcomes occur when the staff at service agencies listen to women, carefully explain the options, and then take action. "Women know best about their own safety and well-being, and when they have a greater sense of control while working with agencies, they find the services more helpful and effective."[4]

Ensuring that victim service programs work in conjunction with the legal system and community agencies and that staff address victims' needs in a positive manner will encourage victims to turn to the criminal justice system for assistance and may maximize the potential to break the cycle of violence.

Notes

1. QDC was chosen as a data collection site because it is an acknowledged leader in implementing strategies that favor criminal justice intervention in domestic violence cases. Over a 7-month period in 1999, researchers interviewed victims to obtain their assessments of the role of police, prosecutors, victim advocates, and judges. Researchers also studied victims' satisfaction with various sectors of the criminal justice system.

2. Hotaling, Gerald T., and Eve S. Buzawa, *Forgoing Criminal Justice Assistance: The Non-Reporting of New Incidents of Abuse in a Court Sample of Domestic Violence Victims,* Washington, DC: U.S. Department of Justice, National Institute of Justice, 2003: 25 (NCJ 195667).

3. Zweig, Janine, Martha R. Burt, and Ashley Van Ness, *Effects on Victims of Victim Service Programs Funded by the STOP Formula Grants Program,* Washington, DC: U.S. Department of Justice, National Institute of Justice, 2003: 16 (NCJ 202903).

4. Ibid., 19.

Critical Thinking

1. Does it matter significantly to law enforcement that victims may not be satisfied with the outcomes of their cases?

2. What did researchers learn about women who take advantage of victim service programs?

From *National Institute of Justice Journal,* January 2006. Published by U.S. Department of Justice.

UNIT 3
The Police

Unit Selections

Learning Outcomes

After reading this unit, you will be able to:

• Discuss some of the problems faced by Arab-Americans since the attacks of 9/11.

• Understand why racial profiling isn't good police work.

• Be able to explain the importance of conducting interrogations in a manner that will instill confidence in the validity of any statements that are obtained.

• Explain the concept of behavioral mirroring when conducting interviews.

• Know what the national standards are that govern visibility for fire trucks and ambulances.

Student Website
www.mhhe.com/cls

Internet References

ACLU Criminal Justice Home Page
    www.aclu.org/CriminalJustice/CriminalJusticeMain.cfm
Law Enforcement Guide to the World Wide Web
    http://leolinks.com
Violent Criminal Apprehension Program (VICAP)
    www.state.ma.us/msp/unitpage/vicap.htm

P olice officers are the guardians of our rights under the Constitution and the law, and as such they have an awesome task. They are asked to prevent crime, protect citizens, arrest wrongdoers, preserve the peace, aid the sick, control juveniles, control traffic, and provide emergency services on a moment's notice. They are also asked to be ready to lay down their lives, if necessary.

In recent years, the job of the police officer has become even more complex and dangerous. Illegal drug use and trafficking are still major problems; racial tensions are explosive; and terrorism is now an alarming reality. As our population grows more numerous and diverse, the role of the police in America becomes ever more challenging, requiring skills that can only be obtained by greater training and professionalism.

The lead article in this section, "Policing in Arab-American Communities after September 11," examines how the terrorist attacks of September 11 changed the face of law enforcement in the United States, including the effect on Arab-American communities brought about by these changes. The typical offender in violent crime categories is white, as pointed out by Tim Wise in "Racial Profiling and Its Apologists."

In the next article, "Our Oath of Office, A Solemn Promise," Rudd focuses on the oath of office that law enforcement officers take, in order to illuminate the purpose and history of the oath and to show its relevance to our Constitution. In "Police Investigations of the Use of Deadly Force Can Influence Perceptions and Outcomes," Bohrer and Chaney examine the process

© Getty Images/Steve Allen

followed by police departments when a police officer kills someone in the line of duty. Next, Dreeke and Navarro discuss a technique that will help investigators create and build rapport when interviewing informants in "Behavioral Mirroring in Interviewing."

The last article in this section, "Keeping Officers Safe on the Road," is an article in which Beth Pearsall writes about steps that can be taken to make investigating traffic incidents safer for police officers.

Policing in Arab-American Communities after September 11

Nicole J. Henderson et al.

For the past 20 years, local police agencies have worked to build stronger ties with the communities they serve. These "community policing" efforts have increased public safety and security as partnerships between law enforcement agencies and community groups have been effective at identifying and defusing community disputes.

However, the Sept. 11 terrorist attacks have led to a host of new concerns about public safety. Communities across the nation—from small towns to sprawling cities—are wrestling with security issues that did not exist a decade ago. These issues are especially complex for communities with significant Arab-American populations.

After Sept. 11, law enforcement agencies on both the local and federal levels experienced great pressure to prevent further attacks. Some researchers and law enforcement officials suggested that local law enforcement agencies should play a greater role in intelligence-gathering and immigration enforcement. In addition, the FBI began to stress counterterrorism efforts, with Joint Terrorism Task Forces working in concert with local law enforcement agencies. Often, these efforts focused on Arab-American communities.

At the same time, local law enforcement agencies were called on to protect the Arab-American community. After the attacks, some people of Arab descent said they experienced increased levels of harassment, ranging from workplace discrimination to verbal abuse and vandalism to severe hate crimes such as assault and homicide. To ensure the safety of Arab-Americans, some local law enforcement agencies felt it necessary to step up their outreach efforts.

Finally, some Arab-Americans and law enforcement officers said that public suspicion of Arab-Americans had led to an increase in false reporting. As one FBI special agent said, "The general public calls in some ridiculous stuff—it's really guilt by being Muslim." Because officers have to look into all reports, false reporting can be a significant strain on law enforcement agencies.

Arab-American communities have been deeply affected by the events of Sept. 11 in other ways. Before the attacks, many Arab-Americans were well assimilated into the American mainstream.[2] But after Sept. 11, some members of Arab-American

Study Methods

The study was conducted in 16 sites across the country, each of which is home to a geographically concentrated Arab-American community. For each site, researchers did telephone interviews with people from three groups: local law enforcement officers, FBI agents assigned to local field offices, and members of the Arab-American community. Researchers then held focus group discussions and in-person interviews at four sites.

What Were the Study's Limitations?

This study focused on Arab-American communities that are concentrated in specific regions, and the law enforcement agencies that serve them. However, such concentrated communities are not necessarily representative of the Arab-American population as a whole. In addition, although researchers interviewed FBI agents from local field offices at each site, they did not interview agents from other federal law enforcement agencies, such as Immigration and Customs Enforcement or the U.S. Attorney's Offices.

communities came to believe that many of their fellow citizens—not to mention some in the media and government—regarded them with suspicion. Although Arab-Americans report a fair amount of goodwill towards local law enforcement agencies, some Arab-Americans said these developments have strained relations between their communities and those agencies. Also, some members of Arab-American communities said they fear federal policies and practices more than violence.

Researchers from the Vera Institute of Justice, examining how post-Sept. 11 law enforcement changes have affected policing in Arab-American neighborhoods (see "Study Methods"), identified four primary and interrelated obstacles to improved relations between law enforcement and the Arab-American community:

- Distrust between Arab-American communities and law enforcement.
- Lack of cultural awareness.

- Language barriers.
- Concerns about immigration status and fear of deportation.

Fortunately, many law enforcement officials and community leaders generally agree on how to address these obstacles.

Distrust

Distrust between Arab-American communities and law enforcement was by far the most commonly cited barrier to improved relations. Although most respondents stressed distrust of law enforcement by the local Arab-American community, a few officers mentioned that the distrust is reciprocal.

Although much of the distrust in Arab-American communities stems from post-Sept. 11 developments, not all of it does. Recent immigrants often feel uncomfortable about approaching law enforcement.[3] This is especially true of immigrants from countries with brutal governments or widespread police corruption. As one local business leader explained, "[Many] Arabs come from [countries with] very authoritarian, dictatorial regimes. The police are run by the state. So from [their] perspective, [approaching law enforcement] is bad news."

The surveys suggest a number of practices that can help:

Begin or improve communication. Reaching out to the local community is the key to building trust. As one sergeant in the public affairs division of a department with an active outreach program noted, "Having a good relationship with the community helps patrol officers do their jobs." In setting up an outreach effort, law enforcement agencies will want to consider the following points:

- *Reach out in person.* Several people stressed the importance of face-to-face meetings as opposed to phone or e-mail contact. One community leader pointed out that "fliers aren't enough," while another explained that the Arab-American community has a strong "oral culture." Outreach efforts were most successful when they used a three-pronged approach: first send a letter, then make a phone call and finally follow up with a personal visit.
- *Meet with the community regularly.* Regular contact between the community and law enforcement agencies is important, and helps break down misconceptions and build trust. At one site, a potentially volatile instance of miscommunication was resolved by discussions in a series of regularly scheduled community forums.
- *Use community contacts to set up meetings.* When arranging meetings, it can help to have a member of the Arab-American community set up the contact: "A non-Arab who invites [members of the Arab-American] community to dinner or to a function will not have the same turnout as if someone from the Arab-American community invites them on [law enforcement's] behalf."

- *Hold meetings in the community as opposed to the precinct headquarters.* This is an effective way to address the fear and hesitation that community members may feel about contacting the police.
- *Include patrol officers in community meetings.* Patrol officers said that community meetings are important. However, some felt that they should play a larger role in these events. One patrol officer described a meeting in which he and his colleagues "were sent in at the beginning to show our faces and meet and greet, but when the meeting started they sent us on our way." Including patrol officers in community meetings gives them a stake in building stronger relations between law enforcement and the community.
- *Set up an open-door policy.* At one site, the chief of police held office hours for community members once a week. He said this policy allowed him to engage community members in "one-on-one dialogue."
- *Schedule community meetings for suitable times.* Often, certain times—such as Friday prayer for Arab-Muslim communities—are not suitable for community meetings.

Create a police-community liaison position. By registering complaints, giving advice or just meeting with community members, liaison officers can address potential problems before they intensify and require the intervention of patrol officers. The status of liaison officers varies from one location to another. Some are appointed by the chief of police or another administrator, while others assume the role on their own initiative and work in a more informal capacity. In creating a liaison position, agencies will want to consider the following points:

- *Get institutional support and backing of the police chief.* Liaison officers who report directly to the police chief and enjoy the institutional support of the department are the most effective in building trust between law enforcement and the Arab-American community. Because these officers are freed from their regular duties, they can focus all of their time and energy on community concerns.
- *Promote visibility and accessibility.* A successful liaison officer is accessible to the community. One effective liaison officer gave out his cell phone number, home number and e-mail address, and set up a website where the community could learn about the police department and send questions to the department. Holding office hours in the community is another way to increase accessibility.
- *Foster a connection to the community.* The liaison officer needs to be culturally competent. Most of the liaison officers interviewed for this study either spoke Arabic or were of Arab descent.

Recruit within Arab-American communities. Officers and community members agreed that having more Arab-Americans on the police force would help overcome fear of law enforcement. In jurisdictions with little precedent for cooperation between law enforcement and the community, recruitment efforts are likely to be greeted with suspicion. "I've seen ads for officer recruitment in our local Arabic newspapers," one community member told researchers. "Why didn't they want to recruit us before?"

The following measures are likely to boost recruitment among Arab-Americans:

- *Focus on young people.* Because young people are less likely to have had negative experiences with law enforcement, reaching out to them by having officers work in schools can help break down barriers.
- *Translate recruiting materials into Arabic.* At one site, the police department translated recruiting materials into Arabic and gave them out at police-community forums.

Be aware that officers may face skepticism when they first reach out to communities. Cultural training programs, advisory councils, regular meetings with the community and other outreach efforts all help build trust. However, officers should be prepared to face some skepticism when they first reach out to the Arab-American community. If their commitment is genuine, even skeptics can be won over.

Lack of Cultural Awareness

Many community leaders stressed the need for improved cultural awareness among law enforcement personnel. Police officers also felt that a deeper knowledge of Arab-American culture would make it easier to respond to calls and mediate disputes.

Setting up cultural awareness training and education is one promising practice. Law enforcement agencies have traditionally responded to their officers' changing vocational needs by offering comprehensive training programs. Such programs are well-suited to educating officers about Arab-American culture. When asked what makes a cultural awareness program effective, officers stressed that it must be both practical and relevant to their everyday work. In particular, officers wanted to learn more about the following topics:

- Islam and religious practices.
- Arab culture.
- Basic Arabic words and phrases.
- Cultural considerations when questioning someone.
- Cultural considerations when arresting someone.

The most successful training programs set the following goals:

Collaborate with the community. Leaders from the local Arab-American community played a role in developing the training programs that were most effective. Programs that are developed this way are better equipped to address a community's specific needs. Because many community leaders are eager and willing to teach others about Islam and Arab culture, they are valuable partners.

Reach rank-and-file officers. Cultural awareness programs need to target the patrol officers who work with the Arab-American community regularly. At one site, an officer remarked that relations between law enforcement administrators and the community were good, but that "among the rank and file there are serious problems . . . local police officers do not know the community."

Bring training sessions into the community. In one innovative training program, officers left the classroom to visit local Arab-American and American Muslim communities. Officers met with community members and visited a mosque.

Language Barriers

Reaching out to those with limited knowledge of English is important, especially for agencies that serve communities with large immigrant populations. Although language barriers can significantly undermine police-community relations, most barriers can be effectively broken down through simple measures.[4] Community leaders are often willing to help out with translation or language training. Inviting them to do so strengthens relations between the local community and law enforcement.

Offer basic language training. For officers working in Arab-American neighborhoods, basic language training is essential. As one community member explained, "The new immigrant hardly speaks any English. When they encounter an officer, they cannot understand them and that causes a problem."

Encourage officers to learn Arabic. Some police departments offer incentives (such as compensatory time) for officers who enroll in Spanish classes. It makes sense to do the same for those who study Arabic.

Provide incentives for Arabic-speaking officers. In police departments across the country, Spanish-speaking officers receive pay bonuses. However, none of the police departments under study offered bonuses for Arabic speakers.

Translate written materials and provide interpreters. Having Arabic interpreters at community meetings and providing Arabic translations of commonly used forms and informational pamphlets is helpful.

Concerns about Immigration Status and Fear of Deportation

Many community leaders expressed concern about the involvement of local law enforcement agencies in immigration enforcement. They noted that threats of deportation or other forms of pressure related to immigration status have been used to seek information. As a result, they said, some members of the community hesitate to report crimes.

Survey responses favored one practice: set up clear and consistent policies. Because immigration and counterterrorism enforcement practices vary from one police department to another, and even from one FBI field office to another, many Arab-Americans are unclear about the enforcement practices of their local police. This lack of clarity can significantly undermine a department's ability to build strong community ties. As one community leader explained, "The police need to establish ground rules. We don't know what the local and federal police will and won't do." Local police departments should carefully consider whether to engage in immigration enforcement, and then communicate their policies to the community. They should also develop policies against racial profiling or, if they already have such policies, reinforce them.

What Can Communities Do?

Efforts by law enforcement organizations are unlikely to succeed without active involvement from the community itself. Law enforcement agencies and communities need to work together. As one community leader put it, "We have to educate [the police] about our culture, and they have to educate us about [police] culture." The research suggests several activities for community leaders who want to reach out to local law enforcement agencies:

Start making contacts with law enforcement. Community leaders can invite police officials to events in the community and attend precinct or station meetings in the neighborhood.

Offer cultural and linguistic support services. Leaders can offer to help develop culturally suitable training materials for police officers. They can help lead training sessions that focus on cultural awareness and offer translation services.

Help with recruiting efforts. Leaders can work with law enforcement on recruiting initiatives in their communities.

Promote community awareness about police practices. Leaders can take part in training sessions the police department offers for community members. They can tell the community about such topics as local laws and codes, and how and when to contact the police.

Lobby for a liaison position. Leaders can let their local police department know that a liaison officer would help build trust, and identify community leaders who might fill such a role informally.

Strengthen community organization within and across communities. Leaders can build community solidarity and reach out to other communities in their area. Law enforcement agencies look for strong community leaders who are easily identifiable.

Renewed dedication to the principles of community policing can lead to positive, trusting relations between law enforcement and the Arab-American community—even in the current environment of concern about national security. Both groups want improved relations, and both groups agree that the practices outlined here are a good place to start.

Notes

1. Henderson, Nicole J., Christopher W. Ortiz, Naomi F. Sugie, and Joel Miller, *Law Enforcement & Arab American Community Relations After September 11, 2001: Engagement in a Time of Uncertainty.* New York: Vera Institute of Justice, 2006. Available online at www.vera.org/publication_pdf/353_636.pdf.

2. Naber, N., "Ambiguous Insiders: An Investigation of Arab American Invisibility," *Ethnic and Racial Studies* 23 (2000): 37–61.

3. See Davis, Robert C., and Nicole J. Henderson, "Willingness to Report Crimes: The Role of Ethnic Group Membership and Community Efficacy," *Crime and Delinquency* 49 (4) (October 2003): 564–580; Pogrebin, M.A., and E.D. Poole, "Culture Conflict and Crime in the Korean-American Community," *Criminal Justice Policy Review* 4 (1990): 69–78; Song, J., "Attitudes of Chinese Immigrants and Vietnamese Refugees Toward Law Enforcement in the United States," *Justice Quarterly* 9 (1992): 703–719.

4. Shah, Susan, Insha Rahman, and Anita Khashu, *Overcoming Language Barriers: Solutions for Law Enforcement,* New York: Vera Institute of Justice, and Washington: U.S. Department of Justice, Office of Community Oriented Policing Services, 2007. Available online at www.vera.org/ publication_pdf/ 382_735.pdf.

Critical Thinking

1. Why is false reporting about Arab-Americans a problem for law enforcement?

2. Should American police officers be encouraged to speak languages other than English?

Nicole J. Henderson, Christopher W. Ortiz, and Naomi F. Sugie were with the Vera Institute of Justice when this research was conducted. Joel Miller is currently with the Vera Institute of Justice.

From *NIJ Research for Practice,* July 2008, published by U.S. Department of Justice, Office of Justice Programs, www.ojp.usdoj.gov. Based on "Law Enforcement and Arab-American Community Relations After September 11, 2001: Engagement in a Time of Uncertainty," June 2006 final report to the National Institute of Justice, NCJ 214607. Copyright © 2006 by Vera Institute of Justice, www.vera.org.

Racial Profiling and Its Apologists

Racist law enforcement is rooted in deceptive statistics, slippery logic, and telling indifference.

TIM WISE

"It's just good police work." So comes the insistence by many—usually whites—that concentrating law enforcement efforts on blacks and Latinos is a perfectly legitimate idea. To listen to some folks tell it, the fact that people of color commit a disproportionate amount of crime (a claim that is true for some but not all offenses) is enough to warrant heightened suspicion of such persons. As for the humiliation experienced by those innocents unfairly singled out, stopped, and searched? Well, they should understand that such mistreatment is the price they'll have to pay, as long as others who look like them are heavily represented in various categories of criminal mischief.

Of course, the attempt to rationalize racism and discriminatory treatment has a long pedigree. Segregationists offer up many "rational" arguments for separation and even slaveowners found high-minded justifications for their control over persons of African descent. In the modern day, excuses for unequal treatment may be more nuanced and couched in calm, dispassionate, even academic jargon; but they remain fundamentally no more legitimate than the claims of racists past. From overt white supremacists to respected social scientists and political commentators, the soft-pedaling of racist law enforcement is a growing cottage industry: one rooted in deceptive statistics, slippery logic, and telling indifference to the victims of such practices.

As demonstrated convincingly in David Harris's new book *Profiles in Injustice: Why Racial Profiling Cannot Work* (New Press, 2002), racial profiling is neither ethically acceptable nor logical as a law enforcement tool. But try telling that to the practice's apologists.

According to racial separatist Jared Taylor of American Renaissance—a relatively highbrow white supremacist organization—black crime rates are so disproportionate relative to those of whites that it is perfectly acceptable for police to profile African Americans in the hopes of uncovering criminal activity. His group's report "The Color of Crime"—which has been touted by mainstream conservatives like Walter Williams—purports to demonstrate just how dangerous blacks are, what with murder, robbery, and assault rates that are considerably higher than the rates for whites. That these higher crime rates are the result of economic conditions disproportionately faced by people of color Taylor does not dispute in the report. But he insists that the reasons for the disparities hardly matter. All that need be known is that one group is statistically more dangerous than the other and avoiding those persons or stopping them for searches is not evidence of racism, but rather the result of rational calculations by citizens and police.

Although in simple numerical terms, whites commit three times more violent crimes each year than blacks, and whites are five to six times more likely to be attacked by another white person than by a black person, to Taylor, this is irrelevant. As he has explained about these white criminals: "They may be boobs, but they're our boobs."

Likewise, Heather MacDonald of the conservative Manhattan Institute has written that racial profiling is a "myth." Police, according to MacDonald—whose treatment of the subject was trumpeted in a column by George Will last year—merely play the odds, knowing "from experience" that blacks are likely to be the ones carrying drugs.

Michael Levin, a professor of philosophy at the City College of New York, argues it is rational for whites to fear young black men since one in four are either in prison, on probation, or on parole on any given day. According to Levin, the assumption that one in four black males encountered are therefore likely to be dangerous is logical and hardly indicates racism. Levin has also said that blacks should be treated as adults earlier by the justice system because they mature faster and trials should be shorter for blacks because they have a "shorter time horizon."

Conservative commentator Dinesh D'Souza says that "rational discrimination against young black men can be fully eradicated only by getting rid of destructive conduct by the group that forms the basis for statistically valid group distinctions. It is difficult to compel people to admire groups many of whose members do not act admirably."

Even when the profiling turns deadly, conservatives show little concern. Writing about Amadou Diallo, recipient of 19 bullets (out of 41 fired) from the NYPD Street Crimes Unit, columnist Mona Charen explained that he died for the sins of his black brethren, whose criminal proclivities gave the officers good reason to suspect that he was up to no good.

Putting aside the obvious racial hostility that forms the core of many if not all of these statements, racial profiling cannot be justified on the basis of general crime rate data showing that blacks commit a disproportionate amount of certain crimes, relative to their numbers in the population. Before making this point clear, it is worth clarifying what is meant by racial profiling.

Racial profiling means one of two things. First, the over-application of an incident-specific criminal description in a way that results in the stopping, searching, and harassment of people based solely or mostly on skin color alone. An example would be the decision by police in one upstate New York college town a few years ago to question every black male in the local university after an elderly white woman claimed to have been raped by a black man (turns out he was white).

So while there is nothing wrong with stopping black men who are 6'2", 200 pounds, driving Ford Escorts, if the perp in a particular local crime is known to be 6'2", 200 pounds, and driving a Ford Escort, but when that description is used to randomly stop black men, even who aren't 6'2", aren't close to 200 pounds, and who are driving totally different cars, then that becomes a problem.

The second and more common form of racial profiling is the disproportionate stopping, searching, frisking, and harassment of people of color in the hopes of uncovering a crime, even when there is no crime already in evidence for which a particular description might be available. In other words: stopping black folks or Latinos and searching for drugs.

This is why general crime rates are irrelevant to the profiling issue. Police generally don't randomly stop and search people in the hopes of turning up last night's convenience store hold-up man. They tend to have more specific information to go on in those cases. As such, the fact that blacks commit a higher share of some crimes (robbery, murder, assault) than their population numbers is of no consequence to the issue of whether profiling them is legitimate. The "crime" for which people of color are being profiled mostly is drug possession. In that case, people of color are not a disproportionate number of violators and police do not find such contraband disproportionately on people of color.

All available evidence indicates that whites are equally or more likely to use (and thus possess at any given time) illegal narcotics. This is especially true for young adults and teenagers, in which categories whites are disproportionate among users.

Although black youth and young adults are more likely than white youth to have been approached by someone offering to give them or sell them drugs during the past month, they are less likely to have actually used drugs in the last 30 days. Among adults, data from California is instructive: although whites over the age of 30 are only 36 percent of the state's population, they comprise 60 percent of all heavy drug users in the state.

Although blacks and Latinos often control large drug sale networks, roughly eight in ten drug busts are not for dealing, but for possession. Drug busts for narcotics trafficking rarely stem from random searches of persons or vehicles—the kind of practice rightly labeled profiling—but rather, tend to take place after a carefully devised sting operation and intelligence gathering, leading to focused law enforcement efforts. As such, the usage numbers are the more pertinent when discussing the kinds of police stops and searches covered by the pejorative label of "profiling."

A Department of Justice study released in 2001 notes that although blacks are twice as likely as whites to have their cars stopped and searched, police are actually twice as likely to find evidence of illegal activity in cars driven by whites.

In New Jersey, for 2000, although blacks and Latinos were 78 percent of persons stopped and searched on the southern portion of the Jersey Turnpike, police were twice as likely to discover evidence of illegal activity in cars driven by whites, relative to blacks, and whites were five times more likely to be in possession of drugs, guns, or other illegal items relative to Latinos. In North Carolina, black drivers are two-thirds more likely than whites to be stopped and searched by the State Highway Patrol, but contraband is discovered in cars driven by whites 27 percent more often.

In New York City, even after controlling for the higher crime rates by blacks and Latinos and local demographics (after all, people of color will be the ones stopped and searched most often in communities where they make up most of the residents), police are still two to three times more likely to search them than whites. Yet, police hunches about who is in possession of drugs, guns, other illegal contraband, or who is wanted for commission of a violent crime turn out to be horribly inaccurate. Despite being stopped and searched more often, blacks and Latinos are less likely to be arrested because they are less likely to be found with evidence of criminal wrongdoing.

So much for MacDonald's "rational" police officers, operating from their personal experiences. Despite police claims that they only stop and search people of color more often because such folks engage in suspicious behavior more often, if the "hit rates" for such persons are no higher than, and even lower than the rates for whites, this calls into question the validity of the suspicious action criteria. If blacks seem suspicious more often, but are actually hiding something less often, then by definition the actions deemed suspicious should be reexamined, as they are not proving to be logical at all, let alone the result of good police work. Indeed, they appear to be proxies for racial stops and searches.

Nor can the disproportionate stopping of black vehicles be justified by differential driving behavior. Every study done on the subject has been clear: there are no significant differences between people of color and whites when it comes to the commission of moving or other violations. Police acknowledge that virtually every driver violates any number of minor laws every time they take to the road. But these violations are not enforced equally and that is the problem.

In one New Jersey study, for example, despite no observed differences in driving behavior, African Americans were 73 percent of all drivers stopped on the Jersey Turnpike, despite being less than 14 percent of the drivers on the road: a rate that is 27 times greater than what would be expected by random chance. Similar results were found in a study of stops in Maryland. On a particular stretch of Interstate 95 in Florida, known for being a drug trafficking route, blacks and Latinos comprise only 5 percent of drivers, but 70 percent of those stopped by members of the Highway Patrol. These stops were hardly justified, as only nine drivers, out of 1,100 stopped during the study, were ever ticketed for any violation, let alone arrested for possession of illegal contraband.

As for Levin's claim that whites should properly consider one in four black males encountered to be a threat to their personal safety, because of their involvement with the criminal justice system, it should be remembered that most of these have been arrested for non-violent offenses like drug possession. Blacks comprise 35 percent of all possession arrests and 75 percent of those sent to prison for a drug offense, despite being only 14 percent of users.

When it comes to truly dangerous violent crime, only a miniscule share of African Americans will commit such offenses in a given year and less than half of these will choose a white victim.

With about 1.5 million violent crimes committed by blacks each year (about 90 percent of these by males) and 70 percent of the crimes committed by just 7 percent of the offenders—a commonly accepted figure by criminologists—this means that less than 2 percent of blacks over age 12 (the cutoff for collecting crime data) and less than 3.5 percent of black males over 12 could even theoretically be considered dangerous. Less than 1.5 percent of black males will attack a white person in a given year, hardly lending credence to Levin's claim about the rationality of white panic.

The fact remains that the typical offender in violent crime categories is white. So even if black rates are disproportionate to their population percentages, any "profile" that tends to involve a black or Latino face is likely to be wrong more than half the time. Whites commit roughly 60 percent of violent crimes, for example. So if 6 in 10 violent criminals are white, how logical could it be to deploy a profile—either for purposes of law enforcement or merely personal purposes of avoiding certain people—that is only going to be correct 40 percent of the time? So too with drugs, where any profile that involves a person of color will be wrong three out of four times?

Additionally, the apologists for profiling are typically selective in terms of the kinds of profiling they support. Although whites are a disproportionate percentage of all drunk drivers, for example, and although drunk driving contributes to the deaths of more than 10,000 people each year, none of the defenders of anti-black or brown profiling suggests that drunk driving roadblocks be set up in white suburbs where the "hit rates" for catching violators would be highest.

Likewise, though white college students are considerably more likely to binge drink (often underage) and use narcotics than college students of color, no one suggests that police or campus cops should regularly stage raids on white fraternity houses or dorm rooms occupied by whites, even though

the raw data would suggest such actions might be statistically justified.

Whites are also nearly twice as likely to engage in child sexual molestation, relative to blacks. Yet how would the Heather MacDonalds and Dinesh D'Souzas of the world react to an announcement that adoption agencies were going to begin screening out white couples seeking to adopt, or subjecting them to extra scrutiny, as a result of such factual information?

Similarly, those seeking to now justify intensified profiling of Arabs or Muslims since September 11 were hardly clamoring for the same treatment of white males in the wake of Oklahoma City. Even now, in the wake of anthrax incidents that the FBI says have almost certainly been domestic, possibly white supremacist in origin, no one is calling for heightened suspicion of whites as a result. .

The absurdity of anti-Arab profiling is particularly obvious in the case of trying to catch members of al-Qaeda. The group, after all, operates in 64 countries, many of them non-Arab, and from which group members would not look anything like the image of a terrorist currently locked in the minds of so many. Likewise, Richard Reid, the would-be shoe bomber recently captured was able to get on the plane he sought to bring down precisely because he had a "proper English name," likely spoke with a proper English accent, and thus, didn't fit the description.

The bottom line is that racial profiling doesn't happen because data justifies the practice, but rather because those with power are able to get away with it, and find it functional to do so as a mechanism of social control over those who are less powerful. By typifying certain "others" as dangerous or undesirable, those seeking to maintain divisions between people whose economic and social interests are actually quite similar can successfully maintain those cleavages.

No conspiracy here, mind you: just the system working as intended, keeping people afraid of one another and committed to the maintenance of the system, by convincing us that certain folks are a danger to our well-being, which then must be safeguarded by a growing prison-industrial complex and draconian legal sanctions; or in the case of terrorist "profiles," by the imposition of unconstitutional detentions, beefed-up military and intelligence spending, and the creation of a paranoiac wartime footing.

Until and unless the stereotypes that underlie racial profiling are attacked and exposed as a fraud, the practice will likely continue: not because it makes good sense, but because racist assumptions about danger—reinforced by media and politicians looking for votes—lead us to think that it does.

Critical Thinking

1. What's wrong with racial profiling to catch drug dealers?
2. What are the arguements in favour of racial profiling?
3. Are the conservatives' arguments adequately addressed?

TIM WISE is a Nashville-based writer, lecturer and antiracist activist. Footnotes for this article can be obtained at tjwise@mindspring.com.

Our Oath of Office: A Solemn Promise

JONATHAN L. RUDD

Early in the morning, on their first full day at the FBI Academy, 50 new-agent trainees, dressed in conservative suits and more than a little anxious about their new careers, stand as instructed by the assistant director of the FBI and raise their right hands. In unison, the trainees repeat the following words as they are sworn in as employees of the federal government:

> I [name] do solemnly swear (or affirm) that I will support and defend the Constitution of the United States against all enemies, foreign and domestic; that I will bear true faith and allegiance to the same; that I take this obligation freely, without any mental reservation or purpose of evasion; and that I will well and faithfully discharge the duties of the office on which I am about to enter. So help me God.

At the end of their academy training, and as part of the official graduation ceremony, these same new-agent trainees once again will stand, raise their right hands, and repeat the same oath. This time, however, the oath will be administered by the director of the FBI, and the trainees will be sworn in as special agents of the Federal Bureau of Investigation.[1] Similar types of ceremonies are conducted in every state, by every law enforcement agency, for every officer across the country. And, each officer promises to do one fundamentally important thing—support and defend the Constitution of the United States.

All too often in our culture, we participate in ceremonies and follow instructions without taking the time to contemplate and understand the meaning and significance of our actions. This article attempts to shed some light on the purpose and history of the oath and to further enhance our understanding of the Constitution that we as law enforcement officers solemnly swear to uphold.

Origins of the Oath

The idea of taking an oath in support of a government, ruler, or cause was not new to the founding fathers. The practice stems from ancient times and was common in England and in the American colonies. "During the American Revolution, General George Washington required all officers to subscribe to an oath renouncing any allegiance to King George III and pledging their fidelity to the United States."[2]

When asked where the requirement that all law enforcement officers take an oath to support and defend the Constitution comes from, some have speculated that it is linked to the presidential oath found in the Constitution.[3] They reason that because the president is the chief executive and law enforcement officers are generally seen as members of the executive branch of government, the requirement to take an oath is inferred from Article II of the Constitution. Others assume that it comes from statutes enacted by Congress and the various state legislatures. Most are surprised to learn that the requirement to take an oath is found in the Constitution itself. Article VI mandates that both federal and state officers of all three branches of government (legislative, executive, and judicial) take an oath to support the Constitution of the United States.

> The Senators and Representatives [. . .], and the Members of the several State Legislatures, and all executive and judicial Officers, both of the United States and of the several States, shall be bound by Oath or Affirmation, to support this Constitution [. . .].[4]

Wording of the Oath

Unlike the presidential oath, the particular wording of this oath is not delineated in the Constitution, merely the requirement that an oath be taken. As suspected, the wording of the oath has been formulated by the federal and state legislatures.

The significance the founding generation placed on the requirement to take an oath as mandated in Article VI is highlighted by the fact that the very first act of the first Congress of the United States was to establish a simple 14-word oath: "I do solemnly swear (or affirm) that I will support the Constitution of the United States."[5]

From the founding of our new government until the Civil War era, this simple oath adequately served its intended purpose. However, in April 1861, in light of the conflicts surrounding the Civil War, President Abraham Lincoln demanded that all federal, executive branch employees take an expanded oath in support of the Union. Shortly thereafter, at an emergency session of Congress, legislation was enacted requiring all employees to take the expanded oath. By the end of the year, Congress had revised the expanded oath and added a new section, creating what came to be known as the Ironclad Test Oath or Test Oath.[6] "The war-inspired Test Oath, signed into law on July 2, 1862, required 'every person elected or appointed to any office . . . under the Government of the United States . . . excepting the President of the United States' to swear or affirm that they had never previously engaged in criminal or disloyal conduct."[7]

As early as 1868, Congress created an alternative oath for individuals unable to take the Test Oath "on account of their participation in the late rebellion."[8] Nearly two decades later, Congress repealed the Test Oath and mandated the federal oath of office we have today.[9] This oath, taken by most federal employees, can be found in Title 5, U.S. Code, § 3331.[10]

State officers, on the other hand, are required by federal statute to take the original oath first promulgated in 1789.[11] In addition to this requirement, state constitutions and legislatures have generally added words and sentiments appropriate to their respective states. One obvious addition is the dual requirement to support and defend not only the federal Constitution but also the constitution and laws of the individual state.[12]

Meaning of the Oath

At the core of each of these oaths, whether the federal oath in its current form or the various state oaths with their additional obligations, lies the simple language put forth by our first Congress: "I do solemnly swear that I will support and defend the Constitution of the United States."

A brief analysis of these words and their meanings may help to solidify their significance. "I . . . "—an individual, person, citizen, one member of the whole, officer; "do"—perform, accomplish, act, carry out, complete, achieve, execute; "solemnly"—somberly, gravely, seriously, earnestly, sincerely, firmly, fervently, with thought and ceremony; "swear (or affirm)"[13]—vow, pledge, promise, guarantee; "that I will"—a positive phrase confirming present and future action, momentum, determination, resolve, responsibility, willpower, and intention; "support"—uphold, bear, carry, sustain, maintain; "and defend"—protect, guard, preserve, secure, shield, look after; "the Constitution of the United States."

The Constitution of the United States

It is significant that we take an oath to support and defend the Constitution and not an individual leader, ruler, office, or entity. This is true for the simple reason that the Constitution is based on lasting principles of sound government that provide balance, stability, and consistency through time. A government based on individuals—who are inconsistent, fallible, and often prone to error—too easily leads to tyranny on the one extreme or anarchy on the other. The founding fathers sought to avoid these extremes and create a balanced government based on constitutional principles.

The American colonists were all too familiar with the harmful effects of unbalanced government and oaths to individual rulers. For example, the English were required to swear loyalty to the crown, and many of the early colonial documents commanded oaths of allegiance to the king.[14] The founding fathers saw that such a system was detrimental to the continued liberties of a free people. A study of both ancient and modern history illustrates this point. One fairly recent example can be seen in the oaths of Nazi Germany. On August 19, 1934, 90 percent of Germany voted for Hitler to assume complete power. The very next day, Hitler's cabinet decreed the Law On the Allegiance of Civil Servants and Soldiers of the Armed Forces. This law abolished all former oaths and required that all soldiers and public servants declare an oath of unquestioned obedience to "Adolf Hitler, Fuhrer of the German Reich and people."[15] Although many of the officers in Hitler's regime came to realize the error of his plans, they were reluctant to stop him because of the oath of loyalty they had taken to the Fuhrer.[16]

The founding fathers diligently sought to avoid the mistakes of other nations and, for the first time in history, form a balanced government where freedom could reign. To appreciate this ideal, we first must acknowledge what some have called the preface or architectural blueprint to the Constitution—the Declaration of Independence.[17] "While the Declaration of Independence, as promulgated on July 4, 1776, did not bring this nation into existence or establish the government of the United States of America, it magnificently enunciated the fundamental principles of republican or constitutional government—principals that are not stated explicitly in the Constitution itself."[18] The essence of these fundamental principles were memorialized when Thomas Jefferson penned the famous words

> We hold these truths to be self-evident, that all men are created equal, that they are endowed by their Creator with certain unalienable Rights, that among these are Life, Liberty and the pursuit of Happiness. That to secure these rights, Governments are instituted among Men, deriving their just powers from the consent of the governed. . . .[19]

Once the colonists declared their independence from Great Britain, they knew they needed a form of government that would keep the 13 colonies united. However, many were skeptical of creating a central government that would destroy their independence as separate and sovereign states. The result was the creation of the Articles of Confederation and Perpetual Union, which lasted only 7 years. This document provided for a weak legislative body and no judicial or executive branch.

Although some have referred to the Articles of Confederation as America's first constitution, it never was given that status by the colonists. American colonists were familiar with, and placed great emphasis on, the supremacy of written constitutions. Immediately following the Declaration of Independence, in addition to creating the Articles of Confederation, 11 of the 13 colonies drafted and ratified state constitutions. The inferiority of the Articles of Confederation can be seen by the fact that "[m]ost of the new state constitutions included elaborate oaths that tied allegiance to and provided a summary of the basic constitutional principles animating American constitutionalism. There was no oath in the Articles of Confederation."[20]

> The Articles of Confederation provided the Federal Government with too little authority to maintain law, order and equality among the new states. So America's best minds came together once again in Philadelphia, where they had declared their independence from Britain 11 years before, and hammered together a far better government for themselves, creating a Constitution that has served Americans well for more than 200 years now.[21]

The Constitution was not miraculously formulated by ideas invented by the founding fathers during the Constitutional Convention. To the contrary, in the years preceding the "Miracle at Philadelphia," Thomas Jefferson, James Madison, Benjamin Franklin, Samuel Adams, John Adams, John Jay, Alexander Hamilton, George Wythe, James Wilson, and others made every effort to study and comprehend the nature and politics of truly free government.[22] During the Revolutionary War, John Adams wrote the following to his wife:

> The science of government is my duty to study, more than all other sciences; the arts of legislation and administration and

negotiation ought to take [the] place of, indeed to exclude, in manner, all other arts. I must study politics and war, that my sons may have liberty to study mathematics and philosophy. My sons ought to study mathematics and philosophy, geography, natural history and naval architecture, navigation, commerce, and agriculture, in order to give their children the right to study painting, poetry, music, architecture, statuary, tapestry, and porcelain.[23]

Based on these studies and the collective wisdom of these men, the Constitution our founding fathers created was an amazingly concise, yet comprehensive, document. Comprising a mere seven articles, it embodies the fundamental principles of popular sovereignty, separation of powers, and federalism, allows for a process of amendment, and provides a system of checks and balances. A closer look at these principles and how they apply to law enforcement today may be instructive.

The Preamble and Popular Sovereignty

It has been said that the Preamble sets forth the goals or purposes of the Constitution.[24] When read from the perspective of a law enforcement officer, the purposes described therein could be seen as a mission statement for today's law enforcement community.

> . . . in Order to form a more perfect Union, establish Justice, insure domestic Tranquility, provide for the common defense, promote the general Welfare, and secure the Blessings of Liberty to ourselves and our Posterity. . . .

The opening and closing words of the Preamble—"We the people of the United States [. . .] do ordain and establish this Constitution for the United States of America"—embrace the idea of "popular sovereignty," a government ordained and established by the consent of the people. From the outset, then, we see that this new government was to be different from any government then in existence. It was not a monarchy where the rule of one could easily lead to tyranny; it was not an aristocracy where the rule of a privileged few could descend into oligarchy, nor was it even to be a pure democracy where mob rule could slip into anarchy.[25] The American dream was to be founded on a constitutional republic where elected representatives swear to uphold the Constitution as they serve at the will and by the consent of the people. This was something "[s]o rare that some historians maintain it has been accomplished only three times during all of human history: Old Testament Israel, the Golden Age of Greece, and the era of emergence of the United States of America."[26]

Separation of Powers and Federalism

The structure of the Constitution itself emphasizes the principle of separation of powers. Article I established the legislative branch with the power to make laws; Article II, the executive branch with the authority to enforce the laws; and Article III, the judicial branch with jurisdiction over legal disputes. "It is important to note that the Constitution in no way granted the federal courts the power of judicial review, or an ultimate interpretive power over the constitutional issues. Modern federal courts possess this

huge power thanks to a long series of precedents beginning with the 1803 case of Marbury v. Madison."[27] Under the doctrine of separation of powers, each branch of government specializes in its particular area of expertise with no one branch having ultimate power over the whole.

Another aspect of the separation of powers, which is of significance to law enforcement today, is the principle of federalism. Federalism is a legal and political system where the national or federal government shares power with the state governments while each maintains some degree of sovereignty.[28] The Constitution helps to delineate the roles of the federal government by spelling out, to some degree, its limited powers, which are outlined in the first three Articles. Section 10 of Article I also places specific, limited restrictions on the states; however, these restrictions actually serve to emphasize the powers reserved exclusively to the federal government (e.g., the power to make treaties with other nations). Article IV delineates a few fundamental requirements incumbent upon state governments, as well as guaranteeing to each state a republican form of government. Other than the limited guidance given to the states, the Constitution does not direct the states on the establishment and functions of state governments. The idea is that there are certain limited activities the federal government is best situated to handle; there are other activities that are best left to the states; and still others best dealt with by counties, cities, families, and individuals.

Under this system of government, the founding fathers realized that conflicts between state and federal jurisdiction would arise. Accordingly, in Article VI of the Constitution, they designated the Constitution itself and other federal laws as "the supreme Law of the Land."[29] This clause (known as the supremacy clause) serves as a "conflict-of-laws rule specifying that certain national acts take priority over any state acts that conflict with national law."[30]

The Bill of Rights and the Fourteenth Amendment

Although the federal government was intended to be a government of limited powers, there were many who feared the inevitable expansion of those powers, particularly in light of the supremacy clause. Without the promise of a Bill of Rights limiting the power of the federal government, the Constitution never would have been ratified. Accordingly, "a total of 189 suggested amendments were submitted to [the first] Congress. James Madison boiled these down to 17, but the Congress approved only 12 of them."[31] The states ended up ratifying 10 as amendments to the Constitution, which became known as the Bill of Rights.

Included within the Bill of Rights are a number of provisions that have had a great impact on criminal law enforcement. In particular, the First Amendment freedoms of religion, speech, press, and assembly; the Fourth Amendment restrictions on unreasonable searches and seizures; the Fifth Amendment protection against compelled self-incrimination; and the Sixth Amendment guarantee of the right to counsel in all criminal prosecutions. The Bill of Rights, however, initially served only as a limitation on the federal government and did not apply to the states. While states had their own state constitutions with their own bills of rights, individual state officers were not bound to provide the protections afforded the people under the federal Constitution. This changed, however, with the adoption of the Fourteenth Amendment in 1868, just 3 years after the end of the Civil War.[32]

Over time, via the Fourteenth Amendment's due process clause, the Supreme Court has selectively incorporated most of the provisions of the Bill of Rights and applied them to the states, thereby unifying fundamental criminal procedure law throughout the United States.

> Today, every law enforcement academy in America provides training in constitutional law, because virtually every aspect of an officer's job touches that area where the authority of government and the liberty of the individual meet. Arrests, searches and seizures, investigative detentions, eyewitness identification, interrogations—all of these everyday law enforcement tasks, and more, are governed by the Federal Constitution. Under their own constitutions, the States may provide greater protections to their people; but by virtue of the Due Process Clause of the 14th amendment, they cannot provide less.[33]

Due, in part, to major paradigm shifts regarding the rights and freedoms of individuals, which gained momentum during the Civil War, the enactment of the Fourteenth Amendment and the Supreme Court's interpretation of its due process clause, and the many advances in the area of technology, communication, and transportation, the federalism that prevailed in the first half of our country's existence is very different from the federalism of today. "Since the New Deal of the 1930s, more and more areas of American law, government, and life have crossed an invisible line from state responsibility into the federal domain."[34] While some lament the far-reaching power of today's federal government, in the area of law enforcement, most of these changes have been welcome, particularly when they have allowed local, state, and federal law enforcement agencies to pool their resources and fight crime, which itself continues to defy jurisdictional boundaries.

Checks and Balances

Finally, the founding fathers built a system of checks and balances into the Constitution, whereby the executive, legislative, and judiciary would check and balance each other and state governments would balance the federal while it, in turn, would maintain a check on the states.[35] When considering our system of checks and balances, obvious examples surface, such as when the president (executive) nominates judges to serve on the Supreme Court (judicial) with the advice and consent of the Senate (legislative). However, nowhere is the use and effect of checks and balances more poignantly illustrated than in the everyday lives of today's law enforcement officers. For example, when officers determine that they have enough probable cause to search a home or make an arrest, barring special limited circumstances, they do not execute the search or arrest of their own accord and based on their singular authority as members of the executive branch. To the contrary, they seek the review and approval of a neutral and detached magistrate—a member of the judicial branch. Even though they may not realize it, every time officers prepare an affidavit and request approval of a warrant, they are engaging in the process of checks and balances so painstakingly advanced by our founding fathers over two centuries ago.

While debates were raging among colonists over whether or not to ratify the Constitution, which had recently been adopted by the Constitutional Convention, the father of the Constitution, James Madison, wrote the following insightful words:

> Ambition must be made to counteract ambition. The interest of the man must be connected with the constitutional rights of the place. . . . If men were angels, no government would be necessary. If angels were to govern men, neither external nor internal controls on government would be necessary. In framing a government which is to be administered by men over men, the great difficulty lies in this: you must first enable the government to control the governed; and in the next place oblige it to control itself.[36]

The most fundamental of the many checks and balances in our system of government is the power to control oneself. At no time is a commitment to this principle more eloquently expressed than when individual officers raise their hands and solemnly swear to support and defend the Constitution of the United States. May all of us do so with a firm understanding of the principles we have determined to defend and a clear recognition of the people we promise to protect.

Conclusion

We owe an incomparable debt of gratitude to the men and women who fought to bring us the Constitution, and those who have fought to preserve it to this day. In memory of the federal, state, and local law enforcement officers who have made the ultimate sacrifice in the service of this country, may we read the words of President Lincoln anew and rededicate our lives to the privilege of protecting and defending the Constitution of the United States.

> Four score and seven years ago our fathers brought forth on this continent a new nation, conceived in liberty and dedicated to the proposition that all men are created equal.
>
> Now we are engaged in a great civil war, testing whether that nation, or any nation so conceived and so dedicated, can long endure. We are met on a great battlefield of that war. We have come to dedicate a portion of that field as a final resting place for those who here gave their lives that that nation might live. It is altogether fitting and proper that we should do this.
>
> But in a larger sense, we cannot dedicate—we cannot consecrate—we cannot hallow—this ground. The brave men, living and dead, who struggled here have consecrated it far above our poor power to add or detract. The world will little note nor long remember what we say here, but it can never forget what they did here. It is for us the living, rather, to be dedicated here to the unfinished work which they who fought here have thus far so nobly advanced.
>
> It is rather for us to be here dedicated to the great task remaining before us—that from these honored dead we take increased devotion to that cause for which they gave the last full measure of devotion; that we here highly resolve that these dead shall not have died in vain; that this nation, under God, shall have a new birth of freedom; and that government of the people, by the people, for the people shall not perish from the earth.[37]

Notes

1. 5 U.S.C. § 3331, infra at endnote 10. See also 5 U.S.C. § 2905 (a) which leaves the decision of whether or not to renew the oath due to a change in status to the discretion of the head of the executive agency.

2. Edwin Meese III et al. eds., 2005, *The Heritage Guide to the Constitution*, Article VI, Oaths Clause by Matthew Spalding, 294–295.

3. *U.S. Const.*, art. II, § 1, cl. 8, which states

   Before he enter on the Execution of his Office, he shall take the following Oath or Affirmation:—"I do solemnly swear (or affirm) that I will faithfully execute the Office of President of the United States, and will to the best of my ability, preserve, protect and defend the Constitution of the United States."

   (For insight regarding whether or not George Washington added the words so help me God to the end of the oath of office he took in 1789, see Forrester Church, *So Help Me God: The Founding Fathers and the First Great Battle Over Church and State*, 2007, 445.).

4. *U.S. Const.*, art. VI, cl. 3.

5. *United States Statutes at Large*, Vol. I, Statute I, Chapter 1, §§ 1–5, June 1, 1789, which, in pertinent part reads

   STATUTE I.
   Chapter I.—An Act to regulate the Time and Manner of administering certain Oaths.

   Sec. 1. Be it enacted by the Senate and [House of] Representatives of the United States of America in Congress assembled. That the oath or affirmation required by the sixth article of the Constitution of the United States, shall be administered in the form following, to wit: "I, A.B. do solemnly swear or affirm (as the case may be) that I will support the Constitution of the United States." [. . .]

   Sec. 3. And be it further enacted, That the members of the several State legislatures [. . .], and all executive and judicial officers of the several States, who have been heretofore chosen or appointed, or who shall be chosen or appointed [. . .] shall, before they proceed to execute the duties of their respective offices, take the foregoing oath or affirmation [. . .].

   Sec. 4. And be it further enacted, That all officers appointed, or hereafter to be appointed under the authority of the United States, shall, before they act in their respective offices, take the same oath or affirmation [. . .].

6. *Revised Statutes of the United States: First Session of the 43rd Congress*, 1873–74, Part 1, 1st Edition, 1875, Title XIX, Section 1756, which states the July 2, 1862, statute as follows:

   Every person elected or appointed to any office of honor or profit, either in the civil, military, or naval service, excepting the President [. . .], shall, before entering upon the duties of such office, and before being entitled to any part of the salary or other emoluments thereof, take and subscribe the following oath: "I, AB, do solemnly swear (or affirm) that I have never voluntarily borne arms against the United States since I have been a citizen thereof; that I have voluntarily given no aid, countenance, counsel, or encouragement to persons engaged in armed hostility thereto; that I have neither sought, nor accepted, nor attempted to exercise the functions of any office whatever, under any authority, or pretended authority, in hostility to the United States; that I have not yielded a voluntary support to any pretended government, authority, power, or constitution within the United States, hostile or inimical thereto. And I do further swear (or affirm) that, to the best of my knowledge and ability, I will support and defend the Constitution of the United States against all enemies, foreign and domestic; that I will bear true faith and allegiance to the same; that I take this obligation freely, without any mental reservation or purpose of evasion, and that I will well and faithfully discharge the duties of the office on which I am about to enter, so help me God."

7. U.S. Senate: Oath of Office (http://www.senate.gov/artandhistory/history/common/briefing/Oath_Office.htm).

8. *Revised Statutes of the United States: First Session of the 43rd Congress*, 1873–74, Part 1, 1st Edition, 1875, Title XIX, Section 1757, which states the July 11, 1868, statute as

   Whenever any person who is not rendered ineligible to office by the provisions of the Fourteenth Amendment to the Constitution is elected or appointed to any office of honor or trust under the Government of the United States, and is not able, on account of his participation in the late rebellion, to take the oath prescribed in the preceding section, he shall, before entering upon the duties of his office, take and subscribe in lieu of that oath the following oath: "I, AB, do solemnly swear (or affirm) that I will support and defend the Constitution of the United States against all enemies, foreign and domestic; that I will bear true faith and allegiance to the same; that I take this obligation freely, without any mental reservation or purpose of evasion, and that I will well and faithfully discharge the duties of the office on which I am about to enter. So help me God."

9. *United States Statutes at Large*, Vol. 23, p. 22, Chapter 46, Sec. 2 (May 13, 1884).

10. 5 U.S.C. § 3331, which states

    An individual, except the President, elected or appointed to an office of honor or profit in the civil service or uniformed services, shall take the following oath: "I, AB, do solemnly swear (or affirm) that I will support and defend the Constitution of the United States against all enemies, foreign and domestic: that I will bear true faith and allegiance to the same; that I take this obligation freely, without any mental reservation or purpose of evasion, and that I will well and faithfully discharge the duties of the office on which I am about to enter. So help me God." This section does not affect other oaths required by law.

11. 4 U.S.C. § 101 (July 30, 1947), which states

    Every member of a State legislature, and every executive and judicial officer of a State, shall, before he proceeds to execute the duties of his office, take an oath in the following form, to wit: "I, AB, do solemnly swear that I will support the Constitution of the United States."

12. For example, see *Constitution of Kentucky* § 228 Oath of Officers [. . .] as ratified and revised 1891

    Members of the General Assembly and all officers, before they enter upon the execution of the duties of their respective offices [. . .], shall take the following oath or affirmation: I do solemnly swear (or affirm, as the case may be) that I will support the Constitution of the United States, and the Constitution of this Commonwealth, and be faithful and true to the Commonwealth of Kentucky so long as I continue a citizen thereof, and that I will faithfully execute, to the best of my ability, the office of_____according to law: and I do further solemnly swear (or affirm) that since the adoption of the present Constitution. I, being a citizen of this State, have not fought a duel with deadly weapons within this State nor out of it. Nor have I sent or accepted a challenge to fight a duel with deadly weapons, nor have I acted as second in carrying a challenge, nor aided or assisted a person thus offending, so help me God.

13. The delegates to the first Congress allowed for the word affirm to be used instead of swear to appease those whose religious beliefs forbid them from taking oaths. See *Heritage Guide*, 295.

14. *Heritage Guide*, 294.

15. William Shirer, *The Rise and Fall of the Third Reich*. New York, NY: Simon & Schuster, 1990, 226–230.

    Service oath for soldiers of the armed forces: "I swear by God this sacred oath that I shall render unconditional obedience to Adolf Hitler, the Fuhrer of the German Reich and people, supreme commander of the armed forces, and that I shall at all times be ready, as a brave soldier, to give my life for this oath." Service oath for public servants: "I swear: I will be faithful and obedient to Adolf Hitler, Fuhrer of the German Reich and people, to observe the law, and to conscientiously fulfil, my official duties, so help me God."

16. Id.

17. Mortimer J. Adler, *We Hold These Truths: Understanding the Ideas and Ideals of the Constitution*, Collier Books. Macmillan Publishing Company (1987).

18. Id. at 7.

19. *The Declaration of Independence* (July 4, 1776).

20. *Heritage Guide*, 295.

21. *The Making of America: Life, Liberty and the Pursuit of a Nation*, by the Editors of Time, vi.

22. W. Cleon Skousen, *The Making of America: The Substance and Meaning of the Constitution*, The National Center For Constitutional Studies (1986). 41.

23. W. Cleon Skousen, *The Five Thousand Year Leap: 28 Great Ideas that Changed the World* (1981, 2009), p. 146, quoting from Adrienne Koch, ed., *The American Enlightenment*, George Braziller, New York, 1965, 163.

24. "The Preamble was placed in the Constitution more or less as an afterthought. It was not proposed or discussed on the floor of the Constitution. Rather, Gouverneur Morris, a delegate from Pennsylvania who as a member of the Committee of Style actually drafted the near-final text of the Constitution, composed it at the last moment. It was Morris who gave the considered purposes of the Constitution coherent shape, and the Preamble was the capstone of his expository gift. The Preamble did not, in itself, have any substantive legal meaning." *Heritage Guide*, 43.

25. Referencing the teachings of the Greek Historian Polybius who lived from 204 to 122 B.C. as quoted in Skousen, *The Five Thousand Year Leap*, 142.

26. Floyd G. Cullop, *The Constitution of the United States: An Introduction*, Mentor (1999), preface to the third edition. (The United States is the oldest continuous government based on a written constitution in the world.)

27. Larry Schweikart and Michael Allen, *A Patriot's History of the United States: From Columbus's Great Discovery to the War on Terror*, Sentinel, Penguin Group (2004), 117.

28. Lawrence M. Friedman, *American Law: An Introduction*, Second Edition, W. W. Norton & Company (1998), 146.

29. *U.S. Const.*, art. VI, cl. 2.

30. *Heritage Guide*, 291.

31. Skousen, *The Making of America*. 673.

32. John C. Hall, "The Constitution and Criminal Procedure," FBI Law Enforcement Bulletin, September 1986. 24–30.

33. Id. at 30.

34. Friedman. *American Law*, 160.

35. Id, at 161.

36. Charles R. Kesler ed., *The Federalist Papers*, No. 51: The Structure of the Government Must Furnish the Proper Checks and Balances Between the Different Departments (Madison).

37. *The Gettysburg Address*, by President Abraham Lincoln, November 19, 1863.

Critical Thinking

1. Do you believe FBI agents are aware of the oath as they go about their daily activities?

2. Should the oath contain anything else?

3. Should the oath be suspended in order to deal with emergency situations?

Law enforcement officers of other than federal jurisdiction who are interested in this article should consult their legal advisors. Some police procedures ruled permissible under federal constitutional law are of questionable legality under state law or are not permitted at all.

From *FBI Law Enforcement Bulletin*, September 1, 2009. Written by Jonathan L. Rudd. Published by Federal Bureau of Investigation. www.fbi.gov

Police Investigations of the Use of Deadly Force Can Influence Perceptions and Outcomes

"When a police officer kills someone in the line of duty—or is killed—it sets in motion a series of internal and external reviews and public debate that normally does not end until several years later when the civil and criminal court trials are over."[1]

SHANNON BOHRER, MBA AND ROBERT CHANEY

Basic law enforcement training covers using force, including deadly force, and investigating crimes, even those involving assaults and shootings by police. The relationship between these two events—the use of force and the police investigation of this use of force—can have far-reaching consequences, both good and bad, for the public, the department, and the officers involved.[2]

The law enforcement profession spends considerable time and resources training officers to use firearms and other weapons and to understand the constitutional standards and agency policies concerning when they can employ such force. Society expects this effort because of the possible consequences of officers not having the skills they need if and when they become involved in a critical incident.

In addition to receiving instruction about the use of force, officers are taught investigative techniques. They must reconstruct the incident, find the facts, and gather evidence to prosecute the offenders. And, historically, they have done this extremely well. But, is the same amount of attention paid to examining the investigative process of the use of deadly force and how this can affect what occurs after such an event? Are there any reasons why the police should approach the investigation of an officer involved shooting differently? To help answer these questions, the authors present an overview of perceptions about these events and some elements that law enforcement agencies can incorporate into investigations of officer-involved shootings that can help ensure fair and judicious outcomes.

Perceptions of Deadly Force

All law enforcement training is based on the two elements of criticality and frequency. Skills that officers need and are required to have to perform their duties fall into both: 1) how often they use them and 2) how crucial it is to have them. Training officers to handle potentially lethal incidents, by nature, is vitally important. Investigating officer involved shootings constitutes a critical function, but, for most departments, it does not occur that frequently. Only examining training needs from the perspective of preparation for the event does not necessarily take into account what can occur afterward. Just because the officer had the right to shoot and the evidence supports the officer's actions may not guarantee a positive, or even a neutral, reception from the public.

In addition, *who* the police shoot seems to mold some perceptions. For example, a bank robber armed with a shotgun presents a different connotation than a 14-year-old thief wielding a knife.[3] Sometimes, it is who the police shoot that also can set the tone for the direction of the investigation surrounding the incident.

The Officer's Perception

Interviews conducted with officers who have been involved in shootings have revealed that while many were well trained for the event, they often were not prepared for the investigation afterward.[4] Some believed that these investigations centered on finding something that officers did wrong so they could be charged with a crime or a violation of departmental policy.[5] Others felt that the investigations were for the protection of the agency and not necessarily the officers involved.[6]

Officers can have broad perceptions that often depend upon their experiences of being involved in a critical incident or knowledge of what has happened to other officers. A trooper with the Arizona Department of Public Safety commented, "I did not choose to take that man's life. . . . He chose to die when he drew a gun on an officer. It was not my choice; it was his."[7]

The Public's Perception

Perceptions by the public of officer-involved shootings usually are as wide and diverse as the population, often driven by media coverage, and sometimes influenced by a long-standing bias and mistrust of government.[8] Documented cases of riots, property damage, and loss of life have occurred in communities where residents have perceived a police shooting as unjustified. Some members of the public seem to automatically assume that the officer did something wrong before any investigation into the incident begins. Conversely, others believe that if the police shot somebody, the individual must not have given the officer any choice.

The Department's Perception

Departmental perceptions can prove diverse and difficult to express. For example, when interviewed, one chief of police advised that "it is sometimes easier to go through an officer being killed in the line of duty than a questionable police shooting."[9] The chief was referring to the public's response, including civil unrest, to what was perceived as an unjustified police shooting. At various levels, however, administrators may feel that a full and fair investigation will clear up any negative perceptions by the public. While not all-inclusive, departmental perceptions include many instances when an officer-involved shooting was viewed with clear and objective clarity before, during, and after the investigation.[10]

Perceptions by the public of officer-involved shootings usually are as wide and diverse as the population . . .

Elements of the Investigation

Few events in law enforcement attract the attention of the media, the political establishment, and the police administration more than an officer-involved shooting. In some instances, such intense interest can affect the investigation. Is this scrutiny related to the incident, the investigation, or both? Does it affect the focus and outcome of the investigation? And, conversely, can the investigative process influence this close observation of the incident?[11]

With these issues in mind, the authors offer six elements for investigating officer-involved shootings. While they are not meant to be all-inclusive or broad enough to cover every conceivable situation, they can be useful as a guide.

The Investigators

The first element involves investigators who have correct and neutral attitudes. Not all officers are suited to conducting police-shooting investigations. Examining such incidents requires open-minded, experienced investigators who have empathy toward the involved officers and members of the general public. Starting with the right investigators will ensure that the process has a solid foundation.

If possible, at least two primary investigators should oversee the case from the beginning until the end. They should be responsible for such activities as supervising the crime scene investigation, reviewing witness statements and evidence and laboratory reports, and coordinating with the criminal justice system. They should not be heavily involved in the initial routine investigation except for handling the interaction with the involved officers, including taking statements.

The Crime Scene

The second element entails the appropriate response to and protection of the crime scene. Homicide or criminal investigators should protect the site. They need to take their time and broaden the protected area, possibly adding a safety zone beyond the immediate vicinity. They should establish a press area with a public information officer available to respond to media inquiries.

Before inspecting the crime scene, the investigators should videotape it and the surroundings and then periodically videotape the area, along with any crowds and parked vehicles, during the course of the examination. Such information may prove valuable later in locating additional witnesses. They should use up-to-date technology and evidence-gathering methods, calling on experts as needed.

Before releasing the crime scene, the investigators should consult with the criminal justice officials who will be responsible for the case. It can be easier to explain the circumstances of the incident while still in control of the location where it occurred.[12]

The Involved Officers

Removing the involved officers from the scene as soon as possible and taking them to a secure location away from other witnesses and media personnel constitute the third element. The investigators need to explain to the officers that these actions will help maintain the integrity of the case. They also should invite the officers to stay within a protected area to participate in the follow-up investigation. When possible, they should only take statements from the involved officers once they clearly understand all of the facts and crime scene information. Moreover, in the initial and early stages of the investigation, authorities never should release the names or any personal information of the involved officers.[13]

Interviews conducted with officers who have been involved in shootings have revealed that . . . they often were not prepared for the investigation afterward.

Sometimes, it is beneficial for involved officers to revisit the crime scene later to help them recall events. If at all possible, the investigators should accompany them.

It is important to keep the involved officers informed. Someone should contact them on a regular basis. In many agencies, the officers have advocates, including peer support, union representation, and legal aid. Keeping the officers advised may require the investigators to go through the advocate.[14]

The Civilian Witnesses

The fourth element highlights the importance of investigators gaining the confidence and respect of civilian witnesses. After all, they need their assistance. In most cases, investigators should handle them the same way as involved officers.

Before interviewing the witnesses, investigators should have a full understanding of the crime scene and the facts of the shooting. If any statements conflict with the crime scene examination or information from other people who observed the incident, investigators should have the witnesses view a crime scene videotape or take them back to the site to help them recall events. They may wish to consult with the criminal justice investigating authority beforehand to ensure that the revisit does not invade the privacy or cause harm to the witnesses. And, of course, investigating authorities never should release any information concerning the witnesses.

The Criminal Justice Authorities

The fifth element, the need to have these cases vetted through the criminal justice process as soon as possible, proves critical to the involved officers, their families, and their employing agencies. Sometimes, backlogs may delay report completion but should not hinder clearance procedures.[15] Close consultation with the appropriate criminal justice authority may alleviate the need for a completed formal report if a written statement for the proper authority confirms the facts. For example, medical examiners and ballistic experts can provide their findings to investigators with formal reports to follow.

Presentations of the investigation should include all videotapes, photographs, and copies of all statements, investigative reports, and other necessary documents. Throughout the criminal justice proceedings, investigators should update the involved officers and their departments about the progress of the case.

The Media

As the final element, the department's public information officer should contact the media before their representatives approach the agency.[16] In the early stages of the investigation, the department should demonstrate that it wants to cooperate with the media. By informing the public through press releases and interviews, the agency shows that it is investigating the incident and that as information *can* be released, it *will* be. Departments should remember that the proverbial "no comment" often gives the impression that the police are hiding something.

Without a positive relationship with the media, poor communication between the public and the police can develop, creating a lack of faith in the management and operations of the department and mistrust from all parties. The time to prepare press releases for officer-involved shootings is *before* one occurs.

In addition, agencies should encourage the media to print and air stories on the responsibilities of officers and the training

conducted to enhance their abilities. General information on past shootings, simulator experiences, and the perspective of the reasonable objective officer can help develop a cooperative association.[17] Such a collaborative effort between the police and the media is not a magic pill and will not alleviate all of the public misperceptions and problems. However, it may reduce or prevent false perceptions, especially with officer involved shootings.[18]

Finally, investigators should review all of the related printed materials and media interviews to identify further witnesses and, if needed, interview them as soon as possible. Sometimes, these individuals may not understand why the police would want to interview them after they have talked to the media, so a diplomatic approach can prove helpful. This highlights the importance of a positive working relationship that often can result in shared information between the media and the police.

Conclusion

Often, it is not a law enforcement shooting that generates negative consequences, but, rather, it is how the involved agency handles the incident that can foster and feed misperceptions. As a Santa Monica, California, police officer pointed out, "No one knows about the hundreds of instances when a police officer decides not to shoot. Perhaps, no one cares. After all, people say we're trained to handle such things, as if training somehow removes or dilutes our humanity."[19]

While the six elements presented in this article may not be all-inclusive, they offer an outline that may reduce the negative events that sometimes occur in these situations. Having the appropriate investigators and a positive working relationship with the media constitute the bookends of an effective process. After all, the right investigators are the foundation for a thorough investigation, and a cooperative connection with the media forms the basis of public understanding. Joining together and sharing information can help both the police and the media deal with officer-involved shootings in a fair and judicious manner.

Few events in law enforcement attract the attention of the media, the political establishment, and the police administration more than an officer-involved shooting.

Notes

1. Darrel W. Stephens, foreword to *Deadly Force: What We Know*, by William A. Geller and Michael S. Scott (Washington, DC: Police Executive Research Forum, 1992).

2. For an overview of legal concerns, see Thomas D. Petrowski, "Use-of-Force Policies and Training: A Reasoned Approach," *FBI Law Enforcement Bulletin*, October 2002, 25–32 and Part Two, November 2002, 24–32.

3. Shannon Bohrer, Harry Kern, and Edward Davis, "The Deadly Dilemma: Shoot or Don't Shoot," *FBI Law Enforcement*

Bulletin, March 2008, 7–12; Larry C. Brubaker, "Deadly Force: A 20-Year Study of Fatal Encounters," *FBI Law Enforcement Bulletin,* April 2002, 6–13; and George T. Williams, "Reluctance to Use Deadly Force: Causes, Consequences, and Cures," *FBI Law Enforcement Bulletin,* October 1999, 1–5.

4. Anthony J. Pinizzotto, Edward F. Davis, and Charles E. Miller III, U.S. Department of Justice, Federal Bureau of Investigation, *In the Line of Fire: Violence Against Law Enforcement* (Washington, DC, 1997); and *Violent Encounters: A Study of Felonious Assaults on Our Nation's Law Enforcement Officers* (Washington, DC, 2006).

5. Interviews with students attending the Management Issues: Law Enforcement's Use of Deadly Force course taught at the FBI's National Academy from 1995 through 1999. The FBI hosts four 10-week National Academy sessions each year during which law enforcement executives from around the world come together to attend classes in various criminal justice subjects.

6. Feedback from students attending the Instructor Training Liability Issues course taught at the Firearms Instructor Schools, Sykesville, Maryland, from 2001 through 2009.

7. American Association of State Troopers, *AAST Trooper Connection,* September 2008.

8. U.S. Department of Justice, Community Relations Service, *Police Use of Excessive Force: A Conciliation Handbook for the Police and the Community* (Washington, DC, June 1999). This publication provides options for addressing controversy surrounding the use of excessive or deadly force and offers guidelines for resolving community disputes. Readers can access www.usdoj.gov/crs/pubs/pdexcess.htm for the June 2002 updated version.

9. In 1993, Edward F. Davis was an instructor in the FBI Academy's Behavioral Science Unit when he interviewed the chief about police and the use of force. The chief's comment could be misconstrued because it was part of a larger dialogue about police use of force and community relations, although it demonstrates perceived and sometimes real concerns. Specifically, the chief was referring to the fact that the department seemed to pull together when an officer is killed and the opposite often occurs when the shooting is questioned in the media.

10. Because of Robert Chaney's (one of this article's authors) extensive experience in investigating police shootings while serving with the Washington, DC, Metropolitan Police Department and then reviewing such incidents for final disposition when later employed by the U.S. Attorney's Office for the District of Columbia, he understands the value of the process and how this can affect public perceptions and investigative outcomes.

11. William A. Geller and Michael S. Scott, *Deadly Force: What We Know* (Washington, DC: Police Executive Research Forum, 1992).

12. Robert Chaney's (one of this article's authors) experience includes a close working relationship with the criminal justice authority (in his case, the criminal justice authority was the U.S. Attorney's Office). The close working relationship can be critical with shootings that have the potential for negative publicity.

13. U.S. Department of Justice, Community Relations Service, *Police Use of Excessive Force: A Conciliation Handbook for the Police and the Community.*

14. Laurence Miller, "Officer-Involved Shooting: Reaction Patterns, Response Protocols, and Psychological Intervention Strategies," *International Journal of Emergency Mental Health* 8, no. 4 (2006): 239–254.

15. Henry Pierson Curtis, "Deadly Force Investigations Can Take Years in Some Florida Counties," *Orlando Sentinel,* November 11, 2007; Todd Coleman, "Documenting the Use of Force," *FBI Law Enforcement Bulletin,* November 2007, 18–23; and Geller and Scott.

16. For additional information, see Brian Parsi Boetig and Penny A. Parrish, "Proactive Media Relations: The Visual Library Initiative," *FBI Low Enforcement Bulletin,* November 2008, 7–9; James D. Sewell, "Working with the Media in Times of Crisis: Key Principles for Law Enforcement," *FBI Law Enforcement Bulletin,* March 2007, 1–6; and Dennis Staszak, "Media Trends and the Public Information Officer," *FBI Law Enforcement Bulletin,* March 2001, 10–13.

17. Brook A. Masters, "Under the Gun: I Died, I Killed, and I Saw the Nature of Deadly Force," *Washington Post,* February 13, 2000.

18. Anthony J. Pinizzotto, Edward Davis, Shannon Bohrer, and Robert Chaney, "Law Enforcement Perspective on the Use of Force: Hands-On, Experiential Training for Prosecuting Attorneys," *FBI Law Enforcement Bulletin,* April 2009, 16–21.

19. Geller and Scott, 1.

Critical Thinking

1. What do you think about the Arizona trooper's comment?

2. Should a police officer be required to give up the Fifth Amendment right to remain silent when he is the subject of an investigation?

3. Why is it valuable for police to have good relations with the media?

Mr. Bohrer, a retired Maryland State Police sergeant, is the range master for the Maryland Police and Correctional Training Commissions in Sykesville. **Mr. Chaney,** a retired homicide detective, currently serves as the deputy director of the Office of Intergovernmental and Public Liaison, U.S. Department of Justice.

From *FBI Law Enforcement Bulletin* by Shannon Bohrer and Robert Chaney, January 2010, pp. 1–7. Published by Federal Bureau of Investigation, www.fbi.gov.

Judging Honesty by Words, Not Fidgets

BENEDICT CAREY

Before any interrogation, before the two-way mirrors or bargaining or good-cop, bad-cop routines, police officers investigating a crime have to make a very tricky determination: Is the person I'm interviewing being honest, or spinning fairy tales?

The answer is crucial, not only for identifying potential suspects and credible witnesses but also for the fate of the person being questioned. Those who come across poorly may become potential suspects and spend hours on the business end of a confrontational, life-changing interrogation—whether or not they are guilty.

Until recently, police departments have had little solid research to guide their instincts. But now forensic scientists have begun testing techniques they hope will give officers, interrogators and others a kind of honesty screen, an improved method of sorting doctored stories from truthful ones.

The new work focuses on what people say, not how they act. It has already changed police work in other countries, and some new techniques are making their way into interrogations in the United States.

In part, the work grows out of a frustration with other methods. Liars do not avert their eyes in an interview on average any more than people telling the truth do, researchers report; they do not fidget, sweat or slump in a chair any more often. They may produce distinct, fleeting changes in expression, experts say, but it is not clear yet how useful it is to analyze those.

Nor have technological advances proved very helpful. No brain-imaging machine can reliably distinguish a doctored story from the truthful one, for instance; ditto for polygraphs, which track changes in physiology as an indirect measure of lying.

"Focusing on content is a very good idea," given the limitations of what is currently being done, said Saul Kassin, a professor of psychology at John Jay College of Criminal Justice.

One broad, straightforward principle has changed police work in Britain: seek information, not a confession. In the mid-1980s, following cases of false confessions, British courts prohibited officers from using some aggressive techniques, like lying about evidence to provoke suspects, and required that interrogations be taped. Officers now work to gather as much evidence as possible before interviewing a suspect, and they make no real distinction between this so-called investigative interview and an interrogation, said Ray Bull, a professor of forensic psychology at the University of Leicester.

"These interviews sound much more like a chat in a bar," said Dr. Bull, who, with colleagues like Aldert Vrij at the University of Portsmouth, has pioneered much of the research in this area. "It's a lot like the old 'Columbo' show, you know, where he pretends to be an idiot but he's gathered a lot of evidence."

Dr. Bull, who has analyzed scores of interrogation tapes, said the police had reported no drop-off in the number of confessions, nor major miscarriages of justice arising from false confessions. In one 2002 survey, researchers in Sweden found that less-confrontational interrogations were associated with a higher likelihood of confession.

Still, forensic researchers have not abandoned the search for verbal clues in interrogations. In analyses of what people say when they are lying and when they are telling the truth, they have found tantalizing differences.

Kevin Colwell, a psychologist at Southern Connecticut State University, has advised police departments, Pentagon officials and child protection workers, who need to check the veracity of conflicting accounts from parents and children. He says that people concocting a story prepare a script that is tight and lacking in detail.

"It's like when your mom busted you as a kid, and you made really obvious mistakes," Dr. Colwell said. "Well, now you're working to avoid those."

By contrast, people telling the truth have no script, and tend to recall more extraneous details and may even make mistakes. They are sloppier.

Psychologists have long studied methods for amplifying this contrast. Drawing on work by Dr. Vrij and Dr. Marcia K. Johnson of Yale, among others, Dr. Colwell and Dr. Cheryl Hiscock-Anisman of National University in La Jolla, Calif., have developed an interview technique that appears to help distinguish a tall tale from a true one.

The interview is low-key but demanding. First, the person recalls a vivid memory, like the first day at college, so researchers have a baseline reading for how the person communicates. The person then freely recounts the event being investigated, recalling all that happened. After several pointed questions ("Would a police officer say a crime was committed?" for example), the interviewee describes the event in question again, adding sounds, smells and other details. Several more stages follow, including one in which the person is asked to recall what happened in reverse.

In several studies, Dr. Colwell and Dr. Hiscock-Anisman have reported one consistent difference: People telling the truth tend to add 20 to 30 percent more external detail than do those who are lying. "This is how memory works, by association," Dr. Hiscock-Anisman said. "If you're telling the truth, this mental reinstatement of contexts triggers more and more external details."

Not so if you've got a concocted story and you're sticking to it. "It's the difference between a tree in full flower in the summer and a barren stick in winter," said Dr. Charles Morgan, a psychiatrist at the National Center for Post-Traumatic Stress Disorder, who has tested it for trauma claims and among special-operations soldiers.

In one recent study, the psychologists had 38 undergraduates enter a professor's office and either steal an exam or replace one that had been stolen. A week later, half told the truth in this structured interview, and the other half tried not to incriminate themselves by lying in the interview. A prize of $20 was offered to the most believable liars.

The researchers had four trained raters who did not know which students were lying analyze the transcripts for response length and richness of added detail, among other things. They correctly categorized 33 of the 38 stories as truthful or deceitful.

The study, whose co-authors were Amina Memon, Laura Taylor and Jessica Prewett, is one of several showing positive results of about 75 percent correct or higher.

This summer, Dr. Colwell and Dr. Hiscock-Anisman are scheduled to teach the technique at the San Diego Police Department, which has a force of some 2,000 officers. "You really develop your own antenna when interviewing people over the years," said Chris Ellis, a lieutenant on the force who invited the researchers to give training. "But we're very open to anything that will make our jobs easier and make us more accurate."

This approach, as promising as it is, has limitations. It applies only to a person talking about what happened during a specific time—not to individual facts, like, "Did you see a red suitcase on the floor?" It may be poorly suited, too, for someone who has been traumatized and is not interested in talking, Dr. Morgan said. And it is not likely to flag the person who changes one small but crucial detail in a story—"Sure, I was there, I threw some punches, but I know nothing about no knife"—or, for that matter, the expert or pathological liar.

But the science is evolving fast. Dr. Bull, Dr. Vrij and Par-Anders Granhag at Goteborg University in Sweden are finding that challenging people with pieces of previously gathered evidence, gradually introduced throughout an investigative interview, increases the strain on liars.

And it all can be done without threats or abuse, which is easier on officers and suspects. Detective Columbo, it turns out, was not just made for TV.

Critical Thinking

1. Should it be a requirement in the United States, as it is in other countries, that interrogations be recorded?

2. When questioning a suspect, should investigators be focused on obtaining a confession that will help the case, or seeking more information?

Behavioral Mirroring in Interviewing

ROBIN K. DREEKE AND JOE NAVARRO, MA

Whether preparing for an interview or meeting with an informant, investigators should spend a significant amount of time planning for the most important part of any human interaction—creating and building rapport. Consistently building rapport with various individuals of different genders and ages who represent diverse backgrounds, educational levels, experiences, ethnicities, and mental health concerns proves challenging to many law enforcement professionals. Everyone has their own personality and preference for how they like to give and receive information.[1]

One of the most powerful and proven ways of establishing rapport is isopraxis, or mirroring another's behavior.[2] From the time people are born, they learn to share mirroring behaviors. When a mother smiles, her baby smiles; when she giggles, her baby giggles; when she arches her eyes, her baby does the same. These mirroring behaviors continue into courtship behaviors reflected back as part of the mating game. People find comfort in and, therefore, seek mirroring behaviors. They also discover solace in processing information presented consistent with their personality and preferences.[3]

Personality mirroring corresponds with nonverbal mirroring—it tries to match the thought process and style of communication a person prefers. Some people like to socialize as part of the communication process, while others prefer a more direct, task-oriented tact. People tend to favor information that they receive in a pleasing manner, and, consequently, they become more attentive and receptive. Studies have shown that individuals have different personality types for processing information, as well as preferences for how they give and receive information.[4] Investigators who assess for such traits can effortlessly mirror communication styles to conduct more effective interviews and better develop informants. To demonstrate this concept, the authors offer an overview of a law enforcement professional's attempts to develop a source and his partner's assistance in doing so.

People tend to favor information that they receive in a pleasing manner, and, consequently, they become more attentive and receptive.

Background

Wilson has worked with the Joint Terrorism Task Force for a number of years, and, because of the great relationship with and mentoring from his training agent and partner, Smith, he has become one of the squad's more notable interviewers and source developers.[5] His techniques include active listening skills, personality and emotional assessments, and a consideration of the best tools to use when dealing with individuals.

Despite Wilson's excellent track record in conducting interviews and developing sources, his encounters occasionally did not go as well as he hoped or planned. Sometimes, despite his best and concentrated efforts and the open minds of individuals he interacted with, his ability to develop a relationship proved elusive. Wilson typically dismissed these infrequent anomalies as part of the unpredictability of human nature. Because he had numerous successful results, he never fully explored the possibility that he may have had some responsibility in his occasional failures until he had one interview that forced him to reflect on and rethink his process.

The Interview

Wilson has been working on an investigation for some time and desperately wants an informant close to his subject who will help him gain a valuable personality assessment on the individual, as well as some firsthand knowledge of his criminal activity. One morning, Wilson asks his partner, Smith, if he has a few minutes to talk about his case.

"OK, so what do we have?" inquires Smith. Wilson briefly explains the investigation as Smith begins flipping through some of the surveillance logs. Smith quickly notes that the subject frequents a local tavern that he is familiar with from a case he worked years earlier and asks Wilson if he has had any success trying to get a source there. Wilson says that he has struck out in that area. Smith details the case he had a few years ago, describing how his subject frequently hung out at the tavern for hours and socialized with patrons who came in after work. Smith had talked with the owner, formed a professional relationship, and opened him as a confidential source who provided valuable assistance to Smith's investigation. After the case ended, Smith closed the source but occasionally reached out to him to check in and ask about him, his work, and his research. Smith says that although some time has passed, he feels

Active listening involves numerous nonverbal communications, such as reflecting eye gaze behavior, sitting attentively (leaning forward), listening to words used and registering their frequency and priority, mirroring body behavior to complement the transmitter of information, using head tilt to indicate receptiveness, and restraining facial indicators of disagreement or contempt.

confident that the owner, and former source, will give Wilson a hand. Wilson asks Smith to arrange an introduction.

A few days later, Smith sets up a coffee meeting between Wilson and the former source. Wilson begins preparing for the interview and asks Smith to tell him a little about the source. Smith informs Wilson that the owner is very busy running the tavern while pursuing research for his PhD. Further, he is a serious, analytical person with well-determined, long-range goals. Wilson asks Smith if the source likes baseball or any other sport that they might talk about to break the ice and develop some rapport. Smith replies, "I don't think so; he is more studious. Because my background is in engineering like the source's, that is generally what we talked about." Wilson shrugs it off and says, "That's OK. I'm sure I can find something he's interested in." Wilson thinks to himself that this should be no big deal. He will just "chat him up" and touch upon myriad topics until one seems to strike a cord and work. Wilson thinks his high energy approach should win the day.

Wilson arrives at the designated coffee shop a little early, like he usually does for a source meeting, and finds that the source has arrived before him and is sitting in an appropriate quiet back table looking at his watch and tapping his foot. Wilson strides toward him and introduces himself with his trademark broad smile and firm handshake, stating, "It's a pleasure to meet you. My friend Smith said you are a great guy and sends his regards." The source stands, slightly bows, and tightens his lips momentarily as he asks quizzically, "Do you mean Agent Smith?" Wilson responds, "Of course, our friend Agent Smith." He gestures for the source to sit down and then offers to get them coffee. The source declines, stating that he does not have much time today.

Wilson thanks the source for coming and says he understands that he is busy and does not plan to take a lot of his time at this first meeting. Without giving him much time to respond, Wilson asks the source to tell him something about himself, his work, and his PhD research. The source again forces a half smile and shifts his chair so that he is not facing Wilson directly anymore but somewhat angled toward the front of the coffee shop and the exit. The source then sits up straight and places his hands on his lap as he thoroughly describes the nature of his research and studies.

Despite Wilson's lack of knowledge of the source's topic, he attempts to listen intently. But, before the source finishes speaking, he quickly interjects a question of where the source was born and grew up. "Oh, Riverdale in the Bronx, New York City," the source responds. Wilson seizes what he perceives as his first opportunity to develop some rapport and quickly asks, "Ah, so you must be a Yankee fan? I also was born in New York and am an avid New York Yankee fan. We should try to catch

a game together sometime. As a matter of fact, the Yankees are playing at home against the Boston Red Sox next week, and I have a buddy who has two extra tickets I could get. That sounds great doesn't it?" The source leans back and away from Wilson and simply responds that his research and the tavern keep him occupied, and he does not really enjoy baseball anyway. Wilson responds, "That's a shame; you'd love it. I'll work on getting us some tickets for later in the season. We'll coordinate your schedule to make it happen for you." The source angles himself more toward the door as he looks at his watch and begins to lean toward the door. Wilson again starts into a monologue about New York sports and what he perceives as some great rapport building with the source.

Wilson finally takes a break from his monologue long enough for the source to look at his watch again and ask Wilson what exactly he can do for him. Wilson nods and says, "Well, I'm just interested in your thoughts and opinions from time to time about some individuals who may be frequenting your tavern." The source again reminds Wilson that he is very busy with his PhD research and asks if Wilson has any specific needs or tasks in mind for the source to review to determine if he can accommodate them in his schedule. Wilson shrugs his shoulders and says, "Not really. I'm not that organized yet. I just wanted to chat with you and give you a brief idea of what I'm hoping to do and just take some time for us to get to know each other better." The source responds, "I apologize; if you don't mind, I have to be going. I need to get back to my office. I need to prepare for a class this evening and still have to go through last evening's receipts from the tavern."

Wilson stands and says, "Sure, by all means," with another broad, somewhat nervous smile. Wilson then thanks him for taking the time to meet. He asks the source if they can get together again in a few weeks to possibly discuss some more details of how the source could provide assistance. The source responds that he is not sure because his schedule can be quite busy, so Wilson asks if it is OK to call him and set something up in a day or so after he reviews his schedule. The source agrees, and Wilson again thanks him for his time and the productive meeting while enthusiastically shaking his hand.

Back at the office, Smith asks Wilson about the meeting. Wilson replies that he thinks it went well and that he will try to get baseball tickets for a game for them to go to in a few weeks to help build some rapport. Smith gives a quizzical look and asks Wilson to keep him posted.

Wilson documents what he perceives was a good interview and completes the necessary paperwork to reopen the confidential human source. After about a week, he attempts to contact the source but can only leave messages on his voicemail. After a few more days, Wilson finally reaches the source on the telephone and comments that he must be a very busy man. The source responds that he is and his research is in a critical stage. Wilson advises that he understands and adds that the source probably could use a break. Wilson quickly interjects that they should grab lunch together, so they both can unwind. The source says that he really does not have time.

Wilson politely presses for some sort of get-together. The source finally states that he does not think that he will be able to help him. Stunned, Wilson respectfully responds that he understands and asks if he might contact him again in the future when his schedule allows. The source pauses and reluctantly agrees but advises that it will not be anytime soon.

The Problem

Wilson slowly hangs up the telephone, feeling extremely low and dejected. He had high hopes for both his case and the working relationship with the source. Now, he faces the embarrassment of closing a source he just opened. He decides that before he takes any action, he will talk to Smith. Maybe his mentor can shed some light on this puzzling problem.

Wilson relates the story of his contact with the source. Surprised, Smith asks details about their conversation. Wilson conveys these and explains how he tried to get the source to go to a baseball game and out to lunch but that the source absolutely refused, saying he would not be able to help him at all. Smith is shocked and says that the source had just completed his master's degree when they met. He asks Wilson what the source's PhD research is about and how it is going. Wilson shrugs his shoulders and says, "I don't know, we didn't talk much about it." Smith then asks Wilson what plan he proposed to the source that was not agreeable for them to work on together. Again, Wilson advises that they had not spoken about it. Smith begins to nod. Slowly, Smith looks up and says, "I think I know the problem." Wilson exclaims, "Great! What should I do?" Smith offers that first, he would like to explain some of the highpoints of how he and the source used to work together on his case. Smith describes the case and how he had brought a detailed list

> Private individuals may avoid eye contact or stare unblinking. Their chins may not jut out, and their arms may be still or even restrained. They may orient their attention slightly away as they do not like to be stared at; look down at their feet; give short, rather than long, answers; and tend to touch less and illustrate less with their hands. Idle chatter is generally wasted on them.

and plan to the source for them to go over together. Following their planning session, the source had contacted Smith using the protocols they established, and they met for a businesslike, organized debriefing. The source always was well prepared and thorough, checking off items on his list of points to cover. The source had stated it was a great diversion from his work, the different challenge was mentally stimulating, and he really enjoyed it. Smith adds that because the source's contributions were so significant, he was able to get him a signed letter of appreciation from the director. Smith asks if any of this sounds familiar to the type of dialogue Wilson had with the source. Wilson replies, "Not even close." Smith says, "That's the problem."

The Solution

Smith asks Wilson to remember the first interview they conducted together a number of years ago. Wilson recalls that Smith had acted more chatty and gregarious than he does around the

office and in his personal life, and Smith had said he was practicing the "Platinum Rule." Smith had explained that people want to be communicated with as they like to communicate, and four basic personality styles define how people prefer to give and receive information: directors, socializers, relaters, or thinkers.[6]

Smith asks Wilson to recall his interaction with the source and describes how individuals are either people oriented or task oriented in how they prefer to communicate. He opens a notebook and shows Wilson a chart containing descriptors of the two (see Chart 1).[7] Smith asks Wilson to think of the source in his work setting and, between the two columns, how he would best describe him. Wilson remembers the beginning of the interview when he introduced himself. The source corrected Wilson by stating Smith's full title and then slightly bowed. Wilson circles the words *formal, proper* and regards the rest of the list, talking with Smith about each choice. He chooses *focuses on facts* and *task oriented* and describes how the source wanted to know Wilson's specific task or plan. Wilson regards the next set, *readily shares feelings* and *keeps feelings private* and says that he does not know the source well enough from the one meeting to make an educated guess. Smith nods and suggests that people may not always be able to choose accurately between the two columns because these represent only illustrators of tendencies and are not definite.

Smith asks Wilson to describe how the source sat and communicated nonverbally. Wilson advises that the source seemed to look stiff in his chair with a straight posture, kept his elbows tucked into his sides, and was not very animated with his hands. Smith commends Wilson on his excellent observations and says that the source most likely fits the category of *keeps feelings private* based on several closed nonverbal displays.

Smith reminds Wilson to just look for tendencies in the source's personality based upon a majority of observations, not 100 percent accuracy in any one column. Wilson quickly circles the phrases *disciplined about time* and *prefers planning*. He believes that the source most likely was *thinking oriented*, rather than *feeling oriented*, but he leaves that blank for now as well.

Smith then asks Wilson to tally the results. Wilson has five in the *task-oriented* column and two undecided. "Perfect," Smith says, "I think we can safely say we are dealing with

Chart 1
Communication Description

People oriented	Task oriented
relaxed, warm	formal, proper
likes opinions	focuses on facts
relationship oriented	task oriented
readily shares feelings	keeps feelings private
flexible about time	disciplined about time
feeling oriented	thinking oriented
spontaneous	prefers planning

Chart 2
Communication Categories

Direct	Indirect
takes risks	avoids risks
swift decisions	cautious decisions
confronting, expressive	less assertive
impatient	easygoing, patient
talks and tells	listens and asks
outgoing	reserved
offers opinions freely	keeps opinions private

a predominantly task-oriented individual and not a people-oriented one. Therefore, the source is either categorized as a thinker or director." Smith uses another chart to determine whether the source prefers to be direct or indirect (see Chart 2).[8]

Chart 3
Personality Model

Director	Socializer
Thinker	Relater

Wilson regards the list and, from his conversation with Smith and the source, quickly discerns that the source makes *cautious decisions,* is *less assertive* and *reserved, listens and asks,* and *keeps opinions private.* Smith states, "Again, we don't have 100 percent, but we definitely can see a trend." Smith then suggests that based on his knowledge of the source, he believes he *takes risks* and tends to be *impatient.* Smith explains to Wilson that having a mix is both normal and expected. Smith asks Wilson where he thinks the source falls in the four domain personality model he described earlier (see Chart 3).[9]

Wilson notes that the source is predominantly task oriented and indirect and, therefore, confident that the source is a thinker. "Exactly what I also would assess," states Smith, who turns to another page in his notebook and shows Wilson another chart (see Chart 4).[10]

Wilson determines that he is a socializer and chuckles as he regards the chart—he does not see the socializer personality type near the thinker. "I guess I was a bit off when trying to relate and develop rapport with the source," Wilson said. "I probably would have gotten the nonverbal message over some time with the source, but I just went in there with my socializer style blazing away." Smith explains that this review helps assess how individuals prefer to give and receive information,

Chart 4
Compatible Combinations

Best combinations at task compatibility	Second best combinations at task compatibility
Thinker – Relater	Thinker – Thinker
Director – Relater	Relater – Relater
Socializer – Relater	Socializer – Thinker

enabling investigators to more rapidly match, or mirror, it. With this powerful understanding of how people prefer to communicate, interviewers and human source developers can more rapidly adapt to someone's style to develop better and quicker rapport.

"This is a powerful tool," Wilson declares. Smith adds that the lists they used to identify the communication style help interviewers mirror observable traits. Interviewers who adapt and mirror both before and during the interview greatly enhance their chances of success.

To Communicate with Directors—

- support their goals and objectives, if possible;
- remain businesslike in your dealings;
- use facts, not feelings, to convey your thoughts if you do not agree with them;
- be precise and well organized;
- remain brief with supporting analysis when recommending other actions;
- get to points quickly;
- do not repeat—they understand quickly; and
- emphasize winning results and growth potential.

Greet directors appropriately, use manners, be formal and precise, ensure nonverbals support your message, and use your hands to illustrate and demark what is important. Respect their space and use your body as a shield from others as they prefer privacy. Time is important to directors, so do not waste it. Use demonstrative materials sparingly; sit at angles but not too close; mirror their behavior; and look for intentional signals that indicate "We are done." Avoid unnecessary touching; it is not usually welcome.

Source: Tony Alessandra and Michael J. O'Conner, *The Platinum Rule* (New York, NY: Warner Books, Inc., 2001), 144.

To Communicate with Relaters—

- be warm and genuine;
- support their feelings by showing personal interest;
- assume that they will take personally whatever facts you state;
- give them enough time to develop trust in you;
- if you disagree with them, do so with more personal feelings and not facts;
- communicate in a steady, slower, and informal manner;
- use active listening skills and encouragers; and
- give assurances of minimizing risks if possible.

With a relater, nonverbal communications are easier to mirror—take the lead from them. You can use more eye gaze behavior, sit closer, touch more often, interject more thoughts, and use hands to illustrate and punctuate with more frequency. These motions will be well received, as well as your emphasis with voice and such behaviors as arching of the eyes. Listen for the pace at which they deliver their message and match their speech and loudness.

Source: Tony Alessandra and Michael J. O'Conner, *The Platinum Rule* (New York, NY: Warner Books, Inc., 2001), 145.

Smith says, "So, let's look at the source again and devise encounter plans based on what we know behaviorally." Wilson responds, "I'll definitely adapt myself to communicating with a thinker as we have described here. The source likes procedures and protocols. I'll have a detailed, accurate, and logical agenda so I don't waste his time. I'll then try to mirror him by being more formal and proper, fact focused, task oriented, and disciplined about time, especially his. I'll also tone back my own personality and be less assertive, listen and ask questions more, and be more reserved. I'll avoid the areas that we were unsure about until I can discover what his preferences are, but this is a great place to start."

Both Smith and Wilson lean back in their chairs and breathe a long sigh. Smith feels good about being able to pass along this vital key he has successfully used over the years. Wilson appreciates Smith's insight and is excited to recontact the source and put his new tools into practice.

Conclusion

The challenge that Wilson faced often occurs in the law enforcement profession. Investigators encounter individuals with whom they just cannot seem to make a connection or develop rapport, not only during the interview but in human source development as well. Analyzing people for particular personality and communication styles and then mirroring those traits can prove key when investigators attempt to build relationships. Law enforcement personnel who use this behavioral tool will foster stronger rapport and glean valuable information in the furtherance of their cases.

To Communicate with Socializers—

- focus your interest on them;
- support their ideas, thoughts, and opinions when possible;
- communicate with a fast-paced, upbeat, stimulating conversation;
- be tolerant of digressions and allow time for the discussion to go on as long as possible;
- avoid arguing;
- be enthusiastic and casual;
- articulate how actions can enhance image and reputation; and
- avoid details.

Socializers generally appreciate comments about appearance or inquiries regarding their family. They tend to sit closer and even communicate while walking, often feel free to interject thoughts, which, at times, may not have any relevance (communication and fellowship are more important), usually interrupt more and expect you to chime in with thoughts. But, give socializers the last word. They maintain eye contact but will look away when relaxed. Socializers liberally use hand gestures and allow for touching to emphasize, especially hand-to-arm touching; share food and drinks as this is well received; and, although they view time as more flexible, investigators should not abuse this privilege.

Source: Tony Alessandra and Michael J. O'Conner, *The Platinum Rule* (New York, NY: Warner Books, Inc., 2001), 149.

To Communicate with Thinkers—

- be thorough and well prepared;
- support their organized and thoughtful approach;
- use actions, not just words;
- remain detailed, accurate, and logical;
- discuss pros and cons of actions;
- provide solid, tangible evidence, not broad speculations;
- have and adhere to established procedures; and
- assure them that decisions will not backfire.

Thinkers appreciate timeliness and brevity, seeking to minimize, rather than maximize, it. Once they understand, leave them to think. Do not interject; be ready with information, do not delay answers; be emphatic but not loud, and confident but not cocky. Avoid arrogance; limit amount of touch; allow for distance between parties; and, when seated, try to sit at 90 degrees. When the encounter is complete, shake hands briefly and leave promptly.

Source: Tony Alessandra and Michael J. O'Conner, *The Platinum Rule* (New York, NY: Warner Books, Inc., 2001), 150.

Notes

1. Tony Alessandra and Michael J. O'Conner, *The Platinum Rule* (New York, NY: Warner Books, Inc., 2001), 4–6. Special Agent Dreeke draws upon his vast experience as a qualified practitioner of the Myers-Briggs Type Indicator and the Personality DISCernment Instrument for information in this article regarding personality and communication styles.

2. Joe Navarro, *What Every Body Is Saying* (New York, NY: Harper Collins, 2008), 27, 90.

3. John R. Schafer and Joe Navarro, *Advanced Interviewing Techniques* (Springfield, IL: Charles C. Thomas, 2004), 39–43.

4. Allesandra and O'Conner, 5–6.

5. Robin Dreeke, "It's All About Them: Tools and Techniques for Interviewing and Human Source Development," *FBI Law Enforcement Bulletin,* June 2009, 1–9.

6. Allesandra and O'Conner, 5–6.

7. Ibid., 63.

8. Ibid., 61.

9. Ibid., 63.

10. Ibid., 119.

Critical Thinking

1. What is the goal of behavioral mirroring?

2. Is the technique practical for law enforcement officers?

3. Should it be taught to investigators?

Special Agent **ROBIN K. DREEKE** serves in the FBI's Counterintelligence Division. **MR. JOE NAVARRO**, a retired FBI special agent with the National Security Division's Behavioral Analysis Program, currently provides private consultation to the intelligence community.

The author invites readers interested in discussing this topic to e-mail him at Robin.Dreeke@ic.fbi.gov.

From *FBI Law Enforcement Bulletin* by Robert Dreeke and Joe Navarro, December 2009, pp. 1–10. Published by Federal Bureau of Investigation, www.fbi.gov.

Keeping Officers Safe on the Road

Several reports highlight visibility issues for law enforcement and safety personnel responding to roadside incidents.

BETH PEARSALL

O*ct. 21, 2008, began like any other day on the job for police officer David Tome.*

Early that Tuesday morning, Tome and the rest of the accident reconstruction team from the Northern York County Regional Police Department were on Route 15 in York County, Pa., investigating a fatal crash that had occurred days earlier. The team set up traffic cones to close the right lane of the road and began the investigation.

However, around 9 a.m., a passing sport-utility vehicle hit Tome where he stood in the right lane, sending him flying over a guardrail. Tome—a five-year veteran of the force, a husband and a father of two young children—died instantly. He was 31 years old.[1]

David Tome's story is tragic and sadly common. Every week, new stories emerge of law enforcement officers, firefighters and other first responders who are injured or killed in roadside crashes throughout the United States.

The National Institute of Justice has collaborated with fire service and automotive engineering agencies on several studies that address roadway safety. Increasing emergency vehicle visibility and developing training and tools aimed at keeping first responders safe on the road have emerged as next steps in the effort to prevent future tragedies.

Alarming Numbers

Preliminary data for 2009 from the National Law Enforcement Officers Memorial Fund show that for the 12th year in a row, more officers were killed in the line of duty in traffic incidents than from any other cause of death, including shootings. These incidents comprise automobile and motorcycle crashes as well as officers struck while outside their vehicles. In 2009, 56 law enforcement officers had died in traffic-related incidents, accounting for close to 50 percent of officer deaths for the year.[2]

Preliminary data for 2009 show that for the 12th year in row, more officers were killed in traffic incidents than from any other cause of death, including shootings.

In the previous year, 28 out of the 118 firefighters who died while on duty were killed in vehicle crashes. Another five firefighters were struck and killed by vehicles.[3]

These sobering numbers clearly show the need to protect law enforcement officers, firefighters and other first responders as they perform their duties on the nation's streets and highways.

Vehicle Visibility

Visibility is essential to roadside safety for emergency responders. Can drivers see and recognize an emergency vehicle as it navigates through traffic on its way to the scene of an accident or fire? When the first responder has reached the scene and is on the side of the road, can drivers clearly see both the person and the vehicle?

Several factors affect a vehicle's visibility—its size and color, for example. Environmental conditions, such as the weather and time of day, also play a role in whether drivers can easily see emergency vehicles along the road.

Emergency vehicles have features designed to draw attention to their presence even when drivers are not actively looking for them. These include warning lights, sirens and horns, and retroreflective striping, which reflects light back to its source. Such features provide information about the vehicle's size, position, speed and direction of travel so drivers can take suitable action.[4]

Some emergency response fields have national standards that govern the visibility of vehicles. The National Fire Protection Association's (NFPA's) Standard for Automotive Fire Apparatus requires fire trucks and ambulances in the United States to have retroreflective striping and markings in multiple locations, including at least:

- Fifty percent of the cab and body length on each side.
- Twenty-five percent of the front width of the vehicle.
- Fifty percent of rear-facing surfaces, in a 45-degree down-and-away "chevron" pattern.

Although compliance with the NFPA standard is voluntary, vehicle manufacturers typically comply to limit liability and ensure the marketability of their products.[5]

Law enforcement does not have a similar national standard. However, many law enforcement agencies apply retroreflective markings to patrol cars, motorcycles and other vehicles.[6]

The demands of the law enforcement profession also create unique visibility issues. Sometimes personnel do not want their cars to be readily detectable. Officers may want to be almost invisible to other drivers under certain circumstances. The need for high visibility at certain times must be balanced against a need for stealth at other times.

Using Reflectors to Improve Visibility

A recent study took a closer look at some commercially available products to determine whether they help increase emergency vehicle visibility and improve roadway safety for emergency responders and the public. The NIJ-funded research was conducted by the U.S. Fire Administration and the International Fire Service Training Association.[7]

Looking specifically at retroreflective striping, high-visibility paint, built-in lighting and other reflectors on emergency vehicles, the researchers found that:

- Retroreflective materials can help heighten emergency vehicle visibility, especially during nighttime conditions.
- Using contrasting colors can help civilian drivers find a hazard amid the visual clutter of the roadway.
- Fluorescent colors (especially fluorescent yellow-green and orange) offer higher visibility during daylight hours.

Researchers also identified ways for first responders to improve the ability of civilian drivers to see and recognize emergency vehicles during all phases of an emergency. These include:

- Using retroreflective material to outline an emergency vehicle with "contour" or "edge" markings, especially on large vehicles.
- Placing retroreflective material lower on emergency vehicles to take advantage of headlights from approaching vehicles. Researchers noted that law enforcement could concentrate retro-reflective material on the rear of vehicles to preserve stealth when facing traffic or patrolling
- Using fluorescent retroreflective material when responders want a high degree of day- and nighttime visibility.
- Applying distinctive logos or emblems made with retro-reflective material to improve emergency vehicle visibility and recognition.

Warning Lights: Help or Hindrance?

USFA and the Society of Automotive Engineers conducted a separate NIJ-funded study to examine another important feature of emergency vehicles—warning lights.[8]

Researchers in this study looked specifically at how the color and intensity of warning lights affect driver vision and emergency vehicle safety during the day and night. They examined whether the lights alerted drivers to the presence and location of an emergency vehicle as intended or whether they unnecessarily distracted drivers or hindered their ability to detect emergency responders on foot.

"Right now, emergency lighting used by some departments is based on tradition and opinion," said Bill Troup, a fire program specialist at the USFA National Fire Data Center. "Some agencies use red warning lights; others use blue, and some use a combination of colors. Why are the colors this way? Because that's the way it's been done. It's tradition, and in some cases, this tradition has become state law. With this study, we wanted to add some science to the 'why' of emergency lighting."

Emergency lighting used by some departments is based on tradition and opinion . . . with this study, we wanted to add some science to the 'why' of emergency lighting.

The researchers asked study participants, who were representative of the driving public, to perform three tasks while viewing a simulated traffic scene:

- Look for emergency warning lights.
- Look for pedestrian emergency responders near the warning lights.
- Rate the ability of the warning lights to draw attention to the emergency scene.

During this field experiment, the researchers varied the color and intensity of the warning lights (using white, yellow, red and blue lights at low and high intensities). They also varied the location of the emergency vehicle (placing it to the left or right of participants) and the surrounding light (creating day and nighttime lighting conditions). The emergency responders wore two different sets of protective clothing. Both sets had standard retroreflective markings; however, the background material on one set was black, and the other was yellow.

The most significant difference occurred between day and night: Researchers found that participants' ability to find warning lights at night was uniformly good and did not improve when they increased the lights' intensity. During the day, however, a higher intensity of each of the four colors improved participants' ability to spot the lights. Blue was the easiest light color for participants to see, day and night.

Even though the responders outside the emergency vehicles wore protective clothing with retroreflective markings, participants had substantially more difficulty finding the responders at night than during the day. Researchers found no difference in participants' ability to find responders wearing the black versus yellow clothing in either the day or night. The warning lights had little effect on participants' ability to see the responders during both lighting conditions.

Based on these findings, the researchers offered three recommendations for improving safety during roadside emergencies:

- **Consider different intensity levels of warning lights for day and night.** Researchers noted that finding a single intensity for warning lights—one that is intense enough for daytime conditions but not too intense for nighttime conditions—can be difficult. Using at least two levels of intensity might be a more effective choice.
- **Make more overall use of blue lights, day and night.** According to the researchers, strong agreement already exists about the advantages of using blue lights at night. In this study, they found that when participants searched for warning

lights in the daytime, blue was more effective than any of the three other colors tested. This finding provides more evidence in favor of using blue lights during all lighting conditions.

- **Use color to make a clear visual distinction between parked emergency vehicles in two different paths.** Researchers suggest using one color of light for vehicles that are parked in the normal path of traffic (for example, red lights). Another color could be used for vehicles that may be near the normal path of traffic but are not obstructing it.

More Tools to Improve Safety

Aside from research studies on vehicle visibility, NIJ also has supported developing Web-based tools that will help improve the safety of law enforcement officers, firefighters and other emergency responders on the roadways.

With support from NIJ, USFA collaborated with the Cumberland Valley Volunteer Firemen's Association's Emergency Responder Safety Institute to create ResponderSafety.com. This Web site contains the latest news and training on roadside safety as well as recent cases of responders who were injured or killed by vehicles while on duty. The site aims to be a place where transportation, public safety and emergency personnel around the country can share lessons learned, thus helping them to respond more safely and effectively to roadway incidents.

USFA also collaborated with the International Association of Firefighters to develop a separate Web-based training program called "Improving Apparatus Response and Roadway Operations Safety for the Career Fire Service." NIJ and USFA are working to expand this roadside-safety training program to cover all emergency responders, including law enforcement. The program is scheduled to launch in 2010.

Roadside Safety: A Multifaceted Issue

Roadside safety issues are complex. Using warning lights and retroreflective material to increase an emergency vehicle's visibility is just one important focus area. Setting up a proper safety zone at the scene of an accident or other roadside hazard, as well as increasing the visibility of emergency responders on foot, is also critical. Perhaps one of the most essential parts of the equation is the alertness of civilian drivers and their ability to recognize an emergency vehicle and take suitable action to avoid a collision. NIJ will continue to work with law enforcement, firefighters and other emergency responders—and the public—to address these concerns and help improve safety for everyone on the road.

Perhaps one of the most essential parts of the equation is the alertness of civilian drivers and their ability to recognize an emergency vehicle and take suitable action to avoid a collision.

For More Information

- www.ResponderSafety.com.
- USFA, *Emergency Vehicle Visibility and Conspicuity Study,* FA-323/August 2009, www.usfa.dhs.gov/downloads/pdf/publications/fa_323.pdf.
- USFA and SAE International, *Effects of Warning Lamp Color and Intensity on Driver Vision,* October 2008, www.sae.org/standardsdev/tsb/cooperative/warninglamp0810.pdf.
- USFA's emergency vehicle safety efforts: www.usfa.dhs.gov/fireservice/research/safety/vehicle.shtm.
- USFA's roadway safety efforts: www.usfa.dhs.gov/fireservice/research/safety/roadway.shtm.

Notes

1. Northern York County Regional Police Department, "David Tome Memorial Page," www.nycrpd.org/tome.html; and "Officer Investigating Fatal Crash Struck, Killed," *WGAL.com,* Oct. 22, 2008, www.wgal.com/news/17769185/detail.html.
2. National Law Enforcement Officers Memorial Fund, "Law Enforcement Officer Fatalities Fall Sharply During Third Quarter of 2009," Oct. 2, 2009, www.nleomf.com.
3. U.S. Fire Administration, *Firefighter Fatalities in the United States in 2008,* Emmitsburg, MD: U.S. Department of Homeland Security, Federal Emergency Management Agency, September 2009, www.usfa.dhs.gov/downloads/pdf/publications/ff_fat08.pdf.
4. U.S. Fire Administration, *Emergency Vehicle Visibility and Conspicuity Study,* Emmitsburg, MD: U.S. Department of Homeland Security, Federal Emergency Management Agency, FA-323/August 2009, www.usfa.dhs.gov/downloads/pdf/publications/fa_323.pdf.
5. Ibid.
6. Ibid.
7. Ibid.
8. Flannagan, M.J., D.F. Blower, and J.M. Devonshire, *Effects of Warning Lamp Color and Intensity on Driver Vision,* Warrendale, PA: SAE International, October 2008, www.sae.org/standardsdev/tsb/cooperative/warninglamp0810.pdf.

Critical Thinking

1. Why are roads and highways especially dangerous places for emergency responders?
2. Should law enforcement vehicles have national standards to govern visibility as do fire trucks and ambulances?

BETH PEARSALL is a freelance writer. She is a former managing editor of the *NIJ Journal.*

From *National Institute of Justice Journal,* issue 265, April 2010, pp. 10–14. Published by U.S. Department of Justice.

UNIT 4

The Judicial System

Unit Selections

Learning Outcomes

After reading this unit, you will be able to:

- Describe how the American bail system can invite corruption.

- Discuss the Constitutional issues involved when government seizes a person's assets.

- Understand the ways that the use of DNA evidence can be a forceful tool for justice, but also can be the cause of serious injustice.

- Know the Constitutional issues surrounding confessions.

- Become more familiar with the thinking of one of our Supreme Court Justices.

Student Website

www.mhhe.com/cls

Internet References

Center for Rational Correctional Policy
    www.correctionalpolicy.com
Justice Information Center (JIC)
    www.ncjrs.org
National Center for Policy Analysis (NCPA)
    www.public-policy.org/~ncpa/pd/law/index3.html
U.S. Department of Justice (DOJ)
    www.usdoj.gov

The courts are an equal partner in the American justice system. Just as the police have the responsibility of guarding our liberties by enforcing the law, the courts play an important role in defending these liberties by applying and interpreting the law. The courts are the battlegrounds where civilized "wars" are fought without bloodshed, to protect individual rights and to settle disputes.

The articles in this unit discuss several issues concerning the judicial process. Ours is an adversary system of justice, and the protagonists—the state and the defendant—are usually represented by counsel.

In the opening article of this section, Adam Liptak informs us that in England and Canada, posting bail for people accused of crimes in exchange for a fee is a crime, as he examines the uniquely American system of bail in "Illegal Globally, Bail for Profit Remains In U.S." Following is "The Forfeiture Racket," where Radley Balko criticizes the practice by law enforcement agencies of confiscating property, a practice he says is unconstitutional.

In "When Our Eyes Deceive Us" the problem of wrongful convictions as a result of eyewitness identifications by victims is looked at by Dahlia Lithwick. Sarah Hammond reports that various state lawmakers are expanding their DNA databases to aid in the battle against crime in "The DNA Factor." Michael Bobelian, in the next article, "DNA's Dirty Little Secret," points out that DNA evidence may actually be putting innocent people in prison.

Next, Carl Benoit discusses the value of confessions and the importance of avoiding Constitutional violations in "Confessions and the Constitution: The Remedy for Violating Constitutional

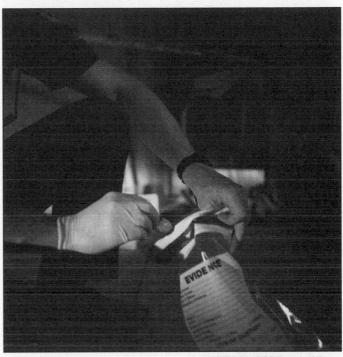

© JUPITERIMAGES/Brand X/Alamy

Safeguards." This unit concludes with "Justice & Antonin Scalia," where the author sketches a picture of the provocative Supreme Court Justice Antonin Scalia.

Illegal Globally, Bail for Profit Remains in U.S.

Adam Liptak

Wayne Spath is a bail bondsman, which means he is an insurance salesman, a social worker, a lightly regulated law enforcement agent, a real estate appraiser—and a for-profit wing of the American justice system.

What he does, which is posting bail for people accused of crimes in exchange for a fee, is all but unknown in the rest of the world. In England, Canada and other countries, agreeing to pay a defendant's bond in exchange for money is a crime akin to witness tampering or bribing a juror—a form of obstruction of justice.

Mr. Spath, who is burly, gregarious and intense, owns Brandy Bail Bonds, and he sees his clients in a pleasant and sterile office building just down the street from the courthouse here. But for the handcuffs on the sign out front, it could be a dentist's office.

"I've got to run, but I'll never leave you in jail," Mr. Spath said, greeting a frequent customer in his reception area one morning a couple of weeks ago. He turned to a second man and said, "Now, don't you miss court on me."

Other countries almost universally reject and condemn Mr. Spath's trade, in which defendants who are presumed innocent but cannot make bail on their own pay an outsider a nonrefundable fee for their freedom.

"It's a very American invention," John Goldkamp, a professor of criminal justice at Temple University, said of the commercial bail bond system. "It's really the only place in the criminal justice system where a liberty decision is governed by a profit-making businessman who will or will not take your business."

Although the system is remarkably effective at what it does, four states—Illinois, Kentucky, Oregon and Wisconsin—have abolished commercial bail bonds, relying instead on systems that require deposits to courts instead of payments to private businesses, or that simply trust defendants to return for trial.

Most of the legal establishment, including the American Bar Association and the National District Attorneys Association, hates the bail bond business, saying it discriminates against poor and middle-class defendants, does nothing for public safety, and usurps decisions that ought to be made by the justice system.

Here as in many other areas of the law, the United States goes it alone. American law is, by international standards, a series of innovations and exceptions. From the central role played by juries in civil cases to the election of judges to punitive damages to the disproportionate number of people in prison, the United States has charted a distinctive and idiosyncratic legal path.

Bail is meant to make sure defendants show up for trial. It has ancient roots in English common law, which relied on sworn promises and on pledges of land or property from the defendants or their relatives to make sure they did not flee.

America's open frontier and entrepreneurial spirit injected an innovation into the process: by the early 1800s, private businesses were allowed to post bail in exchange for payments from the defendants and the promise that they would hunt down the defendants and return them if they failed to appear.

Commercial bail bond companies dominate the pretrial release systems of only two nations, the United States and the Philippines.

The flaw in the system most often cited by critics is that defendants who have not been convicted of a crime and who turn up for every court appearance are nonetheless required to pay a nonrefundable fee to a private business, assuming they do not want to remain in jail.

"Life is not fair, and I probably would feel the same way if I were a defendant," said Bill Kreins, a spokesman for the Professional Bail Agents of the United States, a trade group. "But the system is the best in the world."

The system costs taxpayers nothing, Mr. Kreins said, and it is exceptionally effective at ensuring that defendants appear for court.

Mr. Spath's experience confirms that.

If Mr. Spath considers a potential client a good risk, he will post bail in exchange for a nonrefundable 10 percent fee. In a 35-month period ending in November, his records show, Mr. Spath posted about $37 million in bonds—7,934 of them. That would suggest revenues of about $1.3 million a year, given his fee.

Mr. Spath, who is 62, has seven bail agents working for him, including his daughters Tia and Mia. "It probably costs me 50 grand a month to run this business," he said.

Mr. Spath hounds his clients relentlessly to make sure they appear for court. If they do not, he must pay the court the full amount unless he can find them and bring them back in short order.

Only 434 of his clients failed to appear for a court date over that period, and Mr. Spath straightened out 338 of those cases within the 60 days allowed by Florida law. In the end, he had to pay up only 76 times.

That is a failure rate of less than 1 percent.

But he had just taken a $100,000 hit. "Everything I worked for this year, I lost because of that one guy," he said. "If I write a bad bond, it takes me 17 to make it right."

Mr. Spath had thought the defendant, accused of drug trafficking, was a good bet because he had been cooperating with the government. The defendant is in Brazil now, but Mr. Spath is very good at finding people, and he is not giving up. He is working travel records, phone companies and a former girlfriend, and he is getting closer.

He sometimes requires collateral in addition to his fee, and has accepted rugs, an airplane and a winning Rhode Island lottery ticket. But mostly he is interested in houses.

"In this business, you have to understand real estate," Mr. Spath said. When the real estate market goes south, he said, bail bondsmen get hurt.

According to the Justice Department and academic studies, the clients of commercial bail bond agencies are more likely to appear for court in the first place and more likely to be captured if they flee than those released under other forms of supervision.

That may be because bail bond companies have financial incentives and choose their clients carefully. They also have more power. In many states, bond enforcement agents, sometimes called bounty hunters, may break into homes of defendants without a warrant, temporarily imprison them and move them across state lines without entering into the extradition process.

Still, critics say, efficiency and business considerations should not trump the evenhanded application of justice.

The experiences in states that have abolished commercial bail bonds, prosecutors say, have been mixed.

"The bail bond system is rife with corruption," said Joshua Marquis, the district attorney in Clatsop County, Ore. Since bond companies do not compete on price, they have every incentive to collude with lawyers, the police, jail officials and even judges to make sure that bail is high and that attractive clients are funneled to them.

Mr. Kreins, the industry spokesman, acknowledged scandals in Illinois, where "basically all the agents were in collusion with the judges," and in Louisiana, where sheriffs were also in the mix.

"We have acted responsibly every time an incident has occurred to seek stronger legislation," Mr. Kreins said. Mr. Marquis, the Oregon prosecutor, said doing away with commercial bonds had affected the justice system in a negative way as well. "The fact of the matter is," he said, "that in states like Oregon the failure-to-appear rate has skyrocketed." Oregon uses a combination of court deposits, promises to appear and restrictions on where defendants can live and work.

The rest of the world considers the American system a warning of how not to set up a pretrial release system, F. E. Devine wrote in "Commercial Bail Bonding," a 1991 book that remains the only comprehensive international survey of the subject.

He said that courts in Australia, India and South Africa had disciplined lawyers for professional misconduct for setting up commercial bail arrangements.

Other countries use a mix of methods to ensure that defendants appear for trial.

Some simply keep defendants in jail until trial. Others ask defendants to promise to turn up for trial. Some make failure to appear a separate crime. Some impose strict conditions on release, like reporting to the police frequently. Some make defendants liable for a given sum should they fail to appear but do not collect it up front. Others require a deposit in cash from the defendant, family members or friends, which is returned when the defendant appears.

But injecting money into the equation, even without the bond company's fee, is the exception. "Even purged of commercialism, most countries avoid a bail system based chiefly on financial security deposits," Mr. Devine wrote.

In the United States, the use of commercial bail bonds is rising, and they became the most popular form of pretrial release in 1998. More than 40 percent of felony defendants released before trial paid a bail bond company in 2004, up from 24 percent a decade earlier, according to the Justice Department.

Forty percent of people released on bail are eventually acquitted or have the charges against them dropped. Quite a few of them paid a substantial and nonrefundable fee to remain free in the meantime.

Kate Santana, a 20-year-old waitress, had spent eight days in jail when she found her way to Mr. Spath.

"Me and my husband got into a fight," Ms. Santana explained, "and the cops were called and I was arrested because there was a bite mark on his shoulder."

Mr. Spath took her $200 and posted her $2,000 bail. "I checked her criminal history out," he said. "I found out she was a mother and really she shouldn't be in jail."

But when a friend of a man accused of identity theft and perjury turned up seeking a $16,000 bond, Mr. Spath took a different attitude. "You bet your fanny I'm going to take collateral," he said. "I'll take his firstborn."

Mr. Spath is not much concerned with how the rest of the world views commercial bail bonds, but he was worked up about recent talk of a greater government role in pretrial release here in Broward County.

"Here's what everybody forgets," he said. "The taxpayers have to pay for these programs. Why should they pay for them? Why should they? When we can provide the same service for free. I'd rather see the money spent in parks, mental health issues, the homeless. Let the private sector do it. We do it better."

Critical Thinking

1. What are the arguments in favor of bail?
2. What are the arguments against bail?
3. Is "life is not fair" an adequate response to critics of bail?
4. How does the bail system invite corruption?

The Forfeiture Racket

Police and prosecutors won't give up their license to steal.

RADLEY BALKO

Around 3 in the morning on January 7, 2009, a 22-year-old college student named Anthony Smelley was pulled over on Interstate 70 in Putnam County, Indiana. He and two friends were en route from Detroit to visit Smelley's aunt in St. Louis. Smelley, who had recently received a $50,000 settlement from a car accident, was carrying around $17,500 in cash, according to later court documents. He claims he was bringing the money to buy a new car for his aunt.

The officer who pulled him over, Lt. Dwight Simmons of the Putnam County Sheriff's Department, said that Smelley had made an unsafe lane change and was driving with an obscured license plate. When Simmons asked for a driver's license, Smelley told him he had lost it after the accident. Simmons called in Smelley's name and discovered that his license had actually expired. The policeman asked Smelley to come out of the car, patted him down, and discovered a large roll of cash in his front pocket, in direct contradiction to Smelley's alleged statement in initial questioning that he wasn't, in fact, carrying much money.

A record check indicated that Smelley had previously been arrested (though not charged) for drug possession as a teenager, so the officer called in a K-9 unit to sniff the car for drugs. According to the police report, the dog gave two indications that narcotics might be present. So Smelley and his passengers were detained and the police seized Smelley's $17,500 cash under Indiana's asset forfeiture law.

But a subsequent hand search of the car turned up nothing except an empty glass pipe containing no drug residue in the purse of Smelley's girlfriend. Lacking any other evidence, police never charged anybody in the car with a drug-related crime. Yet not only did Putnam County continue to hold onto Smelley's money, but the authorities initiated legal proceedings to confiscate it permanently.

Smelley's case was no isolated incident. Over the past three decades, it has become routine in the United States for state, local, and federal governments to seize the property of people who were never even charged with, much less convicted of, a crime. Nearly every year, according to Justice Department statistics, the federal government sets new records for asset forfeiture. And under many state laws, the situation is even worse: State officials can seize property without a warrant and need only show "probable cause" that the booty was connected to a drug crime in order to keep it, as opposed to the criminal standard of proof "beyond a reasonable doubt." Instead of being innocent until proven guilty, owners of seized property all too often have a heavier burden of proof than the government officials who stole their stuff.

Municipalities have come to rely on confiscated property for revenue. Police and prosecutors use forfeiture proceeds to fund not only general operations but junkets, parties, and swank office equipment. A cottage industry has sprung up to offer law enforcement agencies instruction on how to take and keep property more efficiently. And in Indiana, where Anthony Smelley is still fighting to get his money back, forfeiture proceeds are enriching attorneys who don't even hold public office, a practice that violates the U.S. Constitution.

Guilty Property, Innocent Owners

Technically, civil asset forfeiture proceedings are brought against the property itself, not the owner. Hence they often have odd case titles, such as *U.S. v. Eight Thousand Eight Hundred and Fifty Dollars* or *U.S. v. One 1987 Jeep Wrangler*. The government need only demonstrate that the seized property is somehow related to a crime, generally either by showing that it was used in the commission of the act (as with a car driven to and from a drug transaction, or a house from which drugs are sold) or that it was purchased with the proceeds.

Because the property itself is on trial, the owner has the status of a third-party claimant. Once the government has shown probable cause of a property's "guilt," the onus is on the owner to prove his innocence. The parents of a drug-dealing teenager, for instance, would have to show they had no knowledge the kid was using the family car to facilitate drug transactions. Homeowners have to show they were unaware that a resident was keeping drugs on the premises. Anyone holding cash in close proximity to illicit drugs may have to document that he earned the money legitimately.

When owners of seized property put up a legal fight (and the majority do not), the cases are almost always heard by judges, not juries. In some states forfeiture claimants don't even have the right to a jury trial. But even in states where they do, owners tend to waive that right, because jury proceedings are longer and more expensive. Federal forfeiture claimants are technically guaranteed a jury trial under the Seventh Amendment, but can lose the right if they fail to reply in a timely manner to sometimes complicated government notices of seizure.

Federal asset forfeiture law dates back to the Racketeer Influenced and Corrupt Organizations (RICO) Act of 1970, a law aimed at seizing profits earned by organized crime. In 1978 Congress broadened RICO to include drug violations. But it was the Comprehensive Crime Control Act of 1984 that made forfeiture the lucrative, widely used law enforcement tool it is today.

"The Crime Control Act did a few things," says the Virginia-based defense attorney David Smith, author of the legal treatise *Prosecution and Defense of Forfeiture Cases*. "First, it corrected some poor drafting in the earlier laws. Second, it created two federal forfeiture funds, one in the Justice Department and one in the Treasury. And most important, it included an earmarking provision that gave forfeiture proceeds back to local law enforcement agencies that helped in a federal forfeiture."

This last bit was key. "The thinking was that this would motivate police agencies to use the forfeiture provisions," Smith says. "They were right. It also basically made law enforcement an interest group. They directly benefited from the law. Since it was passed, they've fought hard to keep it and strengthen it."

The 1984 law lowered the bar for civil forfeiture. To seize property, the government had only to show probable cause to believe that it was connected to drug activity, or the same standard cops use to obtain search warrants. The state was allowed to use hearsay evidence—meaning a federal agent could testify that a drug informant told him a car or home was used in a drug transaction—but property owners were barred from using hearsay, and couldn't even cross-examine some of the government's witnesses. Informants, while being protected from scrutiny, were incentivized monetarily: According to the law, snitches could receive as much as one-quarter of the bounty, up to $50,000 per case.

According to a 1992 Cato Institute study examining the early results of the Comprehensive Crime Control Act, total federal forfeiture revenues increased by 1,500 percent between 1985 and 1991. The Justice Department's forfeiture fund (which doesn't include forfeitures from customs agents) jumped from $27 million in 1985 to $644 million in 1991; by 1996 it crossed the $1 billion line, and as of 2008 assets had increased to $3.1 billion. According to the government's own data, less than 20 percent of federal seizures involved property whose owners were ever prosecuted.

More than 80 percent of federal seizures are never challenged in court, according to Smith. To supporters of forfeiture, this statistic is an indication of the owners' guilt, but opponents argue it simply reflects the fact that in many cases the property was worth less than the legal costs of trying to get it back. Under the 1984 law, forfeiture defendants can't be provided with a court-appointed attorney, meaning an innocent property owner without significant means would have to find a lawyer willing to take his case for free or in exchange for a portion of the property should he succeed in winning it back. And to even get a day in court, owners were forced to post a bond equal to 10 percent of the value of their seized property.

The average Drug Enforcement Administration (DEA) property seizure in 1998 was worth about $25,000. In 2000 a Justice Department source told the PBS series *Frontline* that this figure was also the cutoff under which most forfeiture attorneys advised clients that their cases wouldn't be worth pursuing. So a law aimed at denying drug kingpins their ill-gotten millions ended up affecting mostly those with so little loot it didn't even make sense to hire an attorney to win it back.

Police gradually came to view asset forfeiture as not just a way to minimize drug profits, or even to fill their own coffers, but as a tool to enforce maximum compliance on noncriminals. In one highly publicized example from the 1990s, Jason Brice nearly lost the motel he had bought and renovated in a high-crime area of Houston. At the request of local authorities, Brice hired private security, allowed police to patrol his property (at some cost to his business), and spent tens of thousands of dollars in other measures to prevent drug activity on the premises. But when local police asked Brice to raise his rates to deter criminals, he refused, saying it would put him out of business. Stepped up police harassment of his customers caused Brice to eventually terminate the agreement that had allowed them latitude on his property. In less than a month, local and federal officials tried to seize Brice's motel on the grounds that he was aware of drug dealing taking place there. Brice eventually won, but only after an expensive, drawn-out legal battle.

By the late 1990s, stories such as Brice's finally moved Congress to act. After a series of emotional hearings in 2000, Congress passed the Civil Asset Forfeiture Reform Act (CAFRA), authored by Rep. Henry Hyde (R-Ill.). The bill raised the federal government's burden of proof in forfeiture cases from probable cause to a preponderance of the evidence, the same standard as in other civil cases. It barred the government from using hearsay and allowed owners who won forfeiture challenges to obtain reimbursement for legal expenses.

The bill wasn't perfect. Seizures made by customs agents, as opposed to the DEA or FBI, would still be governed by the old rules. Hyde (who died in 2007) wanted an even heavier burden of proof for the government, the "beyond a reasonable doubt" standard used in criminal cases. That didn't pass. Under CAFRA, the federal government could still take your property without proving beyond a reasonable doubt that *any* crime was committed, much less that you yourself had committed one. But at least the reforms made the process a bit more difficult.

Problem was, the 1984 law had already spawned dozens of imitators on the state level, and CAFRA applied only to the feds. Forfeiture had been sending money to police departments and prosecutors' offices for 16 years, so even in the few states that passed laws to make the process more fair, officials found ways around them. Once the authorities have a license to steal, it turns out to be very difficult to revoke.

Present Punishment for Future Crimes

On February 4, 2009, Anthony Smelley got his first hearing before an Indiana judge. Smelley's attorney, David Kenninger, filed a motion asking for summary judgment against the county, citing a letter from a Detroit law firm stating that the seized money indeed came from an accident settlement, not a drug transaction. Kenninger also argued that because there were no drugs in Smelley's car, the state had failed to show the required "nexus" between the cash and illegal activity. Putnam County Circuit Court Judge Matthew Headley seemed to agree, hitting Christopher Gambill, who represented

Putnam County, with some tough questions. That's when Gambill made an argument that was remarkable even for a forfeiture case.

"You have not alleged that this person was dealing in drugs, right?" Judge Headley said.

"No," Gambill responded. "We alleged this money was being transported for the purpose of being used to be involved in a drug transaction."

Incredibly, Gambill was arguing that the county could seize Smelley's money for a crime that hadn't yet been committed. Asked in a phone interview to clarify, Gambill stands by the general principle. "I can't respond specifically to that case," he says, "but yes, under the state forfeiture statute, we can seize money if we can show that it was intended for use in a drug transaction at a later date." (Smelley himself refused to be interviewed for this article.)

The New York-based attorney Steven Kessler, author of the legal treatise *Civil and Criminal Forfeiture: Federal and State Practice,* says he has never heard the "future crimes" argument. "Can you imagine any judge in America allowing an argument like that to stand?" Kessler says. "It's obscene. It's like something out of that movie *Minority Report.* We don't punish people for crimes they haven't yet committed."

Smelley's fight for his money would only get more bizarre. At the conclusion of the February hearing, Judge Headley temporarily granted the motion for summary judgment, ordering the county to return the money. But there was a catch. Under Indiana law, the county had an additional 10 days to amend its complaint to show a connection between the seized property and illegal activity. If after that 10-day period the state didn't amend its complaint, or if the judge found the amendments insufficient, Smelley could retrieve his cash and be on his way.

But Headley would never rule on the amended complaint. Days after issuing summary judgment, Headley pulled himself off the case without explanation. Smelley's case was then batted around Indiana county courts for months, before finally ending up in front of Special Judge David Bolk. On August 18, more than seven months after Smelley's money was seized, Bolk overturned Headley's summary judgment. The opinion was curt, and didn't offer an explanation. Bolk ordered a civil forfeiture trial for November 13. The trial was then postponed again until January 29, 2010, due to congestion in the court system. That means Putnam County will have held Smelley's money for more than a year before giving him the opportunity to argue that he should get it back.

'Make the Bad Guys Pay!'

A survey of state and federal forfeiture since 2000 shows that CAFRA hasn't stopped the exponential growth of government asset seizure. Adjusted for inflation, the Justice Department's asset forfeiture fund, which includes proceeds from forfeitures carried out by all federal agencies except Immigration and Customs Enforcement, grew from $1.3 billion in 2001 to $3.1 billion in 2008. (The total includes some money left over from previous years, but according to Smith, almost all of the money is doled out to local and federal agencies on an annual basis.) National Public Radio has reported that between 2003 and 2007, the amount of money seized by local law enforcement agencies enrolled in the federal forfeiture program tripled from

$567 million to $1.6 billion. That doesn't include property seized by local law enforcement agencies without involving federal authorities.

While the Hyde bill placed some limits on federal civil forfeiture, it eased the process of seizing property in criminal forfeiture cases. Criminal forfeiture requires a conviction, so the property owner at least has to be found guilty of a crime, but the potential for abuse is widespread here, too. For example, prosecutors can "substitute assets" if they believe a defendant has disposed of seizable property. A court will issue a money judgment based on an estimate of how much the defendant has made through criminal endeavors. In some federal districts, prosecutors can then collect by seizing property that they can't prove was connected to any illegal activity.

Smith, the Virginia-based forfeiture specialist, says courts generally rubber-stamp the government's estimate on substitute assets, putting the defendant on the hook for that amount the rest of his life. This practice can be particularly unfair in conspiracy cases, where unequal defendants can be conjoined under the doctrine of joint and several liability. If 10 defendants are convicted in a drug conspiracy case and a court enters a total money judgment for $10 million, all 10 are liable until the $10 million is paid in full. If the five most responsible parties are sent to prison for 40 years, the remaining five—be they mid-level dealers, foot soldiers, or a girlfriend who forwarded a few phone calls—are liable for the entire $10 million, no matter who actually got the money in the end. "The government is always going to go after the guy with the most money, regardless of culpability," Smith says. "Even if he played only a small role in the conspiracy and earned everything he owns legitimately."

Criminal forfeiture can also prevent defendants from effectively contesting the charges against them. When the DEA accuses a doctor of illegally prescribing pain medication, for example, one of the first actions it takes is to freeze his assets for possible forfeiture. Since most doctors make their entire living from their practice, nearly everything they own can be frozen. Many accused doctors therefore don't have the resources to hire legal representation, much less experts to counter government assertions that they're prescribing controlled substances outside the normal practice of medicine. Forfeiture makes it nearly impossible for them to mount a credible defense.

In addition to raising questions of fairness, forfeiture has warped the priorities of law enforcement agencies. In 2008 the Bureau of Alcohol, Tobacco, Firearms, and Explosives asked for bids from private contractors on 2,000 Leatherman pocket knives for its agents, to be inscribed with the phrase "Always Think Forfeiture," a play on the agency's traditional "ATF" initials. The agency rescinded the order after it was reported in the *Idaho Statesman,* but critics said it betrayed the ethic of an organization more interested in taking people's property than in fighting crime.

Some police agencies come to view forfeiture not just as an occasional windfall for buying guns, police cars, or better equipment, but as a source of funding for basic operations. This is especially true with multijurisdictional drug task forces, some of which have become financially independent of the states, counties, and cities in which they operate, thanks to forfeiture and federal anti-drug grants.

In a 2001 study published in the *Journal of Criminal Justice,* the University of Texas at Dallas criminologist John Worral surveyed 1,400 police departments around the country on their use of forfeiture and the way they incorporated seized assets into their budgets. Worral, who describes himself as agnostic on the issue, concluded that "a substantial proportion of law enforcement agencies are dependent on civil asset forfeiture" and that "forfeiture is coming to be viewed not only as a budgetary supplement, but as a necessary source of income." Almost half of surveyed police departments with more than 100 law enforcement personnel said forfeiture proceeds were "necessary as a budget supplement" for department operations.

Such widespread use of forfeiture has created an industry of facilitators. Organizations such as the International Association for Asset Recovery sponsor conferences where law enforcement officials learn how to maximize their asset-seizing potential. They also offer certifications in forfeiture expertise. Advertising a Florida conference on its website in 2009, an outfit called Asset Recovery Watch (slogan: "Make the bad guys pay!") assures budget-conscious police departments that federal law permits them to use forfeiture funds to send police officers away to forfeiture conferences for training.

Forfeiture may also undermine actual enforcement of the law. In a 1994 study reported in *Justice Quarterly,* criminologists J. Mitchell Miller and Lance H. Selva observed several police agencies that identified drug supplies but delayed making busts to maximize the cash they could seize, since seized cash is more lucrative for police departments than seized drugs. This strategy allowed untold amounts of illicit drugs to be sold and moved into the streets, contrary to the official aims of drug enforcement.

There is also a potential conflict between forfeiture and criminal prosecution. Smith says prosecutors rarely initiate civil forfeiture proceedings against someone who has been acquitted on criminal charges, although the law allows them to do so. "I think the feeling is that a jury would be very skeptical of that—that this person was acquitted in court and that to now try to take his property too is unfair," he says. "If they don't think a jury would be sympathetic, it isn't worth their time to pursue it." If a prosecutor pursues a criminal case, with its higher burden of proof, he risks losing the ability to take the suspect's assets. If he drops the criminal case and just goes after the property with a case that is easier to prove, the suspect goes free, but the government gets to keep his stuff.

"There's also the temptation for prosecutors to offer a plea on the criminal charges in exchange for forfeiting some of the property," says Scott Bullock, an attorney with the Institute for Justice, a libertarian public interest law firm. "If you support the drug laws—and not all of us do—but if you support them, you have to question the incentives."

Highway Robbery in Texas

The Supreme Court this spring will rule on *Alvarez v. Smith,* a challenge to Illinois' forfeiture statute, which mostly mirrors the 1984 federal law—property can be seized without a warrant, retained using only probable cause; the government can use hearsay, defendants cannot; the burden of proof rests largely on those who have their stuff seized; and even victorious defendants cannot recover court costs or attorney fees.

The Supreme Court is unlikely to rule on any of those provisions. Instead it will consider a wrinkle that allows the state to keep property for up to six months before giving the owner his first day in court. Innocent property owners can be kept waiting more than a year before getting a decision, a predicament that critics say imposes an unconstitutional burden, particularly in cases where the police have seized someone's car.

In other states, the problem isn't so much the strict provisions on the books, but rather the relevant law's ambiguity, which can give police and prosecutors too much leeway. Tiny Tenaha, Texas, population 1,046, made national news in 2008 after a series of reports alleged that the town's police force was targeting black and Latino motorists along Highway 84, a busy regional artery that connects Houston to Louisiana's casinos, ensuring a reliable harvest of cash-heavy motorists. The *Chicago Tribune* reported that in just the three years between 2006 and 2008, Tenaha police stopped 140 drivers and asked them to sign waivers agreeing to hand over their cash, cars, jewelry, and other property to avoid arrest and prosecution on drug charges. If the drivers agreed, police took their property and waved them down the highway. If they refused, even innocent motorists faced months of legal hassles and thousands of dollars in attorney fees, usually amounting to far more than the value of the amount seized. One local attorney found court records of 200 cases in which Tenaha police had seized assets from drivers; only 50 were ever criminally charged.

National Public Radio reported in 2008 that in Kingsville, Texas, a town of 25,000, "Police officers drive high-performance Dodge Chargers and use $40,000 digital ticket writers. They'll soon carry military-style assault rifles, and the SWAT team recently acquired sniper rifles." All this equipment was funded with proceeds from highway forfeitures.

Texas prosecutors benefited too. Former Kimble County, Texas, District Attorney Ron Sutton used forfeiture money to pay the travel expenses for him and 198th District Judge Emil Karl Pohl to attend a conference in Hawaii. It was OK, the prosecutor told NPR, because Pohl approved the trip. (The judge later resigned over the incident.) Shelby County, Texas, District Attorney Lynda Kay Russell, whose district includes Tenaha, used forfeiture money to pay for tickets to a motorcycle rally and a Christmas parade. Russell is also attempting to use money from the forfeiture fund to pay for her defense against a civil rights lawsuit brought by several motorists whose property she helped take. In 2005, the district attorney in Montgomery County, Texas, had to admit that his office spent forfeiture money on an office margarita machine. The purchase got attention when the office won first place in a margarita competition at the county fair.

While police departments have been benefiting from forfeiture policies for years, funneling the money to prosecutors raises even more problems. "Police merely seize the property," David Smith says. "They don't determine which cases go forward. It's a violation of due process if the prosecutor, the person actually deciding whether or not to bring a forfeiture case, benefits somehow from the decision. You can't have the same person deciding which cases to take also directly benefiting from those cases."

Smith and the Institute for Justice's Scott Bullock both believe language in the 1982 Supreme Court decision *Marshall v. Jerrico Inc.* suggests that if a law allowing prosecutors' offices to benefit from forfeiture proceeds were challenged in federal court, it might be struck down. "*Jerrico* actually found that a government agency can be reimbursed from the defendant's assets for the cost of an investigation," says Bullock. "But in dicta, the Court indicated that it would strike down a law that allowed a particular public official to benefit from bringing a case." The Institute for Justice brought such a challenge to New Jersey's forfeiture law, which allows proceeds to flow into the general budgets of district attorneys. The New Jersey Supreme Court rejected the argument. So far no one has used *Jerrico* to challenge a state forfeiture law in federal court.

"I think that's where it needs to happen," Smith says. "State courts are made up of former prosecutors and other people who have connections to the community. No one wants to be the one who puts an end to all of this. I think it will take a federal court challenge to do it."

Not every state has kept its old laws intact. Kessler, the New York attorney and forfeiture expert, says 27 states have adopted CAFRA-style reforms. Some go even further, requiring that the proceeds from forfeited property go directly to the state general fund or to a fund earmarked for a specific purpose, such as education.

But here, too, things aren't always as they seem. In Missouri, for example, forfeited property is supposed to go to the state's public schools. But in 1999 a series of reports in *The Kansas City Star* showed how Missouri police agencies were circumventing state law. After seizing property, local police departments would turn it over to the DEA or another federal agency. Under federal law, the federal agency can keep 20 percent or more of the money; the rest, up to 80 percent, goes back to the local police department that conducted the investigation. None of the money in these cases goes to the schools.

The *Kansas City Star* investigation made national news at the time, but Kessler says the practice of circumventing earmarking through federal "adoption" is now common all over the country. "It happens a lot," he says. "It clearly goes against the intent of the state legislatures that passed these laws, but I don't know of any state that has made a serious effort to prevent it from happening."

'It's Blatantly Unconstitutional'

Timothy Bookwalter, the elected chief prosecutor for Putnam County, Indiana, did not represent the county in its effort to keep Anthony Smelley's money. Nor did anyone else in his office. Instead, the case was handled by Christopher Gambill, a local attorney in private practice. Gambill manages civil forfeiture cases for several Indiana counties, and he gets to keep a portion of what he wins in court. "My contingency for my own county is a quarter; for the others it's a third," Gambill says.

The concept is alarming. If allowing public prosecutors to benefit from forfeiture funds brushes up against due process, allowing an unaccountable private attorney to run forfeiture cases and keep a portion of the winnings rams a steamroller straight through the notion. "This is scandalous," Kessler says. "It's blatantly unconstitutional."

Gambill not only argues and briefs Putnam County forfeiture cases; he also determines which cases the county pursues in the first place. That means nongovernmental forfeiture attorneys are making criminal justice decisions that directly bolster

their incomes. "It's really bad policy," David Smith says. "I also don't see how it could possibly be legal."

Mark Rutherford, chairman of the Indiana Public Defender Commission, says he isn't aware of any court challenges to the practice. "It's just sort of accepted here that this is the way things are," Rutherford says. "There are attorneys who have amassed fortunes off of these cases." The office of Indiana Attorney General Greg Zoeller referred inquiries about this contracting system to the Indiana Prosecuting Attorneys Council, which represents the state's prosecutors. That organization did not return several calls seeking comment.

Like Missouri, Indiana theoretically allocates asset forfeiture proceeds to its public schools. In fact, that requirement is spelled out in Indiana's constitution. But there are ways around this restriction. "If you can get someone to settle without having to go to court, under state law that technically isn't a forfeiture," Gambill says. "So it can all go to the police and prosecutors' offices. After the contingency, of course."

'We All Get Greedy'

The country's lurch to the political left won't necessarily mean a greater protection for civil liberties in forfeiture cases. Asset seizure, in fact, is one area where conservatives tend to take a less law-enforcement-friendly position than liberals. "Conservatives value property," Kessler says, "so they tend to be sympathetic to property owners in these cases. If you look back at the Supreme Court cases putting limits on forfeiture, most were written by conservative justices. And of course Rep. Hyde was a conservative Republican."

Don't be surprised, then, if forfeiture power expands in the coming years, particularly with respect to financial fraud, tax evasion, and other white-collar crimes. "It's always a pendulum, swinging back and forth," Kessler says. "I think we are in the pro-government phase now."

But over the long term, Kessler is more optimistic about reform. Expanding unjust forfeiture laws to include new classes of people makes the members of those classes aware of just how unfair those laws can be. And the government always overplays its hand. "We all get greedy, and the government is no exception," he says. "I think that in this climate, they'll go for too much, and then the courts will rein them in. It's unfortunate that that's the way it has to happen."

As for Anthony Smelley: As of this writing, more than a year after the police took $17,500 of his money, he has yet to have his day in court.

Critical Thinking

1. What Constitutional provisions are violated by asset forfeiture?

2. Was the pat-down of Mr. Smelley lawful?

3. Describe the differences between civil and criminal forfeiture.

4. What are the problems with CAFRA?

RADLEY BALKO (rbalko@reason.com) is a senior editor at *Reason*.

When Our Eyes Deceive Us

Dahlia Lithwick

Describe the last person who served you coffee. What if I helped refresh your memory? Showed you some photos of local baristas? Pulled together a helpful lineup? Cheered exuberantly when you picked the "right" one? Now imagine that instead of identifying the person who made your venti latte last week, we had just worked together to nail a robber or a rapist. Imagine how good we would feel. Now imagine what would happen if we were wrong.

Last month, a Texas judge cleared Timothy Cole of the aggravated-sexual-assault conviction that sent him to prison in 1986. Although his victim positively identified him three times—twice in police lineups and again at trial—Cole was ultimately exonerated by DNA testing. The real rapist, Jerry Wayne Johnson, had been confessing to the crime since 1995. Unfortunately for Cole, he died in prison in 1999, long before his name was cleared.

Our eyes deceive us. Social scientists have insisted for decades that our eyewitness-identification process is unreliable at best and can be the cause of grievous injustice. A study published last month by Gary Wells and Deah Quinlivan in Law and Human Behavior, the journal of the American Psychology-Law Society, reveals just how often those injustices occur: of the more than 230 people in the United States who were wrongfully convicted and later exonerated by DNA evidence, approximately 77 percent involved cases of mistaken eyewitness identification, more than any other single factor.

Wells has been studying mistaken identifications for decades, and his objection to the eyewitness-identification system is not that people make mistakes. In an interview, he explains that eyewitness evidence is important, but should be treated—like blood, fingerprints and fiber evidence—as trace evidence, subject to contamination, deterioration and corruption. Our current criminal-justice system allows juries to hear eyewitness-identification evidence shaped by suggestive police procedures. In a 1977 case, *Manson v. Braithwaite,* the Supreme Court held that such evidence could be used if deemed "reliable." Today we know you can have a good long look, be certain you have the right guy and also be wrong. But Manson is still considered good law.

Jennifer Thompson was 22 the night she was raped in 1984. Throughout the ordeal, she scrupulously studied her attacker, determined to memorize every detail of his face and voice so that, if she survived, she could help the police catch him. Thompson soon identified Ronald Cotton in a photo lineup. When she—after some hesitation—again picked Cotton out of a physical lineup a few days later, a detective told her she'd picked the same person in the photo lineup.

But in this case Thompson got it wrong, although Cotton served 10 years before DNA evidence exonerated him and decisively implicated another man, Bobby Poole. The curious part of the story is that despite Thompson's determination to memorize every detail, when she first saw Poole in court she was certain she had never seen him before. Indeed, according to Wells and Quinlivan, "even after DNA had exonerated Cotton and Thompson herself had accepted the fact that Poole was her attacker, she had no memory of Poole's face and, when thinking back to the attack, she says, 'I still see Ronald Cotton'."

In their paper, Wells and Quinlivan suggest a host of tricks the mind can play, ranging from incorporating innocent "feedback" from police investigators to increasing certainty in one's shaky memories that become reinforced over time. Add to that Thompson's determination to regain control over her life, and her need to believe that the justice system was just, and it would have been doubly hard for her to look at a police lineup that, as it happened, did not include an image of the real rapist, and walk away. To hear Thompson and other victims tell it, being part of a system that identified and ultimately convicted the wrong man became another form of victimization, and for that reason alone the system needs to be reformed.

Being part of a system that identified and ultimately convicted the wrong man became another form of victimization.

The problems with the eyewitness-identification system cannot be laid at the feet of crime victims any more than they can be blamed on police investigators. Wells's argument for reforming our eyewitness-identification system is that the incentive for the police to subtly nudge our memories is not only uncorrected by the justice system, but also sometimes rewarded by it. Wells wants the Supreme Court to revisit the scientific basis for its 1977 decision. Whether or not the John Roberts court wishes to take up the issue of innocent prisoners—there is one test case percolating through the New Jersey courts—a few states and cities have used innocent-exoneration scandals to rethink their eyewitness-identification practices. Proposed changes include showing victims photos sequentially and explaining that the perpetrator may not be included in the lineup, and ensuring that whoever conducts the lineup has no knowledge of which person is the actual suspect.

This is not an issue that tracks the usual left-right divide. Some of the most zealous reformers of the eyewitness-identification process are lifelong conservatives who recognize that the credibility of the whole justice system is on the line each time an innocent man goes to jail and a guilty one walks free.

Critical Thinking

1. Shouldn't we be able to rely on a rape victim's identification of her attacker?
2. What safeguards can be taken to prevent misidentifications?

DAHLIA LITHWICK is a *Newsweek* contributing editor and a senior writer for *Slate*. A version of this column also appears on Slate.com.

The DNA Factor

Lawmakers are expanding the use of forensic technology to battle crime.

SARAH HAMMOND

Their tragic deaths occurred years apart, but Johnia Berry and Juli Busken have one thing in common. Their murders spurred lawmakers to pass legislation that led to the arrest of their killers, and bolstered a system to catch other criminals.

Berry, 21, lived in Knoxville, Tenn., and was planning to attend graduate school when she was stabbed to death in 2004. Three years later the Johnia Berry Act was enacted. It created a DNA database in Tennessee that led to a DNA match and the arrest of Berry's killer.

"Ironically, he got caught voluntarily giving a DNA sample for an unrelated arrest," says Lieutenant Governor and Senate President Ron Ramsey, the champion of the act.

In Norman, Okla., Busken, a 21-year-old University of Oklahoma dance major and Arkansas native, was abducted, forced into her car, raped and murdered in 1996. Eight years later, a DNA database matched a man who had been charged with rape and second-degree burglary in another case. He was convicted of Busken's rape and murder and sentenced to death.

Last year, Arkansas Senator Dawn Creekmore sponsored the successful Juli's Law, which requires DNA samples to be taken from all suspects charged with murder, kidnapping and sexual assault in the first degree. "We are looking to further expand Juli's law to include burglary," says Creekmore.

Ramsey says there's no question that DNA has become a key tool for criminal investigations. "DNA is the 21st century fingerprint. Without DNA evidence and state databases, bringing these murderers to justice would have not happened."

> **"DNA is the 21st century fingerprint. Without DNA evidence and state databases, bringing these murderers to justice would have not happened."**
>
> Tennessee Senate President Ron Ramsey

DNA's Growing Role

Since the advent of DNA testing in 1985, biological material—skin, hair, blood and other bodily fluids—has emerged as the most reliable physical evidence from a crime scene. In 1987, police in Britain convicted a man of rape based on DNA evidence, the first person ever convicted on that basis.

In 1987, Florida rapist Tommie Lee Andrews became the first person in the United States to be convicted as a result of DNA evidence. The following year, a Virginia man called the "South Side Strangler" was convicted after DNA linked him to rapes and murders near Richmond.

Now, more than 20 years after DNA was first used in criminal investigations, its crime-fighting potential continues to be an important focus of state crime control legislation. Expansive policies for DNA collection have proved successful, and states continue to widen the scope of their statutes. Forty-seven states have laws to collect DNA samples for all convicted felons. With Juli's law, Arkansas joins 20 other states that are expanding DNA collection from those who are arrested for, but not yet convicted of, qualifying offenses. Johnia's law in Tennessee also extends to arrestees.

One reason for the move toward expanding DNA collection is this: Studies show there is a 40 percent chance that burglaries and other nonviolent crimes are being committed by someone who already has committed a violent crime, perhaps even murder.

The more expansive a state's DNA policy, the more likely it is that a new specimen will match or "hit" a DNA sample that already is in the database. The FBI's Combined DNA Index System is a computer program that allows forensic laboratories at the national, state and local levels to compare samples. It contains more than 5 million profiles, making it the largest in the world.

The information obtained for a new DNA sample is matched against two indexes. The first, the convicted offender index, allows criminal justice officials to match evidence found at the scene of an unsolved crime against specimens taken from qualifying criminals and arrestees.

The second, the forensic index, allows samples from those offenders to be compared to specimens recovered from unsolved crime scenes. It also allows crime scenes to be linked, even if the offender's identity is not yet known. Expanding DNA collection to arrestees will increase the number of testable samples in databases.

DNA analysis is regarded as the "gold standard" of forensic science because research for its techniques have been thoroughly tested and heavily financed. The procedures, however,

DNA: All in the Family

The crime-fighting power of DNA is revolutionizing America's criminal justice systems, but some question whether the science sometimes allows investigators to go too far.

Controversy is rising over what lab technicians should do when a DNA sample reveals a partial match to one of the profiles registered in the database. A partial match means the incriminating biological evidence does not belong to that person, but it may belong to one of their relatives. If a lab turns over the partially matched profile to police to investigate family members, have the constitutional rights of those relatives been violated?

"If my brother's DNA ends up in the database, and he's forfeited his privacy rights by becoming a convicted felon," says Stephen Mercer, a Maryland Defense attorney, "has he also forfeited my privacy rights as a wholly innocent family member?"

Maryland is currently the only state with a statute banning the use of partial matches.

Advocates for the use of partial matches, however, believe safeguards can answer privacy concerns.

"Any time privacy and constitutional matters are at play, there is cause for concern," says Delegate Brent Boggs of West Virginia. "But with proper restrictions and regulations, partial matches of DNA profiles can be an effective tool in the toolbox of law enforcement."

West Virginia is considering legislation that would allow leads from partial matches to be used in trying to solve serious crimes, says Senator Jeffrey Kessler. "If all investigative leads have been exhausted, it's important for public safety not to ignore this tool in pursuing violent criminals."

Denver District Attorney Mitch Morrissey is one of the nation's leading proponents for using partial matches. "We're running the risk of another victim," he says, "and it would be a huge loss if the technology was available and wasn't used to stop an offender."

In Colorado, administrative regulations permit the use of partial matches, as well as a procedure known as familial searching, which refines the partial match criteria so that the results are more likely to lead to a family member. This method involves a close examination of the Y chromosome, the male sex chromosome, and works only for men. With this technique, Morrissey says, a genetic link can be established with 90 percent accuracy. In 2009, Denver solved its first case with the aid of familial DNA software, and Morrissey's office has identified potential family matches in 13 other cases. Investigators are still pursuing those leads.

Along with being an effective tool for finding criminals, "DNA is also a powerful investigative tool that is important for determining innocence," Kessler says.

Daryl Hunt was the first person in the United States to be exonerated with the help of a partial match. He was sentenced to life in prison for a brutal rape and murder in North Carolina. After serving 19 years in prison, Hunt is free, and the real murderer was taken into custody because his biological brother's profile was in the North Carolina database.

Still, Mercer warns that just because it's effective, it doesn't make it right.

"If the measure of reasonableness is going to be, 'We got the right guy,' then every search is going to be reasonable. In the name of solving crimes, let's just start going around and kicking down doors," he says. "We're going to solve a lot of crimes. But what's the cost?"

As the capabilities of DNA analysis continue to develop, legislatures will have a role in deciding which scientific procedures are acceptable and under what conditions they can be used in light of privacy concerns.

—Richard Williams, NCSL

still are vulnerable to human error. Cases of lab analysts contaminating samples, mislabeling samples and misreporting samples are not uncommon. These mistakes highlight the need for oversight in forensic science so that avoidable errors do not become roadblocks to justice.

Testing for Innocence

DNA evidence is not all about putting people behind bars, however. It's also about getting others out from behind them.

"Expanding DNA databases is not only speeding up crime solving, it is also exonerating the innocent at a rapid pace," says Creekmore.

> **"Expanding DNA databases is not only speeding up crime solving, it is also exonerating the innocent at a rapid pace."**
>
> Arkansas Senator Dawn Creekmore

At least 39 states have passed laws allowing post-conviction DNA testing. According to the Innocence Project, to date, 251 people in the United States have been exonerated by DNA testing, including 17 who served time on death row.

Federal assistance is also available for post-conviction testing through the 2004 Innocence Project Act. The law includes the Kirk Bloodsworth Post-Conviction DNA Testing Program, which provides funding for states to test prisoners who claim they're innocent. Bloodsworth, who spent eight years in prison for rape and murder, was the first person on death row exonerated by DNA testing.

DNA analysis also helps solve cases of missing or unidentified people. The U.S. Justice Department is working with state and local officials to expand their capacity for forensic DNA technology to match missing persons with unidentified human remains.

The FBI's Missing Persons DNA Database contains samples from relatives of missing people. The system also can accept genetic samples from material known to belong to the victim, such as hair from a comb or a sample taken from the victim's toothbrush.

Victim of Success

The success forensic science analysis has brought to criminal justice also has brought challenges. Some labs cannot keep pace with the expanded policies, resulting in backlogs of DNA samples.

There are two main components at the heart of the backlog issue for crime laboratories. The first, the casework sample backlog, are samples collected from crime scenes, suspects and victims in criminal cases. Backlogged casework samples delay analysis for all kinds of forensic evidence. The second major source is the convicted offender backlog, which consists of samples from those arrested and incarcerated for qualifying crimes. The convicted offender backlog includes as many as 300,000 unanalyzed DNA samples, with more than 500,000 samples yet to be taken, according to the National Institute of Justice.

The federal government has made the Forensic DNA Backlog Reduction Program the centerpiece of its effort. It is part of the DNA Initiative that began in 2004 and has aimed to develop new DNA technologies, eliminate backlogs and train forensic professionals at federal, state and local levels. State and local governments can request money to expand crime laboratories that conduct DNA analysis as well as funds to handle, screen and analyze backlogged forensic DNA casework samples.

State legislatures are also addressing the backlog problem. Lawmakers in Arizona, California, Colorado, Illinois, Kansas, Louisiana, Maryland, Michigan, Texas and Wisconsin have authorized audits of state crime labs to improve efficiency and reduce backlog. Other states are studying the issue or hiring private labs to analyze samples to meet growing forensic demands.

Fiscal Reality Bites

As enthusiastic as many lawmakers are about the potential for DNA technology, they also are mindful that new programs cost money. In the current economic climate, legislators are looking for new revenue to cover the costs.

Tennessee is considering charging a fee to local governments for elective DNA testing. Ramsey says. "No one wants to cut funding for crime labs that are doing such good work putting killers behind bars, but at the same time, as legislators, we need to balance the budget and be fiscally realistic during these tough times."

Advances in forensic science continue to help states increase the effectiveness of their criminal justice systems.

"We need our law enforcement back on the street fighting crime and carrying on their own investigations," Arkansas' Creekmore says. "Let DNA take care of part of that workload."

Critical Thinking

1. Do you believe that all arrestees should have their DNA added to the data base?

2. Do you see any Constitutional issues with Johnia's law?

SARAH HAMMOND tracks criminal justice issues for NCSL.

DNA's Dirty Little Secret

A forensic tool renowned for exonerating the innocent may actually be putting them in prison.

MICHAEL BOBELIAN

Three days before Christmas 1972, a twenty-two-year-old nurse named Diana Sylvester wrapped up her night shift at the University of San Francisco Medical Center and made her way to her apartment, halfway between the hospital and Golden Gate Park. She arrived around 8:00 A.M. and set her newspaper and purse on the kitchen table. A few minutes later, Sylvester's landlord, Helen Nigidoff, heard loud thuds and screams emanating from Sylvester's unit upstairs. With her apron still on, Nigidoff rang the doorbell before opening a door leading up to Sylvester's apartment, where she came face-to-face with a stranger. "Go away," he growled angrily. "We're making love." As Nigidoff raced downstairs to call the police, the man ran out of the building holding a denim jacket over his face.

When the officers arrived a half hour later, they found a gruesome scene. Sylvester lay motionless next to the Christmas tree on her living-room floor, her mouth unnaturally agape, blood oozing from her chest like molten lava. An autopsy revealed that Sylvester's attacker had forced her to perform oral sex and then strangled her, before plunging a knife into her chest two times. One stab pierced her heart. The other tore through her left lung, drowning her in her own blood.

The attacker forced her to perform oral sex and then strangled her, before plunging a knife into her chest two times. One stab pierced her heart. The other tore through her left lung, drowning her in her own blood.

Police immediately scoured Sylvester's apartment and questioned the landlady, who offered a description of the assailant: white, medium height, and heavy-set, with curly brown hair and a beard. But neither these details nor the bits and pieces of evidence they collected in the months-long investigation that followed were enough to pinpoint the culprit. The few leads investigators turned up fizzled, and the case went cold.

Then in early 2003 the San Francisco Police Department, which had received a grant to use DNA technology to crack unsolved crimes, dug Sylvester's case file out of storage and discovered a slide with sperm that had been swabbed from Sylvester's mouth after her death. The sample was badly deteriorated and contained less than half the DNA markers that are normally used to link a suspect to a crime. But investigators ran the profile through California's DNA database and turned up a match: an ailing seventy-year-old man named John Puckett, who had a history of sexual violence. There was no other physical evidence linking him to the crime. But Puckett was arrested, tried, and eventually convicted based mostly on the DNA match, which was portrayed as proof positive of his guilt—the jury was told that the chance that a random person's DNA would match that found at the crime scene was one in 1.1 million.

If Puckett's were an ordinary criminal case, this figure might have been accurate. Indeed, when police use fresh DNA material to link a crime directly to a suspect identified through eyewitness accounts or other evidence, the chances of accidentally hitting on an innocent person are extraordinarily slim. But when suspects are found by combing through large databases, the odds are exponentially higher. In Puckett's case the actual chance of a false match is a staggering one in three, according to the formula endorsed by the FBI's DNA advisory board and the National Research Council, a body created by Congress to advise the government and the public on scientific issues. But the jury that decided Puckett's fate never heard that figure. In fact, his lawyers were explicitly barred from bringing it up.

Over the past quarter century, DNA evidence has transformed criminal justice, freeing hundreds of innocent people and helping unravel countless crimes that might otherwise have gone unsolved. It has also captivated the public imagination: the plots of popular TV crime shows often hinge on the power of DNA to crack impossible cases, which has helped to give this forensic tool an air of infallibility—a phenomenon known in criminal justice circles as "the CSI effect." This fail-safe image is not entirely unfounded, especially when it comes to traditional applications of DNA evidence. But increasingly DNA is being used for a new purpose: target the culprits in cold cases, where other investigative options have been exhausted. All told, U.S. law enforcement agencies have conducted more than 100,000 so-called cold-hit investigations using the federal DNA database and its state-level counterparts, which hold upward of 7.6 million offender profiles. In these instances, where the DNA is often incomplete or degraded and there are few other clues to go on, the reliability of DNA evidence plummets—a fact that jurors weighing such cases are almost never told. As a result, DNA, a tool renowned for exonerating the innocent, may actually be putting a growing number of them behind bars.

When police initially investigated Sylvester's murder in the early 1970s, the lead suspect was a man named Robert Baker, who just a month before the attack had escaped from a mental hospital and was living in a rundown Volkswagen bus near Fisherman's Wharf. Baker matched the description given by Sylvester's landlady, and two weeks before Sylvester's murder he had snuck into the apartment of another woman who lived just four blocks away and forced her to perform oral sex (a crime for which he was later convicted). In that case, as in Sylvester's, there was no sign of forced entry or a struggle. And while he hadn't killed the woman, he had threatened to do so, telling her, "I can rape you now or after you're dead." Days after Sylvester was killed, Baker also allegedly harassed a woman and a young girl, following them to their home just a few doors from Sylvester's apartment.

There was also other evidence linking Baker to the crime. When police searched his van, for instance, they found a blood-spattered parking ticket, and the blood type matched Sylvester's. And there was a good chance he came into contact with Sylvester just before her murder, as he was one of the street vendors peddling wares outside the hospital where she worked. In fact, that morning Sylvester had lingered around the hospital after her shift, waiting for the vendors to open for business so she could buy a candle for her boyfriend. Police suspected Baker saw her shopping and followed her home. Despite this evidence, Baker, who died in 1978, was never charged with Sylvester's murder (the reasons for this are not made clear in the case file), and the investigation eventually went cold.

Then in 2003 police reopened Sylvester's case file and found the DNA sample. When analyzing DNA, scientists ideally focus on thirteen markers, known as loci. The odds of finding two people who share all thirteen is roughly on par with those of being hit by an asteroid—about one in a quadrillion in many cases. But the fewer the markers, the higher the probability that more than one person will match the same profile, since relatives often share a number of markers and even perfect strangers usually share two or three. In Sylvester's case, the DNA was so degraded that the crime lab was only able to identify five and a half markers; California requires a minimum of seven to even run a profile against its felony database. This meant the lab had to rely on inconclusive readings for two markers—one was so inscrutable, in fact, that there were three possible interpretations, each of which presumably could have led to a different suspect.

Part of the reason for the ambiguity was that, besides being deteriorated, the material was what is known as a "mixed sample," meaning it contained DNA from both Sylvester and the perpetrator. Bonnie Cheng, the crime lab technician who did the analysis, argued that this was not a significant stumbling block—outside of the one marker, where she acknowledged a mixture was present, she testified that it was "highly unlikely" that there was much mingling of genetic material. This runs counter to the views of most experts, who insist that mixed samples tend to be blended

throughout, making it exceedingly difficult to separate one person's DNA from another. In 2005, Peter Gill, then a researcher at the Forensic Science Service, which administers the national DNA database for the British police, told a conference of forensic scientists, "If you show ten colleagues a mixture, you will probably end up with ten different answers." Dan Krane, a molecular biologist at Wright State University and a leading critic of the government's stance on DNA evidence, agrees. "There is a public perception that DNA profiles are black and white," he told me. "The reality is that easily in half of all cases—namely, those where the samples are mixed or degraded—there is the potential for subjectivity."

Once the San Francisco crime lab had completed its analysis, police ran it against California's offender database, which at the time contained DNA profiles of 338,000 convicted sex offenders and violent criminals. One name turned up: John Puckett. Puckett had not been a suspect during the original 1972 investigation, and detectives didn't bother looking into any of the twenty men who were. Instead, they relied wholly on the DNA match.

Puckett first learned of the evidence against him in October 2005, when Inspector Joseph Toomey, a veteran of the San Francisco Police Department's homicide unit, made his way to the trailer park where Puckett lived with his wife on the outskirts of Stockton, a gritty, industrial enclave east of San Francisco. The suspect, who was recovering from heart bypass surgery, hobbled to the door clutching a bag of his own urine. Toomey introduced himself, then launched into questioning. Holding up a picture of Sylvester and her boyfriend that had been clipped from an old newspaper article, he asked Puckett whether he knew her. Puckett said no. "You never had sex with that girl?" Toomey prodded. "I don't know her," Puckett insisted. "Never seen her."

In the months that followed, Puckett was questioned several more times. His story never wavered, and he cooperated readily with investigators. When he and his wife decided to move to Oklahoma to be closer to her children and grandchildren, for example, he notified them months in advance. He also volunteered to give them a fresh sample of his DNA. When it matched the sample in the database, he was arrested and charged with first-degree murder.

The case was assigned to the San Francisco public defender's office, which had recently brought on a DNA specialist named Bicka Barlow. Unlike most lawyers, Barlow has a background in science—before going to law school, she earned a master's degree in genetics and molecular biology from Cornell. For years, she had been agitating against what she saw as overreach by law enforcement and prosecutors when it came to the use of DNA evidence in cold-hit cases. She believed Puckett's was the ideal case to draw attention to the issue because the DNA match was weak. "If there was a DNA case that could be won, this was it," she told me, when I met with her at a café across from the San Francisco criminal courthouse last October. "Most jurisdictions would not have even prosecuted this case."

Barlow's main point of contention was statistics. Typically, law enforcement and prosecutors rely on FBI estimates for the rarity of a given DNA profile—a figure can be as remote as one in many trillions when investigators have all thirteen markers to work with. In Puckett's case, where there were only five and a half markers available, the San Francisco crime lab put the figure at one in 1.1 million—still remote enough to erase any reasonable doubt of his guilt. The problem is that, according to most scientists, this statistic is only relevant when DNA material is used to link a crime directly to a suspect identified through eyewitness testimony or other evidence. In cases where a suspect is found by searching through large databases, the chances of accidentally hitting on the wrong person are orders of magnitude higher.

The reasons for this aren't difficult to grasp: consider what happens when you take a DNA profile that has a rarity of one in a million and run it through a database that contains a million people; chances are you'll get a coincidental match. Given this fact, the two leading scientific bodies that have studied the issue—the National Research Council and the FBI's DNA advisory board—have recommended that law enforcement and prosecutors calculate the probability of a coincidental match differently in cold-hit cases. In particular, they recommend multiplying the FBI's rarity statistic by the number of profiles in the database, to arrive at a figure known as the Database Match Probability. When this formula is applied to Puckett's case (where a profile with a rarity of one in 1.1 million was run through a database of 338,000 offenders) the chances of a coincidental match climb to one in three.

Such coincidental matches are more than a theoretical possibility, as Chicago police can attest. In 2004, detectives investigating a string of robberies on the city's North Side found some skin cells that the culprit had left behind at one crime scene, which contained six DNA markers. When they ran this profile against Illinois's offender database, they found it matched a woman named Diane Myers. There was just one problem: when the burglaries in question were committed, Myers was already in jail, serving time on drug charges.

Indeed, the little information that has come to light about the actual rate of coincidental matches in offender databases suggests the chances of hitting on the wrong person may be even higher than the Database Match Probability suggests. In 2005, Barlow heard that an Arizona state employee named Kathryn Troyer had run a series of tests on the state's DNA database, which at the time included 65,000 profiles, and found multiple people with nine or more identical markers. If you believe the FBI's rarity statistics, this was all but impossible—the chances of any two people in the general population sharing that many markers was supposed to be about one in 750 million, while the Database Match Probability for a nine-marker match in a system the size of Arizona's is roughly one in 11,000.

Barlow decided to subpoena Troyer's searches, believing the finding would be helpful for a case she was working on. To her surprise, she discovered that Troyer had unearthed not just a couple of pairs who shared nine identical markers, but 122. "That was a 'wow' moment," Barlow recalls.

As it turns out, these findings were no fluke. Searches of databases elsewhere have revealed similarly unsettling numbers. In 2006, for instance, a Chicago judge ordered a search of the Illinois database, which contained 233,000 profiles. It turned up 903 pairs with nine or more matching DNA markers. Among geneticists and statisticians, these findings have eroded faith in the FBI's DNA rarity statistics, which were based on data from just 200 or 300 people and are used by crime labs across the country. Laurence Mueller, an ecology and evolutionary biology professor at University of California, Irvine, told me that anyone who knows statistics finds the figures "laughable."

Rather than try to sort out the disparities between its numbers and database findings, the FBI has fought to keep this information under wraps. After Barlow subpoenaed the Arizona database searches, the agency sent the state's Department of Public Safety a cease-and-desist letter, warning that its conduct was "under review." Eventually, the Arizona attorney general obtained a court order to block Barlow's distribution of the findings. In other instances, the FBI has threatened to revoke access to the bureau's master DNA database if states make the contents of their systems available to defense teams or academics. Agency officials argue they have done so because granting access would violate the privacy of the offenders (although researchers generally request anonymous DNA profiles with no names attached) and tie up the FBI's computers, impeding investigations. These justifications baffle researchers. In the December 2009 issue of the journal *Science,* dozens of biologists, geneticists, and forensic experts urged the FBI to change its secretive policy, saying that there was no way that allowing a handful of researchers to run database searches, each of which takes only a few minutes, would hamper investigations. They also dismissed the agency's privacy concerns, saying, "The government frequently releases sensitive information under controlled conditions to verified researchers." Krane of Wright State University, who was the letter's lead author, believes the real reason the FBI has blocked access is to avoid revealing the shortcomings in its own system. "Analysis of the offender database is sure to expose the misconceptions and errors in the method the FBI used to arrive at its rarity statistics," he told me.

Since the crux of the government's case relied on DNA, Barlow knew that she had to get the data on the probability of coincidental matches in front of the jury to have a shot at winning. Beginning in early 2007, Judge Jerome Benson summoned the parties to his courtroom, a high-security chamber with a bulletproof wall of steel and glass separating the bench from the gallery, for a series of pretrial hearings. Puckett, who had spent the previous year and a half in the medical wing of the local county jail, rolled himself in using a government-issued wheelchair, a Bible tucked between his thigh and the chair's frame.

Barlow pled with the judge to let her present evidence challenging the government's one-in-1.1-million statistic. The inability to reveal this information to the jury, she insisted, would violate Puckett's constitutional right to a fair trial. Prosecutor David Merin, countered by presenting two seminal precedents from other courts, which had refused to admit the Database Match Probability (the one-in-three statistic, in Puckett's case). He also called the Arizona database findings "half baked," and argued that if Barlow's requests were granted, the trial would get bogged down in complex statistical debates that would "likely cause a jury to throw up their hands in confusion." Barlow found this argument infuriating. "Frankly, to sit here and say that it would be too confusing for the jury is insulting," she seethed, according to press reports. "If we can't present this evidence, then the case is gone."

John Puckett was arrested and tried based mostly on the DNA evidence, which was portrayed as proof positive of his guilt; the jury was told that the chances of a false DNA match were one in 1.1 million. In fact, they were one in three.

In the end, the defense lost on all counts. Barlow and her fellow counsel, Kwixuan Maloof, were barred from mentioning that Puckett had been identified through a cold hit and from introducing the statistic on the one-in-three likelihood of a coincidental database match in his case—a figure the judge dismissed as "essentially irrelevant." They were also prohibited from presenting evidence on the high rates of coincidental matches found in DNA databases in places like Arizona.

Juries in cold-hit cases are rarely, if ever, presented with evidence on the high probability of coincidental DNA matches. When they see DNA evidence, most defense attorneys assume the case against their client is airtight and start praying for a plea bargain.

This was not unusual. Juries in cold-hit cases are rarely, if ever, presented with evidence on the high probability of coincidental DNA matches. This is partly because, unlike Barlow, most defense attorneys don't understand the underlying statistical problems. When they see DNA evidence, they assume the case against their client is airtight and start praying for a plea bargain. In the rare instances where defense teams challenge the government figures, judges tend to reject their arguments. Few lawyers are savvy enough about genetics and statistics to make persuasive cases, and even those who are have trouble getting judges to comprehend the complex underlying concepts. Some powerful voices in the forensic community have also actively discouraged courts from considering information that casts doubt on the relevance of FBI rarity statistics. Bruce Budowle, the former head of the FBI's laboratory division, regularly offers testimony and written statements urging courts not to admit the Database Match Probability—a figure Budowle argues can be "very misleading to a jury or to any other layperson"—rather than the FBI's numbers. (Budowle did not respond to requests for an interview, but his stance is consistent with that of FBI crime labs, which have ignored the recommendations of the FBI's own DNA advisory board and continue to use FBI rarity statistics rather than the Database Match Probability.) And because courts are bound by precedent, each time a judge decides to bar information about the shortcomings of DNA evidence, he or she makes it more difficult for defense teams in other cases to get this evidence before juries.

During Puckett's trial, which began in January 2008 and was covered in depth by the *Los Angeles Times,* the defense was also barred from introducing any information about Robert Baker, the escaped mental patient who was the lead suspect during the original investigation. This left them with little to work with. The fragile crime scene DNA had been destroyed during testing, so the defense had no way of double-checking the results. Barlow had hoped to test the bloodstained parking ticket found in Baker's van to see if it matched Sylvester's DNA, but it had gone missing from the evidence file. She and Maloof also seriously considered digging up Baker's corpse and running DNA testing on it, but decided it was probably too decayed to do them any good.

Prosecutors had a similarly shallow trove of information to draw from. Besides the moldered DNA, there was no physical evidence linking the defendant to the crime—none of the twenty-six fingerprints found in Sylvester's apartment belonged to him, for instance. And police hadn't been able to place him in the neighborhood on the day of Sylvester's murder (though at some point he had applied for a job at the medical center where she worked). Ordinarily, prosecutors in murder cases rely heavily on testimony from the police and medical examiners who analyzed the fresh crime scene evidence, but in Puckett's case this, too, was out of the question. Everyone intimately involved with the original investigation was either dead or too senile to take the stand. Sylvester's landlady, Helen Nigidoff, was still alive when police started investigating Puckett, but for some reason was never asked to view pictures of the suspect. By the time the trial rolled around, she had died, too, leaving prosecutors and defense attorneys to haggle endlessly over whether Puckett matched her description—a stash of pictures from the 1970s that was found in Puckett's shed showed that, like the culprit, he was a white man of medium height, but he didn't have a beard or curly hair as Nigidoff described.

Still, the prosecution had some chilling circumstantial evidence to present; in 1977, Puckett had been convicted of raping two women and sexually assaulting a third, crimes for which he later served eight years in prison. Because the revelation of past offenses is highly prejudicial, most courts keep these details from jurors. But California allows prosecutors to present this information to show that a crime matches a pattern of offense. In Puckett's case, all three victims were brought in to testify. Each of them described how Puckett had conned his way into their cars by posing as a police officer and got them to drive out to a deserted area. Using a knife or an ice pick as a weapon, he then forced them to perform oral sex. "He . . . grabbed my throat, and I started to scream," recalled one victim. "He started to squeeze and telling me to shut up, and then I felt a knife at my throat."

Among scientists, the high rates of coincidental matches found in some DNA databases have eroded faith in the FBI's DNA rarity statistics. Laurence Mueller, a biology professor at University of California, Irvine, says anyone who knows statistics finds the figures "laughable."

These agonizing accounts no doubt influenced the jury. But in the end, the prosecution's case hung on the DNA evidence and the damning one-in-1.1-million statistic. Merin brought the figure into sharp relief with a simple calculation: the year Sylvester was murdered, he noted, California had eighteen million residents, about half of them men; given the rarity of the crime scene DNA profile, he argued that there were only eight or nine people living in the state who could have done it—and Puckett was one of them. He hammered this point home during the closing argument. "All of the DNA evidence points to the defendant and no one else," he argued. "They're devastating results that point right at Mr. Puckett, telling us that he's guilty."

The jury finally began deliberating in February 2008. Waiting in a holding tank inside the courthouse, Puckett and his lawyers were resigned to a guilty verdict, though they saw a flicker of hope early on when the jury sent Judge Benson a note asking how the suspect was "identified as a person of interest." Barlow pressed the judge to reveal that he was found through a cold hit. Doing otherwise, she argued, would lead the jury to believe that the evidence against her client was more reliable than it actually was. But Benson would not budge. He insisted, as he had from the beginning, that the information was "irrelevant" and urged the jury not to speculate on the matter.

Puckett was found guilty of murder in the first degree and sentenced to life. When interviewed after the trial, jurors said they might have decided differently had they been presented with the statistic on the high probability of a coincidental DNA match.

After forty-eight hours of deliberations, the jury delivered a verdict. Puckett was found guilty of murder in the first degree and later sentenced to life in prison with a possibility of parole after seven years. Jurors told the *Los Angeles Times* that the one-in-1.1-million statistic had been pivotal to their decision. Asked whether the jury might have reached a different conclusion if they had been presented with the one-in-three figure, juror Joe Deluca replied, "Of course it would have changed things. It would have changed a lot of things."

Today Puckett is locked away in Corcoran State Prison while his case awaits appeal. His lawyers hold out some hope for the next round. Months after Puckett's verdict, the California Supreme Court tackled a similar cold-hit murder case. While the judges backed the prosecution's statistic on the likelihood of a false match—the same calculation proffered by the prosecution in the Puckett case—in a footnote they left the door open to presenting the Database Match Probability in some instances. Depending on how this is interpreted, it may give Puckett and others like him a fighting chance of getting the most relevant exculpatory evidence before the jury. But it still falls far short of the recommendations set out by the National Research Council and the FBI's DNA advisory board, which call for the Database Match Probability to be used in all cold-hit cases. And in most parts of the country, judges continue to prevent jurors from seeing this figure at all.

Outside scientific circles, this perilous distortion of DNA evidence has gotten little attention. This is partly because the underlying mathematics can be difficult to grasp for those with no training in science or statistics. But there may also be another factor at play: so far, those who have been swept up in cold-hit investigations have mostly been convicted felons and sex offenders, because theirs were the only profiles in the databases, and the possibility that people who have committed vicious crimes might be getting shabby treatment from the courts is far less likely to stir public outrage. But the list of groups cropping up in these databases is expanding rapidly. Last year, California and at least fourteen other states started cataloging DNA, not just from convicted felons, but from anyone arrested for a felony. At the same time, the FBI began collecting DNA from detained immigrants and anyone arrested for a federal offense, including those charged with petty misdemeanors, such as loitering on federal property. As a result, more than a million new profiles are being added to our nation's offender databases each year, and as DNA testing becomes more routine, it is likely that these systems will grow to include an even wider cross-section of the public. Of course, as the number of profiles in the databases swell, so do the odds of accidentally fingering innocent people. Given these facts, it's not inconceivable that one day you or someone you know will end up in Puckett's situation.

Critical Thinking

1. Why shouldn't the DNA evidence against Puckett be relied on as accurate?

2. What is the difference between DNA in a cold case and in an ordinary criminal case?

3. Under what circumstances can DNA be relied on as an accurate identifier of an individual?

Michael Bobelian, a freelance writer and lawyer based in New York City, is the author of *Children of Armenia: A Forgotten Genocide and the Century-Long Struggle for Justice,* which was recently published by Simon and Schuster. Research support for this article was provided by the Investigative Fund at the Nation Institute.

From *Washington Monthly,* March/April 2010. Copyright © 2010 by Washington Monthly Publishing, LLC, 1319 F St. NW, Suite 710, Washington DC 20004. (202)393-5155. Reprinted by permission. www.washingtonmonthly.com

Confessions and the Constitution
The Remedy for Violating Constitutional Safeguards

Carl A. Benoit, JD

L aw enforcement officers investigating criminal activity within the United States have increasing amounts of technology to assist them in identifying those responsible for criminal conduct. Advances in DNA collection and testing, automated fingerprint identification, and a multitude of forensic techniques are only a few examples of the scientific tools available to the modern criminal investigator.[1] However, despite all of the physical evidence collected in a particular case and all of the scientific analysis used to tie an individual to the commission of a crime, one nonscientific technique continues to play an important role in the investigation and prosecution of criminal activity: the confession. Confessions made to law enforcement officers continue to hold significant importance within the criminal justice process. Law enforcement officers seek to obtain confessions from individuals suspected of criminal activity even when the physical, scientific, or other evidence against an individual is overwhelming. Criminal defendants, faced with the possibility that their confessions may be used by the prosecution at trial, seek to keep their confessions out of court through legal challenges. Both parties recognize the continued influence of the words uttered by criminal defendants on a judge or a jury. There is something powerful in the words that describe the particular events, as well as the thoughts, actions, emotions, or motives, that would otherwise remain hidden and undiscovered from any scientific or forensic test. In 1961, U.S. Supreme Court Justice Felix Frankfurter made the following statement about confessions that still rings true today:

> **. . . one nonscientific technique continues to play an important role in the investigation and prosecution of criminal activity: the confession.**

Despite modern advances in the technology of crime detection, offenses frequently occur about which things cannot be made to speak. And where there cannot be found innocent human witnesses to such offenses, nothing remains—if police investigation is not to be balked before it has fairly begun—but to seek out possibly guilty witnesses and ask them questions, witnesses, that is, who are suspected of knowing something about the offense precisely because they are suspected of implication in it.[2]

It is when the police officer "seek[s] out possibly guilty witnesses and ask[s] them questions"[3] that the law surrounding confessions must be considered. Because confessions and interrogations are such a recognized and long-standing tool in law enforcement, articles about all aspects of the topic abound. Less frequently addressed, however, is a discussion of the legal effect of obtaining a confession in violation of constitutional safeguards. Because obtaining a confession can implicate different constitutional rights, answering this question involves identifying the particular constitutional safeguard involved—typically a right found within the Fourth, Fifth, or Sixth Amendments to the U.S. Constitution—and then understanding the remedy that each provision imposes for a violation.

In recent years, the U.S. Supreme Court decided three cases that involved confessions obtained in violation of constitutional safeguards. And, in each of these cases, the Supreme Court has made one thing clear: the Constitution imposes different remedies for different violations. Law enforcement officers must be aware of these issues and can find guidance in these Supreme Court cases involving confessions. Armed with this information, law enforcement officers can properly understand the implications of obtaining confessions in violation of constitutional safeguards.

The Fourth Amendment

"The right of the people to be secure in their persons, houses, papers, and effects, against unreasonable searches and seizures, shall not be violated. . . ."[4] Expressly contained within its first sentence, the Fourth Amendment's prohibition against unreasonable searches and seizures are familiar terms to law enforcement officers. What is less clear from the text, however, is the remedy the Fourth Amendment imposes for a violation of its protections. While the Fourth Amendment stands silent on this point, the U.S. Supreme Court has not stood mute. Beginning in 1914, the Supreme Court created a remedy for violations of Fourth Amendment rights—the remedy of suppression.[5] This remedy, however, was limited to the federal government and its agents until 1961 when, in *Mapp v. Ohio,*[6] the Supreme Court held that the states were required to suppress evidence obtained in violation of the Fourth Amendment.

The Suppression Remedy

The judicially created remedy of suppression (also called the exclusionary rule), as defined by the Supreme Court, can be easily stated: evidence obtained in violation of the Fourth Amendment is excluded from use at trial. While there are many exceptions and limits to this general rule[7] (beyond what will be covered within this article), the application of this rule to evidence is well understood in law enforcement circles. And, while the suppression remedy applies more commonly to physical or tangible items, the rule's application clearly encompasses confessions. This became clear in 1963 when the Supreme Court ruled that verbal evidence obtained in violation of the Fourth Amendment is subject to the remedy of suppression. This rule, established in *Wong Sun v. United States,* has come to be known, and very nearly defined, by the phrase "fruit of the poison tree."[8] If a proper understanding of the Fourth Amendment rule of suppression requires a more formal definition, then *Wong Sun* provided that as well.

. . . verbal evidence obtained in violation of the Fourth Amendment is subject to the remedy of suppression.

We need not hold that all evidence is "fruit of the poisonous tree" simply because it would not have come to light but for the illegal actions of the police. Rather, the more apt question in such a case is "whether, granting establishment of the primary illegality, the evidence to which instant objection is made has been come at by exploitation of that illegality or instead by means sufficiently distinguishable to be purged of the primary taint."[9]

Thus, for purposes of the Fourth Amendment exclusionary rule, suppression is not necessarily automatic: to order the suppression of evidence, including a confession, a court is required to determine if the evidence in question was obtained in violation of the Fourth Amendment and then determine whether anything occurred that may have cleansed the evidence from this violation. The 2003 case of *Kaupp v. Texas*[10] best illustrates the application of the remedy of suppression to a confession.

Following the disappearance of 14-year-old Destiny Thetford on January 13, 1999, investigators learned that her 19-year-old half-brother, Nicholas Thetford, had a sexual relationship with her and that both were seen together on the day Destiny went missing. On January 26, 1999, Thetford and Robert Kaupp went to the sheriff's office to be questioned about the disappearance. Kaupp was cooperative during the interview and released. Thetford, after a long interview and failing his third polygraph examination, eventually admitted to stabbing Destiny and hiding her body in a drainage ditch. Thetford also implicated

Kaupp in the crime. After obtaining a written statement from Nicholas, detectives sought an arrest warrant for Kaupp. Their request for a warrant was denied.[11] Undeterred, three detectives and three uniformed officers went to Kaupp's house between 2 and 3 A.M. on the morning of January 27 to "get [Kaupp] in and confront him with what Thetford ha[d] said."[12] Kaupp's father allowed the police officers into the home, and Kaupp was located asleep in his bedroom. Kaupp was told, "we need to go and talk," to which he replied, "OK," before he was handcuffed and escorted from his home into a waiting police car, wearing only boxer shorts and a T-shirt.[13] He then was brought to the scene where Destiny's body was recently located, kept there for between 5 to 10 minutes, driven to the police station, placed in an interview room, unhandcuffed, and read his *Miranda* rights. After initial denials, he admitted his involvement in the crime but denied any role in the murder. Kaupp also provided investigators with a signed statement.[14]

Prior to his trial, Kaupp moved to suppress the oral and written statements he made to investigators on the morning of January 27, claiming that the confession was the result of his unlawful arrest. The trial court denied the motion and ruled that Kaupp was not placed under arrest prior to making the admissions. Kaupp was convicted of murder and sentenced to 55 years. The Texas Court of Appeals upheld the conviction, and the Court of Criminal Appeals denied review of the case.[15] Kaupp appealed to the U.S. Supreme Court.

According to the Supreme Court, the admissibility of Kaupp's confession turned on the issue of whether Kaupp's confession was the product of an illegal arrest. The state did not claim to have probable cause to arrest Kaupp when the officers went to Kaupp's home the morning of January 27, but asserted that Kaupp was not arrested until after he gave the confession. According to the state, Kaupp consented to the encounter with the officers when he said, "OK," and was taken from his bedroom. The facts, however, did not support the state in either position. In essence, the Court held that the events of the morning of January 27—from being woken up in his bedroom, being handcuffed, being transported to the police station, and being given *Miranda* warnings—led to the conclusion that Kaupp was arrested. According to the Court, no "reasonable person in [Kaupp's] situation would have thought he was sitting in the interview room as a matter of choice, free to change his mind and go home to bed."[16] Because Kaupp was arrested without probable cause to support the arrest, this Fourth Amendment violation required suppression of the product of the unlawful arrest—the confession—unless the state could prove the confession was an "act of free will [sufficient] to purge the primary taint" of the unlawful seizure.[17] In this regard, the Court noted that factors to consider include observance of *Miranda,* the length of time between the arrest and the confession, the presence of intervening circumstances, and the level of misconduct.[18] The Court observed that only one of the above factors was present—the application of *Miranda*—to favor the prosecution.[19] No substantial time passed between the arrest and the confession, and there was no allegation by the state that any significant intervening event occurred between the arrest and confession.[20] The Court determined that the application of *Miranda* warnings, standing alone, was insufficient to cleanse Kaupp's statement from the illegal arrest.[21] The Court remanded the case to the state court of appeals. On remand, the state admitted that it was unable to point to any facts that would remove the taint from the unlawful arrest.[22]

The *Kaupp* case provides a simple example of the application of the suppression remedy. Kaupp was seized in violation of the Fourth Amendment when he was arrested without probable cause. The product of that unlawful seizure was the confession that Kaupp gave following his unlawful arrest. Because there was insufficient evidence that any events intervened between the unlawful seizure of Kaupp and the confession made by Kaupp to cleanse the statement from the Fourth Amendment violation, the confession was inadmissible.[23]

The Fifth Amendment

The Fifth Amendment to the U.S. Constitution, as it relates to the taking of confessions, provides that "no person . . . shall be compelled in any criminal case to be a witness against himself."[24] In *Miranda v. Arizona*,[25] the Supreme Court held that the environment present in the setting of a custodial interrogation was so coercive that confessions obtained from a person under these circumstances were presumed to be coerced unless specific warnings were provided and a waiver was obtained. This rule was developed primarily to protect the person's Fifth Amendment privilege against self-incrimination. According to *Miranda*, if the warning and waiving procedures are not followed when a person is in custody and subject to interrogation, any statement obtained is inadmissible in the prosecution's case in chief. Thus,

> The prosecution may not use statements, whether exculpatory or inculpatory, stemming from custodial interrogation, unless it demonstrates the use of procedural safeguards effective to secure the privilege against self-incrimination.[26]

If a statement obtained in violation of *Miranda* procedures cannot be used by the prosecution in its direct case, what is the effect on physical evidence located as a result of such a statement? The Supreme Court answered this question in 2004.

. . . a statement obtained in violation of *Miranda* procedures cannot be used by the prosecution in its direct case. . . .

Samuel Patane came to the attention of a police officer and a detective who were investigating Patane for separate offenses. Both law enforcement officers went to Patane's home together, the police officer to investigate Patane's violation of a temporary order of protection and the detective to investigate whether Patane, a convicted felon, illegally possessed a pistol. After arriving at the residence and speaking to him, Patane was arrested for violating the order of protection. The detective began advising him of his *Miranda* rights, but did not get past the right to remain silent because Patane interrupted him,

claiming that he knew his rights. The advice of rights was never completed.[27] The detective then questioned Patane about the pistol, and, though initially reluctant to discuss the gun, Patane said, "I am not sure I should tell you anything about the [handgun] because I don't want you to take it away from me."[28] The detective persisted in light of this response. Patane admitted that the pistol was in his bedroom and gave the detective permission to take the gun. The detective found and seized the pistol. After his indictment charging him as a felon in possession, Patane sought suppression of the pistol.[29]

The district court suppressed the gun,[30] determining that the officers lacked probable cause for the arrest and the pistol was a fruit of the unlawful arrest. The Tenth Circuit Court of Appeals, while reversing the district court on the issue of probable cause, suppressed the gun on the grounds that it was the fruit of Patane's unwarned statement.[31] The case was then appealed to the U.S. Supreme Court.

The issue before the Supreme Court was "whether a failure to give a suspect the warnings prescribed by *Miranda v. Arizona* requires suppression of the physical fruits of the suspect's unwarned but voluntary statements."[32] To resolve the question of the admissibility of the gun and whether its suppression was required by the exclusionary rule, the Court first determined what constitutional right was implicated. Because the circuit court of appeals held that Patane was lawfully arrested based on probable cause, there was no Fourth Amendment violation. What was clear to the Supreme Court, however, based on the uncontested facts, was that the detective obtained Patane's statements without properly advising Patane of his rights pursuant to *Miranda v. Arizona*. Thus, the legal issue for the Supreme Court focused on the application of the Fifth Amendment to the statements Patane made while in custody.

According to Justice Thomas, writing for the majority of the Supreme Court, the core protection of the Fifth Amendment is its prohibition of "compelling a criminal defendant to testify against himself at trial," and the Fifth Amendment "cannot be violated by the introduction of nontestimonial evidence obtained as a result of voluntary statements."[33] There was no claim that Patane's statements about the pistol were made involuntarily in violation of the Fifth Amendment. But, the Court has provided protection of Fifth Amendment rights beyond the core protections. In this regard, Justice Thomas noted that the Supreme Court has created certain rules designed to protect the Fifth Amendment's privilege against self-incrimination, including the procedures set forth in the *Miranda* decision. According to Justice Thomas,

> . . . in *Miranda,* the Court concluded that the possibility of coercion inherent in custodial interrogations unacceptably raises the risk that the suspect's privilege against self-incrimination might be violated. To protect against this danger, the *Miranda* rule creates a presumption of coercion, in the absence of specific warnings, that is generally irrebuttable for purposes of the prosecution's case in chief.[34]

Because the *Miranda* rule provides protections that go beyond the "actual protections of the Self-Incrimination Clause," the Court noted that statements obtained without compliance with *Miranda,* unlike statements that actually violate the Fifth Amendment, can be used in certain situations because they do not violate the Fifth Amendment.[35] For example, "statements taken without *Miranda* warnings (though not actually compelled) can be used to impeach a defendant's testimony at trial."[36] According to the Court, the failure to give *Miranda* warnings by itself does not violate a suspect's Fifth Amendment rights. A violation of *Miranda* may occur only when the suspect's unwarned statement is introduced at trial, and the proper remedy for such a violation is the exclusion of the unwarned statement.[37] Accordingly, "the nontestimonial fruit of a voluntary statement . . . does not implicate the Self-Incrimination Clause" because the "admission of such fruit presents no risk that a defendant's coerced statements (however defined) will be used against him at a criminal trial."[38] Finally, the Court determined that there was no reason to apply the remedy of suppression to the pistol by noting that it had previously decided not to apply suppression to mere failures to give *Miranda* warnings.[39] Finding that the Glock pistol should not be suppressed, the Supreme Court reversed the decision of the court of appeals.[40]

The *Patane* case provides a straightforward application of the *Miranda* rule to statements and also highlights the distinction between the Fifth Amendment and *Miranda.* In the case, there was no argument that Patane's statement was involuntary or coerced—which would have been a violation of the Fifth Amendment. Neither the officer nor the detective compelled Patane to make a statement about the pistol. Their only omission was in questioning Patane without finishing the required warnings and obtaining a waiver. Patane's statement—unwarned but otherwise voluntary—was not obtained in violation of the Fifth Amendment. According to the Court in *Patane,* the full and complete remedy for the unwarned statement is the exclusion of the statement from the prosecution's direct case. The exclusion of the statement fully protected Patane's Fifth Amendment rights. The nontestimonial evidence—the pistol—obtained as a result of Patane's unwarned statement was not the product of a constitutional violation and, therefore, was admissible.

The Sixth Amendment

The Sixth Amendment to the U.S. Constitution guarantees that "[i]n all criminal prosecutions, the accused shall . . . have the Assistance of Counsel for his defence."[41] To protect this right, the Supreme Court has held that a defendant is entitled to have counsel present at certain critical stages, including postindictment interactions between the defendant and the government.[42] The Sixth Amendment protections only apply at certain critical stages—after the filing of a formal charge (in federal procedure, an Indictment of Information) or after a court appearance on the charge. And, because the right applies to the crimes that are the subject of the formal charges or court appearance, it is said to be crime specific.[43] Once the Sixth Amendment right to counsel attaches to the defendant on a particular charge, statements deliberately elicited from a defendant by the government may not be used at trial unless counsel was present when the

statement was made or unless the defendant properly waived his Sixth Amendment right. But, does a Sixth Amendment violation prohibit the prosecution from using a defendant's statements for impeachment purposes? The Supreme Court answered this question in 2009.

The Sixth Amendment protections only apply at certain critical stages. . . .

In January 2004, Rhonda Theel and Donnie Ray Ventris went to the home of Ernest Hicks likely because they learned that Hicks carried large amounts of cash. One or both killed Hicks, took $300 and his cell phone, and fled in his pickup truck.[44] Theel and Ventris were arrested and charged with various crimes for these acts. Theel pleaded guilty to robbery and agreed to testify against Ventris. Prior to his trial, a police informant was placed in the holding cell with Ventris. After the informant engaged Ventris in conversation by telling Ventris that he looked like he had "something more serious weighing on his mind," Ventris confessed to the informant that he had "shot this man in his head and chest" and stolen some property from him as well.[45] At his trial, Ventris took the stand and blamed Theel for both the robbery and murder.[46] The prosecution, over the defendant's objection, was permitted to call the cell-mate informant to testify to the prior statement Ventris made about the murder. The jury acquitted Ventris of murder, but convicted him of burglary and robbery charges. Ventris appealed his conviction. The Kansas Supreme Court held that the statement made by Ventris to the cell-mate informant was not admissible at trial for any reason, including impeachment, and reversed the conviction.[47] The state appealed to the U.S. Supreme Court.

The Supreme Court agreed to hear the appeal to determine "whether a defendant's incriminating statement to a jailhouse informant, concededly elicited in violation of Sixth Amendment strictures, is admissible at trial to impeach the defendant's conflicting statement."[48] The Court began the opinion by noting that while the Sixth Amendment's core protection is "the opportunity for a defendant to consult with an attorney and to have him investigate the case and prepare a defense for trial,"[49] the right extends further. Also included in the Sixth Amendment is the right to have an attorney at certain "critical interactions between the defendant and the State," including "the deliberate elicitation by law enforcement officers (and their agents) of statements pertaining to the charge."[50] According to the Court, which assumed that Ventris's Sixth Amendment right was violated when he was engaged in a conversation by the cell-mate informant, the question is the scope of the remedy to be imposed for the violation. Here, the Court noted that "excluding tainted evidence for impeachment purposes is not worth the candle."[51] This is so because the interests safeguarded by excluding the evidence for impeachment purposes are "outweighed by the need to prevent perjury and to assure the integrity of the trial process."[52] Thus, while the violation should prevent the State from using the evidence affirmatively, it should not shield the defendant from his contradictions or untruths.[53]

The Court considered the possibility that because the unlawfully obtained statement could be used for impeachment purposes, there is incentive for police officers to obtain the statement in violation of the Sixth Amendment. To this end, the Court believed that police officers have significant incentive to comply with the Constitution because "statements lawfully obtained can be used for all purposes. . . ." Even though there may be some incentive to try to obtain impeachment material, the Court finds that this potential benefit is too speculative and not weighty enough to overcome the cost of permitting a defendant to commit perjury unchallenged.[54] Accordingly, the Court held that the "informant's testimony, concededly elicited in violation of the Sixth Amendment, was admissible to challenge Ventris's inconsistent testimony at trial" and reversed the judgment of the Kansas Supreme Court.[55]

The *Ventris* case also provides a clear application of the Sixth Amendment to a confession obtained in violation of its protections. It is important to note here that the Court accepted the premise that the comments by the jailhouse informant amounted to an interrogation of Ventris. Because Ventris's Sixth Amendment rights had attached by virtue of his indictment, no statement about the pending charge could be deliberately elicited from Ventris unless he had counsel present or if he was advised of his Sixth Amendment rights and voluntarily waived them. Because the questioning by the cell-mate informant was assumed to amount to deliberate elicitation and because Ventris's counsel was not present at that time and Ventris had not waived his Sixth Amendment rights, the statement was taken in violation of the Sixth Amendment, and the informant was prohibited from testifying during the prosecution's direct case. However, once Ventris took the witness stand and testified in contradiction to the statements he made to the informant, the prosecution was entitled to use the statements to impeach Ventris's testimony. If Ventris did not take the witness stand, the prosecution would not have been able to introduce the testimony of the informant.

. . . investigators should ensure that confessions obtained comply with the Constitution's demands.

Conclusion

The cases discussed in this article describe the different costs imposed for obtaining a confession in violation of the safeguards found within the Fourth, Fifth, and Sixth Amendments to the U.S. Constitution. In light of the continued importance of confessions to the successful prosecution of criminals, investigators should ensure that confessions obtained comply with the Constitution's demands. In doing so, investigators can ensure that confessions obtained can be fully and affirmatively used to their fullest potential by the prosecution.

Notes

1. Jim Markey, "After the Match: Dealing with the New Era of DNA," *FBI Law Enforcement Bulletin*, October 2007, 1–4.
2. *Culombe v. Connecticut*, 367 U.S. 568 (1961).
3. *Id.*
4. U.S. CONST. Amend IV.
5. *Weeks v. United States*, 232 U.S. 383 (1913).
6. *Mapp v. Ohio*, 367 U.S. 643 (1961).
7. Exceptions and limitations to the application of the suppression remedy include standing (*Rakas v. Illinois*, 439 U.S. 128 (1978)); good faith reliance on a search warrant (*United States v. Leon*, 468 U.S. 897 (1984)); attenuation (*Wong Sun v. United States*, 371 U.S. 471 (1963)); and independent source and inevitable discovery (*Murray v. U.S.*, 487 U.S. 533 (1988)). *See also Hudson v. Michigan*, 547 U.S. 546 (2006) (Suppression not required for when search warrant executed in violation of knock and announce rule); and *Virginia v. Moore*, 553 U.S. 164 (2008) (Suppression not required for an arrest made in violation of state statute but constitutionally permissible).
8. 371 U.S. 471 (1963).
9. *Id.* at 487, 488.
10. 538 U.S. 626 (2003).
11. *Kaupp v. State of Texas*, 2001 WL 619119 (Tex. App.- Hous. (14 Dist.)) (Unpublished opinion).
12. *Kaupp v. Texas*, 538 U.S. 626, 628 (2003).
13. *Id.* at 629.
14. *Id.* at 628, 629.
15. *Id.* at 629.
16. *Id.* at 632.
17. *Id.*
18. *Id.* at 633.
19. *Id.*
20. *Id.*
21. *Id.*
22. *Kaupp v. State of Texas*, 2004 WL 114979 (Tex.App.Hous. (14 Dist.)) (Unpublished opinion).
23. Events that a court should consider in this regard are set forth in *Brown v. Illinois*, 422 U.S. 590 (1975).
24. U.S. CONST. Amend V.
25. 384 U.S. 436 (1966).
26. *Id.* at 445.
27. *United States v. Patane*, 542 U.S. 630, 634–635 (2004).
28. *Id.* at 635.
29. *Id.*
30. If the arrest of Patane was in violation of the Fourth Amendment, then both his statement and the gun would have been subject to suppression.
31. *Id.* at 635–636.
32. *Id.* at 634, 635.
33. *Id.* at 637.
34. *Id.* at 639 (Citations omitted).
35. *Id.*

36. *Id.*

37. *Id.* at 641. According to the Court, "the Self-Incrimination Clause contains its own exclusionary rule."

38. *Id.* at 643.

39. *Id.* at 644. *See Oregon v. Elstad,* 470 U.S. 298 (1985) and *Michigan v. Tucker,* 417 U.S. 433 (1974).

40. *Id.*

41. U.S. CONST. Amend. VI.

42. *Massiah v. United States,* 377 U.S. 201 (1964).

43. *Texas v. Cobb,* 532 U.S. 162 (2001).

44. *Kansas v. Ventris,* 129 S. Ct. 1841, 1843 (2009).

45. *Id.* at 1843.

46. *Id.*

47. *State of Kansas v. Ventris,* 285 Kan. 595 (2008).

48. *Id.* at 1843.

49. *Id.* at 1844–1845 (quoting *Michigan v. Harvey,* 494 U.S. 344, 348 (1990)).

50. *Id.* at 1845. The Court noted that the State conceded that a Sixth Amendment violation occurred and the Court did not rule that this "concession was necessary." It accepted the concession as the law of the case.

51. *Id.* at 1846.

52. *Id.* (quoting *Stone v. Powell,* 428 U.S. 465, 488 (1976)).

53. *Id.*

54. *Id.* at 1847.

55. *Id.*

Critical Thinking

1. Do you agree with the Supreme Court's decision in *Kaupp*? Explain.

2. Do you agree with the Supreme Court's decision in *Patane*? Explain.

3. Do you agree with the Supreme Court's decision in *Ventris*? Explain.

Special Agent **CARL A. BENOIT** is a legal instructor at the FBI Academy.

Law enforcement officers of other than federal jurisdiction who are interested in this article should consult their legal advisors. Some police procedures ruled permissible under federal constitutional law are of questionable legality under state law or are not permitted at all.

From *FBI Law Enforcement Bulletin* by Carl A. Benoit, April 2010, pp. 23–32. Published by Federal Bureau of Investigation, www.fbi.gov.

Justice and Antonin Scalia
The Supreme Court's Most Strident Catholic

JULIA VITULLO-MARTIN

After being nominated as a Supreme Court Justice by President Ronald Reagan in 1986, Antonin Scalia faced down the Democratic-controlled Senate Judiciary Committee by refusing to discuss his views on any question likely to come before him as a sitting justice. Yet his confirmation hearings became a virtual lovefest. Scalia handled his interrogation so engagingly that the Senate voted ninety-eight to zero to confirm him. Reagan was said to have danced around the Oval Office, singing "Scalia/I've just picked a judge named Scalia," to the tune of *West Side Story*'s "Maria."

Reagan knew what he was getting. Scalia would soon establish himself as one of the most brilliant and belligerent conservatives ever to sit on the high court. The late Justice William Brennan's reputation as the most influential Supreme Court justice of his generation would shortly pass to Scalia, asserted Michael Greve, cofounder of the libertarian Center for Individual Rights, a public-interest law firm in Washington, D.C.

From today's perspective, in which Scalia has emerged as a reliable proponent of hard-right views on issues from property rights to the death penalty, his confirmation hearings seem to have happened in a parallel universe. Some senators even called Scalia by his nickname, Nino. It became clear that Nino was a man of many parts—Nino, the tennis player, opera singer, pianist, poker player, raconteur, man about town, father of nine. Potential enemies were declawed by his accomplishments and affability. Howard Metzenbaum, for example, an outspokenly liberal Ohio Democrat, announced that Scalia's conservatism was irrelevant and that all that mattered was his "fitness." Senator Edward Kennedy worried that Scalia might be "insensitive" on women's rights, but concluded that one could hardly "maintain that Judge Scalia is outside the mainstream."

His immigrant saga—the only child of a Sicilian father and a first-generation Italian-American mother—was lavishly praised. Born in 1936, he spent his early childhood in Trenton, New Jersey, before the family moved to New York, when his father became a professor of Romance languages at Brooklyn College. He graduated first in his class from Saint Francis Xavier, a Jesuit high school in Manhattan, first in his class from Georgetown University, and cum laude from Harvard Law School. He went on to practice law from 1961 to 1967 with Cleveland's most prestigious firm, Jones, Day, Cockley, and Reavis—named after

the city's first family of Virginia, became general counsel to the White House Office Telecommunications Policy, chaired the Administrative Conference of the United States, and became assistant attorney general in the U.S. Department of Justice's Office of Legal Counsel. In 1977, he joined the law faculty at the University of Chicago, from which he was appointed in 1982 to the nation's second most important court, the U.S. Court of Appeals for the D.C. Circuit.

Even the legal press was effusive about Scalia's Supreme Court confirmation. Tony Mauro in the *Legal Times* predicted that Scalia would become the court's "intellectual lodestar."

How, then, did this exemplar of charm and learning become what he is today—the scourge of the country's liberal establishment? *FindLaw* columnist Edward Lazarus, for example, recently questioned Scalia's integrity, arguing that his reputation as "a rigorous and thoroughly principled jurist" has always seemed to him "largely a myth." (Lazarus's own moral claim to fame: he betrayed the ethics of his Supreme Court clerkship by publishing the first and only insider account of the workings of the Court. But that's another story.) Ex-prosecutor and best-selling legal commentator Vincent Bugliosi's inflammatory charge is that "having Justice Antonin Scalia speak on ethics is like having a prostitute speak on sexual abstinence." Peter Laarman, minister at New York's Judson Memorial Church, gave a sermon naming Justices Scalia and Clarence Thomas as members of the "scary lunatic fringe occupying most of the seats of power."

Scoffing at the idea that our "maturing" society's "evolving standards of decency" might in and of themselves make the death penalty unconstitutional, Scalia said that the Constitution he interprets and applies is not living but dead.

But the pièce de résistance of liberal loathing can be found in a July 8, 2002, OpEd in *The New York Times* by Princeton professor Sean Wilentz. Wilentz attacked a speech Scalia had given at the University of Chicago Divinity School (and reworked for the conservative journal, *First Things*), arguing that the Eighth Amendment's prohibition of cruel and unusual punishment does not proscribe the death penalty. Scalia's remarks, wrote Wilentz, "show bitterness against democracy, strong dislike for the Constitution's approach to religion, and eager advocacy for the submission of the individual to the state. It is a chilling mixture for an American."

More important for Wilentz and his political allies, this is a chilling mixture for a chief justice—a job Scalia is rumored to want and that President George W. Bush is rumored to want him to have. While the chief is only first among equals, he has the crucial task of assigning opinions in which he is in the majority. A powerful, congenial chief such as Chief Justice Earl Warren—or William Rehnquist, for that matter—can mold the court in his image through persuasive deliberations and adept assignments. Scalia puts little effort into winning over those who disagree with him. Harvard Professor Lawrence Tribe once pointed out that Scalia's "vigor and occasional viciousness" in his written opinions may "alienate people who might be his allies in moving the Court to the right. I therefore hope he will keep it up." There's little reason to think that as chief Scalia wouldn't keep it up. After all, he recently attacked all his colleagues, asserting that the justices on the Court were no better qualified to rule on the right to die than nine people selected at random from a Kansas City phone book. He also took them on individually. He ridiculed Justice Stephen Breyer, for example, for writing a decision so vague that it gave trial courts "not a clue" as to how to carry it out. He mocked Justice David Souter for resorting "to that last hope of lost interpretive causes, that Saint Jude of the hagiography of statutory construction, legislative history."

Scalia can be particularly provocative, even shocking, on race. In a majority opinion on racially based jury selection, he attacked Justice Thurgood Marshall, saying that his dissent "rolls out the ultimate weapon, the accusation of insensitivity to racial discrimination—which will lose its intimidating effect if it continues to be fired so randomly." Given that Marshall knew far better than Scalia the reality of racial discrimination when he saw it—he was surely the only justice in the history of the Supreme Court to have once been dragged to a river by a lynch mob—even years later Scalia's words seem intemperate and misplaced.

He can also be combative on issues that usually call for compassion. He says that the death penalty, for example, is not a "difficult, soul-wrenching question." Scoffing at the idea that our "maturing" society's "evolving standards of decency" might in and of themselves make the death penalty unconstitutional, Scalia said that the Constitution he interprets and applies is not living but dead. Or, as he prefers to put it, "enduring." It means today not what current society (much less the Court) thinks it ought to mean, but what it meant when it was adopted. Scalia has even affronted his conservative Catholic supporters. He's argued (correctly) that the pope's opposition to the death penalty expressed in *Evangelium vitae* is not "binding teaching" requiring adherence by all Catholics—though they must give it

thoughtful and respectful consideration. When Cardinal Avery Dulles said he agreed with the pope's position, Scalia answered that this was "just the phenomenon of the clerical bureaucracy saying, 'Yes, boss.'"

What the pope has to say is irrelevant to him as a judge, says Scalia, since his own views on the morality of the death penalty have nothing to do with how he votes judicially. However, one's moral views do govern whether or not one can or should be a judge at all. "When I sit on a Court that reviews and affirms capital convictions," said Scalia, "I am part of 'the machinery of death.'" The Supreme Court's ruling is often the last step that permits an execution to proceed. Any judge who believes the death penalty immoral should resign, he says, rather than "simply ignoring duly enacted, constitutional laws and sabotaging death-penalty cases."

How, then, can Scalia continue to serve as a judge in a court that has repeatedly upheld abortion, which he regards as immoral? Capital cases, argues Scalia, are different from the other life-and-death issues the Court might hear, like abortion or legalized suicide. In these instances, it is not the state that is decreeing death, but private individuals whom the state has decided not to restrain. One may argue (as many do) that society has a moral obligation to interfere. That moral obligation may weigh heavily upon the voter, and upon the legislator who enacts the laws, Scalia argues, but a judge "bears no moral guilt for the laws society has failed to enact."

Ironically, despite Scalia's carefully drawn, if dubious, distinctions, Scalia's antagonist Wilentz accuses him of believing that Catholics, as citizens, would be unable to uphold views that contradict church doctrine. A shocked Wilentz says that Scalia "sees submission as desirable." This, Wilentz continues, is "exactly the stereotype of Catholicism as papist mind-control that Catholics have struggled against, and that John F. Kennedy did so much to overcome."

Obedience, for good or ill, is indeed an ongoing Scalia theme. He has joked more than once that the keys to being a good Catholic and a good jurist are the same: being strong enough to obey the relevant law. Still, he has not urged submission on American Catholic citizens.

Wilentz also writes that despite calling himself a strict constructionist—actually, he doesn't—Scalia wants to impose "a religious sense that is directly counter to the abundantly expressed wishes of the men who wrote the Constitution." This is not strict constructionism, says Wilentz. It "is opportunism, and it threatens democracy."

Is Wilentz right? Is Scalia an opportunist who threatens the very democracy whose Constitution he has sworn to uphold? Or is he a brace originalist, seeking to return to the principles of the American Founding Fathers that the Court discarded in the last fifty years?

The answer is not yet clear. Part of the anger Scalia arouses is a result of how successful he has been in restoring respect for the Constitution's actual words. Calling his approach textualism, Scalia argues that primacy must be given to the text, structure, and history of any document—Constitution or statute—being interpreted. Judges, he says, are to eschew their own "intellectual, moral, and personal perceptions." Scalia says he takes the Constitution as it is, not as he wants it to be.

In effect, of course, this is an attack on much of twentieth-century jurisprudence, which has created a host of new constitutional rights by embracing such Holmesian ideas as the "balancing of competing interests" and Justice William Brennan's "living Constitution." This expanded vision of the Constitution gave judges enormous power to assert that their individual policy preferences and social goals—however unpopular—were also the law. As Scalia wrote in his solo, and prescient, dissent in the case recognizing the constitutionality of the now notorious Office of the Special Prosecutor: "Evidently, the governing standard is to be what might be called the unfettered wisdom of a majority of this Court, revealed to an obedient people in a case-by-case basis. This is not only not the government of laws that the Constitution established, it is not a government of laws at all."

Larry Kramer, a law professor at New York University, calls Scalia's belief that judges should renounce their own desires when interpreting the law "judicial asceticism." He argues that Scalia's "formalism, textualism, and originalism are only means: denial and self-control are the reasons."

If Scalia's first sin in the eyes of doctrinaire liberals is his textualism, make no mistake about the fact that his second sin is that he is a practicing Catholic—or, as commentators repeatedly mention, a "devout" Catholic. (How the devotion is known is not clear.) Of course, the sins of textualism and Catholicism are not unrelated—both reflect respect for the written word, an ordered universe, and an attachment to tradition. And both have a long contentious relationship with liberalism. Wilentz probably put his finger on something important when he wrote, "One senses that Mr. Scalia's true priority is to get secular humanists off the federal bench."

Certainly, there is something admirable in Scalia's allegiance to tradition and his stubborn refusal to pander on moral issues—both of which predictably incite his critics to excess. Harvard Law Professor Alan Dershowitz, for example, calls Scalia the "voice of Spanish clerical conservatism." The liberal *American Prospect* magazine scathingly refers to Scalia's "Jesuitical" logic. The editor of Salon.com wrote that defenders of the *Bush v. Gore* decision, in which Scalia played such a large role, "would have to perform feats of casuistry unseen since the days when Ignatius Loyola strode the earth to do so." Calling Scalia a cheap-shot artist, *Washington Post* columnist Richard Cohen maintains that the justice's mind is rigid on constitutional issues between church and state: "Anyone who thinks Scalia will give First Amendment issues a fair and reasoned hearing is, it seems, proceeding in a way Scalia would appreciate: solely on faith."

These knee-jerk liberal denunciations are appalling in a way, but while some of these comments might set off alarms for William Donohue and his Catholic League cohorts, they do not represent a revival of pure, nineteenth-century anti-Catholicism.

No respectable attack was ever leveled at the Catholicism of Scalia's nemesis, Justice William Brennan. Generally thought by legal scholars (including Scalia) to have been the twentieth century's most influential justice, Brennan may well have also been the most loved. He was a brilliant, strategic, persuasive conciliator who more often than not won the day. He once said, "With five votes you can do anything around here." His "living Constitution" is both the dominant liberal constitutional concept and the polar opposite of Scalia's textualism.

Scalia, in contrast, goes out of his way to give speeches like his provocative 1996 "Fools for Christ's Sake" address at the Mississippi College of Law, a Baptist school. Most (perhaps all) of his critics missed the reference to Saint Paul and therefore misinterpreted the speech, but then Scalia pretty much knew they would. Baiting the opposition—whether outside or inside the Court—is basic to his temperament.

As a Catholic who grew up in working-class neighborhoods (even though his father was an academic), Scalia often reveals a different sensibility from his Brahmin peers. In a 1979 law review article he denounced "the Wisdoms and the Powells and the Whites," whose ancestors participated in the oppression of African Americans, and who as justice sought to correct the effects of that ancestral oppression at the expense of newer immigrants. In a 1987 dissent he defended the "unknown, unaffluent, and unorganized" workers ignored by proponents of affirmative action.

And, then, of course, there's abortion, by far the most divisive social issue of our time, and one that Scalia argues should be settled legislatively rather than judicially. Yet the conservative Rehnquist Court has signaled more than once that it's not going to reverse *Roe v. Wade*. It doesn't really matter to a majority of the Court that Scalia was probably correct when he said, "I do not believe—and for two hundred years, no one believed—that the Constitution contains a right to abortion." In *A Matter of Interpretation* (Princeton), his Tanner Lectures at Princeton, he cautions that creating new constitutional rights may trigger a majoritarian reaction. "At the end of the day," he notes, "an evolving Constitution will evolve the way the majority wishes." One has to wonder whether the 2002 elections giving the House, Senate, and (by extension, the Supreme Court) to the Republicans reflect, in part, this prediction come true.

Scalia's third sin is his shockingly bad temper, in print, toward his intellectual opponents. Some of his harshest language concerning his colleagues came in his criticism of *Roe*: "The emptiness of the 'reasoned judgment' that produced *Roe* is displayed in plain view by the fact . . . that the best the Court can do to explain how it is that the word 'liberty' must include the right to destroy human fetuses is to rattle off a collection of adjectives that simply decorate a value judgment and conceal a political choice."

That temper has regularly been directed at centrist Justice Sandra Day O'Connor, who often must be wooed as the crucial fifth vote in a conservative coalition. In dissenting from *Planned Parenthood v. Casey* (1992), Scalia questioned O'Connor's intelligence. "Reason finds no refuge in this jurisprudence of confusion," he wrote.

Such outbursts have been costly. For many years, O'Connor avoided signing majority opinions authored by Scalia, which meant that Chief Justice Rehnquist—who needed her vote—avoided assigning controversial opinions to Scalia.

Perhaps Scalia's most troubling sin is that he does not always hold himself to his own principles. He explains his judicial rigidity by saying that when "I adopt a general rule, and say 'This is the basis of our decision,' I not only constrain lower courts, I constrain myself as well. If the next case should have such different facts that my political or policy preferences regarding the outcome are quite opposite, I will be unable to indulge those preferences; I have committed myself to the governing principle." Such rules can embolden judges to be courageous when having to issue an unpopular ruling, such as one protecting a criminal defendant's rights. All around, an admirable position.

How then to explain *Bush v. Gore*, the 5–4 ruling that effectively handed the presidency to George W. Bush in 2000? Bush may well have won the election fair and square, but we'll never know for sure. This was the first time in American history that the Court decided a presidential election, and it did so by improbably concluding that Florida's diverse standards for counting votes constituted an equal protection violation under the Fourteenth Amendment. Scalia's respect for established precedents and his disdain for catchall uses of the equal protection clause suddenly didn't seem to apply here—nor did his reverence for the separation of powers. As if the decision weren't mischievous enough, the Court also pronounced—amazingly—that "our consideration is limited to the present circumstances, for the problem of equal protection in election processes generally presents many complexities." Since when does the Supreme Court limit its rulings to present circumstances?

Ironically, Scalia's tightly argued dissent in *Casey* eerily foreshadows his own lead role in the scandal of *Bush v. Gore*: "The Imperial Judiciary lives," Scalia wrote. "It is instructive to compare this Nietzschean vision of us unelected, life-tenured judges—leading a Volk who will be 'tested by following,' and whose very 'belief in themselves' is mystically bound up in their 'understanding' of a Court that 'speak[s] before all others for their constitutional ideals'—with the somewhat more modest role envisioned for these lawyers by the Founders."

How can Scalia reconcile his principled views with his vote in *Bush v. Gore*? There aren't many convincing answers. His opponents claim Scalia acted as a ruthless, self-serving politician who put his own boy in power when it looked like the other side might win. Another possible explanation is that Scalia believes deeply something else he said in his *Casey* dissent, which is that *Roe* "fanned into life an issue that has inflamed our national politics in general, and has obscured with its smoke the selection of justices to this Court, in particular, ever since." In other words, the Court has embroiled itself in political issues that should be left to the people and their representatives—and that only a Republican administration would set the Court back on its right course. (It is not at all clear that this will happen.) Thus Scalia saw nothing wrong with the language he used in concurring with the Court's stay (by definition an emergency measure) halting the Florida vote recount. Continuing the manual count, wrote Scalia, would "threaten irreparable harm" to Bush "and to the country, by casting a cloud upon what he claims to be the legitimacy of his election." He may never have written a less convincing justification of one of his positions, but it makes some sense if understood in light of how far wrong he thinks the Court has gone.

Scalia has spent most of his career captivating others, who often let their affection for him overcome their distaste for some of his ideas. He is a social animal, and it is possible that his fury about being correct yet alone over several momentous issues has warped his judgment on others—on which he is probably not right. His wrath is born of his self-confidence in the face of universal opposition. Take two 1988 dissents, *Morrison* and *Mistretta*, which, in the words of Northwestern University Law Professor Thomas Merrill, showed Scalia to be "completely isolated" on the Court. Isolated he may have been, but he was also completely right.

Morrison v. Olson was the decision upholding the Independent Counsel Act. Scalia's colleagues thought he had pretty much lost it when he ferociously wrote, "The institutional design of the Independent Counsel is designed to heighten, not to check, all of the institutional hazards of the dedicated prosecutor; the danger of too narrow a focus, of the loss of perspective, of preoccupation with the pursuit of one alleged suspect to the exclusion of other interests." With unchecked discretionary powers and unlimited funds, the independent counsel would be accountable to no one and would be entirely focused on a single target. The office would encourage the worst tendencies in American democracy. "The context of this statute is acrid with the smell of threatened impeachment," wrote Scalia. Indeed.

The history of the Independent Counsel Act is replete with examples of prosecutorial abuse that would have made the Founders recoil. Scalia accurately predicted, "If the prosecutor is obliged to choose his case, it follows that he can choose his defendants. Therein is the most dangerous power of the prosecutor: that he will pick people that he thinks he should get, rather than cases that need to be prosecuted. . . . It is not a question of discovering the commission of a crime and then looking for the man who has committed it, it is a question of picking the man and then searching the law books, or putting investigators to work, to pin some offense on him."

Mistretta v. U.S., the other dissent that isolated Scalia, concerned a revolution in criminal sentencing that has gone almost unnoticed by most Americans. In 1984, Congress established the U.S. Sentencing Commission as an independent rule-making body to promulgate mandatory guidelines for every federal criminal offense. The act specifically rejected rehabilitation as a goal of imprisonment, and mandated instead "that punishment should serve retributive, educational, deterrent, and incapacitative goals." All sentences would become determinate (fixed), with no parole other than a small credit that could be earned by good behavior.

Indeed, the country has grappled with the gross injustices of federal sentencing. In the past, judges were able to use their discretion to minimize inequities in the law. No longer. Now judges are governed by this new branch of government, by what Scalia mockingly calls "a sort of junior-varsity Congress."

Scalia lost on *Mistretta*, but he eventually won on another crucial sentencing issue—victim impact statements. In the mid-1970s, the Supreme Court had begun requiring that defendants in capital cases be allowed to present "mitigating circumstances" during the sentencing phase of capital trials. Yet while defendants in particularly heinous crimes could present evidence about an abusive childhood, victims and their families had no standing to speak. The Supreme Court repeatedly said victim-impact statements created a constitutionally unacceptable risk of arbitrary and capricious decisions by juries. Worse, they would focus attention not on the moral guilt of the defendant's alleged harms to society but on the emotions and opinions of persons who were not parties to the crime. Scalia dissented, attacking the "recently invented" requirement of mitigating circumstances, asking why the jury could not also take into account "the specific harm visited upon society by a murderer." In 1991, in *Payne v. Tennessee*, the Court finally agreed and overturned the ban on victim-impact statements. Justice Marshall announced his retirement the same day—some said because his heart was broken.

This term the Court has ruled 5 to 4 on another sentencing issue—California's three-strikes law. Like victim-impact statements, added punishment for multiple offenses has a long tradition in the common law. Adopted by referendum in 1994, California's harsh law permits judges to treat crimes that would ordinarily be considered misdemeanors as third felonies. (Most states with three-strikes laws require the third strike to actually be a felony, usually a violent one.) The particular cases before the Court involved life sentences for two men whose third crimes were shoplifting—$1,200 worth of golf clubs in one case, and $154 worth of children's videotapes in the other.

Here was a case with Scalia's favorite elements: the direct voice of the majority expressed via referendum, state sovereignty via its law, and centuries of Anglo-Saxon tradition. All of these considerations were to be weighed in determining the punishment of two career criminals who had led astonishingly unproductive lives. What should society do with such people? It is a testament to the revolution Scalia has wrought that this case even came before the Court, much less that the Court upheld three strikes. No longer do courts cavalierly assume that the Constitution prevents Americans from protecting themselves against known repeat predators. We are reminded, again, that in most matters of criminal justice, Scalia is the people champion—even if this decision was written by his protagonist, Justice O'Connor, leaving him to concur. This, in turn, reminds us of the conundrum of his role in *Bush v. Gore*. There he seemed to place the "irreparable harm" that a Florida recount would do to petitioner George W. Bush above the irreparable harm to citizens whose votes would not even be counted. Is Antonin Scalia an opportunist or an originalist? Perhaps he is both.

Critical Thinking

1. Do you agree with Justice Scalia's statement about the death penalty and society's evolving standards of decency?

2. Is Justice Scalia's decision in *Bush v. Gore* compatible with what he said in the dissenting opinion in *Planned Parenthood v. Casey*?

3. What's your opinion on whether Justice Scalia is an opportunist or an originalist?

JULIA VITULLO-MARTIN writes frequently for *Commonweal*, the *Wall Street Journal*, and other publications. She is working on a book on the American Jury and Criminal Law.

UNIT 5

Juvenile Justice

Unit Selections

Learning Outcomes

After reading this unit, you will be able to:

- Discuss the studies into gang-related behavior.

- Explain the benefits of spending tax dollars on rehabilitating prisoners by making education available to inmates.

- Explain why Americans should be concerned about the way teenagers who commit crimes are treated by the criminal justice system.

- Argue that child abuse should not be ignored regardless of the status of the offender.

Student Website

www.mhhe.com/cls

Internet References

Gang Land: The Jerry Capeci Page
www.ganglandnews.com

Institute for Intergovernmental Research (IIR)
www.iir.com

National Criminal Justice Reference Service (NCJRS)
http://virlib.ncjrs.org/JuvenileJustice.asp

Partnership Against Violence Network
www.pavnet.org

Although there were variations within specific offense categories, the overall arrest rate for juvenile violent crime remained relatively constant for several decades. Then, in the late 1980s, something changed; more and more juveniles charged with a violent offense were brought into the justice system. The juvenile justice system is a twentieth-century response to the problems of dealing with children in trouble with the law, or children who need society's protection.

Juvenile court procedure differs from the procedure in adult courts because juvenile courts are based on the philosophy that their function is to treat and to help, not to punish and abandon the offender. Recently, operations of the juvenile court have received criticism, and a number of significant Supreme Court decisions have changed the way that the courts must approach the rights of children. Despite these changes, however, the major thrust of the juvenile justice system remains one of diversion and treatment, rather than adjudication and incarceration, although there is a trend toward dealing more punitively with serious juvenile offenders.

In this unit's opening article, "Violence in Adolescent Dating Relationships," the authors cover the violent side of dating relationships and why this continues to be a problem. In the next article, "America's Imprisoned Kids," Ari Paul reports that there are some signs of change in the way the United States detains and sentences juvenile offenders. "The Long View of Crime," by Pat Kaufman, shows what research into criminological theories has discovered about reducing deviance.

Nelson and Olcott report, in "Jail Time Is Learning Time," about the efforts of New York State's Onondaga County Justice Center in rehabilitating its inmates by offering them valuable

© Mikael Karlsson/Arresting Images

classroom instruction. In "Lifers as Teenagers, Now Seeking Second Chance," Adam Liptak writes about the unique American practice of convicting young adolescents as adults and sentencing them to live their lives in prison.

According to Patrick Clark, in "Preventing Future Crime with Cognitive Behavioral Therapy," a reduction in future criminal behavior can be accomplished by therapeutic approaches based on counseling, skill building, and other services. This section concludes with an article by Connell and Finnegan, "Interviewing Compliant Adolescent Victims," in which they discuss the difficulty facing investigators when they attempt to interview adolescents who do not see themselves as victims.

Violence in Adolescent Dating Relationships

"The early- to mid-teenage years mark a time in which romantic relationships begin to emerge. From a developmental perspective, these relationships can serve a number of positive functions. However, for many adolescents, there is a darker side: dating violence."

ERNEST N. JOURILES, PhD, CORA PLATT, BA, AND RENEE MCDONALD, PhD

For many, the early- to mid-teenage years mark a time in which romantic relationships begin to emerge. From a developmental perspective, these relationships can serve a number of positive functions. However, for many adolescents, there is a darker side: dating violence. In this article, we discuss the definition and measurement of adolescent dating violence, review epidemiological findings regarding victimization, and describe correlates of victimization experiences. We end with a discussion of prevention and intervention programs designed to address adolescent dating violence and highlight important gaps in our knowledge.

Defining and Measuring Adolescent Dating and Dating Violence

"Dating" among adolescents is complicated to define and measure, in part because the nature of dating changes dramatically over the course of adolescence (Connolly et al., 1999; Feiring, 1996). In early adolescence, dating involves getting together with small groups of friends of both sexes to do things together as a group. From these group experiences, adolescents progress to going out with or dating a single individual. Initial single-dating relationships are typically casual and short-term; more serious, exclusive, and longer-lasting relationships emerge in mid- to late-adolescence.

"Dating" among adolescents is complicated to define and measure.

In research on adolescent dating violence, adolescents are often asked to respond to questions about a "boyfriend" or "girlfriend" or someone with whom they have "been on a date with or gone out with." However, what constitutes a boyfriend or girlfriend or a dating partner is not clear, and these judgments are likely to vary tremendously across adolescents. These judgments are probably also influenced by a number of factors including the amount of time spent with each other, the degree of emotional attachment, and the activities engaged in together (Allen, 2004). They are also likely to change over the course of adolescence, as youth mature and become more experienced with dating.

Most everyone has a general idea about what constitutes "violence" in adolescent dating relationships, but not everyone conceptualizes and defines it the same way. In the empirical literature, multiple types of dating violence have been studied, including physical, sexual, and psychological violence. Definitions for these different types of violence vary from study to study, but each is typically based on adolescents' reports of the occurrence of specific acts. For example, physical violence often refers to adolescents' reports of hits, slaps, or beatings; sexual violence refers to forced kissing, touching, or intercourse; and psychological violence to reports of insults, threats, or the use of control tactics. These different types of violence are sometimes further subdivided. For example, indirect aggression (also referred to as relational or social aggression), which includes spreading hurtful rumors or telling cruel stories about a dating partner, has recently begun to be conceptualized as a form of dating violence that may be distinct from more overt forms of psychological or emotional abuse (Wolfe, Scott, Reitzel-Jaffe et al., 2001). As another example, in a recent prevalence study, sexual assault was distinguished from drug- or alcohol-facilitated rape, with the latter defined as sexual assault that occurred while the victim was "high, drunk, or passed out from drinking or taking drugs" (Wolitzky-Taylor et al., 2008).

In the bulk of studies on adolescent dating violence, the youth are surveyed about the occurrence of specific acts of violence within a particular time period, for example, during the previous 12 months. These surveys are typically administered on a single occasion, in either a questionnaire or interview format. Some include only one or two questions about violence; others include comprehensive scales of relationship violence with excellent psychometric properties (e.g., Wolfe et al., 2001). A handful of investigators have attempted to study adolescent dating violence using other methods, such as laboratory observations (e.g., Capaldi, Kimm, & Shortt, 2007), and repeated interviews over a short, circumscribed period of time (e.g., Jouriles et al., 2005). However, studies using alternatives to one-time, self-report survey assessments are few and far between.

This first section highlights some of the complexities involved in conceptualizing adolescent dating violence and describes how different types of dating violence are often defined and measured, providing a backdrop for understanding and interpreting empirical findings in the literature. As illustrated in the section below, different conceptualizations and definitions of dating violence lead to different research findings and conclusions. Similarly, various data collection methods (such as using more questions and/or repeated questioning) also yield different results. At the present time, there is no gold standard with respect to defining or measuring adolescent dating violence; the field is still developing in this regard.

Prevalence of Adolescent Dating Violence

Over the past decade, data from several different national surveys have been used to estimate the prevalence of the various forms of adolescent dating violence. Surveys conducted by the Centers for Disease Control suggest that 9–10% of students in grades 9–12 indicate that a boyfriend or girlfriend has hit, slapped, or physically hurt them on purpose during the previous 12 months, and approximately 8% report having been physically forced to have sexual intercourse against their wishes (Howard, Wang, & Yan, 2007a, 2007b). The 2005 National Survey of Adolescents (NSA) indicates that 1.6% of adolescents between 12 and 17 years of age have experienced "serious dating violence" (Wolitzky-Taylor et al., 2008). Serious dating violence was defined as experiencing one or more of the following forms of violence from a dating partner: physical violence (badly injured, beaten up, or threatened with a knife or gun), sexual violence (forced anal, vaginal, or oral sex; forced penetration with a digit or an object; forced touching of genitalia), or drug/alcohol-facilitated rape.

Most studies in this area ask about male-to-female and female-to-male violence or include gender-neutral questions without assessing whether a respondent is in an opposite-sex or same-sex relationship. The National Longitudinal Study of Adolescent Health is unique in that it reports data on violence

Table 1 Prevalence of Dating Violence in Same-Sex and Opposite-Sex Romantic Relationships

Data from National Longitudinal Study of Adolescent Health		
In the previous 18 months partner had been:	Opposite-sex relationship	Same-sex relationship
Physically violent	12%	11%
Psychologically violent	29%	21%

Halpern, Oslak, Young, Martin, & Kupper, 2001; Halpern, Young, Waller, Martin, & Kupper, 2004.

in opposite-sex as well as same-sex romantic relationships. As can be seen in Table 1, prevalence rates for both physical and psychological violence are similar in opposite-sex and same-sex romantic relationships among adolescents in grades 7–12.

Prevalence rates for both physical and psychological violence are similar in opposite-sex and same-sex romantic relationships among adolescents in grades 7–12.

The prevalence of physical dating violence appears to be fairly similar across studies of national samples. Variation across estimates most likely reflects differences in how violence is defined, and perhaps differences in the samples from which the estimates were derived (e.g., different age ranges sampled). It should be noted that prevalence estimates based on smaller, less representative, localized samples tend to be higher than those based on national samples. In fact, a number of researchers have reported prevalence estimates for physical dating violence among adolescents (over a one-year period or less) to be over 40% (Hickman, Jaycox, & Aronoff, 2004). These elevated estimates might stem directly from sampling differences, but also perhaps from differences in the conceptualization and measurement of dating violence. For example, in many of the smaller samples, investigators assessed dating violence more extensively (such as using more questions and/or through repeated questioning), which might contribute to higher prevalence estimates.

Taken together, the results across studies yield some general conclusions about the nature and scope of adolescent dating violence. Regardless of how it is defined, it appears that a substantial number of United States youth are affected by dating violence. Even with very conservative definitions, such as the one used in the NSA, it was projected that approximately 400,000 adolescents have been victims, at some point in their lives, of serious dating violence (Wolitzky-Taylor et al., 2008).

Psychological violence appears to be much more common than either physical or sexual violence. Data are mixed on the relative prevalence of physical and sexual violence, but some of the national surveys suggest that they are approximately equal in prevalence.

Onset and Course

Dating violence appears to emerge well before high school. For example, cross-sex teasing and harassment, which involve behaviors often construed as either psychological or sexual violence, is evident among 6th graders and increases in prevalence over time (McMaster et al., 2002). One-third of a sample of 7th graders who indicated that they had started dating also reported that they had committed acts of aggression (physical, sexual, or psychological) toward a dating partner; in over half of these cases, physical or sexual aggression was involved (Sears et al., 2007). In the NSA, serious dating violence victimization was not reported by 12-year-olds, but it was by 13-year-olds (Wolitzky-Taylor et al., 2008).

Longitudinal data on the course of adolescent dating violence are scarce, but there is evidence that psychological aggression predicts subsequent physical aggression (O'Leary & Slep, 2003). In fact, different types of dating violence commonly co-occur within adolescent relationships, with the occurrence of one type of violence (physical, psychological, or sexual) associated with an increased likelihood of other types of violence (Sears, Byers, & Price, 2007). In research on interpersonal victimization in general, victims of violence are known to be at increased risk for subsequent victimization. This appears to be true for victims of adolescent dating violence as well (Smith, White, & Holland, 2003).

Demographics of Adolescent Dating Violence

Certain demographic variables including age, race and ethnicity, geographic location, and sex are associated with increased risk for victimization. Specifically, the risk for dating violence victimization increases with age, at least through the middle and high school years. This trend appears to be true for physical, psychological, and sexual violence (e.g., Halpern et al., 2001; Howard et al., 2007a, 2007b; Wolitzky-Taylor et al., 2008). This might be attributable to a number of things, including the changing nature of dating over the course of adolescence. Some evidence has emerged pointing to racial and ethnic differences in adolescents' experiences of dating violence, but other recent, large-scale studies call these findings into question. For example, a number of investigators have found Black adolescents to be more likely than their White counterparts to experience physical and sexual dating violence (e.g., Howard et al., 2007a, 2007b). However, these differences have sometimes disappeared when other variables, such as prior exposures to violence, are considered (Malik, Sorenson, & Aneshensel, 1997). Moreover, recent, well-designed studies of very large samples have found no evidence of racial or ethnic differences in adolescent victimization

(e.g., O'Leary et al., 2008; Wolitzky-Taylor et al., 2008). There do appear to be regional differences in dating violence, with adolescents in southern states at substantially greater risk for experiencing dating violence than adolescents in other regions of the U.S. (Marquart, et al., 2007). Although the reasons for regional differences are not known, it is interesting to note that the South has a higher prevalence rate of overall violence than other regions in the U.S. In short, there may be factors in the Southern U.S. that facilitate the promotion, acceptance, or tolerance of violent behavior.

When violence is defined broadly, prevalence rates for male and female victimization tend to be similar (e.g., Halpern et al., 2001). However, narrower definitions of violence point to some sex differences in the experience of violence. For example, female adolescents are more likely than males to experience severe physical violence (violent acts that are likely to result, or actually have resulted, in physical injuries) and sexual violence (e.g., Molidor & Tolman, 1998; Wolitzky-Taylor et al., 2008). Females are also more likely than males to experience fear, hurt, and the desire to leave the situation for self-protection (Molidor & Tolman, 1998; Jackson, Cram, & Seymour, 2000). In addition, females are more likely to report physical injuries and more harmful and persistent psychological distress after being victimized (O'Keefe, 1997).

Correlates of Adolescent Dating Violence

Most of the findings on the correlates of adolescent dating violence come from studies in which data were collected at a single point in time. Thus, it is difficult to discern if observed correlates are precursors or consequences of the violence, or if they are simply related to experiencing violence, but not in a cause-and-effect manner. Although it is tempting to interpret some of these associations in a causal, unidirectional manner, more often than not, alternative explanations can also be offered. For example, the documented association between dating violence and psychological distress is typically interpreted to mean that experiencing dating violence causes psychological distress (e.g., Howard et al., 2007a, 2007b; Molidor & Tolman, 1998). However, it is not too difficult to imagine how feelings of psychological distress might influence an adolescent's decision about whom to go out with (i.e., adolescents who are psychologically distressed, compared with those who are not, may make different choices about whom to date) and, perhaps, lead an adolescent to an abusive relationship.

Many adolescents engage in antisocial or illegal activities, but those who do so consistently and frequently are at increased risk of dating violence victimization (e.g., Howard et al., 2007a, 2007b). In addition, simply having antisocial friends increases risk for victimization. For example, females who associate with violent or victimized peers appear to be at increased risk for dating violence victimization (Gagne, Lavoie, & Hebert, 2005). Similarly, male and female adolescents exposed to peer-drinking activities within the past 30 days (e.g., "Hanging out with friends who drank") were victimized more often than their counterparts who were not exposed to such activities (Howard, Qiu, & Boekeloo, 2003).

Many other adolescent experiences have also been associated with dating violence victimization. For example, earlier exposures to violence, both within and outside of the family, are associated with victimization (e.g., Gagne et al., 2005; Malik et al., 1997). Negative parent-child interactions and parent-child boundary violations at age 13 predict victimization at age 21 (Linder & Collins, 2005). Trauma symptoms, which may result from violence exposure and untoward parent-child interactions, are posited to interfere with emotional and cognitive processes important in interpreting abusive behavior, and possibly to heighten tolerance for abuse (Capaldi & Gorman-Smith, 2003). Having had prior sexual relationships with peers increases adolescent females' risk for experiencing relationship violence (e.g., Howard et al., 2007a, 2007b). Also, the likelihood of victimization increases as the number of dating partners increases (Halpern et al., 2001).

Several different dimensions of adolescent relationships have been examined in relation to dating violence. For example, physical violence is often reciprocated within relationships, meaning that when dating violence is reported, both partners are typically violent toward one another (e.g., O'Leary, Slep, Avery-Leaf, Cascardi, 2008). Relationship violence is more likely to happen in serious or special romantic relationships, rather than more casual ones (O'Leary et al., 2008; Roberts, Auinger, & Klein, 2006). It is also more likely to occur in relationships with problems, conflict, and power struggles (Bentley et al., 2007; O'Keefe, 1997).

Relationship violence is more likely to happen in serious or special romantic relationships, rather than more casual ones.

Although there are many risk factors for adolescent dating violence, some protective factors have emerged as well. For instance, having high-quality friendships at age 16 is associated with reduced likelihood of experiencing dating violence in romantic relationships at age 21 (Linder & Collins, 2005). High-quality friendships are characterized by security, disclosure, closeness, low levels of conflict, and the effective resolution of conflict that does occur. Also, adolescents who do well in school and those who attend religious services are at decreased risk for experiencing dating violence (Halpern et al., 2001; Howard et al., 2003).

Prevention and Intervention

Much of the prevention research in this area is directed at an entire population (e.g., 9th grade at a school) with the goal of preventing violence from occurring. However, the prevalence data indicate that a sizable number of adolescents in high school, and even middle school, have already perpetrated and/or experienced dating violence. Thus, in most cases the research is not technically universal prevention, from the standpoint of preventing violence before it ever occurs. Rather, it is an attempt to reduce dating violence, by preventing its initial occurrence as well as preventing its re-occurrence among those who have already experienced it.

A sizable number of adolescents in high school, and even middle school, have already perpetrated and/or experienced dating violence.

Many of the school-based prevention programs share a number of commonalities, in addition to the joint focus on prevention and intervention (Whitaker et al., 2006). Most are designed to address perpetration and victimization simultaneously. Many are incorporated into mandatory health classes in middle or high school. Most are based on a combination of feminist and social learning principles, and involve didactic methods to increase knowledge and change attitudes regarding dating violence. Despite these similarities, there are potentially important differences in the structure (e.g., duration) and content of these various programs. Unfortunately, most of these school-based programs have not undergone rigorous empirical evaluation to determine whether they actually reduce occurrences of violence.

A notable exception is Safe Dates, a program developed for 8th and 9th grade students (Foshee, Bauman, Arriaga et al., 1998) that has undergone a fairly rigorous evaluation. Safe Dates includes: (a) ten interactive classroom sessions covering topics such as dating violence norms, gender stereotyping, and conflict management skills, (b) group activities such as peer-performed theater productions and a poster contest, and (c) information about community resources for adolescents in abusive relationships. Evaluation results indicate that Safe Dates reduces psychological and physical violence perpetration, but not victimization, among the students who participated in the program. At first glance, this result might be puzzling: How can the perpetration of violence go down, without a commensurate reduction in victimization? This might be explained, in part, by the fact that not all individuals who participated in Safe Dates dated other Safe Date participants. Although the Safe Dates participants were less likely to commit acts of dating violence after completing the program, they were not necessarily less likely to date individuals who commit violent acts.

Evaluations of other school-based programs using techniques similar to those employed in Safe Dates have not had demonstrable effects on violence perpetration or victimization. Some of these evaluations simply did not include measures of perpetration or victimization as outcomes. Others, however, have attempted to measure intervention effects on violent behavior and victimization, but have found no effects (e.g., Avery-Leaf et al., 1997; Hilton et al., 1998). Many of these school-based programs, however, *have* achieved changes in knowledge or attitudes regarding dating violence (e.g., Avery-Leaf et al., 1997; Hilton et al., 1998; Krajewski et al., 1996; Weisz & Black, 2001).

Another program with demonstrated results is The Youth Relationships Project (YRP) (Wolfe et al., 2003). YRP is a community-based intervention designed for 14–16 year olds who were maltreated as children and were thus at increased risk of being in abusive relationships in the future. YRP is an 18-session, group-based program with three primary components: (a) education about abusive relationships and power dynamics within these relationships, (b) skills development, and (c) social action. The skills targeted in this program include communication skills and conflict resolution. The social action portion of the program includes, among other things, allowing program participants the opportunity to become familiar with and to practice utilizing resources for individuals in violent relationships, as well as the chance to develop a project to raise awareness of dating violence within the community. Sessions include skills practice, guest speakers, videos, and visits to relevant community agencies. Evaluation results indicate that YRP reduces physical dating violence perpetration and physical, emotional, and threatening abuse victimization.

It is encouraging that Safe Dates and the YRP have yielded promising results in reducing dating violence among adolescents. However, given the current state of the prevention literature in this area, it would be erroneous to suggest that we know how to prevent adolescent dating violence. Systematic reviews of this literature indicate that the vast majority of studies attempting to evaluate a dating violence prevention program have *not* found intervention effects on behavioral measures, and even though changes in knowledge and attitudes are often documented, it is not really clear if such changes lead to changes in either perpetration or victimization (Hickman et al., 2004; Whitaker et al., 2006). The promising findings of the Safe Dates and YRP programs require replication, and more information is needed on how these programs accomplished their positive effects. Researchers and practitioners can use these programs as a starting point in their own efforts at preventing relationship violence, but it is still important to continue exploring new ideas about prevention in this area.

Concluding Remarks

It is clear that violence in adolescent dating relationships is a prevalent problem with potentially devastating consequences. We also know a great deal about correlates of such violence. On the other hand, there are still important gaps in our knowledge. For example, longitudinal research on this topic is extremely scarce; thus, we know little about the emergence and unfolding of dating violence and victimization over time. This is particularly true for high-risk groups, such as children from violent homes and other groups potentially at risk. In addition, we know very little about how to address the problem of adolescent dating violence effectively. This might be due, in part, to the dearth of well-designed longitudinal studies on this topic, which are necessary to develop a solid knowledge base on the causes of relationship violence and targets for intervention. Although there are promising and notable efforts in the area of understanding and preventing violence in adolescent dating relationships, we still have much to learn.

Longitudinal research on this topic is extremely scarce; thus, we know little about the emergence and unfolding of dating violence and victimization over time.

References

Allen, L. (2004). "Getting off" and "going out": Young people's conceptions of (hetero) sexual relationships. *Health & Sexuality, 6,* 463–481.

Avery-Leaf, S., Cascardi, M., O'Leary, K.D., & Cano, A. (1997). Efficacy of a dating violence prevention program on attitudes justifying aggression. *Journal of Adolescent Health, 21,* 11–17.

Bentley, C.G., Galliher, R.V., & Ferguson, T.J. (2007). Associations among aspects of interpersonal power and relationship functioning in adolescent romantic couples. *Sex Roles, 57,* 483–495.

Capaldi, D.M., & Gorman-Smith, D. (2003). The development of aggression in young male/female couples. In P. Florsheim (Ed.), *Adolescent Romantic Relations and Sexual Behavior: Theory, Research, and Practical implications* (pp. 243–278). Lawrence Erlbaum Associates, Publishers.

Capaldi, D.M., Kim, H.K., & Shortt, J.W. (2007). Observed initiation and reciprocity of physical aggression in young, at risk couples. *Journal of Family Violence, 22,* 101–111.

Connolly, J., Craig, W., Goldberg, A., & Pepler, D. (1999). Conceptions of cross-sex friendships and romantic relationships in early adolescence. *Journal of Youth and Adolescence, 28,* 481–494.

Feiring, C. (1996). Concept of romance in 15-year-old adolescents. *Journal of Research on Adolescence, 6,* 181–200.

Foshee, V., Bauman, K.E., Arriaga, X.B., Helms, R.W., Koch, G.G., & Linder, G.F. (1998). An evaluation of safe dates, an adolescent dating violence prevention program. *American Journal of Public Health, 88,* 45–50.

Gagne, M., Lavoie, F., & Hebert, M. (2005). Victimization during childhood and revictimization in dating relationships in adolescent girls. *Child Abuse & Neglect, 29,* 1,155–1,172.

Halpern, C.T., Oslak, S.G., Young, M.L., Martin, S.L., & Kupper, L.L. (2001). Partner violence among adolescents in opposite-sex romantic relationships: Findings from the national longitudinal study of adolescent health. *American Journal of Public Health, 91,* 1,679–1,685.

Halpern, C.T., Young, M.L., Wallet, M.W., Martin S.L., & Kupper, L.L. (2004). Prevalence of partner violence in same-sex romantic and sexual relationships in a national sample of adolescents. *Journal of Adolescent Health, 35,* 131.

Hickman, L.J., Jaycox, L.H., & Aranoff, J. (2004). Dating violence among adolescents: Prevalence, gender distribution, and prevention program effectiveness. *Trauma, Violence, and Abuse, 5,* 123–142.

Hilton, N.Z., Harris, G.T., Rice, M.E., Krans, T.S., & Lavigne, S.E. (1998). Antiviolence education in high schools: Implementation and evaluation. *Journal of interpersonal Violence, 13,* 726–742.

Howard, D.E., Qiu, Y., & Boekeloo, B. (2003). Personal and social contextual correlates of adolescent dating violence. *Journal of Adolescent Health, 33,* 9–17.

Howard, D.E., Wang, M. Q., & Yan, F. (2007a). Psychosocial factors associated with reports of physical dating violence among U.S. adolescent females. *Adolescence, 42,* 311–324.

Howard, D.E., Wang, M.Q., & Yan, F. (2007b). Prevalence and psychosocial correlates of forced sexual intercourse among U.S. high school adolescents. *Adolescence, 42,* 629–643.

Jackson, S.M., Cram, F., & Seymour, F.W. (2000). Violence and sexual coercion in high school students' dating relationships. *Journal of Family Violence, 15,* 23–36.

Jouriles, E.N., McDonald, R., Garrido, E., Rosenfield, D., & Brown, A.S. (2005). Assessing aggression in adolescent romantic relationships: Can we do it better? *Psychological Assessment, 17,* 469–475.

Krajewsky, S.S., Rybarik, M.F., Dosch, M.F., & Gilmore, G.D. (1996) Results of a curriculum intervention with seventh graders regarding violence in relationships. *Journal of Family Violence, 11,* 93–112.

Linder, J.R., & Collins, W.A. (2005). Parent and peer predictors of physical aggression and conflict management in romantic relationships in early adulthood. *Journal of Family Psychology, 19,* 252–262.

Malik, S., Sorenson, S.B., & Aneshensel, C.S. (1997). Community and dating violence among adolescents: Perpetration and victimization. *Journal of Adolescent Health, 21,* 291–302.

Marquart, B.S., Nannini, D.K., Edwards, R.W., Stanley, L.R., & Wayman, J.C. (2007). Prevalence of dating violence and victimization: Regional and gender differences. *Adolescence, 12,* 645–657.

McMaster, L.E., Connolly, J., Pepler, D., & Craig, W.M. (2002). Peer to peer sexual harassment in early adolescence: A developmental perspective. *Development and Psychopathology, 14,* 91–105.

Molidor, C., & Tolman, R.M. (1998). Gender and contextual factors in adolescent dating violence. *Violence Against Women, 4,* 180–194.

O'Keefe. M. (1997). Predictors of dating violence among high school students. *Journal of Interpersonal Violence, 12,* 546–568.

O'Leary, K D., & Slep, A.M.S. (2003). A dyadic longitudinal model of adolescent dating aggression. *Journal of Clinical Child and Adolescent Psychology, 32,* 314–327.

O'Leary, K.D., Slep, A.M., Avery-Leaf, S., & Cascardi, M. (2008). Gender differences in dating aggression among multiethnic high school students. *Journal of Adolescent Health, 42,* 473–479.

Roberts, T.A., Auinger, M.S., & Klein, J.D. (2006). Predictors of partner abuse in a nationally representative sample of adolescents involved in heterosexual dating relationships. *Violence and Victims, 21,* 81–89.

Sears, H.A., Byers, E.S., & Price, E.L. (2007). The co-occurrence of adolescent boys' and girls' use of psychologically, physically, and sexually abusive behaviours in their dating relationships. *Journal of Adolescence, 30,* 487–504.

Smith, P.H., White, J.W., & Holland, L.J. (2003). A longitudinal perspective on dating violence among adolescent and college-age women. *American Journal of Public Health, 93,* 1,104–1,109.

Weisz, A.N., & Black, B.M. (2001). Evaluating a sexual assault and dating violence prevention program for urban youths. *Social Work Research, 25,* 89–102.

Whitaker, D.J., Morrison, S., Lindquist, C., Hawkins, S.R., O'Neil, J.A., Nesius, A.M., Mathew, A., & Reese, L. (2006). A critical review of interventions for the primary prevention of perpetration of partner violence. *Aggression and Violent Behavior, 11,* 151–166.

Wolfe, D.A., Scott, K., Reitzel-Jaffe, D., Wekerle, C., Grasley, C., & Straatman, A.-L. (2001). Development and validation of the conflict in adolescent dating relationships inventory. *Psychological Assessment, 13,* 277–293.

Wolfe, D.A., Wekerle, C., Scott, K., Straatman, A. L., Grasley, C., & Reitzel-Jaffe, D. (2003). Dating violence prevention with at-risk youth: A controlled outcome evaluation. *Journal of Consulting and Clinical Psychology, 71,* 279–291.

Wolitzky-Taylor, M.A., Ruggiero, K.J., Danielson, C.K., Resnick, H.S., Hanson, R.F., Smith, D.W., Saunders, B.E., & Kilpatrick, D.G. (2008). Prevalence and correlates of dating violence in a national sample of adolescents. *Journal of the American Academy of Child and Adolescent Psychiatry, 47,* 755–762.

Critical Thinking

1. How would you define violence in dating?

2. Why do you think it is difficult to reduce the number of violent dating incidents?

3. What would you do if a friend of yours was victimized by a violent dating partner?

ERNEST N. JOURILES, PhD is Professor in the Department of Psychology and Co-Director of the Family Research Center at Southern Methodist University. **CORA PLATT** is a doctoral student in the Department of Psychology at Southern Methodist University. **RENEE MCDONALD,** PhD is Associate Professor in the Department of Psychology and Co-Director of the Family Research Center at Southern Methodist University.

America's Imprisoned Kids

The United States is an outlier in the world when it comes to detaining and sentencing juvenile offenders as adults. But there are finally signs of change.

ARI PAUL

There can only be a few issues where government policies in countries like Libya and Burma appear more progressive than those in the United States. Juvenile sentencing is one of them.

The United States currently imprisons 2,270 people who have life sentences without the chance for parole for crimes they committed when they were minors, according to both Human Rights Watch and Amnesty International; in all other nations on Earth, there are a combined total of only 12 such prisoners, HRW says. These are grim figures to prison reform advocates in the United States, who have long battled with the punitive, get-tough ethos that dominates American political discussion about criminal justice issues. But there are notable signs of a turn in the political winds.

Alison Parker, a researcher for HRW, has documented this kind of sentencing, and the United States is far behind the curve when it comes to the rights of child prisoners. The United Nation's Convention on the Rights of the Child provides that children may not receive life sentences without parole or the death penalty. All member states have ratified the CRC—except Somalia and the United States. (Both have signed the treaty but have not ratified it.)

The reality, she maintains, is that most countries do not even contemplate sanctioning this kind of punishment. (This isn't to say that the rest of the world is perfect on the matter. "Israel, South Africa and Tanzania reported that they were in violation of the treaty," Parker says.) Domestically, what is just as disturbing for Parker is that her research has found that African American criminal youths in California receive life without parole at a rate 22 times that for their white counterparts.

For Babe Howell, a law professor at New York University and a former criminal defense attorney, this is a symptom of something larger in the United States. "I think we are so punitive in terms of juvenile sentencing for the same reasons why we are so punitive in terms of all other sentencing," she says. "The reason why we are so punitive otherwise is the harder question, although I think it may have to do with how diverse our society is and that criminal sentences generally fall on people regarded as 'other.' I also think that politics have a lot to do with it. Being

soft on crime is untenable and voting for sentencing increases is just so easy."

Indeed, the trend in trying juveniles as adults started in earnest in the 1980s, when homicide rates in the nation started to soar. (Those rates have come down dramatically since.) By the late 1990s most states had made reforms to make the trial of juveniles as adults easier. And it was at this time that Senator Orrin Hatch of Utah introduced the get-tough Violent and Repeat Juvenile Offender Act, which passed in 1999.

But there are some signs of a potential shift in that prevailing political culture. To take one of the most notable examples, a bill in the California Senate that would make it impossible for the state's judges to sentence criminals younger than 18 to life without the chance of parole is now moving forward. In April 2007 the California Senate Committee on Public Safety passed the Juvenile Life Without Parole Reform Act. The state senator behind it is Leland Yee, a Democrat who has a doctorate in child psychology. He says that the human brain is still maturing during adolescence, and therefore minors are more likely to rehabilitate. "We should always sentence kids a little differently," says Adam Keigwin, a spokesperson for Sen. Yee.

A vote before the full state Senate should take place by mid-May. Some of the bill's supporters are hopeful about its eventual passage. In fact, Republican Governor Arnold Schwarzenegger has made at least some efforts to refocus the state's prison system towards rehabilitation. But Keigwin knows the supporters have to win over conservatives in the legislature, especially those allied with the Christian right. "The message of redemption is very important to them," Parker says. Meanwhile, to appeal to fiscally conservative lawmakers, Yee and the bill's supporters are arguing that it will cost the state $500 million to imprison the current population of minors sentenced without the chance of parole until their deaths.

But it remains the case that any such attempt to reform aspects of America's prison-industrial complex will involve tussling with powerful and entrenched interests. Moreover, the culture of excessive punishment pervades all parts of the American political spectrum.

For example, while the Supreme Court, in the 2005 case *Roper v. Simmons,* ended by a vote of 5–4 the practice of putting to death inmates for crimes committed when they were minors, the written dissents are telling. Sandra Day O'Connor, then the court's famed moderate, said that a difference in maturity levels was not a compelling enough reason to rob the state's ability of executing such convicts. Antonin Scalia scoffed at the majority opinion's comparison to what other countries do. "'Acknowledgement' of foreign approval has no place in the legal opinion of this Court," he wrote. Rhetoric like that is an attempt to neuter the ability of attorneys to use an international standard in charging that specific punishments are 'cruel and unusual' and thus unconstitutional.

While many are hopeful about Yee's proposed legislation in California, if it too fails to pass, it will serve as an all-too-typical illustration of the shame that is America's sentencing policy.

"Given current politics it is not clear to me that there are any promising arguments against these sentencing norms but human rights law," says Howell. "International embarrassment may someday put us in a position where life sentences for juveniles become as embarrassing as Jim Crow did in the 1950s and 1960s."

Critical Thinking

1. Shouldn't kids "do the time" if they choose to "do the crime"?
2. Why is the U.S. so punitive?

ARI PAUL is a reporter for *The Chief-Leader,* a weekly newspaper covering municipal labor unions in New York City. He has also written for *Z, In These Times,* and many other publications.

The Long View of Crime

Information collected over time provides valuable insight into criminal behavior.

PAT KAUFMAN

Many findings of longitudinal studies run counter to long-held beliefs about adolescent offending.

For a new edited volume, criminologist Akiva Lieberman assembled an impressive group of scholars to present conclusions from more than 60 studies on crime and delinquency in adolescence. He collected their essays into a book titled *The Long View of Crime: A Synthesis of Longitudinal Research*. Many of the findings challenge the conventional wisdom and could have significant implications for future policy and practice.

Longitudinal studies, which follow people for extended periods, are valuable because they provide information about offending behavior over time. By contrast, cross-sectional studies provide information about one particular period. It is the difference between a panoramic view and a snapshot. The wide-angle lens of longitudinal research is a powerful tool for sorting out some of the chicken-and-egg, "which came first" issues at the heart of criminal research.

> **The wide-angle lens of longitudinal research is a powerful tool for sorting out some of the chicken-and-egg, "which came first" issues at the heart of criminal research.**

Street Gangs: Why Do Gang Members Commit Crime?

No one disputes that gang members commit more crime than non-members. Two schools of thought have emerged to explain why the crime rate is higher among gang members. One theory, the "selection model," suggests that adolescents who are already predisposed toward delinquency and violence are the ones most likely to join gangs. The opposing theory, the "facilitation model," assumes that gang members are no more disposed toward delinquency and violence than others are and would not contribute to higher crime rates if they did not join a gang. However, when they do join a gang, peer pressures promote their increased involvement in delinquency.

Some longitudinal studies have tested these two competing approaches, and the uniformity of results is impressive. The studies show no evidence to support a pure selection model. The weight of the evidence favors the facilitation model, suggesting that street gangs promote delinquent behavior. A corollary finding that further supports the facilitation model is that delinquency (except that related to drug sales) typically declines after the member leaves the gang.

Longitudinal studies have exposed some other possible misconceptions about gang-related behavior. Several factors thought to be associated with gang membership, such as family poverty, family structure, low self-esteem and neighborhood crime, were not supported by the empirical evidence. Studies show that gang membership in "emerging gang" cities is transitory, typically lasting no more than a year. Traditional gang cities such as LA and Chicago were not included in the set of longitudinal studies and their gangs may function differently, with reports of long-duration and multigenerational gang membership.

These findings could have important implications for designing gang prevention and intervention programs. Delinquent behavior may stem more from gang membership than from any delinquent leanings of the gang members themselves.

Arrest and Sanctions: Do They Deter Delinquency or Make It Worse?

Two conflicting views have emerged about the effect of arrest on delinquent offenders. One is that arrest should deter or even end offending behavior because it makes offenders understand that their behavior is socially disapproved of and that they could be arrested again if they do not reform. The opposite view is that arrest increases offending behavior because arrestees begin to view themselves as bad people, which leads them to continue committing crimes. A similar debate rages about the deterrent effect of sanctions that might be imposed after arrest, such as fines, community service, making restitution, attending treatment programs or imprisonment.

The data from longitudinal studies on this question are robust and consistent. More than a dozen studies found that people who have been arrested are at least as likely to be arrested in the future as those who have not. Thus, rather than being a deterrent, arrest resulted in similar or higher rates of later offending. Fourteen studies that examined the effect of sanctions uniformly found that sanctions either had no effect on or increased later offending. Interestingly, as the severity of sanctions increased, later offending was flat or increased. In addition, several studies have suggested that arrest and sanctions have a negative effect on later employment and increase juveniles' chances of becoming high school dropouts.

Several factors may help to explain why arrest and sanctions do not have the expected deterrent effect. On release, most offenders return to the same risky environment that influenced their delinquency. They already have a well-established history of offending before their first arrest, and some offenders have psychological characteristics that decrease their susceptibility to influence from a prior arrest.

The findings from these studies challenge some deeply entrenched notions about the deterrent effect of arrest and sanctions on offending adolescents. More longitudinal studies that employ samples from general populations and examine different kinds of offenders (e.g., classified by age, sex, social class or stage of delinquent career) are needed to inform policy discussions about the possible benefit of more lenient interventions.

Hard Work: How Does Adolescent Employment Affect Offending?

Employment has long been viewed as a solution to the problems of crime and delinquency. However, studies have shown that the relationship between work and crime is far more complex than originally thought. Longitudinal studies now show that employment effects are likely to depend on the age of the person, and the importance of work varies for different groups (e.g., at-risk adolescents as opposed to older former offenders) at different life stages.

One firmly fixed finding over the years has been that intensive work by adolescents (i.e., 20 or more hours per week) increases delinquent behavior. Researchers believed that intensive work made youths less engaged in school, less supervised by their parents and more likely to meet delinquent peers. However, even this formerly secure belief has been challenged by recent longitudinal studies. They suggest that sample selection—that is, the characteristics of the adolescents studied—may have skewed the findings. Perhaps adolescents who work intensively were already poor students, unsupervised at home and prone to harmful behavior and were therefore likely to be delinquent even without work.

Longitudinal studies also show that employment quality may be more important for crime reduction than the simple presence or absence of a job. Those at high risk for crime have many opportunities to earn money illegally. Recent longitudinal studies on adolescent employment and delinquency suggest the old rules about how jobs affect delinquency may be too simplistic.

Growing Up: Does Moving to Adult Roles Affect Delinquent Behavior?

One observation that has stood the test of time is that the prevalence of criminal offenses rises during adolescence and decreases in the early twenties. This age-related crime curve has led researchers to examine the transition to adult roles, such as marriage, cohabitation and parenthood, as a potential explanation for giving up delinquent ways. Theories abound about why taking on adult roles might reduce offending. Some suggest the transitions themselves are the cause for the change in offending behavior because they reorganize adolescents' lives in ways that limit unstructured socializing (i.e., time hanging out with deviant friends). Others postulate that a "cognitive shift" that precedes the transition, rather than the transition itself, causes the change in offending. They theorize that adolescents first must come to view their deviant lifestyles as undesirable. Only then can they embrace role transitions that will create conventional lifestyles.

Of all the role transitions examined, marriage most effectively and consistently reduces deviance. What is not yet clear is why this is so. Citing one study that showed that marriages to criminal spouses might increase offending, some have questioned whether the strength of the marital bond is as important as the spouses' own characteristics and conventionality.

Because studies show that marriage reduces offending, one might expect to see a similar effect from stable romantic partnerships. However, studies have found exactly the opposite: Individuals commit more crimes while living with romantic partners. One study suggests that this might be because adults who were delinquent youths choose antisocial romantic partners, which contributes to continued offending in young adulthood.

> Of all the role transitions examined, marriage most effectively and consistently reduces deviance.

Recent longitudinal studies have also examined the "parenthood effect." Many theorists have expected a negative effect from parenthood on crime, either because new parents become invested in their children or, as with the marriage effect, because the demands of parenthood reduce unstructured socializing. However, the few studies that have looked at this role transition have not found that having children reduces offending. Although people intentionally enter marriage, the same is not always true of parenthood.

The Long View Ahead

Many of the longitudinal studies described in *The Long View of Crime* shed new light on or even skewer time-honored criminological theories. These findings may provide an impetus for further analysis of existing data. They may also spark a new wave of longitudinal studies that incorporate both advances in statistical methods and innovative designs. Structuring longitudinal studies to advance knowledge about the causes of delinquency could lead to a clearer understanding of the explanation, prevention and treatment of offending and antisocial behavior and more targeted policies to address them.

For More Information

- Liberman, A.M., *The Long View of Crime: A Synthesis of Longitudinal Research*, Washington, D.C.: Springer, 2008.

Critical Thinking

1. What are some misconceptions about gang-related behavior that have been exposed by longitudinal studies?

2. What is the difference between longitudinal studies and cross-sectional studies?

PAT KAUFMAN is a freelance writer and frequent contributor to the *NIJ Journal*.

From *National Institute of Justice Journal*, issue 265, April 2010, pp. 26–28. Published by U.S. Department of Justice.

Jail Time Is Learning Time

SIGNE NELSON AND LYNN OLCOTT

There is excitement in the large, well-lit classroom. Student work, including history posters and artwork, adorn the walls. A polite shuffling of feet can be heard, as names are called and certificates presented. It is the graduation ceremony at the Onondaga County Justice Center in Syracuse, N.Y. The ceremony is held several times a year, recognizing inmates in the Incarcerated Education Program who have passed the GED exam or completed a 108-hour vocational program. The courses in the Incarcerated Education Program are geared to prepare inmates to transition successfully to several different settings.

The Incarcerated Education Program is a joint effort by the Syracuse City School District and the Onondaga County Sheriff's Office, and is housed inside the nine-story Onondaga County Justice Center in downtown Syracuse. The Justice Center is a 250,000 square-foot maximum-security, nonsentenced facility, completed and opened in 1995. The facility was built to contain 616 beds, but currently houses 745 inmates. Between 13,000 and 14,000 inmates passed through booking during 2004. About 2,500 of them were minors.

The Justice Center

The Justice Center is a state-of-the-art facility, designed for and operating on the direct supervision model. Direct supervision is a method of inmate management developed by the federal government in 1974 for presentenced inmates in the Federal Bureau of Prisons. There are about 140 such facilities operating throughout the United States and a few hundred currently under construction. Direct supervision places a single deputy directly in a "housing pod" with between 32 and 64 inmates. Maximum pod capacity in the Onondaga County Justice Center is 56 inmates. Inmates are given either relative freedom of movement within the pod or confined to their cells based on their behavior.

The program has been providing courses and classes at the Justice Center for 10 years, but this partnership between the school district and the sheriff's office began almost 30 years ago with the provision of GED instruction. The Incarcerated Education Program was originally conceived to ensure education for inmates who are minors. The program has grown tremendously and now has more than 20 offerings in academic, vocational and life management areas.

The Syracuse City School District professional staff includes six full-time and 18 part-time teachers and staff members. The program is unique in that there are three Onondaga County Sheriff's sergeants who hold New York State Adult Education certification and who teach classes in the vocational component. An average of 250 inmates, or about one-third of the Justice Center's incarcerated population, are enrolled in day and/or evening classes. There are about 250 hours of class time in the facility per week.

Varied Educational and Training Opportunities

As in the public education sector, vocational programs have evolved with the times. The Basic Office Skills class now offers two sections, and includes computer repair and office production skills. A course in building maintenance can be complemented by a course in pre-application to pre-apprenticeship plumbing, or in painting and surface preparation, a class that includes furniture refinishing. A baking class and nail technology have been added in the past few years. All vocational courses, before implementation, are approved by the New York State Education Department and are designed to be consistent with New York State Department of Labor employment projections for Onondaga County. No vocational programming is implemented without first identifying whether the occupation is an area of growth in the community.

Additionally, a broadly inclusive advisory board, made up of community representatives who are stakeholders in the local economy and in the quality of life in the Syracuse metropolitan area has been established. The Incarcerated Education Advisory Board meets approximately three times a year to discuss the perceived needs of the community and to address strategies for transitioning students into employment. Ongoing topics of study are issues surrounding employment, continuing education and housing.

Incarcerated Education Program planners are very aware that job skills are ineffective without proper work attitudes. Job Readiness Training addresses work ethic, proper work behavior, communication and critical behavior skills. Vocational classes are voluntary for the nonsentenced population. However, because of their popularity, a waiting list is maintained for several courses. Among these popular courses are Basic Office Skills and Small Engine Repair. An additional section of Small Engine Repair has been added for female inmates in the class to ensure gender equity in this training opportunity.

New York State law requires that incarcerated minors continue their education while incarcerated. The Incarcerated Education Program enrolls inmates, ages 16 to 21, in Adult Basic Education/GED classes and addresses students with special needs. Other adult inmates attend on a voluntary basis. Inmates are given an initial placement test to determine math and reading skill levels. Because inmates work at a wide range of ability levels, instruction is individualized and materials are geared to independent work. English as a Second Language and English Literacy/Civics are complementary offerings for inmates who are in need of assistance in English language proficiency and knowledge of American culture and history.

The GED exam is given at the Justice Center every 60 days or more often as needed. In the past three years, 225 students have taken the exam. Passing rates fluctuate between 63 percent and 72 percent. The average passing rate for correctional institutions in New York is about 51 percent. The state average passing rate for the general public in community-based courses is fairly stable at 50 percent.[1]

Of course, not everyone will take the GED. Student turnover is high, as inmates are released, bailed out, sent to treatment centers, or sentenced to county, state and federal correctional facilities. Judy Fiorini is a GED teacher who has been with the program for more than 10 years. "Many go back out into our community. We try to teach them something useful for their lives," Fiorini explains.

Transition services form an integral part of the program. The focus is on minors, but help is available for everyone. Two fulltime staff members assist people upon release, with such important tasks as acquiring a driver's license, seeking housing, reenrolling in high school or preparing for job interviews. A very important part of transition services is helping people acquire birth certificates, social security cards and other documents crucial for identification.

Tackling Cognitive Issues

Corrections professionals and educators are aware that it is not enough to improve the skill base of an inmate. There must be cognitive changes as well. The justice center is not a treatment facility, but it has been evolving into a therapeutic community. As the Incarcerated Education Program has grown, there has been the flexibility to add several important courses dealing with life issues, attitude and decision-making. According to data provided by the justice center, about 80 percent of inmates have substance abuse-related issues at the time of their arrest. To support desired cognitive changes, the justice center began establishing "clean and sober" pods in 2002. Currently, there

are several clean and sober pods, including pods for adult men, women and youths. There are waiting lists for placement in the clean and sober pods.

The Incarcerated Education Program has been offering anger management groups for several years. Anger management helps group members deal with compulsive behavior and focus on long-term goals. Other life management offerings include family education, action for personal choice and a course called Parent and Child Together. Most courses of study are developed inhouse by experienced professional faculty. Additionally, the program established gender-specific courses, Men's Issues and Women's Issues, to help inmates become more directly aware of their own responsibilities, separate from the role of a partner or significant other in their lives. The Men's Issues class is led by certified professionals and focuses on actions and their consequences. As in most jails, male inmates significantly outnumber female inmates. Courses and groups continue to be added, though it is sometimes difficult to find space for the abundance of activity in the program.

The program is financially supported, using state and federal funds, via nine carefully coordinated grants. Also significant for the success of the program has been ongoing encouragement and technical assistance from the New York State Education Department, the New York State Association of Incarcerated Education Programs and support from the New York State Sheriffs' Association.[2]

The Incarcerated Education Program continues to encounter challenges. It takes energy and dedication to keep the varied curricula substantial and cohesive, despite high student turnover and complex student needs. With a large civilian staff, the program requires close coordination between security and civilian concerns to help civilian staff work most effectively within the safety and security priorities of the facility. Biweekly meetings facilitate ongoing communication.

Making the Most of Time

Every available square inch of classroom space is in constant use. Classes have exceeded available space and some classes meet in core areas of the justice center as well. Several classes are held in the residence pods, where heavy, white tables are pulled together and portable white-boards are erected to create nomadic classrooms. Overall, the program is succeeding in several ways. Incarcerated minors are directly and meaningfully involved in high school equivalency classes, and inmates older than 21 receive academic and vocational services on a voluntary basis. All inmates are offered the opportunity for life-skills classes and for transitional services upon release. Time served at the Onondaga County Justice Center can also be time used for valuable academic, vocational and life management achievements.

Notes

1. New York State Department of Education maintains statistics for educational activities at correctional facilities in New York state. Patricia Mooney directs the GED Program for the state

through the GED Testing Office in the State Department of Education. Greg Bayduss is the State Department of Education coordinator in charge of Incarcerated Education Programs throughout New York state.

2. State Professional Organizations: The New York State Association of Incarcerated Education Programs Inc. is a professional organization for teachers, administrators and security personnel (www.nysaiep.org). Its mission is to promote excellence in incarcerated education programs in the state, support research in this field and advocate for incarcerated education initiatives through collaboration with other professional organizations. The authors must mention the valuable assistance of the New York State Sheriffs' Association, supporting each county sheriff, as the chief law enforcement officer in his or her county (www.nyssheriffs.org). The association provides valuable information and technical assistance to county sheriffs to help implement programs in their jails.

Critical Thinking

1. Doesn't the IEP just coddle prisoners?
2. Is this program and others like it a good way to spend tax dollars?

SIGNE NELSON is the coordinator of the Incarcerated Education Program, and **LYNN OLCOTT** is a teacher at Auburn Correctional Facility in New York, formerly with the Incarcerated Education Program. The program could not have attained its present strength without the vision and support of law enforcement officials Sheriff Kevin Walsh, Chief Anthony Callisto, and Syracuse City School District administrator Al Wolf. Special thanks to Capt. John Woloszyn, commander of Support Services; Sgt. Joseph Powlina, administrative compliance supervisor; and Deputy Joseph Caruso, photographer. Their assistance in the production of this article was crucial and much appreciated.

Lifers as Teenagers, Now Seeking Second Chance

Adam Liptak

In December, the United Nations took up a resolution calling for the abolition of life imprisonment without the possibility of parole for children and young teenagers. The vote was 185 to 1, with the United States the lone dissenter.

Indeed, the United States stands alone in the world in convicting young adolescents as adults and sentencing them to live out their lives in prison. According to a new report, there are 73 Americans serving such sentences for crimes they committed at 13 or 14.

Mary Nalls, an 81-year-old retired social worker here, has some thoughts about the matter. Her granddaughter Ashley Jones was 14 when she helped her boyfriend kill her grandfather and aunt—Mrs. Nalls's husband and daughter—by stabbing and shooting them and then setting them on fire. Ms. Jones also tried to kill her 10-year-old sister.

Mrs. Nalls, who was badly injured in the rampage, showed a visitor to her home a white scar on her forehead, a reminder of the burns that put her into a coma for 30 days. She had also been shot in the shoulder and stabbed in the chest.

"I forgot," she said later. "They stabbed me in the jaw, too."

But Mrs. Nalls thinks her granddaughter, now 22, deserves the possibility of a second chance.

"I believe that she should have gotten 15 or 20 years," Mrs. Nalls said. "If children are under age, sometimes they're not responsible for what they do."

The group that plans to release the report on Oct. 17, the Equal Justice Initiative, based in Montgomery, Ala., is one of several human rights organizations that say states should be required to review sentences of juvenile offenders as the decades go by, looking for cases where parole might be warranted.

But prosecutors and victims' rights groups say there are crimes so terrible and people so dangerous that only life sentences without the possibility of release are a fit moral and practical response.

"I don't think every 14-year-old who killed someone deserves life without parole," said Laura Poston, who prosecuted Ms. Jones. "But Ashley planned to kill four people. I don't think there is a conscience in Ashley, and I certainly think she is a threat to do something similar."

Specialists in comparative law acknowledge that there have been occasions when young murderers who would have served life terms in the United States were released from prison in Europe and went on to kill again. But comparing legal systems is difficult, in part because the United States is a more violent society and in part because many other nations imprison relatively few people and often only for repeat violent offenses.

"I know of no systematic studies of comparative recidivism rates," said James Q. Whitman, who teaches comparative criminal law at Yale. "I believe there are recidivism problems in countries like Germany and France, since those are countries that ordinarily incarcerate only dangerous offenders, but at some point they let them out and bad things can happen."

The differences in the two approaches, legal experts said, are rooted in politics and culture. The European systems emphasize rehabilitation, while the American one stresses individual responsibility and punishment.

Corrections professionals and criminologists here and abroad tend to agree that violent crime is usually a young person's activity, suggesting that eventual parole could be considered in most cases. But the American legal system is more responsive to popular concerns about crime and attitudes about punishment, while justice systems abroad tend to be administered by career civil servants rather than elected legislators, prosecutors and judges.

In its sentencing of juveniles, as in many other areas, the legal system in the United States goes it alone. American law is, by international standards, a series of innovations and exceptions. From the central role played by juries in civil cases to the election of judges to punitive damages to the disproportionate number of people in prison, the United States is an island in the sea of international law.

And the very issue of whether American judges should ever take account of foreign law is hotly disputed. At the hearings on their Supreme Court nominations, both John G. Roberts Jr. and Samuel A. Alito Jr. said they thought it a mistake to consider foreign law in constitutional cases.

But the international consensus against life-without-parole sentences for juvenile offenders may nonetheless help Ms. Jones. In about a dozen cases recently filed around the country on behalf of 13- and 14-year-olds sentenced to life in prison, lawyers for the inmates relied on a 2005 Supreme Court decision that banned the execution of people who committed crimes when they were younger than 18.

That decision, *Roper v. Simmons,* was based in part on international law. Noting that the United States was the only nation in the world to sanction the juvenile death penalty, Justice Anthony M. Kennedy, writing for the majority, said it was appropriate to look to "the laws of other countries and to international authorities as instructive" in interpreting the Eighth Amendment's prohibition of cruel and unusual punishment.

He added that teenagers were different from older criminals—less mature, more susceptible to peer pressure and more likely to change for the better. Those findings, lawyers for the juvenile lifers say, should apply to their clients, too.

"Thirteen- and 14-year-old children should not be condemned to death in prison because there is always hope for a child," said Bryan Stevenson, the executive director of the Equal Justice Initiative, which represents Ms. Jones and several other juvenile lifers.

The 2005 death penalty ruling applied to 72 death-row inmates, almost precisely the same number as the 73 prisoners serving life without parole for crimes committed at 13 or 14.

The Supreme Court did not abolish the juvenile death penalty in a single stroke. The 2005 decision followed one in 1988 that held the death penalty unconstitutional for those who had committed crimes under 16.

The new lawsuits, filed in Alabama, California, Florida, Missouri, North Carolina and Wisconsin, seek to follow a similar progression.

"We're not demanding that all these kids be released tomorrow," Mr. Stevenson said. "I'm not even prepared to say that all of them will get to the point where they should be released. We're asking for some review."

In defending American policy in this area in 2006, the State Department told the United Nations that sentencing is usually a matter of state law. "As a general matter," the department added, juvenile offenders serving life-without-parole terms "were hardened criminals who had committed gravely serious crimes."

Human rights groups have disputed that. According to a 2005 report from Human Rights Watch and Amnesty International, 59 percent of the more than 2,200 prisoners serving life without parole for crimes they committed at 17 or younger had never been convicted of a previous crime. And 26 percent were in for felony murder, meaning they participated in a crime that led to a murder but did not themselves kill anyone.

The new report focuses on the youngest offenders, locating 73 juvenile lifers in 19 states who were 13 and 14 when they committed their crimes. Pennsylvania has the most, with 19, and Florida is next, with 15. In those states and Illinois, Nebraska, North Carolina and Washington, 13-year-olds have been sentenced to die in prison.

In most of the cases, the sentences were mandatory, an automatic consequence of a murder conviction after being tried as an adult.

A federal judge here will soon rule on Ms. Jones's challenge to her sentence. Ms. Poston, who prosecuted her, said Ms. Jones was beyond redemption.

"Between the ages of 2 and 3, you develop a conscience," Ms. Poston said. "She never got the voice that says, 'This is bad, Ashley.'"

"It was a blood bath in there," Ms. Poston said of the night of the murders here, in 1999. "Ashley Jones is not the poster child for the argument that life without parole is too long."

In a telephone interview from the Tutwiler Prison for Women in Wetumpka, Ala., Ms. Jones said she did not recognize the girl who committed her crimes. According to court filings, her mother was a drug addict and her stepfather had sexually molested her. "Everybody I loved, everybody I trusted, I was betrayed by," Ms. Jones said.

"I'm very remorseful about what happened," she said. "I should be punished. I don't feel like I should spend the rest of my life in prison."

Mrs. Nalls, her grandmother, had been married for 53 years when she and her husband, Deroy Nalls, agreed to take Ashley in. She was "a problem child," and Mr. Nalls was a tough man who took a dislike to Ashley's boyfriend, Geramie Hart. Mr. Hart, who was 16 at the time of the murders, is also serving a life term. Mrs. Nalls said he deserved a shot at parole someday as well.

Critical Thinking

1. Do you believe that teenagers who commit violent crimes should be sentenced to life without parole?

2. Should Americans be concerned about the unique position of the United States regarding the way it deals with young adolescents?

3. Can Americans learn from the decisions of other countries?

4. Should minors ever be treated as adults in court?

Preventing Future Crime with Cognitive Behavioral Therapy

One form of psychotherapy stands out in the criminal justice system.

PATRICK CLARK

C ognitive behavioral therapy reduces recidivism in both juveniles and adults.

The therapy assumes that most people can become conscious of their own thoughts and behaviors and then make positive changes to them. A person's thoughts are often the result of experience, and behavior is often influenced and prompted by these thoughts. In addition, thoughts may sometimes become distorted and fail to reflect reality accurately.

Cognitive behavioral therapy has been found to be effective with juvenile and adult offenders; substance abusing and violent offenders, and probationers, prisoners and parolees. It is effective in various criminal justice settings, both in institutions and in the community, and addresses a host of problems associated with criminal behavior. For instance, in most cognitive behavioral therapy programs, offenders improve their social skills, means-ends problem solving, critical reasoning, moral reasoning, cognitive style, self-control, impulse management and self-efficacy.

Recently, Mark Lipsey of Vanderbilt University examined the effectiveness of various approaches to intervention with young offenders.[1] His review analyzed the results of 548 studies from 1958 to 2002 that assessed intervention policies, practices and programs.

Lipsey grouped evaluations into seven categories:

- Counseling
- Deterrence
- Discipline
- Multiple coordinated services
- Restorative programs
- Skill building
- Surveillance

When he combined and compared the effects of these interventions, he found that those based on punishment and deterrence appeared to increase criminal recidivism. On the other hand, therapeutic approaches based on counseling, skill building and multiple services had the greatest impact in reducing further criminal behavior.

Lipsey also examined the effectiveness of various therapeutic interventions. In particular, he compared different counseling and skill-building approaches. He found that cognitive behavioral skill-building approaches were more effective in reducing further criminal behavior than any other intervention.

In a different research review, Nana Landenberger and Lipsey showed that programs based on cognitive behavioral therapy are effective with juvenile and adult criminal offenders in various criminal justice settings, including prison, residential, community probation and parole.[2] They examined research studies published from 1965 through 2005 and found 58 that could be included in their review and analysis. The researchers found that cognitive behavioral therapy significantly reduced recidivism even among high-risk offenders.

Therapeutic approaches based on counseling, skill building and multiple services had the greatest impact in reducing further criminal behavior.

Perceptions Affect Behavior

Beliefs, attitudes and values affect the way people think and how they view problems. These beliefs can distort the way a person views reality, interacts with other people and experiences everyday life.

Cognitive behavioral therapy can help restructure distorted thinking and perception, which in turn changes a person's behavior for the better. Characteristics of distorted thinking may include:

- Immature or developmentally arrested thoughts.
- Poor problem solving and decision making.
- An inability to consider the effects of one's behavior.
- An egocentric viewpoint with a negative view or lack of trust in other people.
- A hampered ability to reason and accept blame for wrongdoing.
- A mistaken belief of entitlement, including an inability to delay gratification, confusing wants and needs, and ignoring the rights of other people.
- A tendency to act on impulse, including a lack of self-control and empathy.
- An inability to manage feelings of anger.
- The use of force and violence as a means to achieve goals.

What is CBT?

Cognitive behavioral therapy is a treatment that focuses on patterns of thinking and the beliefs, attitudes and values that underlie thinking. CBT has only recently come into prominence as one of the few approaches to psychotherapy that has been, broadly validated with research, although it has been used in psychological therapy for more than 40 years. It is reliably effective with a wide variety of personal problems and behaviors, including those important to criminal justice, such as substance abuse and anti-social, aggressive, delinquent and criminal behavior.

Unlike other approaches to psychotherapy, CBT places responsibility in the hands of clients while supplying them with the tools to solve their problems, focusing on the present rather than the past. People taking part in CBT learn specific skills that can be used to solve the problems they confront all the time as well as skills they can use to achieve legitimate goals and objectives. CBT first concentrates on developing skills to recognize distorted or unrealistic thinking when it happens, and then to changing that thinking or belief to mollify or eliminate problematic behavior.

The programs, often offered in small group settings, incorporate lessons and exercises involving role play, modeling or demonstrations. Individual counseling sessions are often part of CBT. Clients are given homework and conduct experiments between sessions. These components are used to gauge the individual's readiness for change and foster engagement in that change. A willingness to change is necessary for CBT or any other treatment to be effective in reducing further criminal behavior.

Brand name programs often limit clients to 20–30 sessions, lasting over a period of up to 20 weeks. The more treatment provided or the more sessions participants attend over time, the greater the impact on and decrease in recidivism.

The typical CBT program is provided by trained professionals or paraprofessionals. Training for non-therapist group facillitators often involves 40 hours or more of specialized lessons and skill building. Licensed and certified therapists are often part of cognitive programs, especially those involving individual counseling.

Characteristics of the counselor are important to a program's effectiveness. Counselor honesty, empathy and sensitivity are helpful traits. Support and encouragement, partnership or alliance, and acceptance are necessary in establishing effective rapport, which is especially important in CBT because counselors often take on the role of coach. It is important that counselors be consistent in modeling and expressing the pro-social attitudes and behaviors, moral values and reasoning that are often part of CBT with criminal offenders.

Positive findings from research on CBT are common. Over the years, studies have shown the therapy is effective with various problems, including mood disorders, anxiety and personality and behavioral disorders. Unlike other traditional and popular therapies, CBT has been the subject of more than 400 clinical trials involving a broad range of conditions and populations. It has successfully addressed many issues experienced by children, including disruptive or noncompliant behavior, aggressiveness, oppositional defiant disorder and attention deficit hyperactivity disorder. For adults, CBT has been shown to help with marital problems, sexual dysfunction, depression, mood disorders and substance abuse. It has also been shown to be as useful as antidepressant medication for individuals with depression and appears to be superior to medication in preventing relapses.

Therapy can help a person address and change these unproductive and detrimental beliefs, views and thoughts.[3]

Cognitive Behavioral Therapy and Criminal Offenders

Landenberger and Lipsey found that even high-risk behavior did not reduce the therapy's effectiveness. For example, some of the greatest effects were among more serious offenders. It may be that the therapy's enabling, self-help approach is more effective in engaging typically resistant clients, that it increases their participation and therefore the benefits of participation. The therapy is more effective in reducing further criminal behavior when clients simultaneously receive other support, such as supervision, employment, education and training, and other mental health counseling.

The cognitive behavioral therapy approach has recently been used in many prepackaged, brand name programs, such as "Reasoning and Rehabilitation," "Aggression Replacement Therapy," "Thinking for Change" and others. The National Institute of Corrections recently published a thorough and comprehensive review of cognitive behavioral therapy, which provides detailed descriptions of these and other programs.[4] Interestingly, although the Landenberger and Lipsey review showed these programs were effective, no single program was superior in reducing recidivism.

More research is needed to determine if it would be effective for offenders to receive cognitive behavioral therapy earlier in their criminal careers or as part of early intervention or parenting training programs.

Notes

1. Lipsey, M.W., "The Primary Factors That Characterize Effective Interventions With Juvenile Offenders: A meta-analytic overview," *Victims and Offenders* 4 (2009): 124–147.

2. Landenberger, N.A., and M. Lipsey, "The positive Effects of Cognitive-behavioral Programs for Offenders: A Meta-analysis of Factors Associated With Effective Treatment," *Journal of Experimental Criminology,* 1 (2005): 451–476.

3. Yochelson, S., and S.E. Samenow, *The Criminal Personality, Volume I: A Profile for Change,* New York: Jason Aronson, 1976; and Walters, G., *The Criminal Lifestyle: Patterns of Serious Criminal Conduct,* Newbury Park, Calif.: Sage Publications, 1990.

4. Milkman, H., and K. Wanberg, *Cognitive-Behavioral Treatment: A Review and Discussion for Correction Professionals,* Washington, DC: U.S. Department of Justice, National Institute of Corrections, 2007, http://nicic.gov/Library/021657.

Critical Thinking

1. In what ways can cognitive behavioral therapy reduce recidivism?
2. What do you think about using CBT in parenting programs?
3. Why are counselors' characteristics important?

PATRICK CLARK is a Social Science Analyst with NIJ's Crime Control and Prevention Division.

From *National Institute of Justice Journal,* issue 265, April 2010, pp. 22–25. Published by U.S. Department of Justice.

Interviewing Compliant Adolescent Victims

Catherine S. Connell, MSW and Martha J. Finnegan, MSW

Many child and adolescent victims of exploitation require interviews significantly different from the ones investigators typically have training and expertise in. Special dynamics surround these situations, and, accordingly, the forensic interviewing of children and adolescents has become a specialized field.[1]

More specifically, law enforcement personnel sometimes find adolescent crime victims who—in various degrees and for different reasons—comply with the perpetrators. While investigators may encounter such juveniles in many types of cases, the authors have chosen to focus on computer-facilitated crimes. Interviewers must understand the development and complexity of these teenagers, as well as the dynamics involved in the relationship between victim and offender.

Victims and Perpetrators

Although they may look and talk like adults, teenagers are at a significant and definitive stage of development. While attempting to reach maturity and independence, they remain immature and dependent. During this time, adolescents' social, emotional, and sexual development and behaviors, such as vulnerability to flattery and attraction to recklessness,[2] can put them at risk for victimization.

In adolescence, the part of the brain responsible for reasoning, inhibiting impulses, controlling emotions, and determining right from wrong has not completely formed.[3] As a result, teenagers tend to be impulsive, use poor judgment, and lack decision-making ability. They also do not always recognize the potential consequences of their choices. Often, they take risks and break rules as they consider themselves invincible.[4] However, they blame themselves for any negative outcomes that ensue.[5]

Also significant, sexual curiosity coincides with the physical changes that occur. Chat rooms and other online methods of communication now offer a resource, although not always accurate, for teens who want to learn or resolve confusion about their sexuality. Perhaps, they have questions pertaining to their sexual orientation and feel they have no family members or friends with whom to relate. Some teenagers seek out an adult online to experiment sexually with. In fact, most adolescents who meet an adult online acquaintance in person know it is for sexual purposes.[6]

Adolescents easily fall prey to the grooming process of online predators who appeal to their need to be "special" and "mature." Teens often know the significant age difference of the person they chat with and, perhaps, send pictures to, but this does not change their behavior. For instance, an adolescent girl may engage in a relationship with a 40-year-old man she met online and not consider it problematic. She may enjoy receiving expensive gifts that a male her age could not provide. Further, in spite of the risks involved, this teen may rather communicate with someone who makes her feel grown-up than with her peer group members who may not have matured yet themselves. While other adults would consider this man a criminal, the girl may view him as her boyfriend.

Rarely do these adults use threats or deception to lure their teenage victims.[7] Online perpetrators groom adolescents in a way that tends to gain complicity. Victims may cooperate in certain acts, but not in others. Some teens might go along reluctantly with sexual contact to receive material benefits from the adult, while others may actively participate in what they consider a relationship.[8]

Investigators and Interviews

Investigators must treat these incidents as crimes despite victims' complicity with the perpetrator. However, they will find that conducting an investigation and interviewing these adolescents pose challenges when the victims do not see themselves as such. Complications and problems may arise if interviewers do not understand and acknowledge the dynamics of or recognize compliant victimization.[9] Further, investigators must avoid turning the victim interview into an interrogation, which could pose problems for both the juvenile and the investigation.

Investigators . . . will find that conducting an investigation and interviewing these adolescents pose challenges when the victims do not see themselves as such.

Interviews of compliant teenagers in computer-related cases differ from other child/adolescent interviews for several reasons: investigators usually uncover evidence of victimization during the investigation leading to the interview; the lack of disclosure prior to the interview tends to result in a greater rate of denial, even despite available evidence; and interviewers usually have media evidence, such as child pornography images and chat logs, to present to the adolescent during questioning. Forensic interviews with compliant teenage victims often require the verbal or tangible presentation of evidence to increase the chance of disclosure.

Investigators should carefully consider where to conduct the interview. Inaccurate statements may result from choosing an inappropriate setting. Interviewers should use a neutral location, such as a child advocacy center, unless it proves inappropriate, is not available, or does not allow for the presentation of evidence or interviewing of adolescents who have not made disclosures. A soft interview room at a local police department can serve as another option.

The interviewer's approach can influence the accuracy of the adolescent's statements. Such tactics as trying to convince compliant teens that they are victims, telling them that their relationship with a perpetrator differs from how they perceive it, passing judgment, or conveying parental advice while interviewing them could affect the disclosure process.

For instance, investigators may think it necessary to explain the dangers of the Internet and to offer safety tips. Although such education can prove valuable, the forensic interview is not the appropriate time for it. Teens may perceive this as blame. Instead, investigators must keep an open mind and allow victims to explain what occurred. If not, adolescents may provide inaccurate responses by, for instance, exaggerating violence or minimizing or denying complicit involvement, depending on their perception of what the investigator wants to hear.[10]

As another example, interviewers may approach compliant victims, such as those who willingly traveled with their online acquaintances, by saying, "What happened to you was a bad thing," or "Your parents have been so worried." In response, the teens might acquiesce to what they think an interviewer wants to hear to avoid trouble with their parents.

Many of these victims became compliant because of the perpetrator's skill in making them see the relationship as a real one based on love, not fantasy. These adolescents truly believe that the perpetrator cares about them. During interviews, these teens may become angry and defiant and not provide information about the person they "love." They may give outright denials even when presented with evidence to the contrary,[11] which can cause frustration for victims and investigators.

By staying focused on the teen as a victim, the forensic interviewer avoids inflicting additional trauma, inhibiting disclosure, and instilling in the adolescent a fear of not being believed. Further, defending the interview in court becomes easier if it does not cross the line into an interrogation. However, interviewers still can confront victims in a developmentally appropriate way. For example, if the adolescent states that no sexual contact with the perpetrator occurred, yet the chat logs have clearly stated it has, the investigator can say to the teen, "I'm confused. You said Joe never touched your body, but in these chat logs you and Joe talk about having sex. Tell me about that." In this example, the interviewer confronts the adolescent without turning the interview into an interrogation by accusing the victim of lying.

Also, investigators must understand that sexual exploitation victims may have participated in criminal activity (e.g., using drugs or transmitting sexual images of themselves) as part of their victimization and anticipate factors, such as shame, guilt, embarrassment, and even thoughts of suicide, before conducting the interview. For example, two 13 year olds involved with the same perpetrator revealed during a forensic interview that one had physical contact with the perpetrator while the other only interacted with the subject via computer. However, both indicated that they had thought of or attempted suicide due to embarrassment.

Conclusion

The process of investigating and interviewing child and teen victims has changed over the past several years. Forensic interviewing protocols and guidelines have developed based on research and in response to several court cases overturned on the basis of poor interviewing. Investigators must conduct forensic interviews in a developmentally sensitive, unbiased manner that will support decisions made in the criminal justice and child welfare systems.[12] They should test, rather than confirm, hypotheses.[13] If investigators interview compliant adolescent victims, they must follow guidelines established for the appropriate state, county, or agency. To avoid possible negative consequences, interviewers should receive training in forensic interviewing and use a trained forensic interviewer, multidisciplinary teams, or such resources as child advocacy centers. Investigators must understand that they cannot approach teenagers like adults and that doing so could adversely impact any statements they hope to obtain from the interview.

While services exist to accommodate younger, actively disclosing children, they are not always conducive to teenagers. Certain mental-health issues need to be addressed postinterview so appropriate services can be offered to the victims and their families. Interviewers should learn about state and federal statutes regarding victim's rights and child protection issues. And, they must provide a defensible forensic interview for the adolescent victim.

Notes

1. Forensic interviews are designed to obtain statements from children in a developmentally sensitive, unbiased, and legally defensible manner that will support accurate and fair decision making in the criminal justice and child welfare systems. There are two overriding features of a forensic interview: they are hypothesis testing, rather than hypothesis confirming, and child centered. Interviewers try to rule out alternative explanations for the allegations, and they go through a series of phases, letting the child dictate the vocabulary and content of the conversation as much as possible. See State of Michigan, Governor's Task Force on Children's Justice and Department

of Human Services, *Forensic Interviewing Protocol;* and M.E. Lamb and D.A. Poole, *Investigative Interviews of Children: A Guide for Helping Professionals* (Washington, DC: American Psychological Association, 1998).

2. W. Deaton and M. Hertica, "Developmental Considerations in Forensic Interviews with Adolescents," *The APSAC Advisor* 6: 5–8; and The Southern California Training Center at the Center for Child Protection, "On the Investigation of Child Maltreatment: Child Forensic Interview Training" (Office for Criminal Justice Planning, 1999).

3. "Adolescent Brains Are Works in Progress," retrieved from www.pbs.org/wgbh/pages/frontline/shows/teenbrain/work/adolescent.html.

4. The Southern California Training Center at the Center for Child Protection, "On the Investigation of Child Maltreatment: Child Forensic Interview Training" (Office for Criminal Justice Planning, 1999).

5. Ibid.

6. D. Finkelhor, K.J. Mitchell, J. Wolak, and M.L. Ybarra, "Online 'Predators' and Their Victims: Myths, Realities, and Implications for Prevention and Treatment," *American Psychologist* 63, no. 2: 111–128.

7. Ibid.

8. K.V. Lanning, "A Law Enforcement Perspective on the Compliant Child Victim," *The APSAC Advisor* 14, no. 2.

9. Ibid.

10. Ibid.

11. Ibid.

12. State of Michigan, Governor's Task Force on Children's Justice and Department of Human Services, *Forensic Interviewing Protocol;* and M.E. Lamb and D.A. Poole, *Investigative Interviews of Children: A Guide for Helping Professionals* (Washington, DC: American Psychological Association, 1998).

13. Ibid.

Critical Thinking

1. How would you describe a compliant victim?

2. Why do they become compliant?

3. What are some challenges investigators may face when interviewing a compliant victim?

Ms. Catherine S. Connell, a licensed social worker, is a child/adolescent forensic interview specialist in the FBI's Macomb County, Michigan, resident agency. **Ms. Martha J. Finnegan,** a licensed social worker, is a child/adolescent forensic interview specialist at FBI Headquarters.

From *FBI Law Enforcement Bulletin* by Catherine S. Connell and Martha J. Finnegan, May 2010. Published by Federal Bureau of Investigation, www.fbi.gov.

UNIT 6

Punishment and Corrections

Unit Selections

Learning Outcomes

After reading this unit, you will be able to:

- Explain the HOPE program.

- Explain Operation Ceasefire.

- Explain why both programs have been effective in treating parolees.

- Discuss what effect the high American rates of incarceration have had on the "war on drugs."

- State the differences between privatization and contracting-out of prisons.

- Show why inmates should have access to education.

Student Website

www.mhhe.com/cls

Internet References

American Probation and Parole Association (APPA)
  www.appa-net.org
The Corrections Connection
  www.corrections.com
Critical Criminology Division of the ASC
  www.critcrim.org
David Willshire's Forensic Psychology & Psychiatry Links
  http://members.optushome.com.au/dwillsh/index.html
Oregon Department of Corrections
  http://egov.oregon.gov/DOC/TRANS/CC/cc_welcome.shtml

In the American system of criminal justice, the term "corrections" has a special meaning. It designates programs and agencies that have legal authority over the custody or supervision of people who have been convicted by the courts of a criminal act. The correctional process begins with the sentencing of the convicted offender. The predominant sentencing pattern in the United States encourages maximum judicial discretion and offers a range of alternatives, from probation (supervised, conditional freedom within the community) through imprisonment, to the death penalty.

Selections in this unit focus on the current condition of the U.S. penal system and the effects that sentencing, probation, imprisonment, and parole have on the rehabilitation of criminals.

This section begins with "Inmate Count in U.S. Dwarfs Other Nations'," in which Liptak writes about the grim statistics that distinguish this country's incarceration rates from those of other countries. Jeffrey Rosen, in "Prisoners of Parole," reports on the apparent success of the HOPE program in reducing prison populations through probation and parole reform.

According to W.W. in "The Perverse Incentives of Private Prisons," private prisons, rather than saving taxpayers money, may cost far more than public institutions. Following is a commencement address given by Jablecki, entitled "Prison Inmates Meet Socrates," in which he spoke about the problems caused by public policy that ignores the benefits of attempting to rehabilitate offenders. In "One Clique," Campbell discusses how the issue of race is handled by prison inmates. In the next article, "The Professor Was a Prison Guard," Jeffrey J. Williams writes about how the time he spent working in a prison compares with his present position as a college professor.

The following article, "Supermax Prisons," by Jeffrey Ian Ross, is a warning about the possible constitutional and human

rights violations occurring in these institutions. Any answer to the question What do we get from imprisonment? has to recognize that U.S. imprisonment operates differently from that in any other democratic state in the world. This point is made in Todd R. Clear's essay, "The Results of American Incarceration." A prison warden says that crime is a social disease that we cannot ignore in the hope it will go away. Finally, "Partnering with Law Enforcement" is an article that reports on some of the positive outcomes that have resulted from partnerships among probation and parole officers and police officers.

Inmate Count in U.S. Dwarfs Other Nations'

ADAM LIPTAK

The United States has less than 5 percent of the world's population. But it has almost a quarter of the world's prisoners.

Indeed, the United States *leads* the world in producing prisoners, a reflection of a relatively recent and now entirely distinctive American approach to crime and punishment. Americans are locked up for crimes—from writing bad checks to using drugs—that would rarely produce prison sentences in other countries. And in particular they are kept incarcerated far longer than prisoners in other nations.

Criminologists and legal scholars in other industrialized nations say they are mystified and appalled by the number and length of American prison sentences.

The United States has, for instance, 2.3 million criminals behind bars, more than any other nation, according to data maintained by the International Center for Prison Studies at King's College London.

China, which is four times more populous than the United States, is a distant second, with 1.6 million people in prison. (That number excludes hundreds of thousands of people held in administrative detention, most of them in China's extrajudicial system of re-education through labor, which often singles out political activists who have not committed crimes.)

San Marino, with a population of about 30,000, is at the end of the long list of 218 countries compiled by the center. It has a single prisoner.

The United States comes in first, too, on a more meaningful list from the prison studies center, the one ranked in order of the incarceration rates. It has 751 people in prison or jail for every 100,000 in population. (If you count only adults, one in 100 Americans is locked up.)

The only other major industrialized nation that even comes close is Russia, with 627 prisoners for every 100,000 people. The others have much lower rates. England's rate is 151; Germany's is 88; and Japan's is 63.

The median among all nations is about 125, roughly a sixth of the American rate.

There is little question that the high incarceration rate here has helped drive down crime, though there is debate about how much.

Criminologists and legal experts here and abroad point to a tangle of factors to explain America's extraordinary incarceration rate: higher levels of violent crime, harsher sentencing laws, a legacy of racial turmoil, a special fervor in combating illegal drugs, the American temperament, and the lack of a social safety net. Even democracy plays a role, as judges—many of whom are elected, another American anomaly—yield to populist demands for tough justice.

Whatever the reason, the gap between American justice and that of the rest of the world is enormous and growing.

It used to be that Europeans came to the United States to study its prison systems. They came away impressed.

"In no country is criminal justice administered with more mildness than in the United States," Alexis de Tocqueville, who toured American penitentiaries in 1831, wrote in "Democracy in America."

No more.

"Far from serving as a model for the world, contemporary America is viewed with horror," James Q. Whitman, a specialist in comparative law at Yale, wrote last year in *Social Research*. "Certainly there are no European governments sending delegations to learn from us about how to manage prisons."

Prison sentences here have become "vastly harsher than in any other country to which the United States would ordinarily be compared," Michael H. Tonry, a leading authority on crime policy, wrote in "The Handbook of Crime and Punishment."

Indeed, said Vivien Stern, a research fellow at the prison studies center in London, the American incarceration rate has made the United States "a rogue state, a country that has made a decision not to follow what is a normal Western approach."

The spike in American incarceration rates is quite recent. From 1925 to 1975, the rate remained stable, around 110 people in prison per 100,000 people. It shot up with the movement to get tough on crime in the late 1970s. (These numbers exclude people held in jails, as comprehensive information on prisoners held in state and local jails was not collected until relatively recently.)

The nation's relatively high violent crime rate, partly driven by the much easier availability of guns here, helps explain the number of people in American prisons.

"The assault rate in New York and London is not that much different," said Marc Mauer, the executive director of the Sentencing Project, a research and advocacy group. "But if you look at the murder rate, particularly with firearms, it's much higher."

Despite the recent decline in the murder rate in the United States, it is still about four times that of many nations in Western Europe.

But that is only a partial explanation. The United States, in fact, has relatively low rates of nonviolent crime. It has lower burglary and robbery rates than Australia, Canada and England.

People who commit nonviolent crimes in the rest of the world are less likely to receive prison time and certainly less likely to receive long sentences. The United States is, for instance, the only advanced country that incarcerates people for minor property crimes like passing bad checks, Mr. Whitman wrote.

Efforts to combat illegal drugs play a major role in explaining long prison sentences in the United States as well. In 1980, there were about 40,000 people in American jails and prisons for drug crimes. These days, there are almost 500,000.

Those figures have drawn contempt from European critics. "The U.S. pursues the war on drugs with an ignorant fanaticism," said Ms. Stern of King's College.

Many American prosecutors, on the other hand, say that locking up people involved in the drug trade is imperative, as it helps thwart demand for illegal drugs and drives down other kinds of crime. Attorney General Michael B. Mukasey, for instance, has fought hard to prevent the early release of people in federal prison on crack cocaine offenses, saying that many of them "are among the most serious and violent offenders."

Still, it is the length of sentences that truly distinguishes American prison policy. Indeed, the mere number of sentences imposed here would not place the United States at the top of the incarceration lists. If lists were compiled based on annual admissions to prison per capita, several European countries would outpace the United States. But

American prison stays are much longer, so the total incarceration rate is higher.

Burglars in the United States serve an average of 16 months in prison, according to Mr. Mauer, compared with 5 months in Canada and 7 months in England.

Many specialists dismissed race as an important distinguishing factor in the American prison rate. It is true that blacks are much more likely to be imprisoned than other groups in the United States, but that is not a particularly distinctive phenomenon. Minorities in Canada, Britain and Australia are also disproportionately represented in those nation's prisons, and the ratios are similar to or larger than those in the United States.

Some scholars have found that English-speaking nations have higher prison rates.

"Although it is not at all clear what it is about Anglo-Saxon culture that makes predominantly English-speaking countries especially punitive, they are," Mr. Tonry wrote last year in "Crime, Punishment and Politics in Comparative Perspective."

"It could be related to economies that are more capitalistic and political cultures that are less social democratic than those of most European countries," Mr. Tonry wrote. "Or it could have something to do with the Protestant religions with strong Calvinist overtones that were long influential."

The American character—self-reliant, independent, judgmental—also plays a role.

"America is a comparatively tough place, which puts a strong emphasis on individual responsibility," Mr. Whitman of Yale wrote. "That attitude has shown up in the American criminal justice of the last 30 years."

French-speaking countries, by contrast, have "comparatively mild penal policies," Mr. Tonry wrote.

Of course, sentencing policies within the United States are not monolithic, and national comparisons can be misleading.

"Minnesota looks more like Sweden than like Texas," said Mr. Mauer of the Sentencing Project. (Sweden imprisons about 80 people per 100,000 of population; Minnesota, about 300; and Texas, almost 1,000. Maine has the lowest incarceration rate in the United States, at 273; and Louisiana the highest, at 1,138.)

Whatever the reasons, there is little dispute that America's exceptional incarceration rate has had an impact on crime.

"As one might expect, a good case can be made that fewer Americans are now being victimized" thanks to the tougher crime policies, Paul G. Cassell, an authority on sentencing and a former federal judge, wrote in *The Stanford Law Review*.

From 1981 to 1996, according to Justice Department statistics, the risk of punishment rose in the United States and fell in England. The crime rates predictably moved in the opposite directions, falling in the United States and rising in England.

"These figures," Mr. Cassell wrote, "should give one pause before too quickly concluding that European sentences are appropriate."

Other commentators were more definitive. "The simple truth is that imprisonment works," wrote Kent Scheidegger and Michael Rushford of the Criminal Justice Legal Foundation in *The Stanford Law and Policy Review*. "Locking up criminals for longer periods reduces the level of crime. The benefits of doing so far offset the costs."

There is a counterexample, however, to the north. "Rises and falls in Canada's crime rate have closely paralleled America's for 40 years," Mr. Tonry wrote last year. "But its imprisonment rate has remained stable."

Several specialists here and abroad pointed to a surprising explanation for the high incarceration rate in the United States: democracy.

Most state court judges and prosecutors in the United States are elected and are therefore sensitive to a public that is, according to opinion polls, generally in favor of tough crime policies. In the rest of the world, criminal justice professionals tend to be civil servants who are insulated from popular demands for tough sentencing.

Mr. Whitman, who has studied Tocqueville's work on American penitentiaries, was asked what accounted for America's booming prison population.

"Unfortunately, a lot of the answer is democracy—just what Tocqueville was talking about," he said. "We have a highly politicized criminal justice system."

Critical Thinking

1. Why does the United States incarcerate more people than the rest of the world?

2. Can Americans learn anything from how other countries deal with crime?

3. Have high incarceration rates had any effect on the "war on drugs"?

4. What do you think about "democracy" being responsible for the high prison population in the United States?

Prisoners of Parole

JEFFREY ROSEN

In 2004, Steven Alm, a state trial judge in Hawaii, was frustrated with the cases on his docket. Nearly half of the people appearing before him were convicted offenders with drug problems who had been sentenced to probation rather than prison and then repeatedly violated the terms of that probation by missing appointments or testing positive for drugs. Whether out of neglect or leniency, probation officers would tend to overlook a probationer's first 5 or 10 violations, giving the offender the impression that he could ignore the rules. But eventually, the officers would get fed up and recommend that Alm revoke probation and send the offender to jail to serve out his sentence. That struck Alm as too harsh, but the alternative—winking at probation violations—struck him as too soft. "I thought, This is crazy, this is a crazy way to change people's behavior," he told me recently.

So Alm decided to try something different. He reasoned that if the offenders knew that a probation violation would lead immediately to some certain punishment, they might shape up. "I thought, What did I do when my son was young?" he recalled. "If he misbehaved, I talked to him and warned him, and if he disregarded the warning, I gave him some kind of consequence right away." Working with U.S. marshals and local police, Alm arranged for a new procedure: if offenders tested positive for drugs or missed an appointment, they would be arrested within hours and most would have a hearing within 72 hours. Those who were found to have violated probation would be quickly sentenced to a short jail term proportionate to the severity of the violation—typically a few days.

Alm mentioned his plan to the public defender, who suggested that it was only fair to warn probationers that the rules were going to be strictly enforced for the first time. Alm agreed, and on Oct. 1, 2004, he held a hearing for 18 sex offenders, followed by another one for 16 drug offenders. Brandishing a laminated "Wanted" poster, he told them: "I can guarantee that everyone in this courtroom wants you to succeed on probation, but you have not been cutting it. From now on, you're going to follow all the rules of probation, and if you don't, you're going to be arrested on the spot and spend some time in jail right away." He called the program HOPE, for Hawaii's Opportunity Probation with Enforcement, and prepared himself for a flood of violation hearings.

But they never materialized. There were only three hearings in the first week, two in the second week and none in the third. The HOPE program was so successful that it inspired scholars to evaluate its methods. Within a six-month period, the rate of positive drug tests fell by 93 percent for HOPE probationers, compared with a fall of 14 percent for probationers in a comparison group.

Alm had stumbled onto an effective strategy for keeping people out of prison, one that puts a fresh twist on some venerable ideas about deterrence. Classical deterrence theory has long held that the threat of a mild punishment imposed reliably and immediately has a much greater deterrent effect than the threat of a severe punishment that is delayed and uncertain. Recent work in behavioral economics has helped to explain this phenomenon: people are more sensitive to the immediate than the slightly deferred future and focus more on how likely an outcome is than how bad it is. In the course of implementing HOPE, Alm discovered another reason why the strategy works: people are most likely to obey the law when they're subject to punishments they perceive as legitimate, fair and consistent, rather than arbitrary and capricious. "When the system isn't consistent and predictable, when people are punished randomly, they think, My probation officer doesn't like me, or, Someone's prejudiced against me," Alm told me, "rather than seeing that everyone who breaks a rule is treated equally, in precisely the same way."

Judge Alm's story is an example of a new approach to keeping people out of prison that is being championed by some of the most innovative scholars studying deterrence today. At its core, the approach focuses on establishing the legitimacy of the criminal-justice system in the eyes of those who have run afoul of it or are likely to. Promising less crime and less punishment, this approach includes elements that should appeal to liberals (it doesn't rely on draconian prison sentences) and to conservatives (it stresses individual choice and moral accountability). But at a time when the size of the U.S. prison population is increasingly seen as unsustainable for both budgetary and moral reasons—the United States represents 5 percent of the world's population and nearly 25 percent of the world's prison population—the fact that this approach seems to work may be its biggest draw.

The HOPE program, if widely adopted as a model for probation and parole reform, could make a surprisingly large contribution to reducing the prison population. In many states, the majority of prison admissions come not from arrests for new crimes, as you might think, but from probation and parole violations. Nationwide, roughly two-thirds of parolees fail to complete parole successfully. Todd Clear, a professor at John Jay College of Criminal Justice in New York, estimates that by eliminating imprisonment across the nation for technical parole violations, reducing the length of parole supervision and ratcheting back prison sentences to their 1988 levels, the United States could reduce its prison population by 50 percent.

Some in government are beginning to take notice. In November, invoking the HOPE program as a model, the Democratic congressman Adam Schiff of California and his Republican colleague Ted Poe of Texas introduced legislation in the House that would create federal grants for states to experiment with courts that deliver swift, predictable and moderate punishment for those who violate probation.

There also appears to be a national audience for a broader conversation about new ways to shrink the prison population. Last year, a three-judge panel in California ordered the overcrowded state prison system—the largest in the country, with more than 170,000 prisoners at its peak—to reduce the inmate population by tens of thousands of prisoners within two years in order to comply with constitutional standards for medical and mental health care. Facing a tightening budget crisis in September, California legislators added to the pressure by demanding a reduction in the prison budget of $1.2 billion. In the U.S. Senate, Jim Webb of Virginia is leading a crusade for prison reform, insisting that fewer jail terms for nonviolent offenders can make America safer and more humane, while also saving money. And in the Obama administration, Attorney General Eric Holder is questioning the value of relentlessly expanding prisons. In July, he declared that "high rates of incarceration have tremendous social costs" and "diminishing marginal returns."

The most effective way to shrink the prison population, of course, is not just to reform probation and parole but also to deter groups of potential lawbreakers from committing crimes in the first place. If, in addition to bringing down the numbers of probation and parole revocations, police officers and judges could also address the core problems of drug arrests and street violence, the United States might even be said to have solved its notorious prison problem. Is such an ambitious goal possible? While it might sound too good to be true, the HOPE-style thinking about deterrence offers a promising road map for addressing all these challenges.

Although he acted on his own, Judge Alm did not design the HOPE program without inspiration. In the mid-1990s, when he was a U.S. attorney in Hawaii, Alm heard a presentation by David M. Kennedy, who is considered the patron saint of the new thinking about deterrence. Kennedy, who now teaches at John Jay College of Criminal Justice, spoke about Operation Ceasefire, a program he was designing to reduce youth violence in Boston. Along with his colleagues Anne M. Piehl and Anthony Braga, Kennedy worked with the head of the Youth Violence Strike Force, a division of the Boston Police Department. The police officer explained that while conventional deterrence hadn't worked, he had begun to persuade gangs to behave by issuing a credible threat: namely, that when a gang attracted attention with notorious acts of violence, the entire gang—all of whose members likely had outstanding warrants or probation, parole or traffic violations—would be rounded up.

Kennedy recalls this today as a breakthrough moment in his thinking. Ever since the days of Cesare Beccaria, the 18th-century philosopher and death-penalty opponent, classical deterrence theorists had focused on credibly threatening individuals; Kennedy's first innovation was to focus on increasing the legitimacy of law enforcement in the eyes of groups. "The legitimacy element has risen in my mind from being an important element of the strategy to the most important element," Kennedy told me. Convinced that the best way to increase legitimacy was to enlist what he calls the "community's moral voice," Kennedy set out to deter the most dangerous young gang members by persuading their friends and neighbors to pressure them into obeying the law.

In May 1996, Kennedy, Piehl and Braga helped to design the first of what came to be known as "call-in" sessions, intended to put gangs on notice that they would face swift and certain punishments. Working with Kennedy, probation and parole officers ordered gang members to attend face-to-face meetings with the police. The gang members were given three warnings. First, they were told that if anyone in their group killed someone, the entire group would suffer consequences. Second, the gang members were told that if they want to escape from street life, they could get help and job training from social service agencies and churches. And finally, they heard from members of their community that violence was wrong and it had to stop. The results of the forums were striking and immediate. Within two years, youth violence in Boston fell by two-thirds and city homicide rates by about half.

Why was Operation Ceasefire so effective? One reason was that the warning hearings gave the gang members a sense of what to expect. Increasingly draconian sentences don't always reduce crime, and sometimes increase it. (After increasing in the 1980s, crime fell by 25 percent in the 1990s, but states that put more people in jail had a smaller decline than states that imprisoned fewer.) In part, this is because many people actually don't know the punishments they face.

In addition to offering knowledge, Operation Ceasefire provided certainty. The small numbers of gang members singled out meant they could trust that the police would be able to follow through on their threats. "If you can get people to behave by threatening them credibly, you'll need less actual punishment than if you let them run wild and punish only occasionally," says Mark A. R. Kleiman, author of the new book "When Brute Force Fails: How to Have Less Crime and Less Punishment." Kleiman, whom Alm consulted soon after initiating the HOPE program, became interested in swift, certain and moderate punishment when he was a colleague of Kennedy's years before. Lastly, Operation Ceasefire gave gang members an incentive to obey the law by promising that they would get positive reinforcement from their families and neighbors for changing their behavior.

In all of this, Kennedy's insights were supported by a variety of recent research suggesting that people are more likely to obey the law when they view law enforcement as fair and legitimate. Tom Tyler, a psychology professor at New York University, has found that compliance with court orders is highest for offenders who perceive that they have experienced a fair process. And in a recent book, "American Homicide," the Ohio State University historian Randolph Roth argues that throughout American history, the homicide rate has decreased when people trust that the government is stable and unbiased and believe in the legitimacy of the officials who run it. Similarly, the legal scholar Paul Butler argues in his new book, "Let's Get Free: A Hip-Hop Theory of Justice," that widespread incarceration in the 1980s and '90s undermined the legitimacy of law enforcement in the eyes of the affected communities by converting a prison term into something heroic rather than stigmatic.

After Operation Ceasefire, Kennedy turned his attention from gangs to open-air drug markets. He set out to change how the criminal-justice system was viewed from the perspective of the offenders and their communities—and how the offenders and their communities were viewed by the police. As Kennedy told me, "I saw law enforcement believing plausible but untrue things about the communities they police"—namely, that the communities were corrupt and didn't care about the violence that was destroying them—"and the communities believing untrue things about the police"—namely, that the cops were part of a racist conspiracy to lock up black offenders while overlooking white ones.

To correct what he calls a "corrosive and tragic mistake," Kennedy came up with the idea of a kind of truth-and-reconciliation commission in which offenders would talk to the police accompanied by the people they trusted the most: their mothers. In 2003, working with James Fealy, the police chief in High Point, N.C., Kennedy arranged some preliminary meetings. Although Fealy had been shocked to learn that the community thought he and his officers were almost as bad as the drug dealers, Fealy, in turn, surprised community members by declaring that no one in law enforcement thought the drug war could be won.

These meetings prepared the groundwork for the strategy that followed. After identifying 16 active drug dealers, Fealy arrested four and then prepared warrants for the other 12 that could be signed whenever the police chose. He then called in the other dealers, nine of whom arrived accompanied by their mothers and other "influentials" like grandmothers, and delivered the following message to them as a group: "You could be in jail tonight. We don't want to do that, we want to help you succeed, but you are out of the drug business." The mothers and grandmothers, seemingly impressed by the decision not to arrest, cheered on the police. In subsequent meetings, the "influentials" shouted down naysayers, including a conspiracymonger who accused the C.I.A. of having created the crack epidemic to oppress black people. The drug market in the area dried up.

In addition to influencing Judge Alm's probation reform, Kennedy's efforts to rethink deterrence have also inspired one of the most powerful recent models for national parole reform, which comes from Tracey Meares, a law professor at Yale. (Unlike probation, which involves a sentence instead of prison, parole involves supervision after part of the prison sentence has been served.) In 2002, Meares, who was then a law professor at the University of Chicago, was asked by the U.S. attorney in Chicago, Patrick Fitzgerald, to analyze how best to address crime in the city. She concluded that they should begin on the West Side, in West Garfield Park and the surrounding area, where rates of murder and gun violence were more than four times the city average. Fitzgerald suggested that they might implement a version of Project Exile, a controversial program in Virginia that sought to deter gun violence by threatening federal prosecutions—and a five-year mandatory minimum sentence—for repeat offenders convicted of illegal gun possession. But Project Exile had experienced only mixed success: federal prosecutors could prosecute only a small proportion of the gun cases submitted by the Richmond police. The threat of a severe sentence was, in effect, something of a bluff.

Meares told Fitzgerald that threats of zero tolerance wouldn't work because they simply weren't credible. Instead, Meares argued that law-enforcement officials should concentrate on specific groups of wrongdoers in ways they could accept as both reasonable and fair. Using Operation Ceasefire in Boston as a model, Meares identified everyone who had committed violent or gun-related crimes and had been released from prison and recently assigned to parole. She gathered them in random groups of no more than 20 for call-in sessions in what Meares calls "places of civic importance"—park buildings, local schools and libraries—where they sat at the same table as the police in order to create an egalitarian, nonconfrontational atmosphere. They then heard a version of Kennedy's three-part presentation. The results of the program were drastic: there was a 37 percent drop in the average monthly homicide rate—the largest drop of any neighborhood in the city. Violent crime in Chicago today is at a 30 year low. "All these strategies are a way of signaling to groups of people that government agents view them with dignity, neutrality and trust, which is the best way of convincing them that the government has the right to hold them accountable for their behavior," Meares told me.

From Kennedy and Kleiman to Alm and Meares, the judges and scholars developing new deterrence strategies are changing the way we think about parole, probation, gang violence and drug markets. But the strategies also present a rare opportunity to persuade the nation's policymakers that the most urgent case for prison reform is not only economic but also moral and practical. Yes, it's an outrage that the United States locks up citizens for so long with such uncertain effect; but

it's also self-defeating, because long sentences give rise to a crisis of legitimacy that can lead to more crime, not less.

A crisis of legitimacy may sound like a huge, perhaps intractable problem, but the tantalizing promise of the new deterrence thinking is that the crisis can actually be solved, practical step by practical step. The relative simplicity of the solutions, it turns out, is at the core of their radical potential.

Critical Thinking

1. How would you explain the HOPE program?
2. What is Operation Ceasefire?
3. Why have both programs been effective?

JEFFREY ROSEN, a law professor at George Washington University, is a frequent contributor to the magazine. He is at work on a book about Louis Brandeis.

American Politics: Democracy in America (Blog)
The Perverse Incentives of Private Prisons

Last week authorities captured two fugitives who had been on the lam for three weeks after escaping from an Arizona prison. The convicts and an accomplice are accused of murdering a holiday-making married couple and stealing their camping trailer during their run from justice. This gruesome incident has raised questions about the wisdom and efficacy of private prisons, such as the one from which the Arizona convicts escaped.

Mother Jones reporter Suzy Khimm, writing at Ezra Klein's spot, observes that the portion of Arizona's prison population now residing in privately owned and operated facilities is 20% and growing. "Nationally," Ms Khimm notes, "there's been a similar surge in private prison construction as the inmate population has tripled between 1987 and 2007: Inmates in private prisons now account for 9% of the total US prison population, up from 6% in 2000." Should we welcome this development?

The dominant argument for private prisons is that they will save taxpayers money, as for-profit owners have an incentive to seek efficiencies bureaucrats overseeing government institutions lack. Anyway, that's the theory. According to the Arizona Republic, the reality is that private prisons in the Grand Canyon State so far cost more on a per-prisoner basis than do public institutions. Some experts contend that firms in the prison business reap profits by billing government for rather more than their initial lowball estimates while scrimping in ways that may make prisons less secure.

Ms Khimm says she doesn't see "anything inherently wrong with privately run prisons," as long as they work as well at a lower cost. But I think I would object to private prisons *especially were they more efficient.*

As the economist and legal theorist Bruce Benson has observed, it is important to distinguish between "privatisation" and "contracting out." To fully privatise a government service is to get the government out of the business altogether. Consider garbage collection. If a municipal government decides to sell its garbage trucks and buy the service from a private company with taxpayer money, that's not privatisation. That's contracting out. In a fully privatised scheme, households deal directly with privately-owned garbage-collection services. In that case, government is cut out of the loop entirely.

From an economic point of view, we should expect firms that compete for and rely on government contracts, such as weapons manufacturers and prison operators, to maximise the spread between the amount billed and the actual cost of delivering the service. If contractors can get away with providing less value for money than would the government-run alternative, they will. Moreover, contractors have every incentive to make themselves seem necessary. It is well-known that public prison employee unions constitute a powerful constituency for tough sentencing policies that lead to larger prison populations requiring additional prisons and personnel. The great hazard of contracting out incarceration "services" is that private firms may well turn out to be even more efficient and effective than unions in lobbying for policies that would increase prison populations.

When we add to the mix the observations that America already puts a larger proportion of its population behind bars than does any other country (often for acts that ought to be legal), and that the US already spends an insane portion of national income on the largely non-productive garrison state, it is hard to see the expansion of a for-profit industry with a permanent interest in putting ever more people in cages as consistent with either efficiency or justice.

Critical Thinking

1. Explain the difference between privatization and contracting-out.
2. What are the dangers of privatizing prisons?

Prison Inmates Meet Socrates

Lawrence T. Jablecki

Since 1986, as an adjunct professor on the faculty of a college and a university in the state of Texas, I have had direct contact with hundreds of prison inmates enrolled in academic programs for the purpose of completing the associate's, bachelor's, and master's degrees. I am persuaded that this experience permits the following assertions: the overwhelming majority of prison inmates in this country, both state and federal, are not incorrigibly mean or evil, and a correct understanding of the "public interest" dictates that they should be given the opportunity to participate in state and federally funded higher-education programs designed to change their thinking and conduct.

If any reader is tempted to brand me with the pejorative label of a liberal weenie who doesn't believe in the hard coinage of punishment, the following brief comments should suffice to assuage that suspicion. Criminal offenders are in conflict with the norms of society; they are not suffering from psychological disorders that both explain and excuse their conduct. They have consciously and deliberately chosen to commit a crime or, in numerous cases, they consciously and deliberately set themselves up for committing a crime by altering their normal mental and physical capacities. They were free to do otherwise and should be held responsible. Violent predators and many career criminals deserve to be incarcerated for many years, and some should be sentenced to life without the possibility of parole. I have no philosophical objection to capital punishment, but I am opposed to it because innocent persons are convicted and executed.

Now that I have exposed most of the philosophical guts of my position on crime and punishment, the specific purpose of this essay is to elucidate the reasons why I believe that an introduction to the gadfly of Athens is a highly potent crime-prevention initiative that should be made available to a multitude of prisoners.

I graduated from high school in 1958 and the thought of pursuing higher education was almost totally foreign to my mind. Primarily to maintain my association with buddies in my graduating class, I enrolled in a local junior college and unceremoniously flunked out after less than a full semester due to a total lack of interest. I went to work full time and made some very foolish choices that brought me dangerously close to becoming a felonious hoodlum. When not working, I was in the neighborhood bowling alley, where I achieved some local notoriety as the kid with a 200-plus average. In the fall of 1959, motivated mainly by the desire for an adventure away from parental oversight, I enrolled in the four-year college in Oklahoma where my mother had been a student.

Although I was not failing any of my classes during my first semester, I refused to allow any serious reflection and study to engage my mind or interfere with fun, so by January 1960 I was determined to drop out and pursue the career of a professional bowler. The passage of very close to forty years has not significantly dimmed the memory of an event during the same month that marks the beginning of a radical transformation in my thinking and conduct.

Walking to class one afternoon I encountered one of the recognized campus intellectuals. In response to my greeting of "Hello, what do you know?" he made an abrupt stop in front of me and said, "Mr. Jablecki, I do not know anything. I am simply attempting to understand." He then marched past me. Not having a clue as to the meaning of his curt remark, I articulated a response in very unscholarly language. Several days later I asked a senior who was majoring in something called philosophy to explain to me the distinction between knowing and understanding. After his learned discourse, most of which I failed to comprehend, he urged me to remain in school and suggested that in the spring semester I sign up for "Introduction to Philosophy."

Inspired by his apparent wisdom I remained in college and enrolled in "Introduction to Philosophy." In that class the instructor explained the perennial problems of philosophy: I was able to grasp the difference between knowledge and understanding, and I was introduced to the life and teachings of Socrates. During the semester my ambitions, my thinking, and even my behavior changed. I sold my prized black-beauty bowling ball and purchased some philosophical works, which are still in my library. In a very brief period of time a Socratic "conversion" changed the entire course of my life. To the teacher, Dr. Mel-Thomas Rothwell (deceased), I owe an immeasurable debt of gratitude for his patient mentoring until my graduation in 1964.

The relevance of this autobiographical snapshot is that it evidences the view that it is impossible to exaggerate the power of ideas and concepts—for example, justice, truth, goodness, virtue, and beauty—to grab a human mind and redirect a person's life in the manner advocated by Socrates. And, at the risk of making a generalization to which I acknowledge numerous exceptions, a Socratic conversion usually requires the inspired communication of a teacher or mentor who has experienced the transformative power of ideas and concepts.

In the 1986–1987 academic year I was given my first opportunity to introduce Socrates to prison inmates under the auspices of what was at the time Brazosport Junior College in Lake Jackson, Texas. This institution, now known as Brazosport College, continues to provide a two-year course of instruction leading to an associate of arts degree. I taught two courses of "Introduction to Philosophy" to approximately thirty male inmates at the Clemens Unit of the Texas Department of Corrections. I possess no knowledge of the success or failure of any of these men, but I do have some vivid recollections of some of the classes, including our lively discussions of Socrates.

The first session of the first class has left a permanent mark in my bank of memories. Standing in front of a group of men convicted of a range of serious felonies and incarcerated for a substantial number of years can be terrifying, to say the least. I told them that I had agreed to teach this class because of my firm commitment to the views of the German philosopher Immanuel Kant concerning "respect" for all persons as moral agents capable of choices and my equally firm belief that they can change the direction of the remainder of their lives if they choose to do so. This is essentially how I introduce myself to all new classes of prison inmates. And if they perceive that I really mean what I say, the path is clear for some existentially meaningful discussions and insights.

Perhaps the most important fact I can report about these men—inclusive of the inmates I have taught to date—is that, except for a mere few, they do not blame society or others for their criminal behavior. This acceptance of guilt and responsibility is probably at odds with the belief of most people about the supposed rationalizations of criminals. Not unexpectedly, many of the inmates vented their resentment about how they believe they were unfairly treated at one or more steps in our system of criminal justice, and any seasoned practitioner in the system is obliged to acknowledge the truth of some of their claims. The pertinent and critical point, however, is their acceptance of the facts that they made real choices to commit crimes and that society has a right to protect itself by incarcerating malefactors.

These intuitive or pre-philosophical beliefs are fertile ground for introducing the free-will-versus-determinism debate and the arguments employed to justify the institution of punishment. And these issues lead straight to what is usually a hotly contested debate of the Socratic view that persons do not voluntarily or knowingly commit evil or unlawful acts because knowledge and wisdom are the most powerful elements in human life.

When the above issues are examined in philosophy classes in what the inmates refer to as the "free world," they do not convey the same sense of urgency and importance as they do for students confined behind steel bars. One version of determinism is that all so-called free choices are illusory because no human actions or decisions are exempt from an unbroken chain of "causes." Realizing that, if true, this theory could exonerate him from blame and punishment, a convicted murderer eagerly stated, "I would like to think that it was determinism" rather than a choice, and the room was filled with soft laughter. Another student, convicted of aggravated robbery, attempted to articulate the centuries-old view that all persons are born with an innate knowledge of right and wrong—that is, a moral compass called the conscience. Confessing much confusion about how it works, he said, "Now, I done something and I know it was wrong." Following a Socratic unpacking of the words cause and compel, the unanimous decision was that none of them were compelled or forced to commit their crime and they were free to do otherwise.

It should come as no surprise that a discussion of the purpose and justification of punishment with prison inmates, many of whom have been incarcerated for a major portion of their lives, reaches a high level of emotional intensity. No student, in either class, claimed or even implied that he did not deserve to be punished. A chorus of voices, however, condemned the enormous disparity in sentences characteristic of an indeterminate sentencing system and the wide range in which judicial discretion is free to roam.

With no hesitation, one of the men expressed the belief that if he stole a car and Dr. Jablecki stole a car the latter would undoubtedly be gently treated with probation and the former would be sentenced to prison. This, he exclaimed, is not justice or equality, as both committed the same crime and deserved the same punishment.

147

Heads nodded in agreement and several voiced the caustic remark that the lovely lady of justice wearing the blindfold of impartiality and equality is never blind to the influences of money and status in the community. Anyone, therefore, who plays the role of a Socratic midwife in a similar situation needs to be prepared to maneuver through an emotional minefield in which they will be made aware of all the ugly warts and blemishes in our system of criminal justice.

Now, as implied earlier, I can still almost hear the initial outbursts of disbelief expressed in response to Socrates' belief that no person voluntarily or knowingly commits an evil or wrong act. Socrates, according to the first consensus, had been drinking too much wine or he was an insane old man. The inmates said they knew exactly what they were doing when they committed a murder, robbed a store at gunpoint, sexually assaulted a woman, or cut a drug deal. Assuming the role of Socrates, I called them a collection of ignorant fools incapable of recognizing their best and permanent interests as human beings.

Needless to say, this enlivened the tone of the discussion and set the stage to unpack the meaning of a cluster of relevant words: knowledge, wisdom, ignorance, self-interest, mistake, voluntary, involuntary, happiness, and virtue. After several hours of defining and analyzing them, the new consensus was a defense of Socrates' sobriety and the belief that he was a very smart old man. Although I don't have current information on any of the inmates, I believe that most of them made some progress in the ascent from the cave of ignorance and have not forgotten their meeting with Socrates.

In 1988 a fortuitous meeting with George Trabing, the director of the prison program for the University of Houston at Clear Lake, resulted in an invitation for me to join the adjunct faculty of the university. My assignment was to teach a variety of undergraduate and graduate courses in philosophy to prison inmates housed in the Ramsey I prison unit in Rosharon, Texas. During the past ten years, missing only one or two semesters, I have taught a number of classes—including "Metaphysics," "Epistemology," "Philosophy and the Law," "Philosophy and Religion," "Political Philosophy," "Ethics," and "Human Rights and the Justification of Punishment"—in which I inject the life and teachings of Socrates.

The university's bachelor's program was established in 1974; the master's program began in 1988. Four degrees are currently offered to inmates: a B.A. in behavioral sciences, a B.A. in the humanities, an M.A. in literature, and an M.A. in the humanities. As Trabing, Jerry Fryre, and Craig White describe in their 1995 report *Five Year Review: Texas Department of Criminal Justice Outreach Component Human Sciences and Humanities,* the degree in behavioral science contributes to the development of the

undergraduate student's skills in analytical thinking, written communication, and research; to provide understanding of the customs, languages, values and behaviors of culturally diverse populations, and to educate students to participate as informed, critical citizens of society.... The primary mission of the undergraduate and graduate plans in Humanities and literature is to promote cultural literacy and interdisciplinary skills through the study of the liberal arts.

The most important dimension of the mission of all of these educational programs, however, is to promote positive changes in the thinking and conduct of inmates and to reduce the recidivism rate of those who are released on parole. The profound relevance of Socrates' teaching that the "unexamined life is not worth living" and his identification of knowledge and virtue are captured in the five-year review's comments regarding the men who earned their degree in the humanities:

These students find that courses in history, literature, and philosophy profoundly deepen their sensitivities and expand their horizons. TDCJ students may come from pockets of economic and intellectual poverty from which they have never escaped—they have literally no knowledge of other ways of living. Humanities courses open new realities to them, wholly changing their perspectives about who they are and what the world is about.... Such courses are truly revelations, showing ways of living and thinking that they have not encountered before.

Now, as every practitioner in the field of criminal justice should know, the verification of an indisputable causal connection between offenders' completion of any crime-prevention strategy and their subsequent conduct is a tricky enterprise. At the outset, the creators of these academic programs for prison inmates were cognizant of the paramount importance of documenting a bank of data from which they could quantify the apparent successes and failures. The university's most current report was released in January 1995 as a twenty-year history of the program. The report found that more than 200 inmates earned a bachelor's degree, while forty-five earned a master's degree. From 1990 to 1995, of the thirty-nine inmates who earned a bachelor's degree, seventeen were released on parole and two were returned to prison—a recidivism rate of 11 percent. During the same period, of the forty-five who earned a master's degree, nineteen were released on parole and one was returned to prison—a recidivism rate of 5 percent.

To argue that their academic accomplishment is the only factor capable of explaining their successful reintegration into society would be a mistake. The only near definitive answer to this issue is to track a control group of parolees in the same age range and duration of incarceration who have not completed a similar academic program. Although the U.S. Department of Justice did not fund a recent grant proposal from the university to conduct such research, studies conducted in Indiana, Maryland, Massachusetts, New York, and other states have all reported significantly low recidivism rates for inmates in correctional higher-education programs, ranging from 1 percent to 15.5 percent. In addition, my contact with the students in the Texas program—some of whom are now on parole confirms a determination to change and make contributions to society totally unmatched by the majority of inmates who spend their idle time playing dominos, watching television, and reflecting on their perceptions that they are the oppressed victims of society.

Fortunately, I experienced my Socratic "conversion" when I was twenty years old and would not entertain benevolent thoughts toward any person casting doubts on the reality and meaning of that experience. Similarly, five of the former inmates who achieved academic success deserve to be heard. Their comments include:

"My new degrees, new self-image, and newfound confidence in society led me to try something I'd never tried before: a straight lifestyle. . . . Without the formal education which was available through the college program I would still be trying to perfect my technique for a life of crime. Instead, I am giving something back."

"I cannot begin to tell you how much my life has changed as a result of the 'awakening' I received from each . . . of my instructors. The accomplishments I have made since my release would not have been possible without an education."

"Because of my educational pursuits started while incarcerated, I find myself with a master's degree, an L.C.D.C. (licensed chemical dependency counselor), and a position as the manager of client services with a large nonprofit organization. I am forever thankful . . . for the opportunity to change my life."

"For me, the college experience . . . has changed my life. It has allowed me to believe in myself. It has forced me to reevaluate my life without the self-pity or excuse making."

"I firmly believe that education is the key to staying out of prison. . . . My parents are proud of me; I am respected and consulted by my colleagues; I pay taxes. . . . I hope that I do make a difference in other peoples' lives as a result of my experiences and achievements."

The latter reference to the payment of taxes by a former inmate exposes the shortsighted and factually incorrect arguments of the politicians in Washington, D.C., who have seen to it that prison inmates are ineligible for federal Pell Grant tuition assistance for higher education. In his July 10, 1995, *New Yorker* article "Teaching Prisoners a Lesson," James S. Kunen draws attention to the critical factual misrepresentations involved in the demise of inmates' eligibility for Pell Grants:

When Bart Gordon, a Democratic representative from Tennessee, sponsored the 1994 crime-bill amendment that barred prisoners from receiving Pell Grants, his aim was to trim the fat in federal education spending. He was under the impression that prisoners were using up something like seventy million dollars a year in Pell Grants that could have gone to more deserving students—those on the outside. Senator Kay Bailey Hutchison of Texas, a Republican who led the fight in the Senate against Pell Grants for prisoners, argued that inmates siphoned off two hundred million dollars and displaced a hundred thousand law-abiding students. In fact, all applicants who meet the grants' need-based eligibility requirements receive Pell Grants, regardless of how many qualifying recipients there are. As a General Accounting Office report explains, "If incarcerated students received no Pell Grants, no student currently denied a Pell award would have received one and no award amount would have been increased." And the amount of money saved by cutting off grants to prisoners is tiny: according to the General Accounting Office, of approximately four million Pell Grant recipients in the 1993–94 academic year, twenty-three thousand were in prison, and they received thirty-five million dollars of the six billion dollars awarded, or about six cents of every ten program dollars.

It would probably be incorrect to suggest that Hutchison and the other members of Congress who helped her destroy hope for thousands of inmates in this country are in the philosophical camp of the ancient Cynics, who were contemptuous of bodily pleasures, sneering fault-finders, and incredulous of human goodness and the capacity to change from vice to virtue. I am persuaded, however, that the policy these politicians approved places them in the category of unmerciful retributivists who sincerely believe in the moral imperative of severe punishment for all criminal offenders—that is, they have no mercy for the wicked.

They are not hypocrites, because they really believe that the construction of new prisons is not a necessary evil but a necessary good. Some of the extremists in this camp probably believe that it would be good policy to literally brand the scarlet letter C (for convict) on the forehead of every prison inmate.

Contrary to the philosophy of unmerciful retributivism, Pell Grants for inmates had the long-range potential of saving billions of tax dollars that will now be spent on the construction and maintenance of prisons and the annual costs of warehousing multitudes of federal and state inmates in what can best be described as toxic waste dumps inhabited by persons with little or no hope for a future that can make life worth living. And equally, if not more important, the advocates of unmerciful retributivism have crafted a policy that unintentionally results in a multitude of new victims of crime perpetrated by parolees who have changed from bad to worse.

Recognizing the existence of an unknown number of contingencies—all of which can influence the success or failure of a parolee armed with a university degree the university's statistics stand in sharp contrast to the fact that, in Texas, between 45 percent and 50 percent of parolees are reincarcerated within three years of the date of their release. Most of them are convicted of new felony offenses, many of which involve victims who suffer (among numerous things) the loss of property, physical injuries, and death. Although it is an expansion of the normal usage of the word, this is an obscenity that in addition to all of the accompanying human suffering is costing taxpayers many millions of dollars every year. In Texas, the annual cost for one prison inmate is close to $20,000—very close to the amount my wife and I pay for our son to attend the prestigious Rice University in Houston—and this cost does not include the maintenance of existing prisons and the construction of new ones. After ten years of almost weekly contact with students in the University of Houston prison program, it has become abundantly clear that if I did not believe in the inmates' capacity to change their totally selfish habits of thought and conduct I would not waste my time on an academic exercise destined to fail. Inmates do not have a "right" to a free university education, nor do they "deserve" it. However, there is an urgent and compelling public interest at stake, justifying the use of tax dollars to create and sustain academic programs for them. Once they grasp the Socratic definition of knowledge and its vast distance from opinions and beliefs, most of my current students articulate the hindsight observation that, had they met Socrates at the age of twenty or earlier, it is not unrealistic to suggest they might not be meeting him now clothed in prison garb. While not willing to fully embrace the contention that during their life of crime they were totally ignorant

and really did not "know" what they were doing, most of my students "see," for the first time, the profound truth of Socrates' doctrine that the possession of knowledge and wisdom can lead to a radical and positive change in both thinking and behavior.

Despite the occasional bitterness aimed at the alleged disparities in the system of criminal justice, during these discussions many of the inmates feel at ease to lay bare their souls and express genuine remorse about the impact of their conduct on parents, spouses, children, and victims. It would be foolhardy to claim or even imply that an encounter with Socrates is a necessary prerequisite to bring the majority of them to a profound existential consciousness of the negative consequences of their crimes. In fact, many of them have previously read several books of Plato's *Republic,* and some have read his *Apology* and *Crito.* But none of them have participated in a methodical unpacking of the content, the profound truth, and the errors in Socratic doctrine and instead have had their emotions shaped by traumatic events in their lives—the death of one or both parents, a divorce decree from a former spouse, children who commit crimes, and a denial of parole. The important claim can be made, however, that the Socratic method of philosophical reflection provides a coherent conceptual framework in which many of these men, for the first time, are "awakened" to a totally new perspective on life.

Prior to my career in criminal justice, when I discovered *Great Visions of Philosophy* by W. P. Montague, a notation of "good" was made by the following passage:

> There is a great deal of wrong conduct by individuals and by groups that owes its wrongness to want of wisdom rather than to want of will. . . . We all know that boys brought up in a slum district may get the notion that gang loyalty is really better than loyalty to society; the stealing, kidnapping, and even murder are justifiable and thrilling adventures; and that pity for the weak is stupid or unmanly. In these groups the only vices recognized as such will be the vices of cowardice and of treachery or "squealing" on one's "pals." To be a "tough guy" and perhaps the leader of a gang is an activating and in a sense a genuinely moral ideal of many a high-spirited lad, whose courage and energy if directed into other channels might make him not merely a useful citizen but even a hero. It is obvious enough that here the kind of moral reform that is called for is educational in the broadest sense, involving destruction of hideous economic conditions and of the cultural squalor and ignorance that go with them. Not all criminals indeed but probably the majority could be reformed or cured by being given a Socratic wisdom or knowledge of the things

in life that are really worthwhile and an environment that would make it possible to achieve them. Moreover the whole philosophy of punishment would be revolutionized. Prevention rather than cure would be emphasized, and when preventive measures had failed the necessary restraint of the criminal would be accompanied by education rather than by social revenge.

My Socratic conversion justified the use of the word good in response to the above claims. Today, however, I can confidently proclaim the truth of Montague's call for a Socratic revolution in the philosophy of punishment.

According to the most recent estimates released by the U.S. Department of Justice, at the close of 1998 there were 1,232,900 federal and state prison inmates. To advocate the belief that the majority of them could be reformed by a strong dose of Socrates appears to be an incredulous form of idealism completely out of touch with reality. Given the facts that the opinion of the public is that prison inmates should be "better" people when released on parole and that high-school equivalency classes and vocational training programs provided to the majority of them are not designed to foster moral reform, the suggestion that a multitude of inmates should be introduced to Socrates is not a fantasy of an unearthly idealism.

More specifically, I am absolutely convinced that the recidivism rate of former prison inmates can be reduced significantly if, while incarcerated, they are skillfully guided through a systematic discussion of the life and teachings of Socrates as presented by Plato in the *Apology, Crito, Phaedo, Protagaras,* and the analysis of the concept of justice in the *Republic.* This is the largely uncultivated and fertile soil in which federal and state authorities should plant the seeds of carefully designed and well-funded programs capable of tracking the lives of the participants (male and female) and those in control groups for three to five years in order to establish some incontrovertible data regarding the power of education to change the thinking and conduct of former criminal offenders.

So I tell all of my students that the only way to silence the voices of the cynics committed to the view that providing a university or college education to prison inmates is flushing clean dollars down a dirty toilet is to remain crime-free following release on parole. I tell them that the continuation of the program is contingent upon years of cumulative success stories and that their moral obligation to succeed is grounded in the lives of the students who remain behind bars. They are encouraged to contact me after their release, as I may be able to assist them in their search for employment. However, if they call me for help after committing another felony offense, I will volunteer to testify against them. As I said on May 13, 1998, in the conclusion of the commencement address I gave to a group of inmates who had earned either an associate's degree from Alvin Community College in Alvin, Texas, or a bachelor's or master's degree from the University of Houston at Clear Lake:

> The profound sense in which Socrates was correct is precisely why we are here this evening. Collectively, your teachers have guided you on the ascent from the cave of ignorance as articulated by Plato in his *Republic.* You have been led out of the abyss of intellectual and moral darkness and our hope is that you have experienced a genuine Socratic "conversion"—that is, that you have accepted total responsibility for the rottenness of your past conduct and are morally prepared to fulfill your obligations as a member of the human community. . . . [However] I am obliged to tell you that, if you have not or do not experience a Socratic conversion prior to your release, you will be nothing more than a hypocritical, educated crook.

Socrates does not hold all the answers. For example, I readily admit to my students that, although he was committed to the view that humankind is essentially good, Socrates failed to recognize what philosopher David Hume called the incurable weakness in human nature. In his essay *Of the Origin of Government,* Hume comments on the nature of humanity and why it was necessary to invent a system of rules to protect lives and property:

> It is impossible to keep men faithfully and unerringly in the paths of justice. Some extraordinary circumstances may happen, in which a man finds his interests to be more promoted by fraud or rapine than hurt by the breach which his injustice makes in the social union. But much more frequently he is seduced from this great and important but distant interest by the allurement of present, though often very frivolous, temptations. This great weakness is incurable in human nature.
>
> Men must, therefore, endeavor to palliate what they cannot cure. They must institute some persons under the appellation of magistrates, whose peculiar office it is to point out the decrees of equity, to punish transgressors, to correct fraud and violence, and to oblige men, however reluctant, to consult their own real and permanent interests. In a word, obedience is a new duty which must be invented to support that of justice, and the ties of equity must be corroborated by those of allegiance.

Hume's view of humanity is consistent with Montague's claim that whether we call it "sin" or "selfishness," wrong conduct is due "not to lack of wisdom, but to lack of will. . . . Insight into the nature of the good . . . may be termed a 'necessary,' but not a 'sufficient,' cause of virtue. Wisdom by itself is not enough and great Socrates was wrong in thinking that it was."

Also, almost invariably during our discussions one or more students realize that Socrates' doctrines of humankind and knowledge and virtue are diametrically opposed to the orthodox Christian belief that humans are sinners whose salvation from evil inclinations requires a supernatural infusion of divine grace. The majority of my students, in widely diverse environments, were nurtured in the tradition of Christian theism, and, not surprisingly, a significant number of them are unwilling to concede that Socratic doctrines inflict any serious damage on their religious commitments.

As was the case when I was introduced to Socrates, he can shake unexamined beliefs and faiths. However, unlike any of their other academic classes, it is important that most of my courses contain opportunities for prison inmates to reflect on the most important and enduring questions of human existence. And I can confidently claim that many of them are surprised by the joy of facing the unfathomed depth of Socrates' message to live an examined life.

Critical Thinking

1. Why should inmates have access to education?

2. How can the writings of Socrates help inmates?

3. What does Professor Jablecki mean when he refers to Montague's call for a Socratic revolution in the philosophy of punishment?

LAWRENCE T. JABLECKI is the director of the Brazoria County Community Supervision and Corrections Department in Angleton Texas, and has a PhD in political philosophy from Manchester University in Manchester, England.

One Clique
Why Rivals on the Streets Become Allies behind Bars

SHARROD CAMPBELL

Like many custodial agencies, the Georgia Department of Corrections recognizes the existence of security threat groups (STGs). Awareness of the activities of these groups helps to improve the overall security of a facility because, by definition, these various types of associations and groups have the potential to cause disruption. There are four commonly accepted major categories of STGs:

- Street Gangs—Organizations that have their strongest memberships in the community;
- Prison Gangs—Organizations formed within a penal setting;
- Extremist/Separatist Groups—Organizations with views that promote separation or superiority of one group over another based on race, religious beliefs or political ideologies; and
- Motorcycle Clubs—Criminal biker organizations that identify with the 1 percent theory (99 percent of bikers are law abiding; therefore, the other 1 percent are outlaws).

Although there are four accepted categories of STGs, the analysis of threats is not limited to inmates who may fall under one of these headings. It is essential that monitoring is not limited to these groups because the culture of a custodial setting often fosters impromptu-situational groups that gravitate together around a particular commonality. These situational groupings and associations must also be monitored because they have the potential to compromise security in correctional settings.

Banding Together

Race is one of the strongest commonality factors among inmates within the correctional system. This primary division is often broken down into other groups or associations within the larger group, and it is where many STG affiliations are found. Within an STG, race or culture is no exception, as evidenced by such groups as the Aryan Brotherhood, Black Guerrilla Family and Mexican Mafia. Although the groups are prison gangs that were founded based on race, there are conflicts that occur between them and other groups organized by race.

For example, there are well-documented conflicts between the Mexican Mafia and La Nuestra Familia, both of which are Hispanic culture/race groups that have a history of violence against each other. Incidents of intra-racial conflicts are not limited to prison gangs formed around race; street gangs also have a history of conflicts between rival groups of the same race. These conflicts often can continue when members of the groups enter the prison system. Conflicts in prisons and in the community between Surenos and Nortenos, Crips and Bloods, and People and Folk gangs have been well-documented by the media. However, in the Georgia correctional system there is a possible factor that appears to cause rival associations within the Hispanic culture to band together. This association has resulted in what appears to be a prison truce within the Hispanic population that includes rival Hispanic STGs.

In Georgia, there has been a steady growth in the general Hispanic population that has affected the overall Hispanic prison population. The Hispanic population currently represents about 5 percent of the incarcerated population. Although 5 percent is a relatively low figure, it is important to note that this percentage also reflects the fact that the population has doubled in number from 2001 to 2006. If that doubling trend continues every six years, it is likely that Hispanics will represent 10 percent of the population by 2013.

This article is not intended to imply that the Hispanic population as a whole inside or outside the Georgia correctional system should be validated as an STG. But, as stated earlier, prison groups associate based on common identifiers and the DOC has noted an alliance among Hispanic inmates that transcends the fiercest street and prison gang alliances for group strength.

The rationale that there is a need for strength among any inmate population is not surprising because it directly relates to a need for security. Although there may be some varied points of view between custodial agencies and inmates as to what constitutes security, both have this need as a primary issue. For the agency, security means equality of safety for all staff, the public and inmates. In inmate circles, security often relates to their ability to control the population because control prevents victimization. Control also gives authority to one group over other weaker inmate populations.

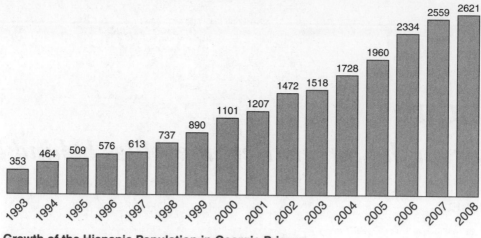

Growth of the Hispanic Population in Georgia Prisons

Within the Georgia penal system, the Hispanic population appears to have the highest overall percentage of STG members. In the general prison population, the security threat population has remained below 4 percent during the past four years, while the percentage of Hispanics in STGs has averaged between 7 percent and 9 percent during the same period.

The higher percentage of STG inmates within the Hispanic population is significant because it supports the possibility that Hispanic STGs have a stronger voice within the larger group. This is critical because validated STGs tend to have a strong organizational structure, which can give the STG a cohesive bond and offer a sense of security to weaker members. Thus, a relationship is developed that creates an atmosphere that forces the individual to remain close to the group. The STG provides security, recreation and a voice to communicate to other groups and prison staff. In return, the member becomes an agent of the STG and must remain loyal. That loyalty may be required in any situation regardless of the type of activity. If the STG has a problem, then the member must be an active part of the solution.

For example, inmates of a race that is outnumbered often believe that they are targeted by the more dominant race. If a minor incident occurs between Hispanic inmates and black inmates, the event may be viewed by the Hispanic inmates as predatory. Events such as thefts are not viewed as isolated events in this perceived power-struggle environment and can trigger group retaliation, which will escalate the conflict. These types of events often reveal that the problem is more complex than the event that triggered the retaliation. There appears to be a collective sense among Hispanic inmates in the Georgia system that this David and Goliath conflict exists because of their small population, which make them appear to be an easy target for black inmates. Their assertion is that banding together will reduce their risk because they will operate as a larger collective—all for one and one for all.

Prison Truce

More than likely, the indoctrination of banding together by race rather than splintering along STG or other variances is instilled early in the incarceration process. In this dynamic,

Hispanic inmates will be advised by other Hispanic inmates already in the system that their associations prior to prison are nonessential. A truce between the rival groups must be maintained during their periods of incarceration. For example, it is not uncommon to find an inmate affiliated with a Surenos gang sharing a cell with a Nortenos-affiliated inmate without any open conflict.

Just like other street gangs, Hispanic-affiliated gangs have a history of interpreting the presence of a rival gang member in their area as a violation. The penalty for those violations can lead to the death of the rival gang member. There are no extensive formal associations between rival gang members, and street truces are not often lasting. But because prison presents a special set of circumstances and the probability of victimization and isolation are high, it is better to be with someone of the same culture even if that person is viewed on the streets as a mortal gang enemy.

This association is apparently recognized only during their incarceration, and upon release their street affiliations are reinstated and a rival prior to incarceration is a rival once again. There has been no indication that this truce happens in county and municipal jails; it appears that this alliance only applies to state facilities.

Concerns

There are some concerns about how long this truce will remain a viable factor among this population. Because it is a volatile situational alliance, there is always the possibility of one STG with more membership overriding the other, creating tension in the group. That tension could be expanded as the group becomes larger and more Hispanics enter the system. If the rate of Hispanic inmates continues trending upward, in the next five years their presence may be significant enough that they will begin to splinter into smaller subsets and their alliance may become severed.

It is also possible that other STGs will begin to view the Hispanic population as a threat. This could present a dangerous situation for Hispanic inmates because although they constitute a higher overall percentage of STG members, they still make up a small percentage of the prison population. Therefore, their ability to defend themselves from a collective assault is limited.

Another concern is that the STG's influence over the actions of Hispanic inmates can potentially undermine the penal system's authority to resolve conflicts and address issues. This can have a huge impact on the climate of a facility and the ability of staff to provide a safe and secure environment.

Language is a primary barrier between staff and Hispanic inmates. When a Spanish-speaking inmate is interviewed about a specific incident, there is usually another inmate serving as an interpreter. The inmate interpreter is also a member of the Hispanic inmate population, which means that he can report the information back to the Hispanic gang leaders if the inmate makes an allegation against the group. That interpreter can even change the statement of the inmate interviewee without staff being aware because of the language barrier.

The Georgia DOC has taken steps to reduce this risk by hiring a bilingual investigator and seeking bilingual staff. This provides the department the resources to respond to a crisis involving Hispanic inmates and ensures that the inmates are afforded privacy while giving statements and that the reported statements are accurate accounts of what was said.

Bilingual staff have had a positive effect on communication between correctional staff and inmates. In addition, several staff members have begun to take a strong interest in improving their bilingual skills. How far reaching the effects bilingual staff will have are yet to be determined in mitigating possible conflicts. What is apparent is that it has improved the DOC's ability to accurately assess the Hispanic population's issues and concerns, which allows Hispanic inmates to seek the help of staff in dealing with their issues.

Critical Thinking

1. Why do inmates feel the need to band together on the basis of race?

2. What are some of the problems Georgia has with its Hispanic inmate population?

SHARROD CAMPBELL is investigator and STG coordinator for the Georgia Department of Corrections' Office of Investigation and Compliance/Intelligence.

The Professor Was a Prison Guard

Jeffrey J. Williams

When I was 20, I left college and took a job in a prison. I went from reading the great books as a Columbia University undergraduate to locking doors and counting inmates as a New York State correction officer. Since I'm an English professor now, people never entirely believe me when the issue comes up, probably because of the horn-rimmed glasses and felicitous implementation of Latinate words. I fancied I'd be like George Orwell, who took a job as an Imperial Police officer in Burma and wrote about it in "Shooting an Elephant." I thought I'd go "up the river" to the "big house" and write "Shooting an Inmate" or some such thing. It didn't quite happen that way, although as a professor, I've worked 14 of 16 years in state institutions.

For the most part, I worked at Downstate Correctional Facility, in Fishkill, N.Y. (You can see it in a hollow along the north side of Interstate 84, just east of the Newburgh-Beacon Bridge.) Newly opened and still under construction when I started, in 1979, the place was billed as the prison of the future. It adopted a "campus" style, with clusters of 36 cells arranged in a split-level horseshoe shape, rather than the traditional warehouse style of long rows of 40 or so cells stacked three or four stories high. The new style presumably granted a more pleasant environment, or simply less chaos. Downstate was also threaded with electronic sensors that would supposedly indicate if a cell door was open, or if someone was walking between the rows of razor wire encircling the facility. The electronics were bruited as a wonder solution to security, as well as being more economical, since the old design of a maximum-security prison required a small island of cement, with walls 30 feet high and 20 feet into the ground. The sensors, however, were moody, a sticky door registering locked and unlocked like a temperamental Christmas-tree light, and a raccoon, a bit of rain, or a poltergeist setting off the ones between the fences. Though annoying, they kept you awake if you drew a shift on the berm overlooking the grounds.

Downstate was designed to replace Sing Sing Correctional Facility, in Ossining, as the "classification and reception center" for New York's state prison system. If you were convicted of a felony and sentenced to a sizable term, you were shipped from a county jail to Downstate. County jails are essentially holding tanks, mixing innocent and guilty awaiting trial, 18-year-old shoplifters and 40-year-old murderers awaiting the next stop. State correction officers looked down on the jails as poorly run zoos, the nursery schools of the prison taxonomy; state officers had substantial training, and state prisons were the higher rehabilitation. Every male inmate in the state system spent his first six weeks at Downstate (women, who at the time numbered less than 5 percent of the prison population, went to Bedford Hills Correctional Facility), taking tests and getting interviewed so counselors could decide where he'd do his time. If he was young, maybe Elmira or Coxsackie; if on a short stretch, a minimum like Taconic; if on a long sentence, behind the high walls of maximums like Great Meadow, Green Haven, Attica, and Clinton. Since most of those convicted came from New York City and environs, Sing Sing had earned the sobriquet "up the river" because it was a 30-mile barge ride up the Hudson. Downstate continued the tradition another 30 miles up, although the present-day conduit is I-84 and the mode of transport a bus.

When you work in prison, just as when you work in academe, you experience a world that has its own language, its own training, its own hierarchy, its own forms of recognition.

Before getting a badge, correction officers did 12 weeks in the training academy in Albany. It was a cross between a military and a technical college, with calisthenics in the morning and classes all day. Wake-up was 6 A.M., with a couple of miles around the track; like in the military, your bed had to be made with crisp corners, belongings neatly stowed in your locker, hair short and face cleanshaven. There were periodic spot inspections, and you got demerits if you missed a step. The academy held hourly classes, punctuated by a bell (lateness was one demerit). One class gave background on the taxonomy and geography of New York's correctional system, from minimum to maximum, prisons dotting the state like community colleges. Another was on relevant law, defining necessary as opposed to excessive use of physical force (one should restrain an inmate from doing harm to himself or others, but not beat him once restrained), and enumerating rights (if an inmate complained of a physical ailment, you had to notify the hospital, even if you thought he was lying). One course covered procedures, detailing how to do a count, how to keep a notebook (in part for legal protection but mostly to pass on information to the next shift), and how to do searches (never ignore an inconvenient corner, even if you don't want to reach, but be careful of hidden pieces of glass or razor blades). One course taught rudimentary psychology, or "interpersonal communication," in which the instructors taught you how to deal with, say, an enraged inmate by responding with something to the effect of, "So you are telling me you're pissed off because. . . . " Although it seemed mindlessly redundant, it was not a bad lesson in how to stop and listen. Prisons, like any social institution, run best when they respond appropriately to needs as well as misdeeds. Contrary to the popular image of sadistic prison guards, the motto the academy drummed into you was "firm, fair, and consistent."

Everyone asks if I carried a gun, but inside the walls you were always outnumbered, and a gun would more likely be used for a takeover or escape. Instead, the most severe weapon was a nightstick. The only place you were issued a gun was on a perimeter post, at one of the gates or on the berm. At the academy, there were classes in weapons—at the time, in the trusty Smith & Wesson .38 revolver, which everyone had to qualify to use; the Remington pump-action shotgun, which you just had to shoot without falling over; and a long-distance .30-30, basically a deer rifle, which granted a special qualification to work in a tower at one of the walled prisons. After you were on the job, you had to qualify with the .38 every year, and, like a field trip, we looked forward to the day we went out to the shooting range. The one part we didn't look forward to was getting tear-gassed, deemed necessary so you knew what it felt like to have the rabid sting of CS or CN gas on your skin and wouldn't panic.

The lessons were usually reinforced with black humor, anecdotes, and morality tales. For example, you can use lethal physical force to prevent an imminent escape but not if an inmate is still on prison grounds. One quip was that if you shot an inmate scaling the fence, you had better make sure he landed on the outside—otherwise you'd end up inside. One story to remind us not to slack off on searches was about an escape from the Fishkill Correctional Facility (actually in Beacon, across the highway from Downstate). The inmate, so the story went, had gotten a gun smuggled in the bottom of a bucket of Kentucky Fried Chicken because the correction officer searching packages had supposedly eaten a piece off the top and passed the bucket through. Another story, to reinforce the rule that you should not eat state food or accept favors, however slight, from inmates, went something like this: An inmate, who worked in the mess hall and prepared the trays that got sent to the blocks for ill or keep-locked inmates, regularly brought BLT's to the correction officer on his block. One day the kitchen officer happened upon the inmate using a bodily fluid as a condiment on the bread. I never knew whether the story was true, but I always brought my lunch.

The first thing you learn when you get behind the walls or concertina wire is that prison has its own language. We received a glossary of terms at the training academy, but, just as with learning a foreign language, the words didn't mean much until you got inside. A prison guard is not a "screw," as in a James Cagney movie, but a "correction officer," or usually just a "CO." A prisoner is not a "convict" but an "inmate." A sentence is a "bid." A cell is a "crib." To calm down is to "chill." A homemade knife is a "shiv."

The university represents the hope, prison the failing, of the meritocracy.

Life in prison is punctuated by counts, three or four for every eight-hour shift. When I was in training at Elmira, which was an old prison with what seemed like mile-long rows of cells three stories high, I remember walking down the narrow runway to take the evening count. There were whispered goads—"CO, you look gooood," "Who you eyeballing?," "Hey motherfucker"—or simply hissing, which was the worst. I didn't turn around to look, since you rarely knew where the voices came from, amidst the echoes of reinforced concrete. Besides, turning would show that they were getting under your skin, which would just fuel the hiss.

What makes time go by in prison is the talk. Talk among the guards was a constant buzz—about life, yesterday's mail, what happened in the visiting room, the food in the mess hall this morning, the lieutenant who was a hard-ass and snuck around at night to catch you sleeping, if you were going fishing on your days off, if you were getting any. With the inmates, though, as in a game of poker, you never let too much show. The one time you worried was when the buzz stopped. You didn't have to know the literary definition of foreshadowing to know that something was aching to happen.

I got good at finding things, as much to stave off boredom as from a sense of duty. Once I found a 10-inch shiv hung in a crevice of cement behind a fuse-box door. It was fashioned from a soup-ladle handle purloined from the kitchen, filed laboriously on cement to a knife edge, its handle wrapped with white athletic tape. I would periodically find jugs of homemade booze, made from fruit and fermented in floor-wax containers, wedged behind a clothes dryer to cook or stowed beneath the bag in a utility vacuum. Once I found a few joints taped under a toilet tank. The joints bothered me more than the rest, not because they were harmful—in fact, one way to still a prison population would be to hand out joints, whereas booze, especially homebrews, tends to prime people for a fight—but because they came from outside. They could have come in through visits, swallowed in a condom, or they could mean a CO or other worker had a business they weren't declaring on their 1040. It violated the boundaries of the place, boundaries that you did not want to get fuzzy.

Prison carries its own set of lessons. One was about how life works, albeit life in a crockpot: mostly by repetition and habit, punctuated by sudden, sometimes scary, but strangely exhilarating moments that shattered the routine. Once when I was at Elmira, whiling away a shift after the inmates were locked in, except for the porters, who did the cleaning, I heard a clomping on the stairs. I looked over to see a porter, head dripping blood, running down the stairs, with another following a few steps back, carrying a piece of jagged glass in his hand. I followed to find two officers on the first tier pinning both inmates to the floor. Danger raises your blood pressure, which isn't good for you over the long term, but acts as a drug in the short.

Another lesson was "Do your job," which was a kind of mantra, repeated by CO's and inmates alike. It meant take your responsibility, don't slough off, don't dump your job on someone else, or you'd be not very tactfully reminded on the cellblock, in the parking lot, or at the next union meeting. The ecological balance of prisons is probably not much more fragile than those of other institutions, or there wouldn't be many prisons still standing, but its imbalances take on a particular intensity. If an inmate had a visitor, you made sure that inmate was escorted to the visiting room right away; otherwise he would have a legitimate beef, which would make life harder for everyone. Especially in the summer, when cement holds heat like barbecue bricks and you didn't want any sparks.

Another lesson was "Don't back down." If an inmate didn't go into his cell at count, you had to confront him and write it up or be ready to hit the beeper you wore on your belt; otherwise, the next day, three people would be lingering at the TV. It was a different kind of lesson than I had learned at Columbia. One might find it in the *Iliad* but not, in my experience, in most academic venues, where aggression is usually served with the sugary coating of passive circumlocution. I miss the clarity of it and, as with single malt, prefer my aggression straight.

Something else to remember was to the effect of "There but for the grace of God go I." There wasn't much room for moral superiority inside the razor wire, and you quickly lost it if you had it. I worked for a time in draft processing, which is where inmates first arrive after coming through the gates. They got a speech, a shower and delousing, a crew cut, and a khaki uniform cut like hospital scrubs, and then were assigned to a block. To avoid bias, officers generally didn't have access to rap sheets, except in draft and transport, when the sheets were like passports that traveled with the inmates. There was a young kid, maybe 18 or 19, who had been returned from Florida after escaping from a minimum. He had gotten three to five for stealing—taking a joy ride in—a dump truck in upstate New York, and the escape would probably double his sentence. On his sheet, there was an entry that read "act attributed to: drinking a case of beer." I'm not exaggerating.

P rison gave me a kind of adult education that, as a scholarship boy, I had not gotten in the humanities sequence at Columbia. It gave me an education about people, how they get by and how they don't. One of the ways they get by is loyalty. The people I worked with, even some of the inmates, "had my back": If a lieutenant gave you a hard time, the union rep would be in his face. If you were out too late and took a nap in the bathroom, another CO would cover for you. If an inmate saw the superintendent coming while you were watching TV and he thought you did your job, he would warn you. The better species of loyalty is, in fact, not blind: If you screw up, someone you work with should tell you. The corruption of loyalty is when no one says anything.

It's always curious to see how colleagues react when they find out about my time—as I like to put it—in prison. Some are fascinated and quote Cool Hand Luke, but clearly it's just a fantasy to them. Some take on a more serious cast and ask what I think of Foucault's *Discipline and Punish,* but then prison has become a disembodied abstraction, something they know as much about as dairy farms (as with most prisons, set a long way from any roads they've been on). Some look away, as if I had a swastika tattooed on my forearm. What they don't seem to realize is that correction officers are of the unionized working classes, like cops, whom my colleagues wouldn't hesitate to call if they had an accident or their house was broken into. It is often said that literature expands your world, but it can also close it off.

It is also often said that the university is not the real world, but in my experience each institutional parcel of life has its own world. When you work in prison, just as when you work in academe, you experience a world that has its own language, its own training, its own hierarchy, its own forms of recognition, its own forms of disrepute, and its own wall from the outside. In some ways, prison is the flip side of meritocracy. Both prisons and universities originated in religious institutions and are based on the model of the cloister; both are transitional institutions; both house and grade people; and both marshal primarily the young. The difference, of course, is that the university represents the hope, prison the failing, of the meritocracy. It's an unseemly sign that we invest more in the underside than in the hope.

Critical Thinking

1. What did the professor learn as a result of his experience as a prison guard?
2. How do you think the experience helped him in the academic world?

JEFFREY J. WILLIAMS is a professor of English and literary and cultural studies at Carnegie Mellon University, and editor of the *Minnesota Review*. His most recent book is the collection *Critics at Work: Interviews, 1993–2003* (New York University Press, 2004).

Supermax Prisons

JEFFREY IAN ROSS, PHD

Each time a crime occurs, an arrest is made, the trial ends, and a person is sentenced to prison, the public has a recurring curiosity about where the convict is sent. Over the past two decades, a phenomenal number of individuals have been sentenced to jails and to state or federal prisons.

But this is just the beginning of the journey. Prisoners are classified into a whole host of various kinds of facilities. They typically vary based on the level of security, from minimum to high. But since the mid-1980s, a dramatic change has underscored corrections in the United States and elsewhere. Correctional systems at all levels have introduced or expanded the use of Supermax prisons.

Supermax prisons, also known as Administrative Control Units, Special (or Security) Handling Units (SHU), or Control Handling Units (CHU) (Here, "CHUs" is pronounced "shoes."), are stand-alone correctional facilities, wings or annexes inside an already existing prison. They are a result of the recent growth in incarceration that has occurred throughout many of the world's advanced industrialized countries.

There is, however, a well-documented turning point in the history of Supermax prisons. In October 1983, after the brutal and fatal stabbings of two correctional officers by inmates at the federal maximum-security prison in Marion, Illinois, the facility implemented a 23-hour-a-day lockdown of all convicts. The institution slowly changed its policies and practices and was retrofitted to become what is now considered a Supermax prison. Then, in 1994, the federal government opened its first Supermax prison in Florence, Colorado, specifically designed to house Supermax prisoners. The facility was dubbed the "Alcatraz of the Rockies."

Research on Supermax Prisons

Although much has been written on jails, prisons, and corrections, the mass media and academic community have been relatively silent with respect to Supermax prisons—and with good reason. It is difficult for journalists and scholars to gain access to prisoners, correctional officers, and administrators inside this type of facility. Reporting on correctional institutions has never been easy, and many editors and reporters shy away from this subject matter. Correctional professionals are also reluctant to talk with outsiders for fear that they may be unnecessarily subjected to public scrutiny.

Numerous books on corrections, jails, and prisons have been published for trade, classroom, and professional audiences; only a few monographs offer an in-depth look at Supermax prisons. In December 2002, the American Correctional Association (the largest professional association for correctional practitioners in the United States) published *Supermax Prisons: Beyond the Rock*. This edited monograph, consisting of seven chapters written by prison officials, is more of a technical guide for prison administrators who run one of these types of facilities. Unfortunately, it suffers from the biases of its sponsor and limited targeted audience. *The Big House: Life Inside a Supermax Security Prison* (June 2004) is a memoir written by Jim Bruton, former warden of the Minnesota Correctional Facility-Oak Park Heights facility. Although pitched as a memoir of a Supermax administrator, Oak Park is without question primarily a maximum-security facility with only one of the nine complexes used as an Administrative Control Unit (or Supermax). Largely because of the numerous entertaining anecdotes, in many respects the book's treatment is superficial. Moreover, Bruton is overly self-congratulatory about his ability to solve problems on his watch and thus serious scholars have easily dismissed the book.

There has also been a handful of publicly available government reports published on the topic of Supermax prisons. These have consisted primarily of statistical compilations outlining the numerous Supermax facilities throughout the United States and the composition of the inmates housed within.

The academic treatments (journal articles or chapters in scholarly books) fall into three groups: general overviews, those that focus on the individuals that are sent to solitary confinement or Supermax prisons, and those that focus on the effects of Supermax prisons. The research centers disproportionately on American Supermax prisons and, while this is a start, this literature treats Supermax prisons in isolation of other countries' experiences. Rigorous comparative examinations of foreign-based Supermax prisons have yet to be performed.

There are many unanswered questions about Supermax prisons. Why are Supermax prisons necessary? What particular circumstances led to the creation of Supermax prisons in different states and countries? Is the construction and increased reliance on Supermax institutions due to the fact that today's prisoners are more incorrigible and dangerous, and thus more difficult to handle? Or is it a reflection of the correctional system's failure or mismanagement, or pressures by the general public for a get-tough stance against dangerous criminals? Who are the typical persons sent to Supermax prisons? Why have the Supermax prisons and similar institutions in other countries engendered intense public outcry? What are the similarities and differences among American supermaxes and comparable facilities elsewhere?

The academic treatments (journal articles or chapters in scholarly books) fall into three groups: general overviews, those that focus on the individuals that are sent to solitary confinement or Supermax prisons, and those that focus on the effects of Supermax prisons.

Why Supermaxes Have Proliferated

Since the mid-1980s, many state departments of corrections have built their own Supermax prisons. Several reasons can account for their proliferation. First, many states had similar experiences to the blood that spilled at Marion. In Minnesota, for example, the escape of a prisoner, kidnapping of correctional officers, fatal stabbing of a warden, and a series of prison disturbances in the early 1970s created an environment that was ripe for the construction of a new facility that would house the "worst of the worst." Another explanation for the growth of Supermax prisons lies in the development of a conservative political ideology that began during the Reagan administration (1981–1989). As a response to an increased public fear of crime and to the demise of the "rehabilitative ideal," a punitive agenda took hold of criminal justice and led to a much larger number of people being incarcerated.

Reagan's Republican successor, George H.W. Bush, continued this approach from 1989 to 1993. Since then several factors prompted a dramatic increase in the number of people entering jails and prisons: the construction of new correctional facilities; new and harsher sentencing guidelines (particularly "truth in sentencing" legislation, mandatory minimums, and determinant sentencing); the passage of "three strikes you're out" laws and the war on drugs.

In short, many of the gains that were part of the so-called "community corrections era" of the 1960s were scaled back. Congress and state legislatures passed draconian laws that reversed such time-honored practices as indeterminate sentencing and invoked a host of laws that lengthened prison sentences for convicted criminals.

Another factor that contributed to the growth of Supermaxes is the careerism of correctional administrators. Some have argued that without the leadership of particular wardens, government rainmakers, and commissioners and/or secretaries of respective state departments of corrections, Supermax facilities would not ever have been built in the first place. Finally, it should be understood that, in many respects, Supermaxes symbolize the failure of rehabilitation and the inability of policymakers and legislators to think and act creatively regarding incarceration. Supermax prisons are excellent examples of the way that America, compared to other countries, has dealt with lawbreakers.

Originally designed to house the most violent, hardened, and escape-prone criminals, Supermaxes are increasingly used for persistent rule-breakers, convicted leaders of criminal organizations (e.g., the mafia) and gangs, serial killers, and political criminals (e.g., spies and terrorists). In some states, the criteria for admission into a Supermax facility and the review of prisoners' time inside (i.e., classification) are very loose or even nonexistent. These facilities are known for their strict lockdown policies, lack of amenities, and prisoner isolation techniques. Escapes from Supermaxes are so rare that they are statistically inconsequential.

In the United States alone, 6.47 million people are under the control of the criminal justice system. Approximately 2.3 million are behind bars in jails or prisons, while 3.8 million are on probation and 725,527 are on parole. The Supermaxes, maintained by the Federal Bureau of Prisons (FBOP) in Marion and Florence, for example, incarcerate 1,710 people—including such notable political criminals as "Unabomber" Ted Kaczynski and Oklahoma City bombing co-conspirator Terry Nichols.

Nevertheless, only a fraction of those incarcerated in state and federal prisons are sent to a Supermax facility. In 1998, approximately 20,000 inmates were locked up in this type of prison, representing less than 2 percent of all the men and women currently incarcerated across the country. Most of the U.S. Supermaxes, such as the federal facility in Florence, are either brand new or nearly so; others, however, are simply free-standing prisons that have been retrofitted. Meanwhile, the number of convicts being sent to Supermax prisons is steadily growing.

Many prisons have earned their individual reputations largely through well-known events that have taken place within their walls and have subsequently been covered by the media. Places like Attica, Folsom, San Quentin, Sing Sing, and Stateville are etched in the consciousness of many Americans. The Supermaxes, on the other hand, are known for their conditions and effects on prisoners within their walls.

Conditions of Confinement

Although cells vary in size and construction, they are generally built to the dimensions of 12 by 7 feet. A cell light usually remains on all night long, and furnishings consist of a bed, a desk, and a stool made out of poured concrete, as well as a stainless steel sink and toilet.

One of the more notable features of all Supermax prisons is the fact that prisoners are usually locked down 23 out of 24 hours a day. The hour outside of the prison is typically used for recreation or bathing/showering. Other than their interaction with the supervising correctional officers (COs), prisoners have virtually no contact with other people (either fellow convicts or visitors). Access to phones and mail is strictly and closely supervised, or even restricted. Reading materials are often prohibited. Supermax prisoners have very limited access to privileges such as watching television or listening to the radio.

Supermax prisons also generally do not allow inmates either to work or congregate during the day. In addition, there is absolutely no personal privacy; everything the convicts do is monitored, usually through a video camera that is on all day and night. Any communication with the correctional officers most often takes place through a narrow window on the steel door of the cell, and/or via an intercom system.

In Supermaxes, inmates rarely have access to educational or religious materials and services. Almost all toiletries (e.g., toothpaste, shaving cream, and razors) are strictly controlled. When an inmate is removed from his cell, he typically has to kneel down with his back to the door. Then he is required to place his hands through the food slot in the door to be handcuffed.

In spite of these simple facilities and the fact that prisoners' rehabilitation is not encouraged (and is next to impossible under these conditions), Supermax prisons are more expensive to build and to run than traditional prisons.

Prisoners are sentenced or transferred to Supermaxes for a variety of reasons that often boil down to a judge's sentence, classification processes, and inmates' behavior while they are incarcerated.

Officially, prison systems design classification categories as a means to designate prisoners to different security levels. Typically, the hard-core, violent convicts serving long sentences are assigned to maximum-security facilities; the incorrigible prisoners serving medium-length sentences are sentenced to medium-security prisons; and the relatively lightweight men serving short sentences are sentenced to minimum-security camps, farms, or community facilities.

For some convicts, the decision of where they will be sent is made long before they hop on their very first prison van. In the sentencing phase of a trial, the judge may specify where the convict will spend his or her time. For example, Ramzi Yousef, the convicted bomber in the 1993 attack on the World Trade Center, was sent directly to the federal Supermax in Florence, Colorado. Depending on sentencing guidelines and an individual's criminal history, officials must determine which security level is most appropriate for each convict. Alternatively, prisoners who are new to the system will be transferred to a receiving and departure setting, where they are classified into the appropriate receiving facility.

The classification of inmates serves many functions for the Department of Corrections (DOC) and the individual correctional institutions. In general, this process determines which facility and security level is best suited to each prisoner. This decision may ultimately facilitate a prisoner's rehabilitation and/or protect correctional officers from being hurt (as officials clearly do not want, for example, a violence-prone convict in a minimum-security prison). Classification also saves taxpayers money (since sending too many prisoners to higher-security prisons, which are more costly to operate, results in a greater expense) and saves the Department of Corrections resources.

Where a convict is sent depends on a number of factors. The division of probation and parole usually prepares a Pre-Sentence Investigation, which is another attempt by the criminal justice system to collect a prisoner's personal information. The probation or parole officer reviews a number of factors relevant to the convict's circumstances, including criminal history. They prepare a report, which makes a recommendation as to which facility would best suit the particular criminal. This report is then shared with the judge, defense attorney, and prosecutor—and the judge retains the ability to accept or dismiss the recommendation. By the same token, some well-heeled and high-profile defendants (e.g., Martha Stewart) or their loved ones may employ the services of sentencing consultants like Herb Hoelter of the National Center for Institutions and Alternatives. For a hefty fee, these hired individuals can prepare a report that recommends where a client should be sentenced. The defendant's attorney then passes the report on to the prosecutor (and judge) in hopes that it may ultimately influence the presiding judge.

In most lock-ups and prisons, the majority of the inmates do not get into trouble because they follow the rules. The problem population comprises approximately 1 percent of the prisoners in an institution. When there is an incident, such as a stabbing on a tier, correctional officers cannot place all of the suspects on administrative segregation (i.e., "in the hole"). But when this type of extreme punishment becomes the norm for a particular prisoner, the administration is usually prompted to transfer the inmate to a higher-security prison. Over time, a prisoner who repeatedly finds himself in this type of situation becomes more and more likely to end up at a Supermax facility.

> **Typically, the hard-core, violent convicts serving long sentences are assigned to maximum-security facilities; the incorrigible prisoners serving medium-length sentences are sentenced to medium-security prisons; and the relatively lightweight men serving short sentences are sentenced to minimum-security camps, farms, or community facilities.**

Effects of Incarceration

All told, the isolation, lack of meaningful activity, and shortage of human contact take their toll on prisoners. Supermax residents often develop severe psychological disorders, though, unfortunately, we do not have specific psychological data, per se, on individuals kept in these facilities. However, numerous reports based on anecdotal information have documented the detrimental effects of these facilities.

The conditions inside Supermax prisons have led several corrections and human rights experts and organizations (like Amnesty International and the American Civil Liberties Union) to question whether these prisons are a violation of (1) the Eighth Amendment of the U.S. Constitution, which prohibits the state from engaging in cruel and unusual punishment, and/or (2) the European Convention on Human Rights and the United Nations'

Universal Declaration of Human Rights, which were established to protect the rights of all individuals, whether living free or incarcerated. According to Roy D. King, in an article published in the 1999 volume of *Punishment and Society,* "Although the effective reach of international human rights standards governing the treatment of prisoners remains uncertain, there seems little doubt that what goes on in a number of Supermax facilities would breach the protections enshrined in these instruments. . . . The International Covenant on Civil and Political Rights, which the United States has ratified, for example, has a more extensive ban on 'torture, cruel, inhuman or degrading treatment or punishment' than the Eighth Amendment prohibition of 'cruel and unusual' punishment, and requires no demonstration of intent or indifference to the risk of harm, on the part of officials" (164).

Supermax prisons have plenty of downsides, and not just as far as the inmates are concerned. Some individuals have suggested that Supermax prisons are all part of the correctional industrial complex (i.e., an informal network of correctional workers, professional organizations, and corporations that keep the jails and prisons system growing). Most of the Supermaxes in the United States are brand new or nearly so. Others are simply freestanding prisons that were retrofitted. According to a study by the Urban Institute, the annual per-cell cost of a Supermax is about $75,000, compared to $25,000 for each cell in an ordinary state prison.

Future Prospects

The United States has plenty of super-expensive Supermax facilities—two-thirds of the states now have them. But these facilities were designed when crime was considered a growing problem; the current lower violent-crime rate shows no real sign of a turn for the worse. However, as good as these prisons are at keeping our worst offenders in check, the purpose of the Supermax is in flux.

No self-respecting state director of corrections or correctional planner will admit that the Supermax concept was a mistake. And you would be wrong to think that these prisons can be replaced by something drastically less costly. But prison experts are beginning to realize that, just like a shrinking city that finds itself with too many schools or fire departments, the Supermax model must be made more flexible in order to justify its size and budget.

One solution is for these facilities to house different types of prisoners. In May 2006, Wisconsin Department of Corrections officials announced that, over the past sixteen years, the state's Supermax facility in Boscobel—which cost $47.5 million (in 1990) and holds 500 inmates—has always stood at 100 cells below its capacity. It is now scheduled to house maximum-security prisoners—serious offenders, but a step down from the worst of the worst.

The Maryland Correctional Adjustment Center, a.k.a. the Baltimore Supermax prison, opened in 1989 at a cost of $21 million with room for 288 inmates. Like its cousin in Wisconsin, the structure has never been at capacity. Not only does it hold the state's most dangerous prisoners, it also houses 100 or so inmates who are working their way through the federal courts and serves as the home for Maryland's ten death row convicts.

Converting cells is one approach, but not the only one. Other ideas include building more regional Supermaxes and filling them by shifting populations from other states. This would allow administrators to completely empty out a given Supermax, and then close it down or convert it to another use.

There is also the possibility that some elements of the Supermax model could be combined with the approaches of more traditional prisons, creating a hybrid that serves a wider population. But different types of prisoners would have to be kept well away from each other—a logistical problem of no small concern.

The invention and adoption of Supermax prisons is perhaps the most significant indictment of the way we run correctional facilities and/or what we accomplish in correctional facilities. Most relatively intelligent people know that the United States incarcerates more people per capita than any other advanced industrialized country. And the average American rarely questions this fact. Then again, many people believe that individuals doing time are probably guilty anyway. Thus reforming or changing prisons is and will remain a constant struggle.

Critical Thinking

1. Do we need more supermax prisons?
2. Do you think the conditions of confinement encourage rehabilitation?
3. What types of inmates are incarcerated in supermax prisons?

JEFFREY IAN ROSS, PhD is an Associate Professor in the Division of Criminology, Criminal Justice and Social Policy, and a Fellow of the Center for International and Comparative Law at the University of Baltimore. He has researched, written, and lectured on national security, political violence, political crime, violent crime, corrections, and policing for over two decades. Ross' work has appeared in many academic journals and books, as well as popular outlets. He is the author, co-author, editor and co-editor of twelve books including most recently *Special Problems in Corrections* (Prentice Hall, 2008). He has also appeared as an expert commentator on crime and policing issues in many media outlets such as newspapers, magazines, and nationally televised shows. His website is www.jeffreyianross.com.

From *Society,* vol. 44, no. 3, March/April 2007, pp. 60–64. Copyright © 2007 by Jeffrey Ian Ross. Reprinted by permission of the author.

The Results of American Incarceration

Any answer to the question "What do we get from imprisonment?" has to recognize that U.S. imprisonment operates differently than it does in any other democratic state in the world.

TODD R. CLEAR

Let's begin with a little thought experiment. Today, there are 1.3 million federal prisoners; over 2 million citizens are incarcerated in state prisons and local jails. Imagine that those numbers grow methodically for the next generation. By the time people born today reach their thirtieth birthday, there will be over 7 million prisoners and, if local jails are counted, more than 10 million locked up on any given day. How are we to react to such daunting numbers?

First, let's agree that the experiment seems unrealistic. This kind of growth would result in about 2 percent of the population incarcerated on any given day. Taken as a percentage of males aged 20–40 (most of those behind bars are from this group), the proportion locked up would be stupefying.

A rational person might say, "State and local governments have trouble affording today's prisons and jails, so how could they pay for such a mind-boggling expansion? What kind of society could justify locking up so many of our young men?"

After a bit more thought, that person might also say, "Well, if we are going to do it, then at least we will eliminate a lot of crime."

This is perhaps a disturbing thought experiment, but it is not a far-fetched one.

The 'War' on Crime

To illustrate, go back a full generation, to the beginning of the 1970s. Richard Nixon is president, and we are having a bit of a "war" on crime (puny, by today's standards). Crime rates seem disturbingly high, and the nightly news seems dominated by stories about disorder in the streets.

Imagine, for a moment, attending a futurist seminar, and the speaker has turned his attention to the topic of social control. He has said a few words about the coming days of electronic surveillance through bracelets on people's ankles and wrists, pictures and home addresses of convicted criminals displayed for all to see at the touch of a keyboard, detention in an offender's home enforced by threat of prison, chemical testing of a person's cells—detectable from saliva left at the scene of a crime—instead of fingerprints to prove guilt at trial, and so on. The audience would rightfully have been a bit awed by the prospect.

Then he makes the most stunning prediction of all. He says, "In the next 30 years, the prison population is going to grow by 600 percent. Instead of today's 200,000 prisoners, we will have more than 1.3 million."

Anyone who heard such predictions in the early 1970s would have been more than a bit skeptical. But they have all come true.

Any answer to the question, "What do we get from imprisonment?" has to begin with a frank recognition that incarceration in the United States today operates differently than in any other modernized or democratic state in the world, and that this phenomenon has resulted from very recent changes in U.S. penal policy. Today, we lock up our fellow citizens at a rate (700 per 100,000) that is between 5 and 10 times higher than in comparable industrial democracies.

A Washington, D.C., prison reform group, the Sentencing Project, has offered these comparisons: European states such as Germany, Sweden, France, the Netherlands, and Switzerland have incarceration rates of less than 100 per 100,000, one-seventh of ours. The big lock-up states—England, Spain, Canada, and Australia—have prison/jail rates of between 100 and 200, or one-fourth of ours. Our only competitors are Russia and South Africa, with prison-use levels that are 90 and 60 percent of ours, respectively.

That is not the whole story. Our world leadership in the use of prison is a fairly recent accomplishment. U.S. prison population statistics go back to 1925, when there were about 100,000 prisoners. Between 1925 and 1940, a period of fairly substantial immigration and U.S. population growth, the number of prisoners doubled. During the years of World War II, the prison population dropped by about a third. (Most observers think this drop was due to the large number of young men in the armed forces and unavailable for imprisonment). Between 1945 and 1961, the number of prisoners grew by 68 percent, to a high of about 210,000 in the early 1960s, staying more or less stable into the 1970s.

U.S. Leads World in Incarceration

- Today, the United States locks up its citizens at a rate (700 per 100,000) that is between 5 and 10 times higher than in comparable industrial democracies.
- In European states such as Germany, Sweden, France, the Netherlands, and Switzerland, incarceration rates are under 100 per 100,000.
- The big lockup states—England, Spain, Canada, and Australia—have prison/jail rates of between 100 and 200, or one-quarter of ours.
- The only competitors for prison and jail use are Russia and South Africa, with levels that are 90 and 60 percent of ours, respectively.
- Since the 1990s, almost all the growth in the prison population has been due to longer sentences, not more crime or prisoners.
- In effect, the U.S. anomaly in prison use results mostly from the policies we enact to deal with crime, much less than from crime itself.

Social scientists looked at these numbers and saw a pattern of profound stability. In 1975, two researchers from Carnegie-Mellon University, Alfred Blumstein and Jacqueline Cohen, argued that after accounting for such factors as war, immigration, and changes in youth population, there had been a "homoeostatic" level of stability in punishment for the first three-quarters of the twentieth century. That theory no longer applies. Between 1971 and 2002, the number of prisoners grew by an astounding 600 percent. Why did everything change?

Why the Growth in Crime?

It is easy to say that prison populations grew because crime—or at least violent crime—grew. But this view turns out to be simplistic. In their recent book, *Crime Is Not the Problem*, UCLA criminologists Franklin Zimring and Gordon Hawkins point out that several countries have violent crime rates that rival ours, yet use prison less readily than we do. Moreover, those European countries with low rates of incarceration seem to have property crime rates that are not so different from ours.

Besides, the growth of the U.S. prison population has been so consistent for a generation that nothing seems to affect it much. Since 1980, for example, prison populations grew during economic boom times and recessions alike; while the baby boomers were entering their crime-prone years and as they exited those years; and as crime dropped and while it soared.

Today's nationally dropping crime rates—a trend in some big cities that is almost a decade long—suggest that prison growth has helped make the streets safer. But when we take the long view, aside from burglary (which has dropped systematically for 20 years), today's crime rates are not very different than at the start of the big prison boom in the 1970s. Since then, crime rates went up for a while, down for a while, back up again, and are now (thankfully) trending downward. Prison populations, by contrast, went only one way during this entire period: up.

Blumstein and Department of Justice statistician Allen Beck have studied trends in criminal justice since the 1980s to better understand what accounts for the recent growth in the prison population. They argue that you can divide the growth into three distinct periods. In the late 1970s and early 1980s, prisons grew because crime was growing and more criminals were being sentenced to prison. In the 1980s into the beginning of the 1990s, prison growth was partly due to crime rates, but it was much more a product of greater numbers of criminals being sentenced to prison and of longer terms for those sentenced there.

By the 1990s and into the early 2000s, the story has changed, and almost all of the growth in the prison population is due to longer sentences, not more crime or more prisoners. In effect, the U.S. anomaly in the use of prison is a result mostly of the policies we enact to deal with crime, and much less of crime itself.

A Street's-Eye View

But all of this exploration looks for broad patterns. What about the view from the streets? John DiIulio of the University of Pennsylvania, former co-director of the White House Office on Faith-Based Initiatives, once observed, "A thug in jail can't shoot my sister." Isn't it apparent on its face that a person behind bars is someone from whom the rest of us are pretty safe?

Yes, but that may not be the most effective way to deter crime. The irony is that while people who are behind bars are less likely to commit crimes, that may not mean those crimes are prevented from occurring.

Drug crime is the obvious example. Almost one-third of those sent to prison are punished for drug-related crimes, and one prisoner in four is serving time for a drug crime. In most of these cases, the criminal activity continued without noticeable interruption, carried out by a replacement. One of the recurrent frustrations of police work is to carry out a drug sweep one day, only to see the drug market return in a matter of hours. Locking up drug offenders is not an efficient strategy for preventing drug crime.

This line of analysis can be misleading, though, because most drug offenders are not specialists in drug crime. Analyses of criminal records show that people in prison who are serving time for drug-related activity typically have arrests and/or convictions for other types of offenses. Doesn't locking them up for drugs prevent the other crimes from happening? At least some other crime is prevented, but not as much as might be thought.

A few years ago, Yale sociologist Albert Reiss reported that about half of all criminal acts are perpetrated by young offenders acting in groups of two or more. Rarely are all of the members of the group prosecuted for the crime. This discovery led to a string of studies of what has been referred to as "co-offending," the commission of crimes by multiple offenders acting in concert. When one person out of a group is arrested and imprisoned, what impact does the arrest have on the crimes the group had been committing? A lot rides on the nature and behavior of criminal groups.

Much research is now under way to better understand how crimes are committed by offenders acting alone and in a group. It would be convenient if criminal groups had stable leaders and were systematic in the way they planned criminal activity. If so, arresting the leaders might break up the groups, and strategies of deterrence might reduce the likelihood of criminal actions. Neither characteristic applies.

Criminologist Mark Warr of the University of Texas has studied the way young males form co-offending groups and engage in criminal acts. He reports that leadership is sporadic and often interchangeable, that criminal actions are spontaneous, and that co-offending groups are loosely formed and vary over time. His findings suggest that well-respected strategies of targeted prosecution and focus on leaders of criminal activity are likely to have diminishing returns in crime prevention. As Rutgers University's Marcus Felson has argued, this analysis of dynamic, spontaneous, loosely organized criminal activity applies not simply to some youth but to most gang behavior. Arresting one person in the network and sending him to prison is far from a guarantee that the crime that person was involved in will stop.

Are Crime and Punishment Connected?

None of this is to argue that imprisonment prevents no crime. Professor David W. Garland of New York University School of Law, one of the most widely respected social critics of imprisonment, puts it well when he says that only the naive would claim that prisons and crime are unrelated. But even if it is recognized that crime and prisons are connected, under close scrutiny, we can find various reasons why wildly growing rates of imprisonment might not lead willy-nilly to wildly reducing rates of crime. Said another way, we can find explanations for the fact that the period in which incarceration has grown so much has not been matched by a corresponding drop in crime.

A new literature is emerging about the unintended consequences of incarceration. Prison populations, for example, are drawn predominantly from the ranks of poor people from minority groups. Today, one in eight black males aged 25–29 is locked up; this rate is almost eight times higher than for white males. Estimates reported by the Department of Justice indicate that of black males born today, 29 percent will go to prison for a felony offense, while currently 17 percent of all African-American males have spent time in prison. These rates are about six times higher than for white males.

Patterns of racial segregation mean that imprisonment also concentrates residentially. James Lynch and William Sabol,

researchers from the Urban Institute, have estimated that in some very poor neighborhoods in Washington, D.C., and Cleveland, Ohio, upwards of 18–20 percent of adult males are locked up on any given day. New York City's Center for Alternative Sentencing and Employment Services reported that in 1998, in two of Brooklyn's poorest Council Districts, one person went to prison or jail for every eight resident males aged 20–40.

These high rates of incarceration, concentrated among poor minority males living in disadvantaged locations, are a new phenomenon that results from a generation of prison population growth in the United States. Social scientists are beginning to investigate whether this socially concentrated use of prison sentences has long-term effects on such factors as neighborhood order, family structure, and child development.

One can imagine, for example, that a neighborhood where a large proportion of parent-age men are missing is a neighborhood that would grapple with a number of problems, from family stability to child supervision. My own research with my colleagues Dina Rose and Elin Waring seems to suggest that high incarceration rates produce socially destabilizing results that may be a factor in sustaining high rates of crime.

The prison is a blunt social instrument, while crime is a much more nuanced social problem. Given what we know about crime, it should not surprise us that so much prison has provided so little in the way of broad public safety.

When trying to weigh the benefits of prison, perhaps we are used to asking the wrong question. We tend to ask about whether prison is a good idea compared to alternative sentencing. In today's America, this may be a fascinating question but it is not a very meaningful one. The more appropriate question would be, "Given our experience with incarceration over the last century, what might we expect from further increases in its use; what might happen if we began to cut back in its use?" This question, which we might perhaps save for another day, would recognize the political reality that U.S. prison rates are going to be internationally out-of-scale for a long time. The only question we face is, how much?

Critical Thinking

1. Should Americans be concerned about the comparisons of incarceration in the U.S. with other countries?

2. How are crime and punishment related?

3. Is incarceration an effective way to deter crime?

Todd R. Clear is Distinguished Professor in Community Justice and Corrections at John Jay College of Criminal Justice in New York City.

Partnering with Law Enforcement

Ashbel T. Wall II and Tracey Z. Poole

The primary mission of law enforcement is to maintain peace and order and provide a safe environment. In these respects, it is fundamentally aligned with the mission of the corrections field. Although each domain has its own role and perspective, the goal of public safety requires integration and activities that interlock and interconnect. The message must be sent, from the top, that this approach is a priority at the highest level.

There are several underlying assumptions that must be in play if prisoner reentry is to be effective. All of them support the argument that corrections and law enforcement must come together to further these important ideas:

- Prisoner reentry is a statewide issue;
- The current approach to corrections is costly and the outcomes are not great;
- Solutions do not lie solely within correctional departments;
- Both human services and law enforcement must join together with corrections;
- Communities and community-based agencies must be part of the process;
- It is possible to create models that cut across existing bureaucratic structures;
- The work must involve changes in organizational culture and attitudes;
- Communication and data-sharing are essential; and
- Success can (and should) be measured.

Perhaps the most important outcome of the partnerships formed between probation and parole officers and police officers is the sense of mutual respect and connection that develops from working in tandem on a regular basis. It is unusual to hear of probation and parole officers described as "the two new rock stars of the city," but that is how Col. Dean Esserman, the Providence police chief, described Rhode Island DOC probation officers Yolanda Harley and Geneva Brown at a recent gathering that included members of his staff, DOC officials and a reporter from *The Providence Journal.* Esserman added, "And I intend to buy tickets to their concert someday."

The chief said he is enthusiastic about this "remarkable partnership" between his department and the DOC and its role in enhancing public safety in the state's largest city. The Providence police officers are now wired into the DOC's inmate database, INFACTS, and can access it from laptops in their cruisers or from police headquarters and substations. Within moments of arrest, police officers can determine whether individuals are on probation or parole, download offenders' photos, and review other important details about their incarceration history.

Meeting probationers where they live is one of the cornerstones of probation. As a result of the partnership between the DOC and the police department, Brown and Harley have moved out of their comfort zone—working previously in the Superior Court and the District Court—and now have offices right alongside the police substation in District 7, a neighborhood with a startlingly high number of probationers. Historically, probation officers had been frustrated because they were desk-bound in the courthouse. Today, these two officers' entire caseloads live within a 10-minute drive. Brown and Harley conduct weekly home visits, participate in ride-alongs with the police and attend weekly staff meetings in Esserman's office to share information about probationers on their caseloads. They say they cannot imagine returning to "the old way" of doing business.

The willingness of District 7's Lt. Michael Correia and his staff to welcome probation officers into their substation and to work hand in glove with them has sent a message across the city that the DOC and the Providence Police Department will partner in every way possible to ensure the safety of the city's residents. Harley and Brown have been pioneers in this effort. Their supervisor and all of the administrators in probation and parole have been instrumental in making this relationship successful.

Once a month, new probationers from the district are invited to the District 7 substation for a "meet 'n greet" attended by critical staff from the police department and probation and parole. Their photos are taken and included in a personalized meet 'n greet flier, which is a handy way for police and probation officers to quickly identify and keep tabs on probationers. "Right away when they come in the room," Correia said, "they know something's different." Micheline Lombardi, who supervises Harley and Brown, sees these gatherings as an opportunity to show probationers that "we're not the enemy. [We want] to help them change the way they look at life and make better choices." Lombardi added: "This is a long-term partnership. We're taking it to the next level. Other districts now want what District 7 has."

Rhode Island's probation officers have among the highest caseloads in the country. While the state needs more officers, its fiscal crisis has made it imperative that new and creative options be considered. Since this partnership has only existed for about seven months, it is too early to generate hard data on the impact the partnership is having on recidivism. However, the sentiment shared by the police department and the DOC is that people behave better when they are being watched, and this collaboration greatly increases the level of supervision.

Of the approximately 20,000 Rhode Islanders on probation or parole in the state's communities, 6,600 lived in the city of Providence as of year-end 2007, according to the Rhode Island DOC's Planning and Research Unit. This partnership is bringing the focus of supervision down to the neighborhood level, and it shows that working together every day really makes the system work. It is a smart investment because it increases the state's ability to prevent re-offending, which involves

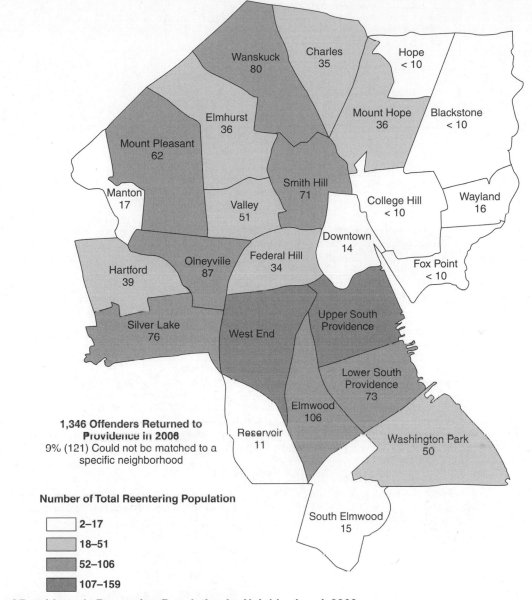

Distribution of Providence's Reentering Population by Neighborhood, 2006

Data Source: R.I. Department of Corrections, 2006 Sentenced Releases.

additional victimization; leads to a churning of offenders through the correctional system; and drives up crowding and costs.

The DOC is interested in developing similar relationships in cities across the state and recently launched an initiative in Warwick, Rhode Island's second largest community. About 75 probationers residing in that city were invited to the police department for a meet 'n greet involving the Warwick Police Department and the DOC's probation and parole staff. They were addressed by A.T. Wall II, the corrections director; Lt. Thomas Hannon, Warwick Police Department; Robert Corrente, U.S. attorney for the state of Rhode Island; Col. Stephen McCartney, Warwick Chief of Police; and Christine Imbriglio, supervisor of Kent County Probation. Several community service providers also attended, including the Kent Center, Kent House, Vantage Point, Assisted Recovery, Addiction Recovery Institute, the Department of Human Services and West Bay Community Action. These providers were available at the conclusion of the presentation to offer assistance and information to attendees. Warwick Mayor Scott Avedesian dropped in on the gathering and also met with local politicians, probation and parole staff, the chief, and others in the neighborhood of

Oakland Beach to discuss expanding the partnership to include more communities. "I'm enthusiastically supporting this and look forward to further expanding the partnership," McCartney said.

Regional Reentry Councils

The battle for successful reentry is ultimately won or lost on the ground in individual communities. The DOC has begun the process of creating local reentry councils in communities with the highest concentration of returning offenders—thus far in Newport, Providence, Pawtucket and Woonsockct. The recntry councils comprise local elected officials, upper managers from local service providers, senior probation and parole staff, law enforcement personnel, and representatives from faith-based organizations and the business sector. These councils are beginning to make an impact on the lives of the men and women in the affected communities who leave prison with the often daunting goal of never coming back.

The purpose of these regional councils is to create a seamless transition for offenders from prison back into their home communities by

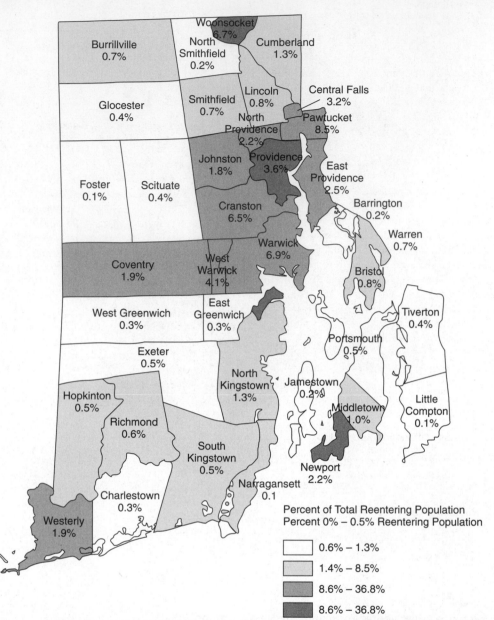

Distribution of Rhode Island's Reentering Population by Municipality, 2006, 3,654 Offenders Returned to Rhode Island in 2006

Data Source: R.I. Department of Corrections, 2006 Sentenced Releases

resolving the specific barriers—finding employment, health care and affordable housing—that often lead to a downward spiral. The councils also serve as advocates for effective inmate reentry. They have the local credibility to point out that reentry is an issue of community safety, and it affects every member of a community, whether directly or indirectly.

Newport's Council

Spearheaded by the faith community in Newport, the regional reentry council there was the first to get off the ground in Rhode Island and has transformed the way the DOC and other social service agencies are able to assist inmates returning to this city.

At a recent meeting of the council, DOC probation and parole and transitional services staff; representatives of local agencies such as a faith-based nonprofit for ex-offenders and a local homeless shelter; the area hospital's social worker; mental health providers; the community police officer; and the city's part-time reentry coordinator

gathered around the table to discuss the list of specific individuals to be released from prison in the next six months.

Newport's Key Players

"All of you are able to tell us things about these people we never would have known otherwise," noted Sister Teresa Foley, professional/transitional services coordinator for the DOC. "The interchange of information has been wonderful and has allowed us to do better planning by knowing all of these interconnections."

Roberta Richman, assistant director for rehabilitative services for the DOC, has been a driving force in getting these regional councils off the ground. She is pleased to see each council taking on a unique shape specific to the character and size of the community. "These people [returning offenders] are not an island unto themselves," Richman said during a council meeting in Newport. "The police know them. Many of you around the table know them. This is where they have grown up and we at the DOC couldn't possibly serve them as well without the helpful information you're all able to provide us with. We share information and the responsibility for being there for people who are trying hard and can't do it alone."

The Rev. Cheryl Robinson runs Turning Around Ministries, a Newport nonprofit that mentors returning offenders for 18 months and helps them with needs such as food, clothing, shelter, and GED preparation or accessing college courses—all of the things that can become stumbling blocks and force someone back into old, harmful patterns. Robinson has been a leader on the Newport Reentry Council since it began.

Cheryl Newsome plays an equally pivotal role as Newport's part-time reentry coordinator. She works with landlords to find housing for clients and accompanies them to court, homeless shelters or mental health appointments. Both Newsome and Robinson travel to the DOC in Cranston once a month to attend discharge-planning meetings.

Tom Reiser is a clinician with CODAC Behavioral Healthcare, and his presence at the council meetings enables his staff to expedite the process of getting offenders enrolled in treatment within days of their release. His agency offers counseling and assessment and acts in coordination with East Bay Community Action. The two agencies work closely with DOC probation and parole staff and provide reports to the courts.

Nancy Hallman, probation and parole supervisor for Newport County, has found the regional council immensely helpful to her and her staff. "Even if someone is on straight probation [never incarcerated]," she noted, "we know we can contact someone from the council for assistance. With our heavy caseloads, having these community networking connections has taken some of the burden off of probation."

Sue Windsor is a social worker with Newport Hospital. She encourages reentering offenders to get a primary care physician if they do not have one and works with discharge planning to ensure that services offenders receive in prison will continue. Windsor also works with probation and parole to ensure that released offenders have the medications they need.

Fernando Comas, probation officer in the sex offender unit who attends council meetings when a sex offender is on the release list, visits these offenders while they are still incarcerated to set them up with the services they will need upon release. "They function much better when people are involved and respond well to a helping hand," he said. "We work to help them reenter society and allow people to observe that they can function normally."

Also in attendance when possible are Christine Green, DOC discharge planner (contracted through the Urban League), who sets up court-ordered treatment and provides follow-up with clients for about a year; and Anna Harrison-Auld, administrator for adult outpatient and emergency services with Newport Country Community Mental Health Center. "We prioritize inmates when they're released," Harrison-Auld explained. "They can walk in on the day of discharge and have an application."

Newport as a Model

Thanks to this partnership, offenders returning to Newport are set up with coordinated services and are better able to function, unlike in past years when they would leave prison and get on a bus with nothing but a trash bag full of their belongings. The hope is to secure additional funding so a reentry center can be set up in downtown Newport and the results of these efforts can be tracked more formally. At one meeting, a discharge planner mentioned that only one of her clients has returned to prison out of all those released to Newport in the previous six or seven months. Robinson is only aware of two of her clients who have returned to prison. They were the ones who refused help.

Perhaps this model is so successful in Newport because of its small size and the close proximity of service providers. Maybe it is the fact that Jimmy Winters, community police officer and another important member of the council, has known most of the returning offenders and their extended families for much of their lives. Whatever the reason, it seems to be working.

Expanding the Effort

Providence Mayor David Cicilline has appointed his police chief to co-chair the reentry council there and has obtained grant money to hire a full-time reentry coordinator. In Pawtucket and Warwick, similar initiatives are just getting off the ground. In order for these efforts to be successful, three legs of the stool need to be in place to provide ex-offenders with the stability they need to reenter society.

Richman, who has been at this work for much of her 30-year DOC career, said: "First, prison officials need to begin preparing [offenders] for life outside the prison walls before they leave us. Then, the community has to put aside the stigma of dealing with people who have been incarcerated. But, most important, the offenders themselves have to want to make the necessary changes."

Perhaps Cicilline said it best in his keynote address to the DOC's offender reentry strategic-planning retreat back in September. The biggest challenge, as he sees it, is on an emotional level. Most Rhode Islanders' gut reaction to the thought of devoting resources to ex-offenders is negative. It does not make sense to them. Those professionals engaged in this work see the benefits, but how do they persuade the public? Clearly not with logic and evidence alone, according to Cicilline. It is really a matter of using different language to talk about this work so that it is not focused on individual offenders. It has to be about communities protecting themselves—people who do not want to be victims or to have their own neighbors victimized again. Any community that neglects this work is risking the safety of its citizens. "We are not building an ex-offender community support system but a community protection strategy," Cicilline argued. "Changing our language in this discussion really isn't political spin. It really is about communities."

The two successful emerging partnerships with law enforcement and the four regional reentry councils in Rhode Island all play a critical role in the state's commitment to effective prisoner reentry. It is through deliberate connections at the ground level that Rhode Island will begin to see a drop in recidivism rates and save taxpayer money by ensuring that the thousands of people released from prison each year will stay out. It is about a whole new way of doing business in corrections, and like any change, there are bound to be growing pains. In the long run, though, the gain will far exceed the pain.

Critical Thinking

1. Describe how the Providence police and the Rhode Island DOC work together.

2. Describe the Newport program.

3. How do regional reentry councils work?

ASHBEL T. WALL II is director of the Rhode Island Department of Corrections. **TRACEY Z. POOLE** is chief of information and public relations for the Rhode Island Department of Corrections.

From *Corrections Today*, April, 2008, pp. 31–37. Copyright © 2008 by American Correctional Association. Reprinted with permission of the American Correctional Association, Alexandria, VA.

Test-Your-Knowledge Form

We encourage you to photocopy and use this page as a tool to assess how the articles in *Annual Editions* expand on the information in your textbook. By reflecting on the articles you will gain enhanced text information. You can also access this useful form on a product's book support website at www.mhhe.com/cls

NAME: _____   DATE: _____

TITLE AND NUMBER OF ARTICLE: _____

BRIEFLY STATE THE MAIN IDEA OF THIS ARTICLE: _____

_____

LIST THREE IMPORTANT FACTS THAT THE AUTHOR USES TO SUPPORT THE MAIN IDEA:

_____

_____

WHAT INFORMATION OR IDEAS DISCUSSED IN THIS ARTICLE ARE ALSO DISCUSSED IN YOUR TEXTBOOK OR OTHER READINGS THAT YOU HAVE DONE? LIST THE TEXTBOOK CHAPTERS AND PAGE NUMBERS:

_____

_____

LIST ANY EXAMPLES OF BIAS OR FAULTY REASONING THAT YOU FOUND IN THE ARTICLE:

_____

_____

LIST ANY NEW TERMS/CONCEPTS THAT WERE DISCUSSED IN THE ARTICLE, AND WRITE A SHORT DEFINITION:

We Want Your Advice

ANNUAL EDITIONS revisions depend on two major opinion sources: one is our Advisory Board, listed in the front of this volume, which works with us in scanning the thousands of articles published in the public press each year; the other is you—the person actually using the book. Please help us and the users of the next edition by completing the prepaid article rating form on this page and returning it to us. Thank you for your help!

ANNUAL EDITIONS: Criminal Justice 11/12

ARTICLE RATING FORM

Here is an opportunity for you to have direct input into the next revision of this volume.
We would like you to rate each of the articles listed below, using the following scale:

1. **Excellent: should definitely be retained**
2. **Above average: should probably be retained**
3. **Below average: should probably be deleted**
4. **Poor: should definitely be deleted**

Your ratings will play a vital part in the next revision.
Please mail this prepaid form to us as soon as possible.
Thanks for your help!

RATING	ARTICLE	RATING	ARTICLE
	1. What Is the Sequence of Events in the Criminal Justice System?		22. Illegal Globally, Bail for Profit Remains in U.S.
	2. Plugging Holes in the Science of Forensics		23. The Forfeiture Racket
	3. Picked from a Lineup, on a Whiff of Evidence		24. When Our Eyes Deceive Us
	4. Organizational Learning and Islamic Militancy		25. The DNA Factor
	5. The Death of the War on Drugs		26. DNA's Dirty Little Secret
	6. The Wrong Man		27. Confessions and the Constitution: The Remedy for Violating Constitutional Safeguards
	7. Universal Policing: Counterterrorism Lessons from Northern Ireland		28. Justice and Antonin Scalia: The Supreme Court's Most Strident Catholic
	8. Telling the Truth about Damned Lies and Statistics		29. Violence in Adolescent Dating Relationships
	9. The Face of Domestic Violence		30. America's Imprisoned Kids
	10. Death by Gender		31. The Long View of Crime
	11. Elder Abuse Emerges from the Shadows of Public Consciousness		32. Jail Time Is Learning Time
	12. Options for Reporting Sexual Violence: Developments over the Past Decade		33. Lifers as Teenagers, Now Seeking Second Chance
	13. The U Visa: An Effective Resource for Law Enforcement		34. Preventing Future Crime with Cognitive Behavioral Therapy
	14. Victim Satisfaction with the Criminal Justice System		35. Interviewing Compliant Adolescent Victims
	15. Policing in Arab-American Communities after September 11		36. Inmate Count in U.S. Dwarfs Other Nations'
	16. Racial Profiling and Its Apologists		37. Prisoners of Parole
	17. Our Oath of Office: A Solemn Promise		38. American Politics: Democracy in America (Blog): The Perverse Incentives of Private Prisons
	18. Police Investigations of the Use of Deadly Force Can Influence Perceptions and Outcomes		39. Prison Inmates Meet Socrates
	19. Judging Honesty by Words, Not Fidgets		40. One Clique: Why Rivals on the Streets Become Allies behind Bars
	20. Behavioral Mirroring in Interviewing		41. The Professor Was a Prison Guard
	21. Keeping Officers Safe on the Road		42. Supermax Prisons
			43. The Results of American Incarceration
			44. Partnering with Law Enforcement

||||

BUSINESS REPLY MAIL
FIRST CLASS MAIL PERMIT NO. 551 DUBUQUE IA

POSTAGE WILL BE PAID BY ADDRESSEE

McGraw-Hill Contemporary Learning Series
501 BELL STREET
DUBUQUE, IA 52001

Iıludıudılllloollıumıllldılıdıdlloouldudll

ABOUT YOU

Name   Date

_____

Are you a teacher? ❏ A student? ❏
Your school's name

_____

Department

_____

Address   City   State   Zip

_____

School telephone #

_____

YOUR COMMENTS ARE IMPORTANT TO US!

Please fill in the following information:
For which course did you use this book?

_____

Did you use a text with this ANNUAL EDITION? ❏ yes ❏ no
What was the title of the text?

_____

What are your general reactions to the Annual Editions concept?

_____

Have you read any pertinent articles recently that you think should be included in the next edition? Explain.

_____

Are there any articles that you feel should be replaced in the next edition? Why?

_____

Are there any World Wide Websites that you feel should be included in the next edition? Please annotate.

_____

May we contact you for editorial input? ❏ yes ❏ no
May we quote your comments? ❏ yes ❏ no

NOTES

NOTES

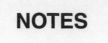

NOTES

NOTES